W9-AUI-130

Nook Farm

MARK TWAIN'S
HARTFORD
CIRCLE

Nook Farm

MARK TWAIN'S HARTFORD CIRCLE

KENNETH R. ANDREWS

UNIVERSITY OF WASHINGTON PRESS
Seattle and London

Washington Paperback edition, 1969, published by arrangement with Harvard University Press
Library of Congress Catalog Card Number 50-9751
Printed in the United States of America

Acknowledgment

I had hardly begun the job of assembling materials for a study of Mark Twain's Hartford environment when I encountered the traditionally open-handed assistance of many institutions and individuals. My sources were to be primarily the unpublished papers of Mark Twain and his neighbors, but I had no willow wand to point out little-known collections. Several libraries helped me search. Those at the University of Illinois, Trinity College, and Harvard, Yale, and Wesleyan Universities are staffed by more persons to whom I owe thanks than I can mention here. To Miss Eugenia M. Henry and Miss Gertrude McKenna of Wesleyan, and to Mrs. Zara Jones Powers and Mrs. Margaret Neeld Coons of the Historical Manuscripts Department, Yale University Library, however, I am in special debt; their generosity far exceeded that literally required by their assignments. I am indebted also to the Connecticut Historical Society and particularly to its librarian, Thompson R. Harlow, and his assistant, Miss Frances A. Hoxie, not only for the location of books and manuscripts but for a hundred other services for which their knowledge of Hartford's past and present qualified them. The Watkinson Library of Reference in Hartford (one of the least used and most highly specialized libraries in the world) is full of rarities and manuscript collections to which Miss Ruth Kerr patiently introduced me. The staffs of the Connecticut State, Hartford Public, and Boston Public Libraries were similarly helpful.

Perhaps the most valuable records of Hartford's community life during the twenty years of Mark Twain's residence there are in private hands. The owners of this material, under no obligation to allow me access to their possessions, were in almost every instance as generous as the librarians in their assistance. To Bernard DeVoto and to his successor as editor of the Mark Twain Papers, Dixon Wecter, I am particularly grateful for access to the magnificent collection of primary sources comprising the literary capital of the Mark Twain Company. Mrs. N. Preston Breed, until recently secretary of the Mark Twain Estate, helped me find my way among its many thousand items. At the time I asked permission, it was not easy or convenient or consonant with policy to let me examine the Mark Twain Papers. Without that privilege this study would have been abortive.

ACKNOWLEDGMENT

The Twichell family, especially Burton Parker Twichell of New Haven, very kindly permitted me to examine the Civil War Letters and many-volumed diary of Joseph Hopkins Twichell, Mark Twain's closest friend. The Twichell Manuscripts (on restricted deposit at the Yale University Library) together with a fourteen-volume scrapbook (in the Connecticut State Library) proved valuable sources for the detailed information I was seeking. Both Mark Twain and Twichell seem to have saved every written memento of their adult lives; the accumulation is wonderful to behold.

The citizens of Hartford — Miss Katharine Seymour Day and the Reverend Joseph Hooker Twichell, in particular — whose reminiscences were guides to additional documentary evidence number more than two dozen. They may not see their hands in the subsequent pages, but they made an important contribution to the mass of material I was eventually to interpret. I hope that my conclusions do little violence to their memories of the society into which they were born.

This book began as a dissertation in American literature, and has been revised for publication by permission of the Graduate School of Arts and Sciences, University of Illinois. I still feel indebted to those who helped me through the doctoral ordeal. To Professor Harold N. Hillebrand, of the University of Illinois, who guided the course of my graduate study until the war, and to Dean Henning Larsen, who subsequently directed the completion of the thesis, I owe much. I am grateful to Professor Howard Mumford Jones of Harvard University not only for the passage in *Ideas in America* which begot this examination of a particular time and place, but more importantly for the detailed criticisms he gave me as he read an early draft of this manuscript. The late Dixon Wecter, in addition to his other kindnesses, also read the manuscript. None of these counselors, of course, is implicated in the shortcomings of the present version.

I thank also Ardis Giffin, Louise Greenleaf, Eleanor Appel, and Helen F. Vinal for their skill and cheerfulness during protracted typing, proofreading, checking, editing, and correspondence, and Mrs. Helen Gray, presently custodian of the Mark Twain Papers, for verifying the accuracy of quotations therefrom.

I have already acknowledged my debt to my wife — whose most important contribution (among many) was the reminder that a single book need not be a life's work — by finally putting an end to this imperfect enterprise.

Most of the quotations in the text are from unpublished papers, but for permission to use copyrighted material quoted from the works of Harriet Beecher Stowe and Mark Twain I acknowledge with thanks the courtesy

ACKNOWLEDGMENT

of Houghton Mifflin Company and Harper and Brothers, respectively. For permission to publish for the first time from manuscripts, I wish to thank the following:

Dixon Wecter, Harper and Brothers, and the Mark Twain Estate for the unpublished passages by Mark Twain and Olivia Clemens and for all passages written by others which were found in the Mark Twain Papers;

The late Burton Parker Twichell and his family for all unpublished passages written by Joseph Hopkins and Harmony Twichell and by others to Joseph Hopkins Twichell;

The Connecticut Historical Society for passages from Isabella Beecher Hooker's diary;

Katharine Seymour Day for all unpublished passages by John and Isabella Beecher Hooker;

The New York Public Library (Henry W. and Albert A. Berg Collection) for passages from letters by Mark Twain;

The Yale University Library for passages from the Morse Collection of Mark Twain Material (Frear Gift) and from the T. R. Lounsbury Papers;

The Watkinson Library of Reference for passages written by and to Charles Dudley Warner in the Warner Papers;

Mary Barton for all unpublished passages by Charles Dudley Warner;

Samuel C. Webster for passages from letters by Mark Twain in his collection;

James B. Pond for the letter written by Major J. B. Pond to Mark Twain;

Thomas N. Fairbanks for passages from letters written by Mrs. A. W. Fairbanks to Mark Twain.

KENNETH R. ANDREWS

Harvard University
July 1, 1950

Contents

ILLUSTRATIONS

ILLUSTRATIONS

Nook Farm

MARK TWAIN'S
HARTFORD
CIRCLE

1

THE COLONIZATION OF NOOK FARM

1851–1871

The Cast of Characters

After 1850 carried the nineteenth century over its chronological crest, a relatively quiet decade of gradual acceleration brought America closer and closer to the Civil War and the arrival of modern times. In these last years of our preindustrial period, a few individuals, who by 1871 had gathered in an apparently provincial corner of Connecticut, were growing up in the widely separated towns where their families had taken root. They were not aware of the chasm between American past and American future that their personal histories would bridge.

In 1851, Samuel Clemens, for example, was at sixteen setting type for his brother Orion's *Hannibal Journal and Western Union* on the Mississippi edge of Missouri. Still before him were the wanderings that were to dislodge him from his village and ultimately deposit him on the banks of the Connecticut. Between Hannibal and Hartford still lay a vast territory of experience. During the next twenty years he was to work in New York and Philadelphia as a journeyman printer, to memorize the Mississippi as a steamboat pilot, to search for silver in Nevada as a prospector and newspaperman, and to examine California and Hawaii, Europe and the Near

East as a traveling journalist. This interval between adolescence and *Innocents Abroad* was to fix his final choice of career, provide him with a more varied substantive experience than any American writer had accumulated before him, and teach him the forms he would apply to it.

In 1851 also, Charles Dudley Warner, whom posterity has already forgotten, was winning first prize in English and a diploma from Hamilton College. In 1829 he had been born a child of New England on a typically untillable farm in Plainfield, Massachusetts. In this hill-town stronghold of Calvinism, he had learned in his childhood the stern faith in which Mark Twain was reared as well as the stubbornness of the rocky soil that other Warners had gone West to escape. After the death of his father in 1834, Charles Warner lived on a more prosperous farm in neighboring Charlemont, where under an otherwise strict regimen he was allowed to read at will. When he was twelve, he rejoined his mother, who was then living in upstate New York. There he made ready for college at the Oneida Conference Seminary, where he met the young Joseph R. Hawley of Connecticut, who was later to bring Warner to Hartford. Warner worked at a variety of occupations, though on a village rather than a continental scale. He had set type in newspaper offices, sold books in stores, and sorted mail in postal stations. T. R. Lounsbury of Yale, his biographer and friend, later said, "He was thus early brought into direct contact with persons of all classes and conditions of life." [1] His village horizons widened by his education and adolescence, Warner now considered literature as a profession. As an undergraduate he had appeared in the *Knickerbocker Magazine*, but still he felt himself better suited to serve ethics than esthetics and inclined toward law as a more practicable career. But first his precarious health, in which he was like his father, detoured him to the Clifton Springs Sanatorium, where he could reflect on the uncertainty of his vocational future and read the works of Washington Irving. He had come straight from devitalized New England, but he was unaware of the inadequacy later attributed to that heritage and looked forward to his maturity as hopefully as any Westerner.

And in 1851, Harriet Beecher Stowe, forty years old, was writing *Uncle Tom's Cabin* in a concentrated passion rather hot for Brunswick, Maine, and was whipping immanent history into a faster pace. She had once lived in Hartford, where, after attending her sister Catharine's female seminary, she had taught from 1827 to 1832. Hartford now must have seemed very remote as she fought the Maine weather, managed her children and her learnedly helpless husband, and transmuted the abstract evils of slavery into the concrete malignance of Simon Legree. She had returned from western scenes of abolitionist violence the year before to accompany Calvin Stowe to his peaceful professorship at Bowdoin. She had known sorrow and turmoil in Cincinnati, but beneath the burden of her experience lay still living a memory of twenty-five years before. Then she had walked one day in the woods near Hartford with her friend Georgiana May and discovered there a wooded knoll near a winding stream. In a reverie soon to come true she built upon it a beautiful dream house.

But also in 1851, John Hooker, of Farmington, Connecticut, took a step which was to narrow the cultural and geographical remoteness separating Hartford and Hannibal and the lesser distances between Maine and upper New York. Always conscious of his ancestry, he found it fitting that as the sixth man in direct descent from Thomas Hooker he should live in Hartford, which his ancestor is credited with founding in 1636. Thomas Hooker had been impelled to lead a band of uncompromising Englishmen out of Massachusetts Colony across the Pequot Wilderness by a gnawing certainty that Cambridge was too small to live in. When he arrived at an abandoned Dutch trading post on the Connecticut River, he established there the thriving colony which promptly drew up the world's first written democratic constitution. Two centuries later, Farmington, a suburb of Hartford, began to seem a tiny village to John Hooker. And for his wife Isabella, of Beecher blood and royal aspirations, it must have been far too simple a town. John had attended Yale, like his father before him and the fathers' sons about him, but a combination of typhoid fever and hard study damaged his eyesight, interrupted his education, and sent him to sea. After two voyages to the Mediterranean and to China and adventures with uncertain pirates who captured his ship and then returned it to its master, he felt strong enough to read law. When he had become fully conscious that in Hartford the opportunity for a more stimulating social life and an extended legal practice awaited him, he and Isabella Beecher Hooker moved from village to city. With his brother-in-law Francis Gillette, John purchased Nook Farm, a tract of 100 acres comprising the estate of William H. Imlay, who had owned it for many years. Intact since Revolutionary days, the farm lay just outside the western city limits and was still, in portions, heavily wooded. Its trees and knolls and its winding stream (traditionally called the Hog or Meandering Swine but variously renamed by the genteel as the Riveret, Little, Woods, or Park River) made it an ideal residential site. Francis Gillette moved into the comfortable farmhouse on the property. John Hooker opened Forest Street among the trees and built a very substantial home upon it. After four years, Gillette built an even larger house near by. Nook Farm was already well on its way to becoming Hartford's choicest residential district and scene of a renewal of the literary primacy that had lapsed with the dispersal of the Hartford Wits.

Hartford grew more rapidly during the fifties than during the sixties and seventies.[2] Hooker had bought shrewdly. As the city pushed westward from the river, the owners were able to subdivide desirable land among congenial persons whom they wished to have as neighbors. From the first, the Hookers looked upon Nook Farm as a small society of their very own. They became noted in the city as proprietary dispensers of hospitality, as cultivated hosts. The first comers were largely relatives. Thomas C. Perkins, then a locally noted lawyer, was eminently eligible to pay a high price for a building lot. His wife Mary was Isabella's sister. Isabella had first met Hooker, then a law student under Perkins, in the latter's downtown house. It was there that the two-year engagement "with the understanding that if either of us found that we had made a mistake we were at liberty to choose elsewhere" [3] was contracted in an atmosphere somewhat more modern than one might expect in Connecticut in 1839. John Hooker's widowed mother occupied a cottage next to her son's house on Forest Street. Elizabeth Gillette, his niece, after marrying George H. Warner, brother of Charles Dudley, settled close by. Joseph R. Hawley, at this time junior partner of John Hooker, met and married in his home Harriet W. Foote, Isabella's cousin from Guilford. The newlyweds settled in the neighborhood. The Hookers' pastor, the Rev. Dr. Nathaniel J. Burton, liberal Congregationalist, lived with the Hooker family for two years. Later he built his own house on the Farm. Mary Hooker, John's sister, married Burton's brother and set up housekeeping there.

This selected society quickly became close knit. "Each of us," said Hooker, "made free of the others' houses . . . each keeping open house, and all of us frequently gathering for a social evening or to welcome some friendly visitor, often some person distinguished in political, literary, or philanthropic life, who had come to some of our houses." [4] The Hartford *Post* many years later referred to the pre-Civil War Nook Farm colony as centered upon the Hooker house, which was distinguished by an "atmosphere of holy domesticity" and by "the brightness, versatility, and enkindling intellectuality of the hosts," which were "commingled with such gentleness, sweetness, and Christian kindness that the guests were ever stimulated, encouraged and refreshed." [5] But more specifically than Christianity, an innate compatibility persisted through emphatic differences of opinion to bind the neighborhood together.

By 1860 the minor characters were all in place; the principals — Warner, Stowe, and Clemens — were soon to arrive. In the neighborhood, a pattern of congeniality had emerged; all doors were open; informality speeded the coming and going. As if by gates, through which only the elect could pass, the rest of the city was kept apart. Within the Farm, conversation sparkled; though frequently forgetting the substance, everybody long remembered the pleasure of it. Given swift current by independent points of view, through the parlors and studies of their houses flowed the main stream of national thought, with eddies of eccentricity forming in the corners. Francis Gillette, for example, descendant of a settler of suburban Windsor, developed through a childhood embittered by a stepfather and a Yale training of formal sterility a combative championship for every lost cause coming his way. Persistently rebuffed by the electorate, he repeatedly sought Abolitionist and Free Soil nominations for public office. Finally a coalition of minority parties, with all of whom he had by this time been identified, got him to the United States Senate to fill an unexpired term in 1854–55. To the conversation of the pre-War Nook Farm he brought interests, edged with reformist zeal, in abolition, temperance, and education. In these areas he subscribed to the convictions of the colony, but he differed from some of his neighbors in his opposition to feminism. Antifeminism was a lost cause in the vicinity of Isabella Hooker, whose championship of women's rights was almost irresistible. Though his arguments with Isabella extended into long public letters in the *Courant*, their friendship was not disturbed. John Hooker himself, styled the Puritanical Wag, was as keenly interested in public questions as in well-turned witticisms. In addition to the mellow glow of Christian charity and moral worth that he was credited with contributing to the discussions of national issues, his rugged persistence as a "brass-mounted Abolitionist" brought him respect. Isabella had a roving mind, later to prove sensationally disruptive of neighborhood equanimity, but through the fifties and sixties she was perfectly attuned to the world and very well informed, like her neighbors, about events and problems in it. Doctor Burton was her ally in arguments on the "woman question." The intellectual content of this group's interaction during the years of Mark Twain's residence will be extensively explored in subsequent pages. At the moment it is significant only that a special society had here formed, which, along with thinking well of itself, found stimulation and satisfaction in its interchanges. The tempo of events was increasing without, but on the Farm the fires were warm and life was leisurely and pleasant.

Charles Dudley Warner

IN 1860 WARNER CAME TO HARTFORD. HE HAD EXPLORED THE WEST DURING TWO years of railroad surveying (experience which he later used in *The Gilded Age*), returned in good health to study law at the University of Pennsylvania, and married brilliant Susan Lee of New York City. In 1858 he returned West to practice law in Chicago. He had not abandoned literature altogether. He had in fact published a *Book of Eloquence*, the first of his compilations, in 1853, and some unpretentious essays had appeared in *Putnam's Magazine*.

Joseph Hawley complicated his own ardent abolitionism in 1856 and crystallized Nook Farm's interest in public affairs by issuing a call for the convention that was to organize the Republican party in Connecticut. It had become apparent to him, to John Hooker, and to most of the other political diagnosticians on Nook Farm that the future of the Free Soil party was negligible, that Know-Nothingism,[6] recently dominant in Hartford, was not only dangerously intolerant but ineffective because of its divergence from abolitionist doctrine. Two hundred men attended the convention to fuse, under the leadership of the Nook Farm nucleus, their Whig, Jeffersonian, and Free Soiler convictions into a unified opposition to the Democrats and the Know-Nothings. The platform adopted was liberally Jeffersonian in tone and the Nook Farm colony became in its support of the program, therefore, Radical Republican. In 1857 Hawley felt the need of a journal for his new party. With William Faxon he founded the *Evening Press* to compete with the Know-Nothing *Courant* and the Democratic *Times*. He soon needed assistance from outside his own circle, and remembered Warner. "In 1860," he said later, "I wrote him that in my opinion he was misplaced as a lawyer and ought rather to enter the literary field. We invited him to join us in the conduct of the 'Press,' and he gladly came to Hartford." [7] Lounsbury recalled at the end of the century that Warner, disillusioned by the discrepancy between untarnished justice and everyday legal traffic, was delighted to become an editor. He and Susan moved first into a cottage near John Hooker, later into a brick house Thomas C. Perkins had built.

The Warners belonged with this active, intelligent, and intensely public-spirited group; they were accepted at once. "Charley's" sense of humor (admirably adapted to fireside conversation) and the rectitude it softened found sympathetic response from the more crusading enthusiasm of his new neighbors. His wife played the piano with almost professional skill — "the best amateur pianist in town," [8] Clara Clemens later called her.

Warner was soon to rise in his new profession. When the Civil War finally capped the local interest in Abolition, the decisive Hawley organized in a few days the first company of Connecticut volunteers, leaving the near-sighted Warner [9] behind to manage the *Evening Press*. The new editor prosecuted the War vigorously, maintaining the original impetus of Radical Republicanism chiefly against cautious advisers to Lincoln like Senator James Dixon and against Dixon's journal, the now Conservative Republican *Courant*. Under Hawley's leadership, exercised through a voluminous correspondence, and influenced in part by his dislike for McClellan, he came to believe the renomination of Lincoln desirable. By the end of the War, however, when Hawley returned a major general on January 15, 1866, Warner was more than glad to relinquish to him the political direction of their paper and to devote his own attention to the more literary and less morally complicated aspects of journalism. Justice had earlier proved tarnished by law; now the pursuit of liberty seemed hampered by politics. As a war hero, Hawley assumed the governorship of Connecticut in 1866; he later went to Congress, where he eventually became an important figure in the Senate. During his public service, he became rapidly as conservative a Republican in the post-War years as he had been radical earlier.[10]

In 1867 Warner and Hawley purchased the Hartford *Courant* and merged the *Press* with it. Warner began the lifetime of leisurely travel recorded in the bulk of his books. In 1868, while Hawley was fighting the demands from the West that government bonds be paid in depreciated currency,[11] Warner was off on his first trip, a fourteen-month survey of the same foreign grounds Mark Twain had toured in five months the year before. He reported his European experiences to the *Courant* with a gentle humor and a pedestrian completeness very unlike the man who was soon to be his neighbor. Until 1870, he was almost unknown except in Hartford. But his was soon to be a household name, as the result not of his travels, his experience in politics, or his acquaintance with our literary past, but of his struggles in the kitchen garden behind the house on Hawthorne Street.

Harriet Beecher Stowe

IN OCTOBER 1862, HARRIET BEECHER STOWE, HEAD OVER HEELS IN AUTHORSHIP, family affairs, and criticism of the conduct of her War, came to Hartford to look for the grove that she and her friend had in their childhood marked for residence. She found it in the southern limits of Nook Farm, bought the plot, and began to plan the mansion she would build. It was very natural to think of Hartford now that Calvin Stowe, low in strength, had retired from the faculty of Andover Theological Seminary. Her sisters Isabella and Mary, and her beloved brother-in-law Thomas Perkins, were there. She was playing with the idea of retirement. "I thought it better to live on less and be in a place of our own, and with no responsibilities except those of common gentlefolk," she wrote Mrs. Fields in the fall of 1862,[12] but the house with eight gables, for which she was virtually construction foreman, was by no means modest. She loved to administer affairs in chaos, and building her first home was a sufficiently complex task to engage her full energies. The ungainly house she built had its history in the childhood which henceforth she was to recall more and more frequently. Its expensive structure was a monument to the fame she had achieved in the world and a symbolic link with the neighborhood in which she felt most at home. With characteristic eagerness she prodded the Irish workmen in the draining and grading of her "four acres and a half of lovely woodland . . . I am busy with drains, sewers, sinks, digging, trenching, and above all with manure!" she wrote Mr. Fields on November 3, 1863. "You should see the joy with which I gaze on manure-heaps, in which the eye of faith sees Delaware grapes and d'Angoulême pears, and all sorts of roses and posies . . ." [13] As she watched and dreamed, she began her *House and Home Papers* for the *Atlantic*, recording her ideas about the construction, decoration, and management of houses for sensible living, and departing from the principles she preached. Oakholm was to prove an expensive and drafty disappointment.

Harriet brought her large family to Nook Farm in April 1864. Calvin was as moody and helpless as ever; his ailing mother was also, at this time, a burden upon the household. Almost as soon as the family was settled, Calvin demonstrated, in this only one of a thousand ways, his facility for getting into ludicrous difficulty. Walking back from downtown along the railroad track, carrying a bottle of whiskey prescribed for his mother, he tripped on a tie and fell to the ground, smashing the bottle to bits and splashing its contents over his clothes. Old and very heavy, he could not get to his feet by himself. Two Irish trackmen helped him up and through the aroma of alcohol supported him home. They winked knowingly at the "Widder Stowe" as they handed him over to her ministrations.

Harriet was exhausted by the move from Andover to Hartford, but now faced with debt, she began to write harder than ever. She succumbed frequently to Victorian "prostrations." But she was in the city she considered home. By the time Mark Twain arrived to live in Hartford, she was ready to give up the struggle at the dream house. The encroaching factories were moving closer; the winding stream was polluted with sewage. In 1870 she abandoned her unheatable mansion for a simpler three-story house abutting the property Mark Twain would purchase. But though her homemaking venture had failed, it had led her to develop further the domestic science in which her elder sister Catharine had been a pioneer and to help make America conscious of home management as a complicated art — a consciousness comprising a striking feature of American social history in this period.

The number of books she wrote after establishing herself on Nook Farm, the family affairs absorbing her attention (like her son Fred's inebriety after his disability in the Union service and her interest in Florida as an investment, a winter home, and a retreat for Fred), must have limited the extent to which Mrs. Stowe could participate in the leisurely social life of her colony of distinguished "gentlefolk."[14] She, like the others, loved conversation before the fire; to Mrs. Fields she said, "Let me put my feet upon the fender, and I can talk till all is blue."[15] Her friends recalled that her face, so plain in her photographs, became beautiful in the full ardor of conversation. But she could not spare many evenings for idle talk or earnest argument. Besides the everyday pressures, she was feeling more explicitly than ever before the consecration of her mission as a writer. For companionship outside her home, she came to depend primarily on her relatives, rather than on the Nook Farm group as a whole, and though she was friendly, she did not become accessible until the seventies, when her labors lightened. By that time she had become the object of reverence.

The chief disaster of these years brought the Nook Farm community rallying behind her. When she rashly published the story of Lord Byron's incest in the *Atlantic*[16] for September 1869, sure that the time had come to reveal confidential conversations with Lady Byron, the storm she provoked recalled in intensity the furor set off by *Uncle Tom's Cabin*. With little charity for her sex and none for her alleged motive, the press heaped upon her name every possible vilification. No other American woman had so suffered. Rather than bow to the attack, she determined to fight the world and publish a long volume in vindication. She engaged David Dudley Field, John Hooker, and Thomas C. Perkins as her legal advisers in an attempt to make her brief thoroughly convincing. Along with twenty other persons hired to read the text critically, she employed Isabella Beecher Hooker as her secretary to handle the voluminous correspondence. Mary Beecher Perkins, who had called with her sister on Lady Byron, but who had not heard the revelations, wrote letters for the volume to attest her sister's accuracy. Harriet actually threw her book together in ten frantic weeks in New York, returned to Hartford for a harried Christmas, awaited anxiously the January publication, and discovered that after all the book had no effect on national opinion. The scandal was not soon forgotten, but, though Mrs. Stowe's fame declined rapidly after 1870, her neighbors did not join in the contempt which elsewhere turned to forgetfulness. By the time Mark Twain came to Hartford, she had been dishonored by the country at large; in Nook Farm she was reverenced until the day of her death. No evidence in the voluminous documents of the period indicates that any of her neighbors was shocked by her daring to write of incest, although many must have recognized the obvious truth that she had made a catastrophic mistake. The old taboos were losing their power, but vulnerability made them only more virulent.

Joseph Hopkins Twichell

JOSEPH HOPKINS TWICHELL, WHO OF ALL THE PEOPLE IN MARK TWAIN'S crowded life was to be his closest friend, became intimate with the Nook Farm colony soon after 1865, the year he assumed the pastorate of the Asylum Hill Congregational Church and settled on near-by Woodland Street.[17] Like most of the rest of this circle, he came from old New England stock. He was born at Southington on May 27, 1838, son of a farmer and leather manufacturer who traced his American ancestry to an Englishman who landed in New England in 1630. The handsome and vigorous boy attended the Lewis Academy in Southington. At seventeen he entered Yale, where he was successful in scholarship, in athletics, and in numerous friendships which he was to keep alive until his death. His popularity, high spirits, and prominence among his fellows brought him recognition of several sorts. When in springtime exuberance he led a traditional undergraduate riot which ended in the accidental death of a fireman, he was rusticated by the Yale authorities. Because he was port-waist oar on the Yale crew, it was considered at the college all the more remarkable that he won "one of the six Townsend premiums for English composition, which are among the most enviable honors of the College course."[18] After his graduation he entered the Union Theological Seminary. The details of his call to the ministry are not known, for his voluminous journals cover later years. Before he had completed his course, the Civil War broke out. On April 22, 1861 he wrote his father that he had volunteered, "for the blood of the Twichells was emphatically up."[19] He accepted the chaplaincy of the roughest regiment he could find, the New York Zouaves, because he had observed that men less obviously "rough and wicked" were very well attended by chaplains already and because he thought himself peculiarly fitted to influence its kind of man. He recognized intuitively that, unlike the paler parson of less adaptable temperament, he could get along with the scourings of the pavement and bring to them a kind of leadership they had never known. He went off to war after writing this lofty sentence, reminiscent of the efforts that had won at Yale the Townsend premium for composition: "God save the Union and grant civilization and Christianity to sit unmolested and fearless under the wide-spreading branches of Constitutional Law."[20]

The War was to widen Twichell's Connecticut horizons and to mature the personality of the man who perhaps otherwise would have been undistinguished as a person, as a counselor, or as a preacher. After his assignment to General Sickles's brigade, when the impetus compelling his enlistment began to fade a little before the enormity of the job he set himself, he was relieved to find that his superior was not only a Congregationalist but a man from Winsted who had breathed Connecticut air. He had feared that the brigade chaplain might be an Episcopalian. Differences of sect were soon to mean very little to him. An enveloping tolerance reduced his theology, never over-elaborate, to a few fundamentals of humanity. His closest friend of the war years was to be the Reverend J. B. O'Hagan, S.J., a priest from Worcester, Massachusetts, who shared his blanket in the field. The Puritan and the Jesuit thought their ecclesiastical differences more amusing than important, and amusing only because of the significance other people attached to them.[21]

With considerable ingenuity and some success, Twichell set out at once to convert his soldiers to active Christianity and to persuade the officers to provide time and facilities for himself and his services. The difficulties were numerous. He approached the members of his regiment through the hearts of the more amenable younger men and optimistically planned, not for a revival, but for a gradual infiltration of higher feelings and a fuller patriotism into his young pagans. (He himself was not yet twenty-three.) He rejoiced that General Sickles was "flat-footed on the matter of temperance among his officers" [22] but was grieved and indignant because the training schedule was not designed to allow him an hour for services on Sunday.

And why? Because, forsooth, it is a fine day for shows and a grand parade has been ordered. Even while I write, the tramp of regiments, the roll of drums, the resonant brass, the shrill fife, rise upon the air, inspiring, even grand at the proper time, but when intruding upon the hours demanded by God for better purposes, a profanation and a shame. It hurts my Puritan ears to listen . . . We learn anew that we must assert ourselves.[23]

His puritan ears pained him less as his sense of values altered and his aggressiveness won him steadily increasing privileges. By June he was making progress, ministering in time allowed to him by the regimental command to as many Catholics as Protestants. He had secured a hundred home-town papers for his men. By July, when his regiment packed to leave Camp Scott for action, he saw that he would have to depart from his standard and send home a carelessly written letter.

From the Potomac his letters to his father came alive with firsthand reporting of the war's confusion. On the trip to the city, the regiment lost men at every stop, for the discipline was abominable. Close to the lines, he was impressed by the processions of supply wagons and troops and by the noise of the frantic last-minute musket drill. At Camp Clendenin, the green troops panicked in false alarm. On the march, as his regiment moved into position along the Potomac, he carried several packs at a time whenever weaker soldiers faltered. This exertion caused him no difficulty, though in the summer sun he "perspired like rain as my Fathers son should . . . That's the sort of chaplain to have, I heard a great many say." [24] He made friends among the officers, too, including an unreligious colonel, lieutenant colonel, and major. He could truly say, however, that in the companionship of these men, he had not compromised himself "as a Christian and clergyman, i.e., so far as I know." [25]

In the autumn of 1861, Twichell battled typhoid and rum, twin scourges of the regiment. In his letters he no longer mentioned profanity, though in volume and variety it could not have diminished. The imminence of action, due on October 27, gave him no qualm; the night before his first battle he slept soundly. When firing began, and he first saw men die, his concerns were more for their lives than for their souls. He was indefatigable in his noncombatant usefulness and unpreoccupied by his own danger from disease or bullet. He had time for occasional moral indignation when the provocation was more fundamental than the minor delinquencies that had bothered him in training camp:

> One of our men Louis McFee of Co H on returning exhausted by 48 hours marching and loss of sleep, procured some vile whiskey and drank it to excess. He was wild drunk all Saturday afternoon — fell into a stupor at about 10 o'clock P.M. and was found dead in his tent the next morning at 9. Apoplexy of the brain, the doctors said — murder and suicide, everybody else. It was awful, horrible. I could not let the occasion pass. A grave was dug near the camp and we buried him that afternoon (Sunday). At my request the whole regiment was paraded and standing beside the coffin of the dead soldier. I spoke my mind freely and I hope in the fear of God. The occasion was one calculated to inspire the preacher and hold the audience. I had the advantage of breathless attention, and I have good reason to believe, that by God's help, my words were not in vain.[26]

In the same month, Twichell was led to explore the complete inefficiency of the hospital at Camp Winfield Scott, for its collapse threatened the welfare of his men. He set out with another officer.

> We wormed our way through the forest of shipping which suddenly had grown up in Poquosin Creek and were landed on the intrenchments. One of the Captains on duty there guided us first to the neat chapel in which the enemy have been praying for success all winter, and there lay eighteen men all very low with the typhoid fever. Two of them were dying, some were insensible, others raving, only one seemed to have his mind, none of them had their clothes off. All of these men except one with some fifty others had the day before been placed in ambulances and driven two miles over corduroy roads to the landing near our camp (it is two miles by land) for transportation to Annapolis. Through some mis-

understanding they lay in the ambulances for hours, and were finally driven back to the hospital and unloaded. One man died during the operation and was taken out a corpse . . . The body lay in a shanty close by, just as it was lifted out of the ambulance — the arms folded over the face — the knees drawn up — one boot on. In a box of rough boards lay another dead man. Our captain had caused this box to be made, as also another for the other body and he assured me that it was with extreme difficulty that nails for the purpose could be procured. A corporals guard of our boys was marched to the shanty. With some difficulty the boot was wrenched from the stiffened foot which was stockingless. Tenderly the body was lifted into the box by men whose hands were coarser than their hearts — we drew his blanket over him (his overcoat had not been taken off) — four nails driven with a spade closed him in — the two were taken up and borne to their graves not six rods distant — just inside the earth-work, near the door of a bomb proof. Already the graves had two feet of water in them and their sides were sliding in. A rope was borrowed from a mule team at hand — they were let down — at first they floated but in a minute filled and sank — a little earth was thrown on — I conducted a short funeral service — a little more work with the spade, and they are left till the resurrection morning. Who they were I knew not . . . The spot will not be still until the army has gone. For weeks as today there will be clatter, and rumbling of wheels and swearing of drivers and all the din of a sudden commerce about them, then the roar of battle, and soon they will be left to deepen the desolation of the peninsula.[27]

On June 4, 1862, Twichell reported to his father the hardships before Richmond, and with the detailed realism and the haste of the passage above describes without emotion the stench of the enemy's unburied dead. In one square rod the bodies of thirteen Confederates lay corrupting in the sun. The Union soldiers who died among them had been interred by a burial party conscious of the limits of its responsibility. On the previous Saturday his brigade had lost 2200 men. Now fully introduced to the meaning of war, Twichell became quickly accustomed to blood, disease, and death and was referring to them in his letters almost casually.

As the War went on, and the campaigns in which he participated plunged deeper into blood, he could not find the time to continue his personal history of the conflict. We are without a record of his experiences at Fredericksburg. But we know that he accompanied General Sickles to the operating room where the latter's leg, shattered by a ball at Gettysburg, was amputated. Growing used to his work in the field, Twichell ceased to reflect extensively upon it, or to think it extraordinary. He found his labors tolerable. The companionship important in any army resulted in many lifelong friendships. Always intensely loyal to Sickles, he later defended him against the charges that he had wasted lives in his attacks. "Fighting Joe" Hooker was "his particular general," a man "not in all respects to be approved," but "exceedingly loveable." [28] He felt himself growing through his battlefield experience, his exposure to action, to filth, to disease and death. On December 11, 1863 he wrote to Theodore Tilton that the *Independent* was partly responsible for his religious development; the latest issue was always in his marching library, along with his Bible and Shakespeare. But the war was his real tutor.

In the letters is ample documentation of Twichell's development from youth to maturity, from confidence to humility, from the provincialism of his Connecticut upbringing and education to an awareness of all kinds of men in all attitudes, from an academic devotion to humanity to an affection and sympathy for human beings, from vague evangelism to an acceptance of men as they are. By the time he was mustered out with his regiment on June 30, 1864, he had undergone an invaluable training for the pastorate to which he would soon be called.

Though he had been ordained in 1863, he now applied to the Andover Theological Seminary (two months after Calvin and Harriet Stowe had left for Nook Farm) for additional courses to complete his training. On leave from the war in 1863, he had met Horace Bushnell in Hartford, in an encounter always remembered because Twichell "fell in love with him" and in his presence was "conscious of sad deficiency at that point, of lack of piety, of consecration," [29] and particularly of a lack of theological views. Bushnell, to whom theology was actually unimportant, was sufficiently impressed by Twichell to offer him tentatively the post as his assistant in the Park Church, but by the time the younger man came out of Andover in 1865, he received from Bushnell a greater favor.

Under the leadership of Gillette and Hooker, Nook Farm grew up. When the westward growth of the city reached Asylum Hill in 1860, it became evident that a neighborhood church had become a necessity. Transportation down to the ancient Main Street churches was at all seasons difficult and in winter uncertain. The first line of horsecars did not appear until 1863, and the old-fashioned omnibus in operation before that time did not run on Sundays. At the instigation of Francis Gillette, rotund Professor Calvin Stowe, in skullcap and flaring white beard, conducted a Bible class in the schoolhouse the city had built in the vicinity.[30] In 1864 Gillette represented the Nook Farm group at a meeting of prosperous and prominent citizens of the larger Asylum Hill neighborhood. The assembled citizens decided to organize a Congregational church, selected a site, and shortly thereafter began to solicit funds. Very soon more than $87,000 was donated to construct a Portland stone church which finally cost $106,000, not including $10,000 for the plot of land.

The 114 original parishioners, who so easily brought the expensive building into being, now applied to Bushnell for recommendations to fill the less expensive pastorate. Bushnell remembered the promise he had seen in Twichell and submitted his name. No other candidates were considered. That the climate of Congregationalism had become springlike in a few years is nowhere more strikingly evident than in the choice of these prosperous laymen of a protégé of the old heretic.[31] Twichell's neutral lack of interest in theological speculation or in religious disputation got him in no trouble before the examining committee, though over his head Bushnell and old Joel Hawes[32] managed to engage in a doctrinal argument. Francis Gillette wrote Twichell that the church had approved him unanimously, with only two members of the society considering that he had "insufficient knowledge."[33] John R. Keep, deacon, sententiously noted that Hartford would provide the young veteran with just the "restraint and stimulus" necessary for growth to the full manhood God intended for him. He had "in the most remarkable manner taken the hearts of all . . ."[34] On August 8, Twichell replied that after "long and prayerful deliberation, aided by the counsels of godly and competent men,"[35] he was pleased to accept. Two weeks later he proposed to Julia Harmony Cushman of New Jersey, whom he had met on leave during the war. The couple were married in November, and on December 13 Twichell was installed in the only pulpit he ever occupied. He and his wife were soon to be part of Nook Farm's fabric.

During the six years before Mark Twain's arrival, Twichell strengthened the impression his parishioners had immediately taken from their first sight of him. His sermons reflected his lack of interest in intellectual Congregationalism and avoided questions of high public policy. He spoke always of what interested him most — of brotherliness, of the Christian ethic as the assurance and foundation of the good life, of the emotional, uncodified relation of man to a God of love, and of his optimistic perception of a growing kindness among humanity. His style was even at this time apparently rhythmic, his voice rich, resounding, and warm. And with the attraction of handsome strength and breeziness, humor, and a touch of earthiness, he completely charmed his parishioners into devotion, greatly increased their numbers, and made it unthinkable that he should ever leave them. They thought him a "memorable man" and responded to his natural directness at once. It is possible that he should have flayed the superficial delusions of his conventional flock, castigated their devotion to prosperity, and led them from the dominant commercialism of the Gilded Age into an appreciation that they and their country were corrupt and complacent. But this course of action did not occur to Twichell. Completely adjusted to his generation and its tides of feeling, he was entirely normal and nothing neurotic. Such a man is not usually very interesting to his posterity, but among his contemporaries Twichell attracted the attention and love of a man not ultimately satisfied with his own world, a man who was not normal and was neurotic, and who interests us very much.

Mark Twain

MARK TWAIN'S MOVE TO HARTFORD OCCASIONED SOME SURPRISE TO HIS contemporaries, but to him it seemed entirely natural, if not the inevitable result of inescapable events. As Henry C. Vedder wrote in his *American Writers of Today*:

It is not surprising that Mr. Warner and Mrs. Stowe should be neighbors in a staid Connecticut town; Mrs. Stowe was born in that State, and Mr. Warner is a New Englander. But that Mark Twain should have drifted to Hartford as a permanent residence is only less astonishing than Mr. Cable's emigration from New Orleans to Northampton, Mass.[36]

For two reasons the threads of relationships and events tapestried behind Mark's arrival are worth tracing. First is the element of the unexpected. But more important is the chagrin exhibited by critics of the 1920's who found in Mark's decision to settle in the East an abject surrender to gentility and an abandonment of his potential powers. These sentimentalists, reacting to the dominance by business of American art in the Gilded Age, considered Mark's selection of "Puritan Hartford" the worst possible of a large number of dubious choices.[37]

Mark Twain had returned from the *Quaker City* voyage late in 1867 to find that his newspaper letters had made him famous. As soon as he reached shore he read a letter from Elisha Bliss, Jr., of Hartford's American Publishing Company, who asked him for a subscription book on his experiences.[38] Other important events clustered around his homecoming. On January 1, 1868, his shipmate Charles Langdon introduced Mark to his sister Olivia, whose picture Mark had admired at Smyrna some months before. Witnesses to this meeting were Isabella Beecher Hooker and her daughter Alice, who had come to New York to see their old friends, the Langdons.[39] Mark was entranced by Olivia, but he still had eyes to note that Alice was "another beautiful girl."

On January 5, Mark was the guest of Henry Ward Beecher, then at the peak of his fame as preacher and public figure. At the Brooklyn Sunday

THE BEECHER FAMILY

LYMAN BEECHER (1775–1863), Congregationalist, preacher, theologian, husband to three wives, father of thirteen children. His nine famous children were:

CATHARINE BEECHER (1800–1878), educator, author, antifeminist, home economist. Lived long in Hartford with her sister Harriet; principal of Hartford Female Seminary.

WILLIAM HENRY BEECHER (1802–1889), preacher, educator, dyspeptic, and failure.

EDWARD BEECHER (1803–1895), preacher, educator, editor, scholar, feminist, believer in the preëxistence of souls.

MARY BEECHER PERKINS (1805–1900), housewife. Lived long in Hartford's Nook Farm as wife of the lawyer, Thomas C. Perkins.

HARRIET BEECHER STOWE (1811–1896), author. Lived in Hartford as a child and in Nook Farm from 1862 until her death.

HENRY WARD BEECHER (1813–1889), preacher, alleged adulterer, editor, author, pastor of the Plymouth Church in Brooklyn.

CHARLES BEECHER (1815–1900), preacher, spiritualist, musician, heretic.

ISABELLA BEECHER HOOKER (1822–1907), suffragist. Wife of John Hooker, lawyer. Lived in Nook Farm from 1852–1907. Daughter of Lyman Beecher's second wife.

THOMAS KINNICUT BEECHER (1824–1900), preacher, liberal, pastor of First Congregational Church of Elmira, New York, and of Olivia Langdon. Son of Lyman Beecher's second wife.

dinner Mark met Harriet Beecher Stowe and Catharine Beecher and extended his acquaintance with Isabella Beecher Hooker. Henry Ward, wily in the accumulation of money, advised the innocent author to drive a sharp bargain with Bliss, the predacious publisher. On January 8, Mark wrote a casual account of his meetings with the great Beechers and announced that he intended to spend some time at Elmira "and a few days at Mrs. Hooker's in Hartford, Conn., shortly." [40] His first visit to Hartford occurred on January 21, 1868.

Mark was immediately liked by most of those who met him in these exciting days. Albert Bigelow Paine, Mark's biographer, dramatizes the contrast between the unkempt Westerner and the urbane cosmopolites, representing Bliss, for example, as disappointed in his appearance.[41] I find no evidence, however, that Mark was not fully accepted from the moment of his introduction to New York and Hartford society. The Beechers and Hookers seemed to notice less eccentricity in his manner and dress than did the Bostonians of his later career. He wore easily the implied honors of the new associations and moved into a new world under a warm welcome.

In turn, Hartford pleased Mark Twain. He recorded his immediately favorable first impression in a letter to *Alta California* dated January 25, 1868,[42] magnifying for a Pacific audience interesting features of the local notions of propriety:

> I think this is the best built and the handsomest town I have ever seen. They call New England the land of steady habits, and I can see the evidence about me that it was not named amiss . . . [He finds that nobody smokes in the streets, that cigar stores are few and far between, and that nobody is visibly drunk.] What a singular country it is! At the hospitable mansion at which I am a guest, I have to smoke surreptitiously when all are in bed, to save my reputation, and then draw suspicion upon the cat when the family detect the unfamiliar odor. I never was so absolutely proper in the broad light of day in my life as I have been for the last day or two. So far I am safe; but I am sorry to say that the cat has lost caste.

He walked about Nook Farm, admired its sights, and ascribed its spaciousness and wealth to the entire city:

> They have the broadest, straightest streets in Hartford, that ever led a sinner to destruction, and the dwelling houses are the amplest in size, and the shapeliest, and have the most capacious ornamental grounds about them. This is the centre of Connecticut wealth. Hartford dollars have a place in half the great moneyed enterprises of the union. All those Phoenix and Charter Oak Insurance Companies, whose gorgeous chromo-lithographic show cards it has been my delight to study in far-away cities, are located here.

Like a good reporter he described Sharp's Rifle Factory and the plant of Samuel Colt, who invented the revolver and manufactured munitions during

ISABELLA BEECHER HOOKER

ISABELLA BEECHER HOOKER AT 75

the Civil War. The chief symbol of Hartford's past, the Charter Oak, was everywhere. He saw enough wood taken from it "to build a plank road from here to Salt Lake City." Hartford was impressive in its physical attractiveness, its generously proportioned prosperity, and the gracious character of its everyday life. "Hartford has a population of 40,000 souls and most of them ride in sleighs. This is a sign of prosperity, and a knowledge of how to live — isn't it?"

On the twenty-fourth of January Mark wrote to Mrs. Fairbanks of Cleveland of his awkwardness during his first introduction to Nook Farm society:

> I am the guest of Mr. Hooker's (Henry Ward Beecher's brother-in-law) family here for a few days, & I tell you I have to walk mighty straight. I desire to have the respect of this sterling old Puritan community, for their respect is well worth having — & so I don't dare to smoke after I go to bed, & in fact I don't dare to do *anything* that's comfortable & natural. It comes a little hard to lead such a sinless life, but then you know it won't be for long — I can let myself out when I get to Washington. I have promised to be Mrs. Hooker's special Washington correspondent, & so I shall have to be particular again.[43]

Mark must have thought the prosperity he admired in Hartford within his own grasp. If he could complete the profitable projects to which he had committed himself in these busy months and finish *Innocents Abroad*, he saw himself a rich man. His Washington secretaryship under Senator Stewart ended soon, but it provided him material for newspaper letters appearing in the Chicago *Republican* and with insight into the politics and manners of the capital that was to sharpen *The Gilded Age*. In the midst of a swarm of journalistic commitments, he sailed for California, ostensibly to negotiate with the *Alta* for release of its copyright on the *Quaker City* letters but perhaps more accurately to seek resolution of the restlessness and indecision that characterized his behavior while he was still uncertain about his future. Once ashore in California, he completed arrangements with the *Alta*, which probably could have been effected by mail, and plunged into a feverish combination of writing and lecturing. By the end of July, he was back in New York. In August he postponed acceptance of Mrs. Fairbanks's invitation to Cleveland; he was too busy. He "did not come east to work, except on the book. I expect to go to Hartford tomorrow, & begin."[44]

On this visit of two weeks, largely devoted to *Innocents Abroad*, he saw Hartford in summer and found it good. Again in the *Alta*, he emphasized the beauty and the impressive public morality of the place. He found after wandering "all over" the town that Hartford was

> composed almost entirely of dwelling houses — not shingle-shaped affairs, stood on end and packed together like a 'deck' of cards, but massive private hotels,

scattered along the broad straight streets, from fifty all the way up to two hundred yards apart. Each house sits in the midst of about an acre of green grass, or flower beds, or ornamental shrubbery, guarded on all sides by the trimmed hedges of arbor-vitae, and by files of huge forest trees that cast a shadow like a thunder-cloud . . . Everywhere the eye turns it is blessed with a vision of refreshing green. You do not know what beauty is if you have not been here.[45]

The quiet setting he admired here was very different from the landscape he had known in Nevada and in San Francisco, or in the wastelands of the Middle East. Fresh from the less ordered natural loveliness of Hannibal, he had been depressed by the bleakness of Washoe, where, he had said, a bird flying over the territory had to carry its own provisions. The burnt summer desolation of the Oakland Bay region and the flimsy construction disfiguring San Francisco made the details he included in these letters particularly significant to a California audience. Mark must have been alert to the problem of choosing a place to live in permanently, and with the image of Olivia in his mind, it must have occurred to him that Hartford was attractive and suitable. But he feared that the income from his newspaper correspondence and his lectures would not be sufficient. The book and its sales became important. "To live in this style one must have his bank account of course," he said in an *Alta* letter, noting that he had observed no poverty. He had not yet walked into the slums on the river flats.

. . . where are the poor in Hartford? I confess I do not know. They are 'corralled' doubtless — corralled in some unsanctified corner of this paradise whither my feet have not yet wandered, I suppose.[46]

Mark was not blind to the possibility that residence in a place like Hartford would mean adjustment to its outward conventionality. In his first newspaper letter he said he had felt the rub as a constant smoker; on this occasion he makes fun of the public morality. The blue-law spirit was not yet dead. In a dubious reference to a restriction that did not exist, he said that the ban on ownership of cards had been repealed only a year earlier — there was not a *whole* pack in Hartford. Another blue law preserved the beauty of the streets, for property owners must submit all building plans to the city government for approval. "People accustomed to large liberties will call this an unjust, unrighteous law . . . I like this law. I exult in it every time I walk abroad in these delightful streets." He found morality as ubiquitous as August huckleberries and proved its strength by citing the young ladies who walked alone in the streets as late as ten o'clock without being molested. Girls swarmed up and down Main Street "with a happy effrontery that is in the last degree entertaining to a stranger. We may expect the lion and the lamb to lie down together shortly in Connecticut, if it be constitutional for the millennium to come in small doses. To me, a sinner, the prospect is anything but inviting." The irony of this passage seems almost to underline his developing identification of himself with this mode of living and to reflect an anxiety about obtaining its sanction.

On August 18, Mark left Hartford for New York on his way to Elmira for "a couple of days" which he was glad to extend to two weeks. After some progress in his courtship he finally visited Mrs. Fairbanks in Cleveland. In October he was back in Hartford again to find that the publication of *Innocents Abroad* had been postponed to March 1869, in order to allow provision of more profuse and commercially advisable illustrations.[47] On this, or the previous visit, he met Joseph Twichell. The Blisses, his hosts, were parishioners of the spireless Asylum Hill Congregational Church, which had appeared as a "stump-tail church" in his August *Alta* letter. According to Paine,[48] Mrs. Bliss introduced Twichell to Mark as the latter was commenting on the commercial pursuits of the Asylum Hill congregation by calling its meetingplace the "Church of the Holy Speculators." On his subsequent visits he saw Twichell each time, and in the friendship taking root lay what was to prove another attraction of Hartford residence. Twichell remembered this meeting when he wrote on Mark's death in the Hartford *Courant*:

We were both young men, and the acquaintance so begun soon grew into a friendship which continued unbroken ever after, and went on strengthening with the flight of years. I cannot say that at that point we were wholly sympathetic in either thought or feeling. Our antecedent conditions and experience in life had been very different, and, in some ways, contrasted. But while originally attracted to him by the brightness of his mind, the incomparable charm of his talk, and his rare companionableness, I was not long in finding out that he had a big, warm and tender heart.[49]

But neither man rationalized the affinity at the time. Mark and Twichell probably hiked to the Talcott Mountain Tower (a permanently pleasant recreation for both during the next twenty years), for Mark soon wrote to the *Alta*: "I have seen a New England forest in October, and so I suppose I have looked upon almost the fairest vision the earth affords."[50] Charles Dudley Warner, Twichell's earlier companion on these twenty-mile walks, was then in Europe. Mark was to meet him later.

Through the next two years, Mark's attraction to Hartford strengthened steadily. He was back at the Blisses' in early March 1869, but earlier he had pursued his courtship whenever the lecturing itinerary provided by James Redpath's Boston Lyceum Bureau brought him near Elmira. On February

4, 1869 his engagement to Livy was finally ratified. In June he brought his fiancée to the wedding of Alice Hooker to John Calvin Day, a Nook Farm celebration presided over by Henry Ward Beecher. This was Olivia's first opportunity to visit her friends in their homes. Mark undoubtedly took pleasure in showing her about the neighborhood, in imagining his living there with her, and in renewing his acquaintance with the Beechers and the Hookers. An *Alta* letter of July 1869 contains no impressions of the city, though it retails a story of the abduction into slavery of the Crown Prince of Timbuctoo, a yarn he had heard at the Hookers. The first copy of *Innocents Abroad* was delivered to him on July 20.[51] In November Mark came back to lecture on the Sandwich Islands in Allyn Hall to a good audience, many of whom were by now his acquaintances or friends.

In spite of the immediate success of *Innocents Abroad*, Mark still did not feel that he could take the risk of supporting Livy by his books alone, nor was he certain that he would compose any more. No American writer had been able to maintain living standards as high as the Langdons' without a private fortune. With this difficulty in mind, he looked for a newspaper in which he might purchase an interest. He had considered buying into the Cleveland *Herald* with his royalties, but by April 1869 he had abandoned the idea. Mr. Fairbanks's interests in the property would be damaged if Fairbanks were to part with any of his half-share of the stock. Mark looked at other papers; it is not surprising that he attempted to buy into the Hartford *Courant*.

I made proposals to an eastern newspaper firm, [he wrote Mrs. Fairbanks] & they wrote to one partner to come home from Europe [52] & see about it. He was to have spent the summer or a part of it abroad, but they say he will now get back in May. Therefore I am reading proof & waiting.[53]

His very careful consideration of his future position and residence is apparent in this next passage:

I wait very patiently, because this thing of settling down for life is the solemnest matter that has ever yet come into my calculations, & I am not inclined to get in a sweat about it, or make a move without looking well into it first. I must not make a mistake in this thing. As I do not quite understand having secrets from you, I will say that the Eastern paper I allude to is the Hartford Courant — though I have a strong impression that I told you about it, or wrote you about it some time ago.

This venture faltered when Charles Dudley Warner and Joseph Hawley, after consulting Samuel Bowles of the Springfield *Republican*, cold-shouldered Mark's offer to buy an interest in the paper in June 1869. A few months later, when *Innocents Abroad* had proved a phenomenal success, the original partners in the *Courant* regretted their exclusiveness.[54] But in the meantime Jervis Langdon, taking a decisive hand, had suggested and financed the purchase for $25,000 of a one-third interest in the Buffalo *Express*. Mark assumed his editorial duties on August 14, 1869, his preference for Hartford deflected but not suppressed.

Mark brought Twichell from Hartford to help Thomas K. Beecher marry him to Livy in Elmira. This gesture is significant of the fast-growing intimacy between these men, who until then could not have seen each other more than a half-dozen times. The occasion was the beginning of friendship between Thomas K. Beecher and Twichell. After the ceremony, the newlyweds were installed in an elaborately expensive house purchased by Langdon and presented to Mark as a surprise wedding gift. Now he was indeed living in a "private hotel," though it was crowded on a small plot of ground in a neighborhood lacking the spacious landscaping and the admirable trees of Nook Farm. He began to learn directly how much it cost to support a mansion of this sort, to pay the servants thoughtfully hired by Jervis Langdon, to act as the substantial householder. Never pausing, apparently, to consider the implications of the problem, he eagerly plunged into the task of supporting Livy on the level to which her father's coal mines and yards had accustomed her.

Hartford moved even closer as Buffalo speedily proved unsatisfactory and the duties for the *Express* an irksome chore. Mark's "settling down," because of a series of misfortunes, proved an unpleasant process. The illness and death of Jervis Langdon were followed by the death in their home of a friend of Livy's and by the premature birth of Mark's son Langdon, after which both mother and child fared badly. The *Express* failed to grow. His editorials, falling on deaf ears, were producing little return on his borrowed invested capital. Mark and Livy made no friends in Buffalo, except the David Grays; the society there provided no compensation for misfortune.

Meanwhile Mark was prodding his brother Orion to move to Hartford. Elisha Bliss agreed to employ Orion at $12.50 per week, a figure suggested by Mark, and in November 1870 was looking forward to Orion's arrival since clerical need for his "expert hand" was great. Mark forwarded Bliss's letter to Orion with the note "I hope you will pack up & leave for Hartford *instantly* & finally."[55] He was pressing Orion to do what he wanted to do himself, for Hartford began to appear more and more a green and pleasant land.[56] Orion went to Hartford to edit a trade paper called *The American Publisher* and to help about the office of the American Publishing Company. After hours he began to work on his inventions: a new paddle wheel to enable a steamboat to cross the Atlantic in twenty-four hours and a flying machine which would cover the distance even more rapidly. Both schemes interested Mark. He himself had just invented an adjustable vest strap.

Mark passed on to Orion and Molly Clemens another interesting assessment of New England life. He wrote them he had asked Twichell to call,

> which he says he will do as soon as a press of botherations gives him a chance. Both of you *go slow* — don't hurry in the matter of making friends, & don't get impatient. Making friends in Yankee land is a slow, slow business, but they are friends worth having when they *are* made. There is no section in America half so good to live in as splendid old New England — & there is no city on this continent so lovely & lovable as Boston, almost in sight of which it is now your high privilege to live.[57]

By the end of 1870, *Innocents Abroad* had sold enormously. Bliss was hungry for another book. Mark finished *Roughing It*, encouraged by the praise of Joe Goodman of the Virginia City *Enterprise*, and delivered the manuscript in the summer of 1871. While in Hartford he looked for a place to live. In March he had written to J. H. Riley [58] from Buffalo, "I mean to store our furniture and build a house in Hartford just like this one" as soon as he could sell his Buffalo residence for the $25,000 it had cost Jervis Langdon. He would not build immediately, for he meant to take his time "in building a house & build it *right*, even if it does cost 25 per cent more." [59] Now, therefore, he wanted a place to rent. He found that the Hookers would lease their home to him for an indefinite period.[60] On October 1, 1871 Mark brought Livy to the home he had entered first on his earliest visit to Hartford. The move was very wearing. Already the Clemens family was heavily burdened with household goods. The baby was sick and continually wailing. Livy was exhausted by the packing and unpacking, for the furniture was brought down from Buffalo for Hartford storage. After he showed his family into the Hooker home and quartered the horse and buggy in the original Nook Farm barn, Mark left at once for a lecture tour in order to reduce the heavy debt confronting him. The Clemenses were to live in this house until April 1874, when a mansion more splendid would be ready for them. Mark had at last arrived in the "handsomest town" he had ever seen, to the place of all the cities of America and Europe which attracted him most, to take his place among the friends he felt most worth having. The earlier realization of the high cost of residing in "this paradise" must have been far more poignant now as he left his exhausted wife and sickly child in order to supplement his royalties with lecture money. In Hartford, one must have his bank account, of course.

2

THE VARIETIES OF RELIGIOUS EXPERIENCE

1871–1891

Liberal Congregationalism: Horace Bushnell

TWENTY YEARS AFTER JOHN HOOKER DETERMINED TO MAKE HIS HOME in Hartford, his Nook Farm community was threatened by alterations in American life which the Civil War had brought. The intellectual unity of the pre-War colony began to disintegrate. In some of its members crusading energy expired with the conquest of slavery. The subsequent campaigns of the still militant conflicted with an increasingly conservative loyalty to old ideas and customs. The external chaos of national reorganization never long ruffled Nook Farm's surface serenity, but in the deep shadows under the old trees the inner peace was permanently disturbed. Religious, ethical, social, and political questions could no longer be answered by reference in concert to stable truth. Many of the new problems seemed entirely insoluble.

In 1871, Mark Twain and his Connecticut intimates began, in contest with the instability of modern times, to improvise ways of achieving an ordered life. The context of ideas and attitudes within which the literary activities of the artists residing in Nook Farm become intelligible is a complex record of individual and community adaptations to a changed Hartford and a changing America.

VARIETIES OF RELIGIOUS EXPERIENCE

Because Nook Farm was in Hartford and Hartford was in New England, it is appropriate to begin study of this context with the religious experience of these people. If a simple uniformity bridged their opinions, if the "Puritan" label could be applied truthfully to this society to end inquiry, it would be possible to say, as some have said, that Mark Twain's ultimate pessimism developed in reaction to the conservative religion of his time and neighborhood, in rebellion against the pressure of mediocre orthodoxy. But the complexity of religious experience in Mark Twain's immediate vicinity forbids such cavalier generalization. This small group included no Calvinists, no literal Puritans, no man who was behind his generation in the way he thought of this world in relation to any other, and few who were not ahead of it.

Religious conservatism, possibly more marked in Hartford than in some other old cities, was not characteristic of the Nook Farm nucleus. The Bushnell Congregationalism, once as radical as possible within the framework of any church system, was most prominent. But we shall find, without looking very hard, departures from the liberal-orthodox, particularly, of all places, in the oldest Nook Farm family. It appears useful to examine religious before secular ideas, for though systematic theology was no longer the preoccupation it had been in the New England that Harriet Beecher Stowe recreates, personal religion still played an important if more and more ill-defined role in everyday secular life and ultimately in the literature of the individuals in whom we are presently interested.

Horace Bushnell, one of the great preachers of the nineteenth century, was the philosopher of what after his time came to be the conventional religion of the Nook Farm community. His ancestry was as long identified with Connecticut as Hooker's or Twichell's. Early in the 1800's his grandmother, like a few others of her generation, renounced Calvinism. She could no longer stand it. Bushnell, thus released from a two-century tradition, and by no means intending to become a minister, went in homespun from a beautiful Connecticut village, where hills and forest had prompted in him Wordsworthian intimations of God in nature, to Yale in 1823. There he succeeded both as athlete and student. Afterwards he taught school, reported for the New York *Journal of Commerce*, and studied law, avoiding the ministry because of his religious doubts. During the Yale revival of 1831, however, he was converted, and in 1833, after graduation from the Yale Divinity School, he was ordained and installed as pastor of the North Church in Hartford. He evaded doctrinal alliance with the warring factions within the Congregational Church. He read Coleridge instead. Under the power of mystical experience he finally perpetrated heresy in his *God in*

Christ in 1849, a book that brought both the new and the old schools of Presbyterianism down upon him. That he was not actually tried is a sign the times were ready for Bushnell; the General Association, noticing his congregation's loyalty, ruled that it existed to support rather than to censure individual churches.

Bushnell had not been content with the liberal but highly logical teaching of Nathaniel W. Taylor, of the much-maligned New Haven school of theology. Through his own intuitive sense of God he developed the doctrine that the spiritual world was incapable of reduction to precise statement, that only to the trained imagination were religious truths perceptible.[1] He argued in *Christian Nurture* (1861) that children should be given religious training, and he progressed to such theses as the principle that the Trinity does not represent permanent differentiation in the Godhead. In his sermons and books he repudiated the penal interpretation of atonement and substituted for it his most influential idea — the "moral influence" theory that Christ's death was self-sacrifice, a sign of God's love so powerful that because of it the power of sin in man is conquered. He came close to the thinkers of the Romantic Movement by arguing the immanence of God in what he had created and defining the essence of God as the spiritual reality in nature and in man. Although this development was common enough in the literature of early nineteenth-century England, Bushnell was apparently the first theologian in New England to develop the religion of nature within the framework of a formal sect.

As the outlines of his doctrine became clear and conservative churchmen, branding Bushnell a heretic, tried to unfrock him, unnamed leaders of Boston Unitarianism, which at the time was in possession of almost all of that city's Congregational churches, asked him to join the movement, asserting that Bushnell was essentially Unitarian. He replied, "Gentlemen, I am much mistaken by many, but by none so much as you. I don't belong with you, but the farthest possible otherwise, if you only knew it."[2] Today, after emotional loyalties have disappeared with the dust of the men they controlled and only the logic of what they said remains, it is difficult to see what he meant or why it was entirely true. Unitarianism was always abortive in Hartford; it may be that Bushnell chose to persuade Congregationalism to his view rather than join an uninfluential and uncongenial minority.

Whatever his motives, Bushnell became a preacher's preacher and in Hartford exercised his influence through younger protégés who dominated the churches until the twentieth century. In the country at large, his greatest disciples were such widely popular preachers as Henry Ward Beecher and Phillips Brooks. Bushnell presided over the repudiation of Calvinism in

Connecticut. By turning religion over to the personal mystical experience of the parishioner, he abdicated the formal position the minister had occupied in old New England. That Twichell, trained by the Civil War in the essential unreality of formal theology, should have been his enthusiastic defender and follower was inevitable, for in Bushnell's authority the young man could find confirmation of his own tentative reflections.

As if in practical illustration of this relegation of religious experience to the individual, Bushnell himself took a lifelong interest in the secular affairs of his day. His participation in the transition from a stable agricultural republic to a fluid industrial democracy took him far beyond Hartford and a set of ideas every Mark Twain student has been content to call provincial. Invalided early in the 1850's, he went to California in 1856, seeking relief from bronchial trouble. As he recuperated, he tramped into the mountains, saw the Gold Rush country before Mark Twain did, picked out the present route of the Southern Pacific railroad's entrance to San Francisco, and actively took part in the establishment of the University of California, choosing the Berkeley location it now occupies. He declined its presidency to return to his Hartford pulpit, but in 1861 he retired to devote what was left of his strength to writing and to the civic affairs of his own city.

As his interest in the transcontinental railway indicates, Bushnell was in sympathy with the material progress of post-Civil War America. Even as early as 1847 he had announced in a Hartford sermon that "prosperity was our duty" and that as a means to its discharge the Connecticut River should be harnessed for power. That the development of national resources and the expansion of trade should be more than reckless exploitation, he took for granted. In a spirited contest with narrow business interests, he transformed the face of Hartford by forcing the clearance of an unsightly area around the railroad station. Waste from the railroads, dumped among tenements, ramshackle factories, and pigsties, had disfigured many acres in the heart of the city. The area of affected land was so valuable to its owners, the problem of elevating the railroad station so repugnant to intrenched interests, that the fight to transfer ownership from private owners to the Park Commission became bitter. Bushnell was angrily accused of arson after two mills, prominent eyesores in the midst of the blighted district, mysteriously burned to their foundations. He defeated his opponents, however, and a public park named after him replaced the slums. Later Bushnell proposed successfully that the city purchase adjoining Trinity College property and locate the state capitol where it now stands.

Hence, of the business interests whose general expansion he favored for the sake of general prosperity, Bushnell was not a tool. He was confident the new age was a momentous one and, though a theologian, was acutely aware of the material world in which he lived. He would have chosen no other.

His catholic tastes and radiating interests made him well known to the laymen of Hartford. His devotion to mountain climbing, in which he persisted during his ill health, brought Charles Dudley Warner into intimacy with him, for Bushnell, like Twichell and Warner, left the malarial city each year to summer in the Adirondacks. Every spring he fished with Charles Hopkins Clark, who in a later time succeeded Warner as editor of the *Courant*. The residents of Nook Farm watched his "elastic, springy walk" change to a halting but determined gait, as illness made inroads on his strength and age marked his delicate face. In the 1870's he still drove fast on Farmington Avenue, passing everybody on the road and shouting to his passenger, if he had one, "My boy, I don't like dust." Although Isabella Beecher Hooker avoided him (Bushnell was unexpectedly conservative in denouncing women's suffrage [3]) and John Hooker remonstrated with him in the press, Nook Farm loved him. Mark Twain was on friendly terms with him, as he was all his life with every minister he personally knew, and in 1872 was characteristically remorseful when he forgot to send him a complimentary copy of *Roughing It*. "You blame yourself over much," Bushnell replied.[4] The old man called to meet Mrs. Langdon, visiting Mark and Livy in the Hooker house in December 1872, and gladly signed Mark's copyright petition, though he wanted his name far down to let the "literary gentlemen" have their lead. In a sense, he had foretold the rise of Mark Twain. At a Yale Commemorative Celebration in 1865 he had said in his principal oration ("Our Obligation to the Dead"): "Henceforth we are not going to write English but American. We have gotten our position, we are now to have our own civilization, think our own thoughts, rhyme our own measures." The development of American literature in his own neighborhood, though he died in 1876 before it had reached the climax, did not escape him.

Here, then, was the Emerson of Hartford, the revered leader of the early days of Mark Twain's residence and the shaper of the community's religious thought. Mark thought of him as "that noble old Roman," the greatest clergyman the nineteenth century produced.[5] The Nook Farm community and its environs were at one time dominated by his ideas. His own solution to the problems of the universe via personal rather than institutional religion led not only to the proliferation of his own interests into secular areas, but paralleled and undoubtedly influenced the gradual decline of religion as the nineteenth century grew older. The disintegration of Calvinism, long overdue, was effectively hastened and in Connecticut completed by Bushnell.

The result, or at least a concomitant change, was to be one he had not foreseen and one that his devotee, Edwin Pond Parker, did not recognize in 1902 when, recalling the inspiration of Bushnell's sermons, he wished that they could put "some edge on the dull faith of this present generation of rather faithless Christian people." [6] For with the dissolution of the iron discipline of the parent church, the individual man or woman, to whose mystical intuitions and instinctive spirituality Bushnell had in optimism and faith entrusted God, apparently ceased to concern himself with the spiritual life, particularly as science proposed mechanistic explanations of universal mysteries. The religious temper of a people was changing, and more than one of the Nook Farm writers was to be absorbed in studying the effects of materialism. All were to be affected by it.

The Religion of Love: Harriet Beecher Stowe

BUSHNELL, AS I HAVE SAID, WAS A PECULIARLY POTENT FORCE IN THE Congregational Church through his influence over colleagues who read his many books and interpreted them in their churches for popular consumption. But, rather than the rebel against the ancient order, he was the spokesman of a people applying the pragmatic test to Calvinism and finding it logically repugnant and increasingly useless in permitting full participation in the life they knew around them. Harriet Beecher Stowe, Bushnell's neighbor, had independently rejected the Calvinism of her father — the most influential preacher of the early years of the nineteenth century. Since she reached directly a far greater audience than Bushnell's and with her brother Henry Ward Beecher carried the new message of God's love to millions, it is essential to consider the nature of her own experience, not only for its biographical interest and its place in the religious thought of Nook Farm, but ultimately for its place in her books and in the emotions of her countrymen.

Catharine Beecher, Harriet's elder sister, who lived long with Harriet in Hartford during her last years, had in her youth made the first break with Lyman Beecher's theology and effected a change in point of view that spread through the whole brilliant family to alter eventually the dogma of the old man himself. When her fiancé, young Professor Fisher of Yale, was drowned before his conversion, it was, of course, Lyman's conviction that he was doomed to an eternal punishment. After a period of profound depression and torment, Catharine finally refused to accept so intolerable an interpretation. The experience had a permanent effect upon Harriet. Through it and her own conversion, which was questioned by Lyman Beecher because it was too easy, she became certain of the validity of her personal religion and sure of the inadequacy of rational theology.

But merely with shaping a set of religious convictions to accommodate her own understanding of the world, Harriet could not content herself. She was moved by the Beecher heredity to reform the world to which her conversion had more nearly adjusted her, and in all her many books she preaches, first and last, in order that her own point of view be accepted by society at large. In *The Minister's Wooing*[7] she used as the climactic incident the Fisher tragedy of her childhood. James Marvyn, with whom Mary is in love, is reported drowned. No evidence justifies hope that at his death he had become one of the Elect. Mary has detected in him only the beginnings of grace. His mother's grief is frightening; her sanity is saved only by the common sense of Candace, the Negro servant, with whose instincts the creed of Calvinism is irreconcilable.[8] James makes a melodramatic reappearance, safe and regenerate, and after marriage to Mary develops under her guidance into a "heroic and Christ-like manhood."

In her other novels of New England, Harriet finds additional opportunity to press the doctrine of God's love for his children, the simple message containing the essence of her own belief. Henry, in *Oldtown Folks*,[9] says, "And my theology is, once penetrate any human soul with the full belief that *God loves him*, and you save him." In *Poganuc People*, the last of the New England novels, Dolly, who is Harriet as she remembers herself as a child, converts stony-hearted Zeph Higgins. Melodrama and message combine to make the incident the most direct illustration of that theology. Dolly's words to the man, "Christ loves you,"

> thrilled through his soul with a strange new power; he opened his eyes and looked astonished into the little earnest, pleading face . . . A tear stole down his hard cheek.
>
> "Thank'e, dear child," he said.
> "You will believe it?"
> "I'll try."
> "You will trust him?"
>
> Zeph paused a moment, then rose up with a new and different expression in his face, and said, in a subdued and earnest voice, "*I will.*"[10]

Her thesis was above all comforting to troubled spirits. The New England tetralogy — *The Minister's Wooing, The Pearl of Orr's Island, Oldtown Folks*, and *Poganuc People* — contains a remarkably detailed analysis of Calvinism and its social implications, ranging from the conflict of Presbyterians and Episcopalians, and its implications in politics,[11] through the preoccupation of congregation and pastor with Calvinist metaphysics,[12] to the poisonous effect of the doctrine upon the people.[13] The popularity of her stories derived, however, not so much from the accuracy of her studies of an anachronistic religion as from the effectiveness of her method for accommodating domestic tragedies. To mothers, who had usually lost one or more infants, she brought the comfort that lives were taken to further the mission of Jesus, that children who die were born

> not for a career and history of their own, but to be proud of life to others. In every household or house have been some of these . . . Fairest . . . and least developed, are the holy innocents who come into our households to smile with the smile of angels, who sleep in our bosoms, and win us with the softness of tender little hands, and pass away like the lamb that was slain before they have ever learned the speech of mortals.[14]

Harriet's point of view toward the death of loved ones must have appealed to many. She had tested it. In 1849 an infant of hers had died of cholera in Cincinnati and in 1857 her son Henry, a Dartmouth student, was drowned in the Connecticut River. She had not faced these trials of her religious faith without anguish. She wrote privately,

> If ever I was conscious of an attack of the Devil trying to separate me from the love of Christ, it was some days after the terrible news came . . . Distressing doubts as to Henry's spiritual state were rudely thrust upon my soul. It was as if a voice had said to me: "You trusted in God, did you? You believed that He loved you! You had perfect confidence that He would never take your child till the work of grace was mature! Now He has hurried him into eternity without a moment's warning, without preparation, and where is he?" [15]

But in time, to which she gives no credit, her world righted and she labored to endow her generation with her own equipoise. When her son Fred disappeared without a trace in 1870, and when her most brilliant daughter later succumbed to a nervous disability and a dependence on drugs, she seemed able to face trouble more easily, but she had been able to see these clouds gathering long in advance. To treat life's sorrows and all its pain, she developed a personal Creator who is vitally interested in his creatures; she based the validity of her belief on her observations. The breadth of her experience and the earthiness of her nondoctrinaire realism saved most of her books from the vacuousness of the goody-goody literature of her times.

The growth of this point of view, a nonintellectual parallel of Bushnell's doctrine, was as evident elsewhere in America as in Nook Farm, in so far as it was allied with the retreat from hell-fire theology. To evaluate this simple creed in terms of its acceptability to intellectuals of the twentieth century is pointless. In its day and in some quarters it served its purpose by providing an orientation to the facts of life: it served Harriet, for example, better at the death of her sons than skepticism served Mark when his daughter died in 1896. So much for the more conventional aspects of Harriet's religion. She was to take part also in the erratic developments of the neighborhood's religious experience.

Harriet's formal allegiance to church was typical of the evolving obliteration of real differences between the Protestant sects. She often attended Twichell's church, with which her husband was historically associated, though she had enrolled as an Episcopalian when she moved to Hartford. More or less absent-mindedly, Calvin remained a Congregationalist. His studies of Biblical history in a way authorized his wife's belief in the Bible as the source of simple religious truth as distinguished from the theological superstructure erected upon it. Harriet's son Charles elected to become a Congregational minister without protest from his mother and eventually settled in Hartford in a parsonage she bought for him. Charles Dudley Warner, a parishioner of Twichell's, also thought of becoming an Episcopalian (or something "further"—perhaps Catholic), but his satisfaction with Twichell and the developing dominance of a nonsectarian Christian ethic over loyalty to a given creed kept him within the fold. His inclination was that of the Nook Farm group, who by 1870 had left far behind the jealous sectarian loyalties of their antediluvian youth. Dr. Burton, Bushnell's successor in the Park Church, before accepting his new post apparently himself considered joining the Episcopal Church. "We are all tending that way," Charles Dudley Warner added. "I mean Susie [his wife]. I should go further if I stirred at all." [16]

The Religion of Love: Henry Ward Beecher

THE DEVELOPMENT OF RELIGIOUS IDEAS AFTER THE CIVIL WAR WAS MULTIfaceted. The collapse of Calvinism and the popularization of optimism and unschematized individual faith prompted a host of departures from the comparatively simple uniformity of the old days. Members of the Beecher family were implicated in the spread of popular evolutionism which would eventually undermine the acceptance of Harriet's moral teachings. Charles Beecher, for example, had been tried during the Civil War (very soon after Darwin's pronouncements) for the heresy in his approval of the doctrines of evolution, the preëxistence of souls, and spiritualism,[17] a combination in which he found no inconsistency. That other Congregational Associations were belatedly approaching the organizational tolerance of Connecticut is indicated in his eventual exoneration after being found guilty. In Brooklyn, Henry Ward Beecher carried Harriet's warmth of faith and Bushnell's doctrine of immanent spirituality (later with an added evolutionary and melioristic twist of his own) to the people so effectively that eagerness to hear him became hysterical. He had no theology, no concern for philosophy, and no dialectical facility. But taking some of the Hartford intuitions to the extreme of sensibility, he gave a whole generation an emotional thrill as love and perfectionism took the place of fear, and hope superseded logic.

In the mind of Henry Ward Beecher, the problem of evil had become almost trivial. Like his brothers and sisters, he had shed the morbid doctrine of total depravity. The Beechers as a family swung almost to the opposite extreme of benignity. Catharine had developed in Hartford her own differences with John Calvin; the human mind, she argued, was a perfect construction, untainted and educable. Edward Beecher used Biblical evidence and complicated metaphysics to reject his father's teaching; he asserted that no predisposition to evil hindered man's evolutionary progress toward utter saintliness. Harriet Beecher recognized only one sin, slavery; once it was eradicated, the sunshine of God's goodness could nurture the inevitable growth of his people.

Under the optimism of the view that the natural is the good, a slow leavening of public morality took place. Thomas K. Beecher, another son of Lyman, distrusted his brother Henry's confidence that no harm would result from relaxing the stern disciplines which once had reinforced moral conduct with the imagery of hell. He deplored the free-love sects, for example, which he saw casting shadows across the country. But his hesitant recognition of the clouds gave him no premonition that out of them disaster was soon to strike like lightning.

Though the revolutionary religious doctrines of the Beecher clan and of Horace Bushnell made steady progress against limited logical opposition, a tremendous explosion was brewing. The new teachings were greeted with an enthusiasm which conceals the disturbance they germinated. The religion of love sanctioned a new kind of religious belief and a whole new orientation to reality. It not only altered the religious philosophy of a generation, but affected deeply its views toward moral conduct. In beneficent affirmation of the goodness of man, it authorized a novel freedom of behavior which was in sharpest conflict with the Calvinist heritage. The inevitable violence, occurring after the religious revolution was well advanced and the arguments of the conservative opposition had become almost inaudible, flared in the most sensational scandal of the nineteenth century — the alleged adultery of Henry Ward Beecher and Elizabeth Tilton.

The tides of feeling which this incident released to sweep the nation washed into Hartford to alter Nook Farm's serenity. Henry Ward Beecher had often visited his three sisters there. He had encouraged Mark Twain before *Innocents Abroad*; he had seen him many times since the first meetings in New York. He knew well both Charles Dudley Warner and Joseph Twichell. His sister Isabella loved him deeply. Since nothing else in the years between 1870 and 1875 loomed so large in Nook Farm's experience as the disaster befalling Henry Ward Beecher, the event belongs in this record of the community's history. And since the occurrence was the inevitable consequence of introducing the religion of love to a nation trained in an austere morality associated with Calvinist asceticism, I have thought it appropriate to include with their religious experience the role of Hartford people in this dramatic catastrophe.

Henry Ward Beecher had been pastor of the Plymouth Church in Brooklyn since 1847. In 1848, as editor of Henry C. Bowen's *Independent*, he began to reach an audience larger than his immediate pastorate. By 1858 he had become intimate with Theodore Tilton, a suffrage advocate who converted Henry to advocacy of women's rights and who succeeded Beecher as editor of the *Independent* in 1861. Gossip began to circulate in New York in the late sixties that Henry Ward Beecher's relation with Tilton's wife was adulterous. In the latter part of 1871, Elizabeth Tilton "confessed" to Susan B. Anthony and Elizabeth Cady Stanton that the stories had foundation in fact. Mrs. Anthony, horrified, was also grimly pleased. She had long wasted no affection on Henry. In 1865 he had denounced her radical wing of the suffrage party and switched his own allegiance to Julia Ward Howe's more conservative faction. Susan repeated Elizabeth Tilton's story to Victoria Woodhull and Isabella Beecher Hooker. Victoria Woodhull, beautiful adventuress, advocate of free love, spiritualism, and feminism, seized the opportunity to strike publicly at hypocrisy. In September of 1872, standing before a breathless convention of Boston spiritualists, she dramatically announced that America's most renowned clergyman was practicing in secret the free-love doctrines he denounced from the pulpit. In November of 1872 she spread the Beecher-Tilton story through an issue of her paper, *Woodhull and Claflin's Weekly*.[18] Within twenty-four hours of publication, copies sold for forty dollars each.

Beecher and Tilton kept complete silence. No reputable newspaper referred to the scandal for a long time, in spite of its having become public property. Finally, in 1873, the Plymouth Church, deciding that the incident could no longer be ignored, dropped Tilton from its rolls. The press took up the story, but still Beecher and Tilton made no statement. In December of 1874, Theodore Tilton, aware that his reputation was indeed suffering, filed suit for alienation of affections. The trial, beginning in January 1875, lasted six lurid months. An enormous amount of contradictory evidence was aired. Beecher's famous letter of contrition, in which he confessed to having wronged Tilton, without saying in what way, was read into the record. The full story of Tilton's and Beecher's curious relation through an intermediary named Moulton explained the long silence as an attempt of both men to avoid publicity. The jury, unable to reach a verdict, returned a majority of nine to three for acquittal and was discharged in July 1875. The Plymouth Church called an "Advisory Council" of Congregational ministers to reëxamine the evidence and settle the case to the satisfaction of the public. The ministers exonerated Beecher.[19]

Alleged infidelity in Brooklyn is inescapably relevant to the story of Nook Farm because of Isabella Beecher Hooker's conviction that her brother had committed the transgression with which he was charged. If Victoria Woodhull thought Henry was guilty, then so would she. Victoria had traveled the West with her sister Tennessee (later Tennie C.) Claflin, dealing in every profitable quackery from spiritualism to faith-healing. Invading the East, the two sisters became, under the sponsorship of Commodore Vanderbilt, the first lady brokers of Wall Street.[20] Notoriously promiscuous, Victoria was hardly the kind of woman who could be expected to enthrall Mrs. Hooker. But in 1870, while Isabella was in Washington running the convention of the National Woman's Suffrage Association, Victoria appeared independently before Congress with her own plea for the ballot. Isabella heard Victoria present the memorial, invited her to join the Association's convention, and almost at once fell under the younger woman's spell. Her subjection was so complete that she could not question Victoria's charge against her brother.

The scandal itself, and Isabella's unconcealed belief in Henry's guilt, brought consternation and heartsickness to Nook Farm. Most of its residents sided with Henry. Their position was in part a matter of personal loyalty to a friend and probably also a nonlogical conviction that such ugliness could not be, except on levels of society lower than their own. They were puzzled by Isabella's prejudice. No brother-sister hostility existed to explain her position. When Henry wrote to her on April 25, 1872, to ask her silence, he added, "Probably you and I are nearer together than any of our family." [21] Isabella, to be sure, did not lightly make her decision to speak out; for a time she was willing to entertain the idea that Henry's offense was wrong only in its surreptitiousness. When she did act, it was with the courage that Theodore Tilton had earlier described in her as providing "new proof that a Calvinistic education, if once the soul which it narrows gets broadened, furnished an intensity of moral conviction." [22] Isabella finally wrote Henry on November 1, 1872 that she had been told of his guilt by Mrs. Woodhull and Mrs. Stanton. "From that day to this I have carried a heavy load, you may be sure. I could not share it with my husband, because he was already overburdened and alarmingly affected brainwise." She had sent John off to Europe with her daughter Mary to spare him the shock, only to learn that independently he had come to her conclusion. When she had heard the story from Mrs. Stanton, her only comment to Henry had been, "if true you had a philosophy of the relation of the sexes so far ahead of the times that you dared not announce it, though you consented to live by it." Before passing judgment, she decided to wait, because she had come to see that "human laws were an impertinence." She could see "glimpses of a new science of life [free love] that at present is revolting to my feelings and my judgment" in the face of which she would keep an open mind. But as fast as she *knew* the truth she would announce it without heed to the social consequences. She begged the whole truth so that if Henry were ready to announce a new social freedom, he and she might do it together. "My own conviction is that the one radical mistake you have made is in supposing that you are so much ahead of your time, and in daring to attempt to lead when you have anything to conceal." Henry must be true to his mental convictions. Again of her anguish:

> I have not told you the half that I have suffered since February [1871], but you can imagine, knowing what my husband is to me, that it was no common love . . . when I decided to nearly break his heart, already lacerated by the course I had been compelled to pursue, by sending him away to die, perhaps, without me at his side.[23]

To her brother Tom in Elmira, she wrote of her perplexity, begged for advice, and alluded to the compulsion in her devotion to Victoria Woodhull which had driven her to side against her brother:

> . . . my heart aches for that woman even as for my own flesh and blood. I do not understand her, but I know her to be pure and unselfish and absolutely driven by some power foreign to herself to these strange utterances [like the accusation against Henry], which are always in behalf of freedom, purity — truth, as she understands it — always to befriend the poor and outcast, and bring low only the proud, the hypocrites in high places.[24]

Thomas replied, knowing Woodhull better than his sister did:

> To allow the devil himself to be crushed for speaking the truth is unspeakably cowardly and contemptible. I respect, *as at present advised* [his italics], Mrs. Woodhull, while I abhor her philosophy. She only carries out Henry's philosophy, against which I recorded my protest twenty years ago, and parted (lovingly and achingly) from him, saying, "We cannot work together." . . . In my judgment Henry is following his slippery doctrines of expediency, and in his cry of progress and the nobleness of human nature has sacrificed clear, exact, ideal integrity.[25]

He declined to participate in the controversy, advised Isabella she could not help Henry (having chosen her principles, she must take the consequences), but warned her she had no legal proof of Henry's guilt.

Undeterred, Isabella acted on her convictions without pondering their validity. Henry became seriously alarmed when Isabella proposed on November 27, 1872 to appear in his pulpit and take sole charge of the services to read a paper she would write "as one commissioned from on high." She was driven to this course by a reference in the Hartford *Times* bringing the scandal close home. She named a meeting place and demanded that Henry come to see her. Theodore Tilton came instead (he was then collaborating with Beecher in keeping silent on the month-old Woodhull charges), and though he later declined to testify how he achieved Isabella's silence, Moulton, the intermediary, reported on the witness stand that Tilton had told him:

> I did go to see Mrs. Hooker [at the home of an unidentified New York friend], and . . . I did for the purpose of quieting her as against making the charge of adultery against him, charging her with adultery . . . I came back and told Mr. Beecher that, and he seemed to be satisfied with it, and was delighted with it.[26]

It is more probable that Isabella gave up her plan of action because it demanded Henry's consent and collaboration. Much as she would like to, she could not, after all, take Henry's pulpit by force.

John Hooker emerges from the events of 1871 and 1872 a pathetic figure. He proved entirely loyal to his wife in the face of provocations not yet fully detailed. Isabella had trained him in the merits of the woman's-rights crusade, but he could not and would not share her admiration for Victoria Woodhull, who was not the symbol of purity to him that she was to Isabella. Unlike his wife, he cultivated respectability; nothing repelled him more than the idea of free love. He wrote his wife from Florence in November 1872, just as *Woodhull and Claflin's Weekly* was announcing the scandal to the world, a letter that refers poignantly to his concern for his own reputation. He implored Isabella to let the report get about, after the scandal is inevitably made public, that she has maintained her friendship with Mrs. Woodhull only to persuade the latter to withhold the story from publication,

> . . . and that you gave up going to Europe with me so as to be at home and comfort H. [Henry] when the truth came out . . . This will give the appearance of self-sacrifice to your affiliation with her, and will explain your not coming abroad with me — a fact which has a very unwife-like look. I know that we will otherwise be regarded as living in some discord, and probably (by many people) as practising her principles. It would be a great relief to me to have your relation to Mrs. W. explained in this way, so creditable to your heart. There is not half the untruth in it that there has been all along in my pretended approval of Mrs. Woodhull's course. And yet people think me an honest man. I have lied enough about that to ruin the character of an average man, and have probably damaged myself by it.[27]

His wife, of course, declined the suggestion; the reign of King John and Queen Isabella over Nook Farm society was at an end.

The other Beecher sisters flew to Henry's defense and broke off relations with Isabella. Mary Beecher Perkins and her husband were staunch advocates of Henry's innocence. Harriet closed her house to Isabella. Only Catharine Beecher, who at 75 would not quarrel with any of her relatives, remained on speaking terms with Mrs. Hooker. Yet Catharine was deep in this affair, having only recently failed to convince Victoria Woodhull (in a face-to-face interview during a Central Park buggy ride) that her views on marriage were unacceptable. Mark Twain, arriving back from a three-month absence from home in November 1872 — a day or two before Isabella notified Henry that she was coming to New York — stormed into town and announced to Livy that they too would ostracize Isabella. Molly Clemens wrote her mother-in-law, "Sam says Livy shall not cross Mrs. Hookers threshold and if he talks to Mrs. H he will tell her in plain words the reason." [28] Thus, after a year in Hartford, the newcomer to the society of the East, instead of being himself rejected, excluded its early leader from the association of his wife. Isabella had been the first of the Hartford people to extend hospitality to him; she was currently his landlady. But she was asserting in public that her own brother had committed adultery. Isabella withstood such obloquy for two years, but in 1874, when Henry publicly called her insane, she fled to Europe to escape the unbearable recriminations.

Her husband meanwhile did his earnest best to reweave the torn relationships, salvage his wife's good name, and defend his own reputation as "that member of the Hartford bar which is the synonym of all that is purest in professional character and lovely in personal virtues." [29] He returned to

Hartford in 1873 and thereafter made every attempt to emphasize the half-truth that Isabella, in love for Henry, was only protecting him against the inevitable explosion and preparing him for it. By October 1874 his efforts to convince Harriet Beecher Stowe had made some progress; she told Twichell that Isabella had become convinced her views of Henry's guilt were entirely wrong.[30] Actually Isabella never changed her mind. Harriet became unconvinced again, apparently, for she told Hooker that Twichell had said Isabella wanted the documents shown to establish Beecher's guilt. Hooker called on Twichell in December to ask what Isabella had said to him when she had showed him in the previous summer some documents bearing on the case. Twichell patiently explained to Hooker that he had said only that Isabella wanted the documents read to prepare those who loved Henry for his approaching downfall. Twichell read them, but found them unconvincing.

Mr. H. said that no one of Mr. B's partizans was doing so much for love of him as Mrs. H. for she was allowing herself to rest under the charge of conspiring against him just because she feared it might work against him to clear herself (as she easily could) of the charge as it was made in the public prints last autumn. Mr. H. gave me the impression that he believed Mr. B. to be guilty.[31]

In February of 1875 Hooker, still busy with the Augean stables, came again to Twichell, carrying a draft of a letter to Mrs. Susan Howard of Brooklyn that he wanted to publish—

a strong, good letter, exhibiting certain dark phazes of the Scandal affair, yet not pronouncing upon them, but keeping to its object of disproving what the newspapers said about Mrs. Hooker as to her mental and moral subjection to Mrs. Woodhull—her having seduced her into the conspiracy against her brother &c. Mr. Hooker showed great feeling of sorrow for his wife and a sense of her being cruelly dealt with. By Mr. Hookers consent showed the letter to Parker and Clemens. Both thought that it looked badly for H.W.B.[32]

This entry marks Hooker's greatest success as a fence mender. Twichell's mind was not entirely made up, and elsewhere in the community John's untiring and earnest pleading bore some fruit.

Twichell's participation in the great scandal grew more direct as time went on. He attended some of the sessions of the trial with Mark, and he studied carefully the maze of conflicting evidence. After the public clamor for clear-cut decision caused the Plymouth Church to call a grand council of ministers to ponder a final verdict, Twichell, one of the Congregational ministers summoned, went to Brooklyn in February of 1876. He boarded the train depressed by his misgivings. The first meeting of the council, however, convinced him that it was "a noble body of men bent on doing righteously without fear or favor." Henry Ward Beecher, who had behaved like a clown through the public trial, bore himself well and seriously now. "He *seemed* like a good man, and I know that many delegates as they listened to him and watched him were conscious of ceasing to doubt his integrity." The council cleared Beecher but criticized his "'inexpressible folly' in falling so easy a prey to his enemies."[33] Twichell found in that formula the solvent of his foreboding.

The proceedings of the council were interrupted by the news of the death of Horace Bushnell, and on February 17, with Edwin Pond Parker, who had also gone from Hartford to sit as judge, Twichell hurried home for the funeral. In ironic timeliness it was a moving occasion for both men. Bushnell, the intellectual, had in a measure prepared the way for Beecher, the vulnerable purveyor of compelling optimism. Bushnell's death marked the moment when some, like Thomas K. Beecher, had come to see that an extension of Bushnell's basic doctrine had social implications. The New York *Times* observed:

> There is only one good result which can possibly follow from this exposure and trial. It may lead people in Brooklyn and elsewhere to distrust the new Gospel of love and to allow no priests or ministers to come between husband and wife, or to interfere with family ties or sully family honor. Lastly it may induce them to return to the older and safer moorings which alone can prevent society from drifting into chaos. If this should be the fruit of the trial, a scandal which poisoned the air for six long months will not have been dragged to the light in vain.[34]

The warning here that the gospel of love should not be confused with erotic fervor[35] was heeded, and a scrupulous abstention from invasion of the individual's privacy was thenceforth the minister's practice. But American society was irrevocably cut loose from "older and safer moorings" and would be compelled to find its religious and ethical bearings at sea. The breaking away from steadfast standards of conduct, in part signalized and in part hastened by the purgative notoriety attending the Beecher trial, came later than the departure from stable religious ideas. Both were inevitable, but the everyday consequences of neither were entirely welcome to those who became unwilling pilgrims over unmapped territory.

Clerical Triumvirate: Burton, Parker, and Twichell

DURING THE SEVENTIES AND EIGHTIES IN HARTFORD, THREE YOUNGER LIBERAL Congregational clergymen stood together in the eyes of the community as the leaders of religious thought and the acknowledged masters of the pulpit. Devoted to the theological legacy of Bushnell and united by strong personal affection, Joseph Hopkins Twichell, Nathaniel Judson Burton, and Edwin Pond Parker exercised a congenial influence over their place and time and became widely known throughout New England as a talented triumvirate. All three were close friends of Mark Twain.

Nathaniel Burton, born in 1822, was the oldest of the group. His father was an itinerant Methodist preacher whose fathers before him had lived in Connecticut since the seventeenth century. After his graduation from Wesleyan University in 1850, he attended the Yale Divinity School, to be ordained in 1852 as a Congregational pastor. He went to Hartford in 1857, where he occupied the pulpit of the Fourth Congregational Church and settled with his family in Nook Farm. After Bushnell's retirement, he succeeded to the leadership of the Park Church and retained it till his death in 1887.

Burton's principal achievement, like that of his younger associates, was the personal influence he wielded over the people of his acquaintance and congregation. He was born and educated a Methodist, ordained a Congregationalist, and later considered becoming an Episcopalian. Theological controversy meant no more to him than did sectarian refinements. He devoted almost all his time to the pleasures of company, elevating companionship as he knew it in Nook Farm to a way of life and a source of spiritual satisfaction. He published nothing substantial, though after his death his son Richard,[36] at Mark Twain's suggestion, edited his lectures delivered at the Yale Divinity School and a dozen of what Mark called "those splendid preachments of his" taken from the barrel. Mark overruled Charles Webster, his business partner,[37] who probably thought the sermons unsalable, and thus preserved some of his friend's life work. His addresses were written with a careless floridity once accepted as elegance and power and were, John Hooker tells us, universally composed at the last minute, with as little time as possible torn from company to permit solitary composition. A passage in one of his sermons characterizes both his point of view and his pulpit style:

> In my judgment the principal thing in the world is its men and women. Great and dear is this green month of June; great the overarch of heavenly blue; great the careering night with its embellishment of stars; great and solemn the outstretch of astronomic spaces; great, and also bewitching, that everlasting march and miscellany of phenomena which constitutes our environment here. Neverthe-

less, let the heart speak, and the greatest interest in God's whole round of fascinations is the people. Multitudes of them I have never gotten hold of in any visible way; but I take a sense of them stretching away beyond my horizon, and I have a feeling of their company present and to come. Many of them to whom I do have access are not superfinely made up, but, then, no more am I.[38]

The people he knew loved him in return. They liked his face (he looked about his nose and eyes and mouth a little like the older Mark Twain, though the top of his head was bald), his generosity and tolerance, the heartiness of his laughter, and the inclusiveness of his optimism and affection. "Burly and magnificent," Mark called him.[39] He vastly amused the Hooker household for two years. "A stranger," Hooker wrote, "certainly a sanctimonious one, would have had his doubts whether such an inclination to hilarity was consistent with the deep, earnest religious thought and feeling that after all was the predominating feature of his life, and I trust was not wholly wanting in mine."[40] Burton liked Mark Twain and enjoyed the complimentary copy of each book Mark sent him. He wrote Mark once to recommend a colored butler to him and said in passing,

And permit me . . . to say I am glad you (and yours) are safely in the country again. I feel a vague kind of moral support when you are anywhere around. Of course I cant analysize it and say why! And why should I? No Sir I accept the blessing & ask no questions. That seems scriptural and safe. And the sooner you come to Htfd the better.[41]

Burton had a "rich and royal nature," Timothy Dwight thought, and he stood out in any company of men. "His very countenance . . . showed his masterful power . . . There was in him a deep-seated confidence in the nobility and real grandeur of the human soul, which made him a believer in the final triumph of good over evil, and gave him a never-failing enthusiasm in his work for this end."[42]

Burton's optimism was deep-rooted in his own temperament and that of his neighborhood, but it was neither provincial nor altogether unstreaked by melancholy. He was not entirely ignorant of the world. He had lived a year in Europe in 1868–69, writing letters back to the *Courant* as shrewd in observation as complex in language, and had seen eastern America on a trip to Florida with John Hooker in 1867. But the further his observations of peoples were widened, the more confident in men he became.

In his last years, however, he knew inexplicably melancholy moods. At these moments, when his pleasure in this world palled, he turned to the next for a renewal of inspiration. Dwight noticed the recurring melancholia in his association with Burton in the Yale Corporation, and Hooker preserved "a soliloquy of some intense mood of his later years" which contains a real note of weariness beneath the characteristic stylistic gingerbread:

> Heaven is rest and joy, and it requires the heart to interpret that and grasp its immeasurable meaning. Oh! when I am tired; when my body is unstrung and my soul is jaded, and my bones flag and my ambitions flicker in their socket . . . when the song of birds is heavy music, and all the trees of the field seem chastened . . . when the beauty of women is vanity to my eyes, and I can see no dignity in the faces of men; when the friends of my youth are scattered and dead . . . when my sympathies are pensive and retrospective, and I live with the dead whom I knew more than with the living whom I know . . . when the love and the hate, and the efforts and delights of men seem small and empty,—oh! when I am tired, and sad, and worn out, I know what is intended by the promise of rest and joy in heaven.[43]

Edwin Pond Parker achieved a position in the Hartford community much like Burton's, though greater reserve in his relations with his neighbors tempered the admiration of his public. He came down from Maine in 1860 to the state of his ancestors to minister for sixty years to the Second Church. When his theology came into dramatic conflict with the elder generation at his initial examination, Joel Hawes rescued him from the jaws of the opponents of Bushnell, who were appalled at Parker's casual treatment of the doctrine of probation. Parker had never thought of probation in the abstract at all and on the spur of the moment supposed that "God would give every man a *fair chance*!"[44] A crusty minority considered this "a most unfortunate expression" and after his installation a battle raged over his head in the *Observer*, the *Independent*, the *Congregationalist*, and the *Recorder*. This flare-up was almost the last protest of the old guard against the new simplicity; the rage of the orthodox professionals was apparently deepened by a bitter realization that theology had lost its dialectical grandeur and its strenuous objectivity. Cubs were coming from the schools, they felt, with soft hearts as their only qualification. Burton sympathized with Parker's naïve directness and between the two began the friendship to which Twichell was admitted five years later.

Parker began his pastorate by celebrating on December 24, 1860 the first Christmas to be observed by a New England Congregational church. He followed this innovation with the introduction of music and ritual without incurring immovable opposition. His sermons, preserved intermittently in Monday's *Courant*, were as fully dependent on the castellated periodic sentence as were Burton's, but his ornamentation was less Gothic. Their messages were no more doctrinal than one might expect; they were intended to create an atmosphere in which perception of the compelling goodness of life might be quickened in the listener. He tried to attract attention to the esthetics of the undifferentiated Christian ethic. Parker had interests more varied than Burton's unalloyed satisfaction in human beings. Where Burton found in Mark Twain's books something for laughter, Parker examined them as an amateur critic, urging Mark to leave humor and move toward the superior excellence of *The Prince and the Pauper*. Their relations were cordial, in spite of the probably unintentional condescension in Parker's manner.[45] He wrote a review of Mark Twain's career for J. R. Osgood (Boston publisher) to use for circular purposes and often chose literary rather than religious subjects for essays read to the Monday Evening Club. He compiled a biography of Harriet Beecher Stowe for *Eminent Women of the Age* (1868). As he grew old at his post, he came to be regarded as an institution, influential in the pulpit and in the Yale Corporation. Satisfied with his role and with his era, his mind was apparently untroubled with misgivings. He took pride in the fact that though Hartford had 200 saloons for 30,000 people in 1860, it supported only half as many in 1892 with twice the population. And the state of the nation was similarly satisfactory.

> Not only do we live amid material comforts that make our world far more endurable and enjoyable than that of former ages, but we possess an intellectual light, a social welfare, a civil and spiritual freedom, of which our forefathers scarcely dreamed.[46]

In Parker, optimism most explicitly became complacence.

Though Twichell came to Hartford five years after Parker, it was not long before he joined his older colleagues in a three-cornered coöperation and a permanent friendship. The three men collaborated in *The Christian Hymnal*, under the leadership of Parker, from 1875 to 1877. Their families were intimate. Twichell, who named his nine children after friends, named one son Burton Parker Twichell; the trio assembled at the christening of their namesake. Twichell read the prayers over the body of Parker's child of two weeks. They were all members of the Yale Corporation. Implicit agreement bound them together in their discharge of clerical responsibilities. They agreed to derive their authority from the acceptance and love of their congregations, whom they would not harass in their leadership.

Of Twichell's religious ideas it is not necessary to say much more. Twichell is more important as a man than as a minister, and it is the man putting the simple religious faith of his place into practice who is presently of interest. Like Parker and Burton, he was devoted to his profession, but in character he surpassed them in complexity.

Mark Twain's ideas of religion were even in 1871 very different from his friend's, but he listened to Twichell's accounts of his work and sympathized with the intensity of his ethical convictions. Twichell was tireless in dealing with individual derelictions, and though bland about the smaller vices of men, was much troubled about addiction to alcohol and sexual immorality. Once he learned that one of his parishioners had seduced a girl who belonged to the literary circle of a large city. The young man refused to accede to Twichell's suggestion that he marry his victim. The miscreant brought another to the church one Sunday as his bride, and Twichell found he could not look at the reptile. "But you ought to have seen Harmony . . . her countenance was a study. She says that she experienced for several minutes . . . the actual physical sensation of nausea and that she couldn't tell at all what the sermon had been about. Oh, Sister Twichell was inspired with a holy wrath, I can assure you." But despite his amused tone he took very seriously this kind of misdemeanor. "It seems to me that never in my life before, in the same space of time, have I had so many *Cases* revealing the woful tragical aspects of human experience, brought to my knowledge, as in the past few months." [47]

But though the Cases were more numerous toward the end of the century than during the seventies and eighties, alcoholism was a pressing problem in the earlier years. It was not only prevalent in the community, but frequent in the congregation. Fred Stowe, after a brain wound in the Civil War had made him an inebriate, stumbled around Nook Farm and the downtown streets until his mother, in the hope that travel might cure him, sent him away on a trip, from which he never was to return. Soon one of Twichell's deacons, a high official in the Farmers and Mechanics Bank, went via drink to embezzlement and ruin — and thence to the penitentiary. Twichell was deeply moved by these and other incidents. He wrote to Mark in 1879:

> The Inebriate Asylum is closed. Cause: lack of funds. Cause of that: the Superintendent a failure, I *think*. Yet new drunkards are blooming all around. I've got another awful secret or two of impending ruin and disgrace loaded onto me, and it is a sick business, I can tell you.
>
> I wish I loved any good thing half as much as I hate Rum, now that I have found it out.
>
> Mark! Mark! *Do you look out for it!*
>
> It is the Arch Deceiver. It *fools* men.[48]

Twichell's weapon was moral suasion; he found it often inadequate. Without the advantage of therapies developed after his time and still not generally accepted, he sometimes despaired. He was always deeply concerned with deviations from the normal among his flock and heartsick when his ministrations failed. But his observations of human fallibility did not deflect his faith in the human race, and in his letters to Mark he took issue with the latter's pessimism, charging that Mark was too "orthodox on the Doctrine of Total Human Depravity." [49]

Besides the devotion to his calling exhibited in his clinical experience, Twichell's personal religion was notable for humility. He was never complacent about his own gifts or satisfied with his own religious development. After reading Mary Bushnell Cheney's life of her father, he wrote in his journal:

> It has caused all Christian truth to appear most true and most beautiful; especially the possibility of man's union with God through Christ by faith. It has given me, I trust, a fresh instigation to try and struggle out of my low estate and reach some higher ground. I am convicted of sin, sin, sin, and emptiness . . . Oh, Lord, must I live on to the end in this poverty? Yet I know the riches are ready to be given if I will make room for them.[50]

Many other entries are devoted to soul searching, not so frequently as to indicate obsessive self-abasement, but often enough to establish the modesty of his self-estimate.

Twichell's diffidence about his sermons and writings was unremitting. On one occasion, Charles Dudley Warner, his parishioner, took issue in a *Courant* editorial [51] with this self-depreciation:

> And I am the more indignant over it because he is so sincere about it. I suppose it never once occurred to him that he was paying an exceedingly poor tribute to the intelligence of his congregation. He confessed that the preparation of his discourse was hard work and cost him time and labor, and he went on to speak as if it were notorious that the result was pretty much a failure.

Warner then sums up Twichell's accomplishments during twenty years of

> uncommon intellectual stir and the agitation and unsettlement of doubt. I happen to know that he has been keenly alive to all this movement, and has given much study and thought to the discussions that have shaken the Christian world. He is of a liberal and receptive mind.

And his sermons, concise, clear, shaded by humor, have literary power.

But it is Warner's last sentence that gives the key to Twichell's place in his community and to the nature of his achievement as a religious leader. "Heaven, in short, does not often send us a real MAN." In a sense this sentence refers also to the power of Burton and Parker, but Twichell differed personally from them in an earthiness that salted the assumption of personal saintliness then made appropriate by his profession. In spite of momentary doubts about his personal salvation, he was exuberantly glad to be alive. In 1882, for example, he wrote to Mark, still at Quarry Farm, of his homecoming from Europe:

> Really I am about as happy as I *thought* I should be: and for the time as content, utterly, thankfully, joyfully content — with my earthly lot, as I felt I must be while contemplating it at a distance of three to four thousand miles. Oh, it is splendid. This year 125 Woodland St is enchanted ground, clear out to the barbed wire fence . . . Harmony and I are having a new honeymoon, and the seven children in the chorus don't seem at all in the way.[52]

Part of this joy was thankfulness that he had got old Newton Case[53] back from an onerous tour of the continent, during which Twichell had to bear with the insufferable dullness of the company who had taken him along as guide, and beyond that had to locate a *pissoir* for the old man every twenty minutes. Paris was the only really convenient city.

Twichell was an enthusiastic outdoor man. In the summer he loved to put a flannel shirt on and indolently enjoy the cool mountains, either in the Adirondacks or in New Hampshire. He often roamed about under an alias so that he could rub elbows with all sorts of disreputable characters without embarrassment by the odor of sanctity. These adventures often became literary material for Mark. Twichell delighted in relaxation. His pleasure in Mark's bawdy *1601* is well known. Mark writes of it:

> It [the MS] made a fat letter. I bundled it up and mailed it to Twichell in Hartford. And in the fall, when we returned to our home in Hartford and Twichell and I resumed the Saturday ten-mile walk to Talcott tower and back, every Saturday as had been our custom for years, we used to carry that letter along. There was a grove of hickory trees by the roadside, six miles out, and close by it was the only place in that whole region where the fringed gentian grew. On our return from the Tower we used to gather the gentians, then lie down on the grass upon the golden carpet of fallen hickory leaves and get out that letter and read it by the help of these poetical surroundings. We used to laugh ourselves lame and sore over the cup-bearers troubles. I wonder if we could laugh over them now? We were so young then — and maybe there was not so much to laugh at . . . as we thought there was.[54]

Somehow I find nothing prurient in Twichell's enjoyment of *1601*, and nothing inconsistent with his whole character as a religious man. He believed that excretion, for example, was not a regrettable human necessity and chided Mark, on at least one occasion, for calling "indelicate" a speech he found himself making as he woke out of a dream. He did not admit any dichotomy between the animal and the higher functions of life. His sense of humor was not bounded by a horror of the vulgar.

This was a man whom his contemporaries, recognizing his earthiness, found effective in the ministry. Charles Hopkins Clark wrote of him in retrospect:

> Nobody stands in dread of him, everybody respects and loves him and to thousands he is still "Joe" Twichell; he is as approachable as one boy is to another, full of interest in the things of this world, and in abundant sympathy with many of them, and all the more influential because his feet touch the ground and he walks the same earth with the rest of us, though on a path that leads upward and along which his leadership draws and has drawn so many others.[55]

By the end of the century, Twichell was nationally known to be genial, eloquent, witty, and yet a Christian. The place of his "religious ideas" in this development may seem to be minor, and certainly his contribution to theology was negligible, but his religious faith encompassed an important tolerance of the whole nature of man.

To assess at this distance a leadership not based on logically enunciated policy is difficult and perhaps irrelevant to a summary of religious experience. Intellectuals of religion Burton, Parker, and Twichell emphatically were not. They were instinctively adapted to the new post-War atmosphere, wholly at home in its values, and entirely disinclined to codify their relationship to society or to alter the values they observed. Their status derived almost entirely from the strength of their personal hold on their fellows. Testimony to their aura is unanimous. They were good men of wide acquaintance and universal popularity. Their message was shaped in rhythmical appeals to an ethical life and their devotion to religion was tempered by a wide humanity. Their churches became institutions for community good works and centers of information and appropriate recreation. The debates of the old time on the nature of God and the relation of his creatures to him had given way to ethical addresses, spelling bees, charity bazaars, and lectures on literature and the arts.

Each of these three ministers had a congregation of professional and business men who subscribed to a code of personal and business ethics and regarded themselves as both sober and responsible citizens. The men were lawyers or merchants or members of the growing insurance business. No robber barons prowled among them, and few, if any, Democrats. Taken as a whole, they were politically conservative, honest and cautious, content with a high return on their investments, and satisfied with conditions that made such returns possible. To charities they subscribed generously, trusting Burton, or Parker, or Twichell to distinguish the worthy causes from those unworthy, but firmly convinced that poverty in general was, under the beneficence of private capitalism, traceable most often to shiftlessness and addiction to drink. Just as the clerical triumvirate had abandoned Calvinist metaphysics to preach a religion of optimistic faith, so the congregations, which in Old New England followed pulpit dialectics with disputatious zeal, were now passive listeners to bland affirmations. Their ministers were of them, not above them, and through twenty years little disturbed the easy relationship.

The Asylum Hill Congregational Church was the focus of what formal religious life we need consider. Mark Twain rented a pew there and in the seventies, though he never joined the congregation as a formal member, usually attended services when he and his family were in Hartford. From the rolls of the congregation came his good friends. Eminent men like Marshall Jewell — thrice governor of Connecticut, minister to Russia, and Grant's postmaster general — were on the lists. Most of the Nook Farm residents, the Hawleys, Gillettes, Warners, Cases, Blisses, and Dunhams, were members. Two or three times a week, most of them met for religious exercises or secular programs. Mark was always on hand for readings or speeches. In May of 1875, for example, Mark made the opening speech at a spelling match, pointing out that, though the temperance epidemic had apparently spared the city, the spelling craze had hit it squarely. Mark and Livy furnished the first prize: "Guizot's exquisitely illustrated History of France, 900 wood engravings, 40 fine steel engravings, published by Estes and Lauriat, Boston in 50 monthly parts, the 'London Art Journal' in monthly parts and 'A Nosegay,' daintily painted upon slate, on a finely polished surface, the invention and handiwork of a New England Lady." [56] Six hundred dollars was cleared in the small fair, of which the spelling match was the climax. Again, on May 31, 1876, Mark gave a reading at the church. Between selections a quintette of parishioners sang such hymns as "Farewell, Annie Darling" and "Fly Away Birdling." During the seventies and eighties the church sponsored many such affairs, including a series of lectures on American literature by young Richard Burton.

Through the years, then, Burton, Parker, and Twichell presided more and more over a "religious" activity turning secular as memory of the old theology grew dim. What William James describes as the religion of healthy-mindedness was in the saddle; these disciples of Bushnell were locally its undisputed leaders. The healthy-minded fear and see no evil, and in the assurance of the dignity rather than the depravity of man they require a

THE JOHN HOOKER HOUSE

ISABELLA BEECHER HOOKER AND JOHN HOOKER, ABOUT 1895

HARMONY CUSHMAN TWICHELL, ABOUT 1875

JOSEPH HOPKINS TWICHELL, ABOUT 1875

secular ministry — a leadership not theological and institutional but social and personal. Twichell, a man's man, broadly tolerant, muscular, and friendly, was particularly well qualified for his role.

It is not surprising, given a leadership adapted so competently to the led, that the religion of these preachers was not evangelical. Hartford's Congregational clergy welcomed Moody and Sankey when the latter arrived in 1878 to conduct daily services in the skating rink, but they did not themselves try to stimulate revivals. Twichell urged the crowds at the final meeting to keep on going to church. Mark liked his representative remarks well enough to record the substance in his notebook. The local preachers themselves, Twichell admitted, could not provide such inspired preaching every week, but it should be remembered that half a loaf is better than no bread. Elijah found the food brought him by the ravens as nutritious as if it had been delivered by a finer bird.[57] Though their congregations continued to grow steadily, it was not the habit of these clergymen to proselytize, for the emotionalism of revival meetings seemed not in the best of taste and the nature of their relation to their congregations did not encourage that form of ministerial zeal.

The fall of Henry Ward Beecher, which some thought a blow to the new doctrines of religious meliorism, did not alter the course of this confident trio of clergymen, for in their eyes and thus in the eyes of their congregations Beecher had not fallen at all. They were full of pity for him because the nation did not share their loyalty. Beecher came to Hartford in 1876 for a meeting of the American Board of Congregational Foreign Missions. Burton, Parker, and Twichell made a concerted move to have him speak but finally desisted in the face of opposition from out-of-town delegates. Twichell's admiration for him grew steadily. In 1885, at the funeral of H. W. Sage, father of his classmate and intimate, Dean Sage, and president of the Plymouth Church Council, Twichell found Beecher's funeral address "an utterance of golden eloquence full of deep sweet music of tender sympathy and Christian hope." He thought that Henry, now past 70, was in the full tide of his power.

> I was glad to have had an opportunity of seeing at close range once more the greatest genius, and on the whole, in my view, the greatest man, this country ever produced.[58]

At this meeting Twichell was particularly interested in Beecher's remarks about the truth of evolution.

In March of 1887 Beecher died. To Twichell, his death was "an occasion of inexpressible sorrow . . . no mind has had such influence on mine, unless it be Dr. Bushnell's; and no character, unless it be my father."[59] On March 13, Twichell preached on Beecher's career, referring to its central calamity:

. . . on the day when he became the subject of such a joy and of such a sorrow as has been seldom witnessed in our communities — the day when the glad, exultant cry went up from all the ranks and haunts of iniquity that he had fallen — and that into a depth of baseness and falseness that was unfathomable, while on the other side, among the hundreds of thousands who had loved and honored him and whose years he had comforted and strengthened, there was equal distress of consternation and grief — I found it practicable in the face of all plausibilities that told against him, to keep my faith in him — as I did — and I have an abiding confidence that as time passes and distance more and more reveals the proportions of his greatness and the nature and magnitude and lasting beneficent consequence of the work he wrought (he is too near now to be measured in his full stature and little men can pick at him), whatever mists cloud his name will dissolve, his integrity will be accepted in the judgment of men, and he will be recognized and felt to have been in his whole life a true-hearted and mighty servant of God and of Christ, all all because he was a mighty believer in God and in Christ.[60]

Immediately after reading his paper on Monday morning, Mark wrote his friend:

Hartford, Mch 14/87

Dear Joe:

It is a noble sermon, & I am glad I did not hear it. The mere reading it moved me more than I like to be moved — or, rather, *would* like to be moved in public. It is great & fine; & worthy of its majestic subject. You struck twelve.

What a pity — that so insignificant a matter as the chastity or unchastity of an Elizabeth Tilton could clip the locks of this Samson & make him as other men, in the estimation of a nation of Lilliputians creeping & climbing about his shoe-soles.

Yrs ever
Mark[61]

The old wounds in the Nook Farm community ached again. While Henry was dying in New York, Isabella Beecher Hooker tried to reach his bedside, but Henry's wife would not admit her. With the closed door standing between Isabella and the deathbed apology she was expecting, she walked the sidewalk with the reporters who were awaiting the aged preacher's death. She was not only thwarted in her final opportunity to grant Henry forgiveness, but barred from his funeral. She joined the long public queue to get a last glimpse of him. Her brother Thomas, sad and thoughtful, came from Elmira to the funeral but did not go with the procession to the cemetery.

Another death that year dissolved the Burton-Parker-Twichell union. On October 13, 1887, Nathaniel Burton, with his faithful deacon, John Hooker, at his bedside, died of pneumonia. Twichell called it "a dark, sad day!! . . . I went at once to his house and found that it was even so. There I met my other brother Dr. Parker. In presence of the astounding fact, which overwhelmed both of us with surprize and distress we found nothing to say, but could only embrace with tears."[62]

Spiritualism: Isabella Beecher Hooker

IT IS IMPORTANT TO NOTE, I THINK, THAT THE CONGREGATIONALISM DESCRIBED in the preceding pages, while achieving acceptance as conventional in the Hartford community, was decidedly liberal in comparison with the general Protestantism of the period. Without engaging in controversy, Burton, Parker, and Twichell and their congregations grew away from Calvinism faster than most churches of the General Associations. The essential tolerance of their point of view was established by 1870. But as late as 1887 the American Board was still battling over a principle which twenty years earlier had been completely settled in Hartford — "whether or no any person doubting the remediless perdition of heathen sinners who died without the knowledge of the Gospel grace, shall be accepted for missionary service." In spite of strong addresses by Doctor Parker and Doctor Walker (the latter another Congregational minister of Hartford), the board voted *no* — two to one. Twichell, feeling the archaism of the question and convinced of the folly of the decision, asked himself, "What will the next generation say of such a contest?"[63]

Liberal though it was, the prevailing orthodoxy still did not satisfy all members of the Nook Farm colony, or of the city at large. On Nook Farm itself, Charles Dudley Warner was, of the important figures, the most content. No other writer satisfied himself so completely with the formal religion or found it so well adapted to his personal needs. But even he became involved in developing divergences. In what is yet to be examined of the religious climate in which Mark Twain lived, we must consider the eccentricities of religious experience that arose, as well as the ultimate rejection of Christianity by Mark Twain.

I cannot encompass here the range of religious experience outside the church which fanned out to embrace every eccentricity as the authority of the established churches diminished through these two decades. Though by 1889 a list of thirty-nine churches in Hartford reads as one might expect (ten Congregational, seven Episcopal, four Methodist, six Baptist, four Catholic, one Jewish, seven miscellaneous), cultism was then at its height. "There is so much going on outside of the regular churches," Warner wrote in the same year,

> . . . wherever I walk in the city of a Sunday afternoon, I am struck with the number of little meetings going on, of the faithful and unfaithful, Adventists, socialists, spiritualists, culturists, Sons and Daughters of Edom; from all the open windows of the tall buildings come notes of praying, of exhortation, the melancholy wail of the inspiring Sankey tunes, total abstinence melodies, songs of entreaty, and songs of praise.[64]

Even Unitarianism was regarded as a cult in Hartford, not because community conservatism starved it, but because in its flexibility local Congregationalism produced few dissidents. A Unitarian society was organized in Hartford in 1844; a church was built two years later. Five hundred people from a population of 11,000 attended the laying of the cornerstone, but soon the peak of interest passed; the church building was sold for debt in 1860. For twenty years the movement languished. In 1877, Martin K. Schermerhorn, who had begun to hold meetings in the Opera House, ascribed his difficulties in the *Christian Register* to the circumstance that though "There is much liberal thought in this very intelligent and refined city . . . it lacks boldness, and disguises itself under the old names."[65] Nevertheless, a regular minister was appointed in 1878, and a new building was built in 1881.

Six years later, in the year of Beecher's and Burton's deaths, and of the American Board's preoccupation with Election and the eligibility of missionaries who did not believe in it, John C. Kimball declared from the Unitarian platform that the hanging of the Haymarket anarchists was comparable to the crucifixion of Christ. He was sustained by his society. A motion to eject him was roundly defeated and a resolution passed that the society was proud to have in its pulpit ministers who "were in advance of the public sentiment . . . and dared again and again to take an unpopular side."[66] The stipulation that the society did not sympathize with anarchy was appended. The society grew very slowly, adding an average of only twelve members a year from 1878 to 1885, and few more thereafter.

The Unitarian movement, however, attracted the attention of Isabella Beecher Hooker. She longed to take over its pulpit in 1876 but could not bring herself to offer her name. After Burton's death in 1887, she and John left the Park Church; eventually both were buried by Unitarian ministers. As by this time one would expect, Isabella's religious ideas comprised the most radical deviation from liberal Congregationalism on Nook Farm. Her eccentricity is of considerable account, for Isabella, a born leader, was always an influence in the community. No pressure of disapproval could suppress the energy of her activities. Her interest in spiritualism was to become an obsession, but the idea of spiritualism in the Nook Farm context is necessarily interesting, and its social complications for the Hookers are important in understanding this society.

Modern spiritualism began in 1848 in Hydesville, near Rochester, New York. There the Fox sisters, said by skeptics to be able to crackle their toes, introduced "intelligent raps" to the populace and made a fortune as reassuring communicants between this changing world and the next. Other mediums soon appeared.[67] The source of "spiritism" was generally supposed by nonbelievers at the time to reside in the transition from a literal to a symbolic religion. When angels and demons were real, and the actuality of another existence was emotionally and intellectually indisputable, social critics said, spiritualism was impossible. The substitution by nineteenth-century Christianity of an indefinable, sometimes transcendental entity for vivid anthropomorphism was held to compel the heart, "sighing for consolation that society could not give — for some inspiration or token from those who had passed beyond — to seek a refuge in spiritualism." [68] According to the contemporary view, spiritualism was a halfway house on the road to complete disbelief in revealed religion, and an emotional refuge for those whose faith had been detached from the rock of old-time simplicity.

However that may be, for Isabella Hooker, conversion to spiritualism was a further step away from Calvinism, an intellectual advance, and a road to literal glory that more than compensated for her deep troubles. When she accepted Victoria Woodhull as a comrade in feminism, she fell so far under her charm as to accept readily Victoria's curious religious beliefs. For Victoria, spiritualism, feminism, free love were all facets of the same enlightenment. Isabella was never to become a free-love advocate, though, as we have seen, she was ready to say that it could be a development of the future. In 1872, Victoria, then president of the National Society of Spiritualists, addressed the convention of the National Suffrage Association on the subject of spiritualism and political reform. Isabella said afterwards that "if the Spiritualists had brains enough and soul enough to come up to the position to which Victoria Woodhull invited them, they would rule the world." [69]

Sometime between 1872 and 1876, while Isabella was in disgrace over her intrusion into Henry Ward Beecher's affairs, Victoria did indeed invite her to rule the world. She accepted the commission and began to prepare herself for her great responsibilities. A remarkable diary extending from May 11, 1876 to January 1877 [70] chronicles Isabella's belief that within the year she would be called to the presidency of a matriarchal government, which would spread from the United States across the whole world and under her leadership be merged with the kingdom of Christ in a great millennial period.[71] Her conviction is supported by ecstatic mystical experience of a highly literal order and by copious assurances from the mouths of her departed friends. As the diary opens, Isabella has decided that John, after all, was to be in her Cabinet, in the department of Foreign Affairs. Gradually, through the year, her visions allowed her to complete the panel of her top advisers. Her nephew Fred Perkins, for example, was to have an important role. With each selection she began a program of training to make the person chosen ready for his responsibilities.

The vehicles for Isabella's insights were conversations with the dead, usually arranged by her mother, who came to her as she lay perfectly still in bed. As accompaniment to the visitations, she heard raps in the bureau and knocks in the adjoining rooms. Her materializations could be consummated alone or through any medium. A psychiatrist would find it illuminating that many of the people who appeared to her asked her forgiveness for wrongs she had suffered at their hands. Bushnell, only lately dead, insisted, in "such words of contrition & self-condemnation" as she never heard, that he was wrong to oppose suffrage for women; he was going to make it right as soon as he could. Her mother had demonstrated in Paris in 1874 that Henry Ward Beecher would one day kneel to her; she felt now in "holy joy" the imminence of that crisis, but when he reported in person her heart was wrung by his agony of remorse for the way he had treated her. She was saddened by the repeated evidence given by all her spirits in passing that her small granddaughter, Kathy Burton, would die before she reached the age of eight, a belief associated with personal difficulties with her son-in-law. In addition to such therapeutic visions, Isabella felt a more abstract guidance influencing her every decision and responded to a generalized power coursing through an active parasol into her body as she took sunbaths, or through a pen as she took messages in automatic longhand. Her converse with spirits was usually about earthly affairs. She had hoped to learn more about the future life, but so far the nature of God had not been revealed to her. "I seem to comprehend how the being who maketh the clouds his pavilion yet noteth the fall of the sparrow & heareth the faintest cry toward 'Our Father.' But oh I do not understand this great nature & sometimes have a fear that it is not a person after all." [72]

Isabella kept, for a time, the prospect of maternal government a closely guarded secret, even from her husband and son. But of her powers as a medium and of her visions she spoke often to her family. She took active part in the circle of mediums and believers which attained some size in Hartford as the avowed and unavowed supporters grew toward the 5,000,000 mark in the United States. Ellen Burr, sister of the publisher of the Hartford *Times*, who lived eventually at the corner of Farmington Avenue and Forest Street next door to Mark Twain's new house, was an ally, in both suffrage and spiritualism. Isabella felt that her friends in Elmira were beginning to see the light and busily extended her acquaintance among the Hartford mediums. A Mrs. Roberts was representative of the latter group. Through her, Isabella talked to Byron, who was suffering terrible punishment in the spirit world for his sneers against Harriet Beecher Stowe. A Laura Blibben could materialize Fred Stowe, though he did not talk through her as he did through Mrs. Roberts. Isabella said, "This is consistent with our human changes of feeling & possibly the mediums qualify the expression also." [73] A young girl, ward of Edward Gillette, could perform extraordinary feats of strength under spiritual control. Most of the mediums were visited primarily by the spirits of Indian warriors, who in transmitting messages from the Hartford dead frequently lapsed into unintelligible gibberish when pressed for embarrassing details. A Chinese medium attained a very limited vogue. Séances involving these professionals were held at regular times at various homes, like organized whist parties of the same period. Isabella experimented by herself to develop her own powers. When she rubbed Will Gillette's weak eyes, she sensed that her nephew was potentially a great medium. Sometimes at the séances the spirits came to Isabella, forcing her to speak. On one occasion Joan of Arc appeared to converse with her son Ned, but Joan had great difficult making her purpose clear in Isabella's feeble French.

Through all this, John was again very patient, though sore tried. He seemed to sympathize with this obsession of his wife's, but she thought him singularly quiet for a believer and noted that he did not derive permanent comfort from the visions she introduced him to in their bed. He felt no different, going on in his old worrying way, she wrote, "except as he leans on me & draws a certain hope & faith from my unwavering courage & simple resignation to the will of God." [74] Most of the time he was probably nervously anticipating the next public embarrassment. Over a period of months, Isabella dreamed that a burglar was to enter the home of Eugene Burton and wound him severely. After several false alarms, she was seized by the certainty that the time had finally come. John went to the chief of police, obtained two policemen, alerted half the neighborhood, and deployed it in the dark one Saturday night to arrest the intruder. The Hooker family stayed up all night, but nothing happened. Her son Ned was gentle on this occasion as always; not believing, he humored his mother. John believed, but he did not want to. Eventually he subscribed with enthusiasm to the new faith, but he retained an aversion to the low class of society from which mediums seemed to be called.

Although she thought that John was generally unaware of her tireless care of him, of her support in his efforts to pull through hard times, she sometimes sympathized with his uneasiness:

> Poor man, he has a hard time I suppose with me — but I am sure that the chief source of all the suffering I experience is the fear of wounding and disturbing him.[75]

In December John came to her in even greater distress than usual, harassed now by his discovery that his Grandfather Hooker had been partially insane in his old age and by his fear that he was going the same road. Isabella pointed out that John had resources in her and in understanding his own case. Attention to diet would alter the inheritance.

The social consequences of her devotion to spiritualism were in one way even more poignant for Isabella than those following her role in the Beecher scandal. In July of 1876, Eugene Burton, certain that Isabella was coming between him and his wife (Mary was being trained by her mother for a cabinet post; the two were reading Darwin together) and appalled by her prediction of his daughter's early death, forbade her to enter his house next door or to see little Kathy under any circumstances. This prohibition broke Isabella's heart. She was reminded of the sorrow every day. Livy Clemens told her one afternoon that Miss Kassie had come to call upon the Clemenses. "How charming," Livy said, "she looks in her dark suit & bright red bows." Isabella choked inwardly but commented impersonally on the change of fashions permitting children to wear dark colors. "Will these things end soon? I think so — or I could not endure with serenity." Sometimes, even so, her endurance faltered, and once her impatience gave power and pathos to her prose:

> This unrest is terrible — this sense of coming glory — & no sign of its advent but the longing of a few weary-hearted women meeting in upper chambers & communing in the deep silences of the night.[76]

But the rifts with her friends, at least, were beginning to heal. In 1876 she detected in Susan Warner possibilities of "development" and thought of trying to materialize Beethoven, to whose music Susan was devoted, so that he could pass judgment on her piano interpretations. Catharine Beecher came over from the Stowe house to talk and talk of clairvoyance and healing, phenomena which she accepted as real, but for which she could not account. Isabella rejoiced that soon Catharine would be forced to recognize the truth of spiritualism in order to explain such facts of experience, but meanwhile she did not urge the point. Catharine would ask her to come over for croquet on the little lawn between the house and Mark Twain's fence and once came with a fifty-dollar bill from Harriet, who had heard of the Hooker financial troubles. Reconciliation followed these overtures. In December 1876 Susan Warner asked her to the first lunch of Nook Farm women to which she had been invited since her return from Europe and the publication of her letters to Henry Ward Beecher. Eating cold chicken, fried oysters, and celery salad with Livy Clemens, Mrs. Langdon, and sixteen other women of the neighborhood, she was reminded of the pleasant, cordial old times and forgot for the moment her family troubles. Her proselytizing for spiritualism did not alter her new relationship, for everyone to whom she gave messages from the other world accepted them without initial surprise and seemed carried along with her as if in sympathy. But she did not inflict her messages on anyone of whose opposition she was convinced. As if the spirit world sympathized with her plight, she was given messages for transmission only to the psychically susceptible. By this time many in Nook Farm trembled before signs from the unseen.

As the year slipped by, the clearing of the social skies seemed to Isabella the surest verification of her peculiar religious experience. She persuaded herself that before the first of January the announcement of her great election would be made from on high. A New Year's Eve party would make an appropriate setting for the celestial ceremonials. To it she invited the Clemenses, both Warner families, the Gillettes, her daughters Mary and Alice — almost the whole neighborhood. Only the Stowes were out of town, at their Florida home. As she heaped apples, nuts, raisins, and cider on the study table on December 31, she thought and thought about the coming event, her heart full. She stopped long enough to write Alice that Kathy, Mary's daughter, would not live now to see the New Year. She sent notes of invitation to her medium friends at the last minute, though John had firmly forbidden it. And as Ned and his fiancée were cracking nuts together in the next room, she paused again to reflect how different all this was from the old-fashioned ways of Sabbath-keeping. As the proper hour struck, friends came in unexpected numbers. Mark Twain appeared early to excuse himself — he wanted to visit with Hjalmar Boyesen at the

Warners'—but reappeared later bringing Livy and Boyesen. By a note delivered by Mark, Isabella persuaded Susan Warner to come too, though Susan had said earlier she was not sufficiently well. General Hawley and Kate Foote (governess of the Clemens children) came with a box of raisins made like a magnificent velvet casket. The parlor was full, and just as the company began to sing hymns, the mediums arrived.

Mrs. Roberts came first, frightened at the size of the party and clothed in an unsuitable dress. Isabella draped one of her own gowns around the woman and deposited her as stealthily as possible in an upper bedroom. She came downstairs to find John admitting Miss Perry and her mother. Miss Perry also had come as she was, in a wrapper. John propelled them into the study and looked frantically around at Isabella. Mrs. Perry grew very noisy, but when Isabella quieted her, her daughter said to John, "We will not do anything to distress you, Sir." Isabella slipped them upstairs, where the pair joined Mrs. Roberts at a worktable in the bedroom. Darting down again to rejoin the singing guests, she discovered morose Dr. Williams (another medium) in the hall. This, she exclaimed to herself, was too much. But, summoning her strength, she sent the newcomer to join the mystified ladies upstairs. Then she went into the parlor, where, as calmer minutes passed, she was satisfied to note a number of powerful mediums, of whom Frank Whitmore[77] appeared to be a new one. The stage was set. The witnesses were properly deployed. Isabella looked at the clock. The millennium hung in breathless balance. There were enough mediums in the house to body forth the Holy Ghost.

Imperceptibly the climactic moment passed, without—most strangely—the commencement of a new world. Dr. Williams, who had not been enjoying himself above with the frightened ladies of his calling, sent word by John, who had been anxiously preserving the isolation of the professionals, that Miss Perry wanted to go home. At this point Alice, who had gone upstairs and noticed the strange group huddled around the little table in her mother's room, came into the hall and said loudly, "Why, what is going on in your room, mother? There is the queerest looking lot up there." Isabella shook her head sharply; Alice stopped. Just as Mark Twain and Livy, with the Warners and Boyesen, came out of the parlor, Dr. Williams came down, stumbled through them, fumbled for his hat, and shouldered his way out the door. Isabella, after a quick moment of pain, began to laugh, enjoying the certainty that the Clemenses had taken him for a coachman. Susie Warner said as she left, "Well, Mrs. Hooker, I give it up—this has been just as pleasant as the old times when you were living here . . . What an evening we have had." For Isabella these were sweet words; they constituted an affirmation of accord in this world which made less needful a dramatic announcement of the next.

In the lull after Mark and Livy and the Warners left, Isabella smuggled Mrs. Perry and her daughter downstairs. The girl, inspired by the strength of her Indian warrior, promptly seized John in the hallway and pommeled him. After this excitement there were no more incidents. When the last guest had gone, John faced his wife to demand an explanation, but Isabella asked postponement till the morning.

Isabella went into the study then, to think about the year's having passed without the appearance of the glory of the Lord. She thought if perhaps she arranged more gatherings like this one and held them in the Stowes' most mediumistic house . . . But John came in. Quietly determined to speak his mind at last, he charged his wife with monomania and said she was thinking too intently on spiritualism. She was consequently not to be trusted. She must henceforth consult him always, particularly in social arrangements. Ned softly assured his father that his mother was not crazy, nor any way disturbed; he should accept the situation and make the best of it.

But Isabella was stirred to anger by the charge, for ever since her brother Henry's accusations she had been sensitive about her sanity. Her reading in spiritualism, she said to John, was not limited to the *Banner of Light* (the Boston publication of the movement); she read in politics, science, and art and made notes for future use. She would have him realize she had other interests, too. She played whist for diversion and, in the words of her later record of this interview,

> was very fond of music & entertaining company — was perfectly devoted to him day & night & helpful in his work to the extent of my ability — while he had confessed to me lately, that he not only was a hypochondriac of *melancholy without a cause* from his grandfather which would make him positively insane in his old age & a burden to his friends. Now I said, simply because I am investigating phenomena that claim the attention of the whole scientific world . . . now *you dare to call me insane* — I think this is the pot calling the kettle black.[78]

While this domestic crisis was taking place, many of Isabella's departed guests were at the Warners', where Twichell, who had not been invited to the Hookers', had also come. Boyesen, Mark and Livy, Hawley and Miss Foote sang and talked for much of the night. Just before dispersal, Twichell offered a benediction. For him it was a most delightful evening; there was no tragedy in it.

Despite the fiasco of this New Year's Eve and the scene following, Isabella remained a faithful spiritualist to the end of her days, deriving particular comfort from it when, after Mary's sudden death in 1887, she was able to talk to her in moments of intense concentration. Her faithful husband forgave her and shared her belief more willingly as time went on.[79] Isabella's monomania faded in intensity. She eventually believed that revelation of her role as the Comforter would be restricted to a very few until the distant future, but with the ultimate result that

> I, like my adorable brother Jesus shall grow into the hearts of men and women & children by the power of God our common Father to whom be all the praise & honor & glory now & forevermore Amen.

With these words she closed the diary and presumably kept no other. Kathy Burton still lived.

Spiritualism: The Warners, the Stowes, and Mark Twain

THE SPIRITUALISM OF ISABELLA BEECHER HOOKER REACHED AN EXCESS OF ABnormality unduplicated in Hartford. But the dichotomy between the conventional religion on the one hand, and the Hooker brand of millennial hysterics on the other, was by no means clean-cut. Into the religious experience of the Warners came echoes of Isabella's ecstasies. The Stowes had studied and experimented with spiritist manifestations for years. The interest in psychic phenomena entered the great house on Farmington Avenue where Mark Twain and Livy lived, fully aware of the Nook Farm points of view toward religion and sensitive to the psychic turbulence in the neighborhood.

The Hookers and the Twichells came to a permanent parting in 1876. Once Twichell's doubts about Henry Ward Beecher were cleared away by the Plymouth Council, John's unceasing explanations of Isabella's behavior must have seemed unconvincing and annoying. A man of his rock-founded normality could have no liking for spiritualism. In any event, Isabella took tenacious hold of the interesting idea that Twichell had told John no one wanted her in the Asylum Hill Church, or John either if she accompanied him. She told the Warners of this development and fancied they seemed shocked and afterwards tenderly kind. Later, though, it appears that Twichell had been "neglecting" the Hookers. John offered to find out whether the neglect were unconscious and unintentional, though Isabella, certain it was deliberate, advised against an interview. She changed her mind when John said he wished to tell Twichell "such Christianity was spurious and worthless . . . & he should not go to Church again—adding 'I may go with you to Mr. Johnson's [Episcopal Church].'"[80] Warner went with her occasionally to the Trinity College Church, but the Hookers settled on the Park Church as soon as Dr. Burton took it over. Later, after Burton's death, they were to break away, severing their connection with formal religion altogether. For his part, Twichell had nothing good to say of Isabella, whom he mentioned often in his letters to Mark Twain after 1891. For a man of so little malevolence, his allusions to his neighbor are extraordinarily bitter.

But Warner, though he was Twichell's nearest friend after Mark Twain, tolerated Isabella. He was utterly kind always, and he doubtless pitied her for her troubles, real and imagined. And his wife, who had taken the lead in reinstating Isabella socially, began, if we can believe the diary, to listen to spiritist persuasions. Thereafter Susan sent for her whenever she was ill. Isabella took her hand on one occasion, intent on finally summoning up Beethoven, but the spirits of Susan's parents appeared instead. When Susan asked her if Dr. Bushnell had appeared to her, Isabella replied he had and adds in her diary that Susan thought his expression wonderfully characteristic. In later meetings she worked on Susan's sympathy, drawing her further and further into spiritual experiences. The Hookers often walked over in the evening to hear Susan play and Ned sing Gluck songs to her accompaniment.

Friendly also with George and Lilly Warner, Isabella plotted for a means to "develop" Lilly. A rather vague guidance led her to suggest to George that she take his wife to Paris for her health, but it became clear to her later that the purpose of the trip would be to convert Lilly to spiritualism. Lilly could not think of leaving George, however, and Isabella gave up her notion, though she thought of it longingly during whist games whenever George was her partner.

Another interesting, but this time familiar, chapter in the religious psychology of a society in transition was being lived in the Stowe house. Old Calvin had been since his boyhood bemused by most distinct apparitions, which he was often unable to distinguish from terrestrial reality. Harriet used his propensity and the visions it permitted in *Oldtown Folks*. Horace Holyoke, her name for Calvin, the narrator, had a spirit friend named Harvey, who, like the mythical rabbit of the modern play, was a great comfort. "I *thought* to him," he says, perhaps indicating a need for affection which may have opened the way to the visions, "and in return received silent demonstrations of sympathy and fellowship from him." At the old burial ground in Natick, he "loved to sit and watch and dream long after sundown or moonrise, and fancy I saw bands of wavering shapes, and hope that some one out of the crowd might have a smile of recognition or a spiritual word for me." In association with these apparitions appeared a habit of indecision, "a habit of looking at everything from so many different sides, that it was difficult to get a settled assent to anything."[81] As Calvin grew older he studied with candid curiosity and detachment his own peculiarity. His friends thought it could not be dismissed as evidence of an unsound mind, for his mentality was obviously impressive, his erudition objectively sound, and his scholarship logical. A professor at Andover was convinced the appearances were due to a disease of the optic nerve "altogether reasonable in consideration of the nervous ebullition which preceded and accompanied his visions."[82] He made no secret of his gift and adopted no dogmatic explanation of its origin.[83]

This capacity naturally attracted Calvin to spiritualism when it came to his attention as a cult. After Henry Stowe's death by drowning, the old man began to feel his son's presence in the vibration of a nonexistent guitar. In 1860 Harriet counseled her husband from Florence, where she had been discussing spiritualism with Elizabeth Barrett Browning. She repeated to Calvin the same advice she had given a Boston lady, whom "the spiritualists would regard as a very powerful medium": to try the spirits whether they were of God. "I have found that when I am with her I receive very strong impressions from the spiritual world, so that I feel . . . comforted, as if I have been near to my Henry and other departed friends." She continued:

> One thing I am convinced of, — that spiritualism is a reaction from the intense materialism of the present age. Luther, when he recognized a personal devil, was much nearer right . . . Circles and spiritual jugglery I regard as the lying signs and wonders . . . but there is a real scriptural spiritualism which has fallen into disuse, and must be revived, and there are, doubtless, people who from some constitutional formation can more readily receive the impressions of the surrounding spiritual world. Such were apostles, prophets, and workers of miracles.

By 1872, she was more impressed with the "facts" of cultist spiritism. She wrote George Eliot on February 8 that, lacking evidence to prove them supplemental to the revelations of Christianity, she did "regard them as an interesting and curious study in psychology."[84] She noted that many more thousand spiritualists existed than showed themselves.

Amid the spiritual phenomena that caught the attention of her generation, in the 1860's she arrived at an interim public conclusion not quite the same as her private view. Harriet wrote Oliver Wendell Holmes in 1876, the year of Isabella's great delusion, that she then believed the "marvels" entirely natural phenomena, the result of imperfectly understood natural laws. She had no faith, she said, in mediums who practiced for money.[85]

She could nevertheless understand and sympathize with those who did believe. Her own Christianity she claimed adequate to the personal tragedies of her life. In opposition to the consolation offered by the more literal spiritualists, she had preached constantly her doctrine to others. But she knew how it could be.

> Each friend takes away a portion of ourselves . . . with involuntary yearning we turn to the door of the sepulchre. We lean against the cold marble, but there is no answer. . .
>
> There are those who would have us think that in *our* day this doom is reversed; that there are those who have the power to restore to us the communion of our lost ones. How many a heart, wrung and tortured with the anguish of this fearful silence, has throbbed with strange, vague hopes at the suggestion! When we hear sometimes of persons of the strongest and clearest minds becoming votaries of certain spiritualist circles, let us not wonder . . . it is only an indication of that heart-hunger which in part it appeases.
>
> Ah *were* it true! Ah, were it so that when we go forth weeping in the gray dawn, bearing spices and odors which we long to pour forth for the beloved dead, we should indeed find the stone rolled away and an angel sitting on it! [86]

She had seen no angel, she said. That our glorified dead should stoop to juggle and rap and squeak, to perform cheap tricks with tables and chairs, was inconceivable. Like Ruskin, who became convinced of the existence of the future life and then had no further use for it because of its low character, Harriet said that an immortality among mountebanks would be worse than annihilation. Communion with Christ gave adequate consolation in sorrow.

Although this view has been often advertised as Mrs. Stowe's mature estimate of spiritualism, it was, according to Forrest Wilson, hers only for a short period. Her letters afterwards show her experimenting endlessly with the occult, more believer than skeptic. In any event, she never made public alliance with the cause of her sister. Her avowed interest, however, was probably partial confession of ultimate inadequacy in her announced beliefs, just as millions of others were turning from conventional points of view to secret solace. Wherever she wrote of it publicly, she remained noncommittal, but the possibilities of spiritualism were never long out of her mind.

Mark Twain was obviously aware of the sweep of psychic manifestations across Nook Farm and the country in the early seventies. Spiritualism as such appealed to him not at all; his growing disbelief in individual immortality held firm. But though he thought the cult ridiculous,[87] he found the growing "scientific" study of extrasensory perception fascinating. In the middle seventies he decided that William Wright (Dan de Quille) of the *Territorial Enterprise* should write a history of the Comstock Lode. Before he could post a letter of instruction, an envelope came from Wright with the identical scheme submitted for Mark's comment. Mark knew the contents of the letter, he said, as soon as he saw the envelope. This incident, after preparation in minor instances of unspoken communication between him and Livy, carried his interest in what he termed "mental telegraphy" to its peak. His dabbling in psychic phenomena appears in later articles—"Mental Telegraphy" and "Mental Telegraphy Again." [88] In 1878, when he and Twichell were traveling in Switzerland, both men noted instances of what they considered thought transference. As Mark read George Eliot's *Romola*, the only scene to impress him was Tito's compromising with his conscience. A few minutes later, Twichell noticed the book and commented at once on the same passage, out of which he had constructed a sermon in 1872.[89] In a much more startling incident, Mark and Joe met around the bend of an Alpine trail an American whom they had been discussing and supposed at home across the sea. Mark's interest grew less compelling in time, but even as late as 1898 he was predicting to Howells that people one day would be communicating in words via mental telegraph. His interest enlivened the table talk in Nook Farm; it was geared to the complex process whereby crude spiritualism was eventually to be refined in societies for psychical research. Mental telegraphy certainly shed no light on and had little relation to the psychology of his religious experience. In later years Mark was to undertake the study of mental healing, but the context of his preoccupation was then, as at this time, not noticeably religious.

The Rejection of Christianity: Mark Twain

AGAINST THE BACKGROUND OF RELIGIOUS IDEAS THAT WE HAVE OBSERVED IN THE Hartford community and in the context of intuitional religious experience pulsing through so wide a range of emotion, the skepticism of Mark Twain cannot be correctly judged as an isolated revolt against complacent orthodoxy. The prevailing Christianity of Hartford, once very radical, was at the beginning of the seventies in advance of popular religion; its modification in some of the individuals whose personal needs were not satisfied by it reflects a turmoil of improvisation that cannot be designated by the most careless imagination as complacent acceptance of a uniform creed. With one or two exceptions, every one of the tenants of Nook Farm had been brought up in the Calvinist tradition. Without exception, every one had rejected the faith of his youth. The severity of the emotional consequences varied with the maturity of the individual. Mark Twain, whose religious training in Hannibal was also Calvinist in outline, went further than most in his rejection, but he was on the same road and was permitted to travel it by his contemporaries and by his intimates in Hartford.

Mark's childhood has been examined from controversial points of view with a zealousness that obscures the paucity of evidence. We know that his mother was a Presbyterian, that she sent him to hear the Presbyterian minister's fire-and-brimstone vocabulary. We know that his sensitive conscience was impressed by the lurid imagery of hell-fire that reaches a mythological incandescence in *Tom Sawyer* and *Huckleberry Finn*. We know also that his father was a freethinker (like the Judge in *Pudd'nhead Wilson*), a man who did not attend church, or speak of religious matters, or participate in family religious exercises, but who scrupulously observed a personal integrity that Mark took over intact.[90] We know that his uncle John Quarles, who owned the farm later recreated also in an atmosphere of mythical alteration, was a Universalist who denied the exclusiveness of the Elect and insisted that all would be saved.[91] We know as well that the subtle influences of his upbringing in the midst of frontier violence, natural beauty, Negro song and superstition, and river-suggested excitement at the crossroads of a continent make assessing the countereffect of his Calvinist training very difficult.

But we know also that the literalness of his childhood religion began to fade when he left his village to wander the country as printer, pilot, miner, and reporter. On the river he read many books, in the print shops many more. Somewhere he was exposed to smatterings of the philosophy of determinism.[92] In Cincinnati, whence he sent one of his "Snodgrass Letters" to Orion, then in Keokuk, he met a Scotchman named Macfarlane, who impressed him with a pre-Darwinian mechanistic evolutionary theory. Mark Twain was much more likely to absorb his philosophy from contacts of this sort than from systematic reading.

At any rate Mark's doubts of the validity of Christianity as he had absorbed it formed early. He knew the Bible thoroughly and could not use in his own world the Old Testament God. In 1860 he wrote Orion: "What a man wants with religion in these breadless times surpasses my comprehension." [93] Calvinism did not square with his developing tolerance for humanity and was not necessary to observance of ethical standards and equable social justice. But his vague determinism did not prevent him, wherever he went, from systematically making friends of preachers. And he made no formal break with the church. For the time being it was not necessary to formulate a philosophy, for there was no need to explain or justify to himself his place in a world full of excitement and promise. Time enough when that world collapsed.

When Mark fell in love with Olivia Langdon, he first decided to accept her Christianity as his, just as he was eager to identify himself with everything she stood for. But even Olivia's religion was not the Calvinism which in Howells' phrase "bowed the neck of most Americans in the early eighteen-seventies,"[94] for it had been shaped by the Langdons' intimate friend and pastor, Thomas K. Beecher, who, though he stayed aloof from his brother Henry's emotionalism, was not a reactionary. Thomas was an unorthodox clergyman who became concerned primarily with the social and ethical implications of Christianity — the area in which Mark was to retain a passionate interest — and who was to rebel against expanding capitalism's exploitation of the working man. He differed from the liberal Congregationalists in Hartford by being more liberal politically and less confident that his age was automatically approaching perfection. But, on the other hand, Livy's faith, untempered by long reflection or wide experience, was not of the caliber of Beecher's. It was passive and esthetic. Mark yielded to it. The details of his deference can be observed in letters published by Clara Clemens in *My Father: Mark Twain* (1931). At one interesting moment, he diluted his Western experience, perhaps with Livy's ingenuous gentility in mind, implied a conventional faith in immortality, and referred to one of his clerical friendships:

> You know the hymn — it is 'Oh, refresh us.' It haunts me now because I am thinking of a steadfast friend whose death I have just learned through the papers . . . the Reverend Franklin Rising . . . He was rector of the Episcopal Church in Virginia City, Nevada — a noble young fellow — and for three years, there, he and I were fast friends. I used to try to teach him how to preach in order to get at the better natures of the rough population about him, and he used to try hard to learn — for I knew them and he did not; he was refined and sensitive and not intended for such a people as that . . . his wanderings are done now, the glories of heaven are about him, and in his ears its mysterious music is sounding — but to me comes no vision but a lonely ship in a great solitude of sea and water; and into my ears comes no sound but the complaining of the waves and the softened cadences of that simple old hymn — but oh, Livy, it comes freighted with infinite pathos!

For Livy's sadness at leaving her home, Mark offered consolation in the imagery of conventional religion:

But I shall so strive all the days of my life to make you happy, and shall try so hard to walk as you did in the light and the love of God, that some of the bitterness of your exile shall be spared you . . . Don't be sad, Livy, we'll model our home after the old home, and make the Spirit of Love lord over all the realm. Smile again, Livy, and be of good heart. Turn toward the Cross and be comforted — I turn with you — What would you more? The peace of God shall rest upon us, and all will be well.[95]

But the radiant mood of surrender to Olivia's religion, to the luxurious softness of sentiment, to the way of life it represented and the satisfaction in it which may somehow be related to the exultation of his courtship were to fade in the first year of his marriage. Amid the minor disasters that were partly responsible for his move to Hartford, Mark rebelled against family Bible reading and confessed his skepticism. In an unpublished article which Paine says was written about 1870 in Buffalo, Mark characterized the God of the Bible as "irascible, vindictive, fierce and ever fickle"[96] and announced that the true God steadfastly and impartially governed his universe by a "beneficent, exact, and changeless" machinery. The justness and fairness of his rule of the world suggested that if there were a future life, we would be justly dealt with. We should demand nothing else. Here was the determinism (still far from the inexorable and amoral mechanism of *What Is Man?*) that Mark may have absorbed in his scattered reading and fitted to life as he knew it. Immortality he questioned indirectly and prayer he ruled out as superfluous. This benign determinism, adequate at the moment and brought to light by the pressure of misfortune, was to be altered by the experience of the next twenty years and by the tragic events thereafter. Olivia suppressed this manuscript but accepted its thesis, and the couple moved to Hartford, never again to belong to a church.

Mark and Livy settled in a society where no one else believed in the God of the Old Testament and where everyone was satisfied to refer to his own convictions for the ultimate authority behind religious belief. The individual's right to determine his own relation to God would not be contested there so long as personal morality, necessary for a secure society, was not threatened and public morality was not undermined. The religious emancipation of his neighbors, to be sure, did not take a satiric turn. Harriet Beecher Stowe, though recognizing the morbid psychology of Calvinist New England and analyzing the unfortunate repressions (her term) that crippled its inhabitants, was not inclined to turn the irony of her antislavery novels on the way of religious life she had helped to alter. Mark, more impatient by nature and more in need of reprisal against the defective point of view he had outgrown, used his pen to jab at it.

Extract from Captain Stormfield's Visit to Heaven was an early satiric attack on the conventional notion of heaven. Captain Stormfield, admitted to the celestial city after the world from which he comes is finally identified as the Wart, discovers that playing a harp on a cloudbank is the most boring of all possible ways to spend eternity, that pain and suffering are necessary to provide the contrast essential to happiness, that class distinctions and a highly stratified hierarchy exist there, and that its rabble is at least as gullible and feckless as on earth. Mark recreates a literal heaven to laugh at the inadequacies of the conventional idea of eternity. In his laughter he moved beyond most of his Nook Farm neighbors, who retained as the focal conception in their relation to the spiritual world a confidence in personal immortality. None of them, however, seems to have visualized heaven in terms of the literal imagery Mark makes fun of in one of his best short pieces. Implicit in the point of view he takes is an impersonality of control of the universe and a derogation of human beings who magnify the importance of their own immortality as being either inevitable or desirable.

But though Mark advanced gradually toward rejection of a beneficent order, he adopted upon his arrival in Hartford the role of Twichell's chief parishioner. This assumption was not a hypocritical evasion of responsibility, for he did not ever feel called upon to conceal the true nature of his religious views from his neighbors, or, for example, from the full membership of the Monday Evening Club, upon which he often practiced his heresies. It was in part, no doubt, a concession to the large public whom he thought it would be suicidal to offend. More crucially, his churchgoing was a way of taking part in the community life, and his identification with the Asylum Hill Congregational Church as a pewholder was a symbol of his membership in the Nook Farm community. Though he had rejected Christianity, his rejection was qualified by his behavior in a way that brings to mind Bushnell's abandonment of the old theology. Mark ruled out all theology, and the supernatural that it attempted to interpret, but he was not contemptuous of Christianity as a basis for an equitable society and not at all at odds with his community's regard for personal and public morality.

In any event, Mark contributed publicly all his life to the Mark Twain-Joe Twichell preacher-parishioner relation. When he took his pastor to Bermuda, to Boston, or to Europe, the papers made much of his maintaining a personal minister. The celebrated walk to Boston in 1874, for example, strengthened an impression, partly humorous, partly serious, which Mark must have intended. In his notebooks, he worked out remarks for public consumption. "I keep a clergyman," he wrote in his *Tramp Abroad* notebook, thinking perhaps of something to say to a reporter, "to remonstrate against my drinking — it gives zest and increase of appetite."[97] Eventually the legend of the association became so widespread that when Twichell went to England again in 1908, he was hailed everywhere as Mark Twain's pastor, widely interviewed, and extensively quoted in the press.

Mark's attraction to Twichell in a relation that was in reality personal rather than professional was not at all inconsistent, peculiar as it might seem that a Westerner funny man should associate himself intimately with an Eastern clergyman. In the West he had deliberately made friends of the ministers in whatever community he lived, taking the initiative in making himself known. "I called on Rev. Dr. Wadsworth last night," he wrote his mother from San Francisco in 1866, "but the old rip wasn't at home."

> I was sorry, because I wanted to make his acquaintance. I am thick as thieves with the Rev. Stebbins, and I am laying for the Rev. Scudder and the Rev. Dr. Stone. I am running on preachers now, altogether. I find them gay . . . I am taking letters of introduction to Henry Ward Beecher . . . and other eminent persons of the east. Whenever anybody offers me a letter to a preacher, now I snaffle it on the spot.[98]

In the *Alta* he wrote on June 10, 1867, "Preachers are always pleasant company when they are off duty."[99] In 1868, writing to Mrs. Fairbanks, he pointed out that though he was being attacked for the Holy Land letters which she had not revised, "It is only the small-fry ministers who assail me. All those of high rank & real influence I visit, dine & swap lies with, [are] just the same as ever."[100] What deeper significance his striking attraction to preachers may signify, I cannot say. Clergymen were educated, articulate, and socially skillful and usually shared conspicuously the sympathetic humanity that at this time appealed to Mark. He would always be more attracted by a fully developed person than repelled by a difference of religious opinion, which would, indeed, add zest to the friendship. That his preference for preachers as companions derives from admiration and envy for men who dared to live without devoting themselves to the accumulation of money, I could not demonstrate. And I am quite certain it does not stem from a feeling of guilt over his apostasy.

Rather than Twichell's parishioner, Mark was Twichell's friend, devoted to him for forty years. Their correspondence is filled with mutual "love, respect & admiration," sometimes expressed in the language of love letters. The two talked endlessly of religion, and every subject, as they walked in the country, and each took sound satisfaction from the other's company and ideas. Twichell, like Mark, was an accomplished talker; each found in the other the "relief of utterance." Each to the other habitually made "a very true disclosure" of his "inside."[101]

Mark Twain's biographer has put into currency a false notion that Twichell did not argue Mark's skepticism with him. Paine dramatically places in Switzerland in 1878 the revelation to Twichell of Mark's disbelief and quotes a paragraph of undocumented conversation in which Mark confesses he had been living a lie in pretending to be a Christian. Paine adds: "So the personal side of religious discussion closed between them and was never afterwards reopened."[102] That this sentence, at least, is inaccurate becomes entirely clear in Twichell's later letters to Mark. When Olivia died in 1904, for example, Twichell, at a time of all others when he might well have deferred to Mark's agnosticism without comment, gently insisted on his confidence that "behind the riddle there is a Hidden and Awful Wisdom . . . that for the mortal spirit there is a practicable victory over the world with all its baffling mysteries."[103]

It is impossible to think that the long talk in which Twichell and Mark discussed the passages from the *Rubaiyat* printed in the *Courant* in 1879 did not include a full discussion of its personal religious implications. Twichell found that Omar expressed certain thoughts and moods of his exactly, that the poem brought to mind a passage of Emerson which Mark had read to him the night before. "Read it," he wrote, "and we'll talk it over." Mark himself took an immense pleasure in the poem. The resulting conversation could hardly have omitted Mark's personal responses to Omar's philosophy. And again in 1881, Twichell, with his usual self-depreciation, wrote Mark, "I'll try to be a better minister than ever to you, Mark, i.e. I'll try to *be* one, which I often fear I haven't been at all. I've got the affection anyhow, whatever else is wanting." It is true, of course, that Twichell was sufficiently mature that he did not attempt to convert Mark with American Mission Board arguments. He was willing to recognize Mark's position; it did not become a sore point, and in their intimacy its frequency as a topic for discussion was not interrupted either by delicate avoidance or by special preoccupations.[104]

It is possible, then, that the rest of Paine's account may be at this particular point similarly inaccurate. I do not know when Mark told Twichell of his religious views. For the first few years, while still he was able to attend church and keep his peace, he may have said nothing. But surely at some period before their intimacy was ten years old the subject would have come up. It was not the custom of Twichell, any more than of the present-day clergyman, to probe uninvited an individual's religious belief; with the religion of individual intuition this had become an effrontery. But in 1875, three years before the European trip, Twichell wrote Mark: "We have had many and many a good time together, my dear old fellow; it has been a bright streak [of] experience to me all through; but, oh dear me, how I do wish I had been a better pastor to you. God bless you, in spite of me,"[105] a passage which in this context suggests that Mark's religious opinions were a matter of regret to Twichell, as it is natural they would be. If so, Twichell must have known what those opinions were. But he did not usually look upon Mark's religion as testimony to his own professional ineffectiveness. It was not essential to his own faith or well-being that Mark share his own views. Twichell's personal balance was keyed to a maturity that did not require public or private evangelism. It is absurd to imply that this attitude was evidence of lack of faith, personal hypocrisy, or shallowness, as is suggested by Edward Wagenknecht.[106]

In the friendship of Mark and Twichell there was then this difference. Later even sharper conflicts on political questions and on the manginess of the human race were to appear in the period after Mark's Hartford residence, when his skepticism had become despair and his doubt of a beneficent God had become certainty of impersonal malignance. No divergences in religious, philosophical, political, or social views, some of which we will have occasion to look at later, interfered with the mutual satisfaction of their intimacy. Later Mark was to pour into Twichell's sympathetic ear the undiluted venom of his bitterness, and Twichell was to rejoice that his listening brought Mark relief and to long, in the interim between the outpourings, for the maledictions that were at the end the background of their affectionate interchanges.

As the two decades progressed, Mark's religion was much of the time, particularly in the seventies, of secondary importance to him. In his skepticism he was well enough content, making of it no great issue and straining it out of his published writings, except for satiric references to Calvinism in *Tom Sawyer*, *Huckleberry Finn*, and such occasional pieces as the "Recent Carnival of Crime in Connecticut." Only on special provocation did his association with the more pious irk him. Thus during his 1885 lecture tour with George Washington Cable, the latter's punctilious observance of the Sabbath proved inconvenient and infuriating. Nobody among his Hartford friends was as sanctimonious as Cable; Mark usually found his own views easily adjustable to those of his neighbors. For on important ideas he was in agreement with them. When, to name an exception, he and Howells did not in 1878 recognize the divinity of Christ, Mark bridged this deviation with the opinion that Christ is nonetheless a sacred personage to whom is due the profoundest reverence.[107] Life at this time, he said generally, was a fairy tale. When John Hay told him that life was a tragedy after forty, he disputed him warmly.[108] And until the success he made for himself collapsed, his dominant mood was a happy exhilaration in which religious speculation was not central.

But even during his most creative years, when he was happiest and best adjusted to the world he had chosen, when he was reveling exuberantly in his prosperity and was writing his greatest books, there were signs of the black despair that the events of the nineties were to magnify into the desperate unhappiness at the heart of his later life. In 1876 he wrote Mrs. Fairbanks in a mood not at all humorous:

Let him [Charley, son of Mrs. Fairbanks] go it now when he's young! Never mind about that grisly future season when he shall have made a dazzling success & shall sit with folded hands in well-earned ease & look around upon his corpses & mine, & contemplate his daughters & mine in the mad-house, & his sons & mine gone to the devil. That is all away yonder — we will not bother about it now.[109]

He had known at this time only the sorrow of his son's death in the first year of his Hartford residence. But he was always to exaggerate almost incredibly the weight of his own misfortunes, and it is little wonder that when they did become from any point of view very heavy, he should have succumbed to desolation.

In the Hartford years, then, Mark's uncertain sense of proportion showed itself as a deeply significant trait that permitted his determinism to unfold in its later bleakness. Of the plentiful evidence, no single piece is so striking as the letter he wrote to Howells in 1886, near the end of the happy years.[110] He refers to a death in the Howells family, acknowledging briefly that as an experience it must have been hard. But he himself has just suffered a thunder-stroke which "for the moment ranged me breast to breast & comraded me as an equal, with all men who have suffered sudden & awful disaster: I found that all their lives my children have been afraid of me!" He extends this anticlimax, which of course did not even resemble actuality, into what he calls a pathetic revelation beside which all the concentrated griefs of his fifty years paled. If he were to live seventy-five years, he says, nothing could equal its shock. Howells, recalling later the troubles of Mark's life, gently recognized Mark's inclination to enlarge his sorrows:

They were of the common lot, and no special tragedy . . . the death of his children would seem to have struck him with a sort of dismay, as if no one else had known the like, and it finds naive utterance in his letters.[111]

This inability to see himself and his misfortunes in perspective is allied to other personal characteristics instinct in the psychological fitness of his religious opinions—his tenderness with humanity and his recurrent sense of guilt. Twichell said—everything in Mark's life attests his accuracy—that Mark, though a man with the bark on, had "exquisite sentiments" underneath: extreme affectionateness, immediate responsiveness to any appeal to his sense of pity, and an easy susceptibility to tears. In illustration of his consideration for others, he said Mark hated to pass another person while walking; he was "exceedingly timid, tremblingly timid, about approaching strangers." [112] His whole life is a record of extreme sensibility. He was outraged by the smallest breach of ethical decency. This sensitivity exacerbated his lack of perspective in that it increased his misery by allowing him to exaggerate the inhumanity he was so quick to discover in others and in himself.

Even more crucial in these happy years is the closely related sense of guilt complicating his relation to everyone he loved. He had blamed himself for the death of his brother Henry, who died attended by Mark after the explosion of the steamboat *Pennsylvania* in 1858. In 1872 he accused himself of allowing his son Langdon to lie a few moments in the cold and falsely attributed the boy's death to this accident. He could twist his participation in these misfortunes into culpable behavior, but he did not need an actual event to evoke his ever-ready remorse. He could invent one.

After the trip with Twichell through Switzerland, an occasion almost the climactic exuberance of his and Twichell's youth and a joyful and extravagantly gay interlude,[113] Mark wrote to Twichell of the richness of the holiday, adding unexpectedly,

> I am putting out of my mind all memory of the times when I misbehaved toward you & hurt you; I am resolved to consider it forgiven, & store up & remember only the charming hours of the journeys, & the times when I was not unworthy to be with you & share a companionship which to me stands first after Livy's. It is justifiable to do this—for why should I let my small infirmities of disposition live & grovel among my mental pictures of the eternal sublimities of the Alps? [114]

Twichell was both puzzled and moved by this passage, so grotesque a commentary on the perfection of their holiday. He replied to it, after expressing again his gratitude:

> But I think we may well despair of producing another chapter of life so barren of matter for conscience to work up into gimcracks of remorse, as that composed by our late six weeks together.
>
> The astounding note I received from you on the Bothnia at Liverpool, which made me, and still makes me laugh and cry by turns, is a dainty bit of literature—it's so natural—just precisely as if it was about something that had happened. You surely didn't mean it for irony, assuming with feigned humility, acknowledg-

ments that were rather due from me? Yet really, I can't make *any* sense of it on any other hypothesis. Confound me, don't I remember the day I got mad at you — and you so mild and unresenting under it? Oh, you dear long suffering Mark, there's nobody I want to travel with henceforth but you.[115]

This self-blame was not an unusual exercise for Mark. Continually assuming guilt for offenses he had not committed, he was sure whenever these frequent moods came upon him that his very presence harassed Livy and that his most innocent act was crude or cruel.

I am not qualified to diagnose the psychic source of this abnormality; but Mark Twain's exaggerated compassion, his powerful impulses to remorse, and his disproportionate valuations of his own misfortunes are at least facets of a personality inharmoniously adjusted to the real world. Here are the early sounds of a private tumult that in vivid contrast to the gaiety at the other extreme of his alternation rose eventually in clamor to drown out his happiness. These characteristics seem symptomatic of a deep disturbance out of which a rickety explanation of the universe emerged. A dogma based on shifting doubts, his amateur philosophy gradually showed itself unsatisfactory as the eighties passed. Mark was unable to let it alone — to formulate his skepticism and turn to other things. It is inevitable that the future development of his religious thought should be away from doubt in the direction of certainty, certainty of the malignant futility in individual endeavor. Mark's religion was as much as his neighbors' the product of his times. Somehow his response to his environment was defective. In his house the same kind of turbulence simmered as at the Stowes' and the Warners' and the Hookers' and in thousands of places in America, where deep entanglements involving the relation of man to his destiny had not vanished with the eradication of a morbid theology.

It is not necessary to the recognition of Mark Twain's literature to answer the questions his experience prompts. The significance of his religious ideas should be evaluated in the context in which they were evolved. Such a view makes his revolt less erratic than if we conceive of it in terms of the Western frontiersman's reaction against a hostile Eastern culture. Mark Twain was at home in this neighborhood. He accepted the ethical ideals of Nook Farm and shared its spiritual uneasiness. In decorous observance of the Christian ethic, he and his contemporaries lived a religion which was continuous through the variety of eccentricities and divergences that multiplied on Nook Farm.

The disintegration in mid-century of a society welded by incontrovertible beliefs to ironclad doctrines enveloped all of Mark Twain's circle. Its religious experience was the mottled reflection of uncertainty. This entire company was now without anchor in an established society. Not only had the stabilizing influence of a tangible future life disappeared, but the coherence of earthly existence was becoming hazy. In Nook Farm no philosophers of a society in flux emerged to build new frameworks; no trained intellectuals assessed coolly the implications for individual well-being of the disruptive developments after the Civil War. Genius was there in generous proportion, but genius is not proof against a disorganized world. Mark Twain was eventually a casualty of the great demoralization. And as we have seen, the poignance of change moved deeply most of the others at Nook Farm. But in the meantime a few books arose out of personal sensitivity and a generation's immaturity to achieve recognition as great literature.

3

THE VARIETIES OF SECULAR EXPERIENCE

1871–1891

Everyday Life in Family and Neighborhood

THE SECULAR ACTIVITY OF NOOK FARM WAS LESS CHAOTIC THAN ITS religious experience. Solitary obsession and individual preoccupation with eternity did not blight the development of an abundant social life from which Mark Twain and his satellites took comfort and pleasure. The everyday life of the seventies and eighties, exhilarated by the achievement of community intimacy, is a significant chapter in our social history. For here in this neighborhood, where a restless Mark Twain voluntarily made his home for twenty years, a talented and cultured group brought to fruition a kind of life sanctioned by the whole history of Hartford and by the shorter experience of other cultured and conservative cities in America. The community devoted its combined imagination to making congeniality a way of life. Under favorable climatic conditions, it cultivated specific ideals observable in detail. Universally acceptable concepts of family happiness, of hospitality, of varied, intelligent, and fresh recreation, of continuous cultural self-improvement, and of material comfort were fully developed by a neighborhood attempting with conscious skill to live a rich life and a happy one. For a considerable period the attainment of a constantly complicating and always stimulating social life accelerated toward apparent perfection. Mark Twain contributed an even more determined energy than his neighbors to the pursuit of community ideals, which quickly became his own. Not willingly would he abandon the life he lived in Hartford; he was never to forget it. And after his going his friends would never be able to rebuild the fellowship in which he had been the key figure.

First of all, Nook Farm gave careful attention to contriving suitable settings for its family activities. The construction and furnishing of homes custom-designed to accommodate the local household gods was a painstaking business. The results reflected the heavy taste of the time; the dark-brown angular houses were weighed down by verandas, cupolas, gables, and balconies. But in Nook Farm the elaborateness of post-War building was less offensive than in most prosperous neighborhoods of American cities, for comfort and spaciousness were more important architectural objectives than richness of gingerbread.

Mrs. Stowe was the community expert in the planning and decoration of Nook Farm's substantial residences and the leading theoretician of the ideal family life. She and Catharine Beecher addressed their home-economics texts to householders poorer than their neighbors, planning $1600, two-bedroom cottages [1] with convenient closets, adequate ventilation, and efficient chimneys. But Harriet's ideas of home decoration were applicable also to the larger houses of Nook Farm. Since beauty was essential to a "higher moral growth," she advised the humble homemaker to paper the parlor walls with sunshiny patterns, to cover the floor with straw matting (cheaper than the elaborate carpets which the broom wore out), to brighten the furniture with lounge covers of matched light colors, to drape white muslin at the windows, to hang varnished chromos (like Bierstadt's "Sunset in the Yo Semite Valley") on the walls, to distribute statuettes and knickknacks everywhere, and above all, to grow ivy around windows, pictures, and statuary. The effect she pursued, with all its quaintness, was an airy, colorful modification of the stuffy Victorian interior. On a more expensive plane, the Nook Farm householders followed her instructions. Instead of putting a carrot or sweet potato in a glass of water, they built into their houses small conservatories (of a pattern invented by Harriet) where fountains played among green plants. They dispensed with stoves in favor of central hot-air heating and replaced earth-closets [2] with flush toilets, but they accepted for themselves the ideals of informality and comfort that Harriet urged upon the nation at large.

The Nook Farm houses were all big enough to require a staff of servants. Harriet concerned herself actively with the critical shortage of houseworkers. Well she might; she was partly responsible for the development of female education, which had made daughters of "plain working-men" contemptuous of domestic service. As a result, she pointed out in *The Chimney-Corner* (1868), schoolteaching and dressmaking, the only occupations creditable for the educated woman, were overcrowded, and many homes like her own were inadequately staffed. She recommended that domestic drudgery somehow be lifted into an alluring science. Individual and unusual women were certainly entitled freedom to develop in their own spheres, but woman's chief talent as a sex is to make and keep a home, and to that end females should welcome training and experience in domestic service as a supplement to their school education.

Charles Dudley Warner agreed with Harriet. He contemplated in melancholy the quality of servants fumbling about his big brown house off Forest Street. "There is surely some defect in the theory of equality in our society which makes domestic service to be shunned as if it were a disgrace," he wrote,[3] thinking perhaps of his discovery of dipsomania among Irish laundresses. His own house was bedecked with Mexican fabrics and rich rugs; the small rooms were crowded with spoils of his travels, arranged in "artistic confusion." Magazines and books, coming in great numbers to the *Courant* for review, were everywhere. The comfortable, heavily cushioned chairs and divans, in contrast to a background of stiffer mahogany pieces and bookshelves, were pulled to the center of the living rooms. Instead of chromolithographs of the "Yo Semite," he hung Vasques's "Martyrdom of Santa Barbara" over the fireplace, and etchings and old prints elsewhere. His Stowe conservatory was designed to filter the sunshine entering the dining room through green leaves, blossoms, and falling water. It was an effective adornment. Mrs. T. B. Aldrich of Boston was much impressed by it;[4] so, in a different way, was Warner. "We don't eat much of anything," he said; "we put our money into our conservatory."[5] The homelike clutter of the house made it attractive to the neighborhood; in summer, the trees outside softened its exterior lines and open doors and windows made it inviting. In winter, wood fires burned constantly on the hearths.

In the Hooker house Isabella prided herself on the tactful management of her servants, of whom she was consciously considerate and to whom she graciously presented Christmas gifts as the small staff lined up for the formal occasion. She maintained her study as a museum of her European trips. In 1876 Mark Twain and Livy made a point of bringing the Fullers of New York to see her collection of bric-a-brac.[6] The ladies were volubly appreciative of Isabella's taste in home decoration. They liked the fresh pine boughs festooning the library, and they approved Isabella's most recent touch — a bright shawl draped about a picture of her mother that Harriet had sent over. The Hooker house was less informal than Warner's and presumably less cozy, but Isabella followed Harriet's practice of growing ivy on the window curtains and utilizing every inch of space for knickknacks. The appointment of her home she regarded as a work of art, and its management an opportunity to practice the administrative skill that world affairs would require of her.

Mrs. Stowe, once she had abandoned baronial Oakholm, lived in a graceful and chaste Quaker-gray house near by. She and her neighbors thought of it as a cottage, but its three stories and dozen rooms seem very spacious to apartment dwellers who visit it today. In the living room on the ground floor, she displayed many of her books. The alcoved, Gothic-topped cases, in which she had arranged a hundred copies of *Uncle Tom's Cabin* — one from every edition and translation — lined an entire wall. The simple furniture (covered with green rep in 1886) of her small parlor was a mixture of antique and Victorian. Souvenirs of her triumphal tours of Europe were everywhere; on the walls hung her own water colors of orange trees and Florida landscapes. The house seemed, in contrast to the neighboring mansions, humbly close to the street; all the others were dignified by greater expanses of grass and shrubbery.

Mark Twain, who had leased the Hooker home in 1871 to allow time to build a house of his own that would be "right," constructed eventually the most sumptuous home in Nook Farm. After a year of careful thought, he purchased a desirable site (later enlarged by a second purchase) for $20,000 and built upon it a mansion with nineteen large rooms and five baths. Although the exterior of the house was deliberately underemphasized to give it a "modest aspect," the modified Gothic design was sufficiently unconventional to attract criticism from a host of sidewalk superintendents. The Hartford *Times* said the house rising on Farmington Avenue was clearly "one of the oddest looking buildings in the State ever designed for a dwelling, if not in the whole country."[7] The main entrance faced the back property of the houses on the east; the servant and kitchen wing faced Farmington Avenue. Because of this arrangement, the library could look out upon a wooded bank at the foot of which flowed the little river; a veranda could extend from the back of the house out into the trees. The turrets, balconies, porches, and miscellaneous lookouts all commanded attractive views.

The interior of the house must have represented the richest intelligent taste of the time, particularly after the original decor was later adjusted to the advancing idea of elegance. The marble floor of the large entrance hall was softened by Persian rugs. An enormous open three-flight staircase of dark oak led upward. The similarly dark woodwork in the parlor, dining room, and library on the main floor was relieved, after 1882, by silver wall decorations from Tiffany's. The conservatory off the library was the most elaborate in the city — a large room supplied with exotic plants from a greenhouse maintained on the property. The library itself, decorated in blue and olive, lined by chest-high bookshelves and statuary, and given additional life and color by the conservatory, was probably the most impressive room in the house. The bedrooms were museums of dark carved furniture brought from Venice and elsewhere in Europe, but the children's rooms were bright and cheerful. Throughout, sphinxes and griffins contorted themselves into lounges and sofas. The hearths in every room supported varied and unusual superstructures; one fireplace was dwarfed by an elaborate mantelpiece transported, like much of the woods and other appointments, from Europe. The general impression was that of an ordered and spacious richness. The completed house became quickly the object of widespread notice and established a lasting influence on Hartford house-building and home decoration. Mark Twain had surpassed by a wide margin, as he had planned to, the elegance of the "private hotels" he had first remarked in Nook Farm. Influenced in part by the taste of the Farm, but also purposely original, he had constructed a unique manor in which he could dispense a lord's hospitality. Though his fortunes were at low ebb when he joined this society, within three years he had been able to install $21,000 worth of furniture in a $70,000 house standing on five acres of land worth $31,000. This achievement was for a time a most satisfactory one.

The architecture and decoration of all the houses in Nook Farm were twenty years ahead of the unimaginative austerity then characteristic of most urban middle-class homes in America. Visitors from other cities — the feminists, politicians, writers, journalists, and artists who came in great numbers to see the Hookers, Hawleys, Stowes, Warners, and Clemenses — were fluently appreciative of the relative originality of Hartford homes. The praise of people from New York and Boston, from Charleston and New Orleans, stimulated the local quest for informal comfort in the humbler houses and for elegant luxury in the mansions. Nook Farm's absorption in the trappings of domesticity produced an appropriate backdrop for the kind of living its residents considered felicitous.

The ideal of a house as the comfortable, spacious, and well-furnished vehicle for living involves a concept of family life which, though familiar, remains interesting. Each of the Nook Farm families conceived of a fully developed family experience as the heart of existence and devoted much energy to living up to this conception. Mrs. Hooker brooded over the hostilities among her kin with a sorrow which demonstrated that love for her family persisted through millennial delusions. Mrs. Stowe, whose family life was always most complex and deeply troubled, defined the management of the family "state" as a sacred profession and attempted to educate her generation to accept the necessity for learning skill in family affairs as the most fruitful of all social endeavors. Harmony Twichell, distressed as she was by nine pregnancies, resigned herself to their frequency in the recognition that her only happiness lay in her husband and children. And Mark Twain was celebrated among his friends and contemporaries for being conspicuously devoted to his wife and daughters.

During the first years Mark lived in Hartford, he was still adjusting himself to marriage, overstating in letters to his friends the strictness of his wife's government — an exaggeration allied to his susceptibilty to unreasonable remorse and to his characteristic assumption, whenever he took up a pen, of a bumpkin clownishness. The letters of Mark Twain have been thoroughly examined in the now-obsolete Brooks–DeVoto contention about Livy's alleged suppression of her husband's real genius; the published evidence of the meaningfulness of family ties to Mark Twain has become very well known. As his family grew again after the death of his son from the births of Susie in 1872 and Clara in 1874 to the arrival of Jean in 1880, and particularly after his children were old enough to listen to stories, play charades, and act in private theatricals, Mark gave much of his time and energy to their entertainment. Since he did not discipline himself in Hartford as he did on Quarry Farm to write a large number of words each day, he was always available, when the children were not in the upstairs schoolroom, for play. He gradually became so completely absorbed by his family, in fact, that after the deaths of his wife and two of his children he was utterly unable to recover from his grief. Family sorrows thus had much to do with the despair of his old age. But while the sun shone on his prosperity and on his loved ones, he was more than content with his role as husband and father. In 1874 he wrote, speaking of his family, "if there is one individual creature on all this footstool who is more thoroughly and uniformly and unceasingly happy than I am I defy the world to produce him and prove him. In my opinion he doesn't exist." [8] And for his felicity he thanked Olivia, grateful for her toleration of what he considered his rough ways.

Mark's domesticity represented his spontaneous conformance to the way of life he adopted when he settled in the East. His progress toward the goal of being worthy of Livy was, of course, watched and encouraged by Mrs. Langdon and Mother Fairbanks. Both approved. Mrs. Fairbanks wrote, after a visit to Hartford in the seventies,

> I am glad to have had this fresh picture of your home life, and to have come again, (as I always do when I am with you) into the inner sanctum where I see your motives, your responsibilities and your inspirations. Perhaps it is the partial verdict of a partial mother, but I do believe if there were more such conscientious wives and faithful mothers, and amiable husbands and fathers as certain ones I could find on a Hartford map, there would be more people walking upon that higher grade to which so many spasmodically aspire.[9]

And in 1876, comparing Nook Farm with Cleveland, she asked, "Don't you think heaven does lie somewhere near Hartford or Boston, and that if I am good I shall sometime go there to stay?"[10]

The Clemens household and the other families of Nook Farm were unified by a cohesiveness more characteristic of their time than of ours. But in this neighborhood the unity of the family was in no sense exclusive. The everyday life of Nook Farm was lived less in the single family sphere than in the social area where families met on common ground. The informality of the old Farm was perpetuated and enlarged in the seventies and eighties. The houses appeared to be irregularly spaced on one enormous fenceless estate. Winding among the trees were paths and shortcuts which neighbors used without going to the street. Doors were always unlocked and residents of the Farm walked in and out of each other's houses at any time of day without knocking.

The ideal of the good life as a happy family life thus warmed the whole neighborhood; the intimacy of the individual family circle intertwined the group of families. Mark and Livy, whose friendship with the Twichells was well advanced by 1871, next became intimate with the Warners. From the first, Livy, unlike Mark, was very fond of Charles Warner, whose gentleness of humor, kindliness of manner, and aura of personal integrity engaged her affections. From this early affinity the collaboration of Warner and Mark in *The Gilded Age* developed to absorb both families for three months in 1873. Another member of the community, the antiquarian J. Hammond Trumbull,[11] added to the book the mottoes that parade dozens of languages in cryptographic chapter headings. Susan Warner and Livy Clemens passed judgment each evening on their husbands' daily production, but though the writing of their first novel was for each of the two writers an enthusiastic coöperative venture, neither was satisfied with the results. Certainly Mark was not entirely happy in the partnership; he had probably interpreted Warner's earlier refusal to sell a share of the *Courant* as a personal rebuff. Mark drew up careful contracts at every stage of the venture and decided to undertake the very profitable dramatization of the book by himself, on the ground that Colonel Sellers was his character. The formality of the contracts suggests coolness between the signatories. But by 1876 Mark was writing Howells that he was liking Warner better and better every day; the prejudices and dislike he had experienced in that relation were wearing out. He was willing to defer to Livy's blind fondness for Warner—her instincts in the perception of character were truer than Mark's.[12] Warner's later reviews of Mark's books in the *Courant* were always friendly; their correspondence was warm. Warner wrote in 1874, for example, when the Clemenses had gone early to Elmira for the birth of Clara: "I hope Livy is thriving. We think of her daily with love. You may believe we miss you—miss is no word for it."[13] And in Hartford Mark enjoyed Warner's conversational facility, his jokes, his valentine to Livy beginning,

> Come out into the slush, dear,
> In your gracious galoshes shod[14]

and spent hours before the fire in the Warner living room talking with the company assembled there.[15] In his autobiography he wrote,

> It is seldom that man is so beloved by both sexes and all ages as Warner was. There was a charm about his spirit, and his ways, and his words, that won all that came within the sphere of its influence. Our children adopted him while they were little creatures, and thenceforth, to the end, he was Cousin Charley to them.[16]

The Twichell-Warner family friendship extended beyond the closeness of the two men, who walked to Talcott Tower and talked together of life, literature, and religion. Warner often strolled over to Woodland Street in the afternoon to lounge about Twichell's study or to talk at length with Harmony, whom he honored as "The Wise Woman." Every Thanksgiving Susan invited the entire Twichell tribe for dinner, and nearly every summer the two families lived side by side in Keene Valley, New York, where they had first met in 1866. There, as in Hartford, Joe and Warner tramped the hills. In 1876, for example, they made a four-day trip through the Catskills,

> . . . a very pleasant trip in the best of company—a great feast of talk—noble exercise—splendid scenery—all the country we passed through W of the Hudson was Irvings land to both of us, and we felt in view of such an example, the great service of a national literature.[17]

While the men were away, Susan and Harmony passed the time together. Later Twichell wrote of his friendship for Warner:

> We may well account such a friendship as his one of life's choicest treasures. I have no words to tell what it has been worth to me.[18]

On October 8, 1886, the neighborhood celebrated the thirtieth anniversary of the Warner marriage in a ceremony typical of the gracefully expressed mutual affection in Nook Farm. At six o'clock Joe and Harmony Twichell, George and Lilly Warner, Miss Fanny Hesse and Annie Price of the Warner household gathered at Mark Twain's. Once assembled, the company moved conspiratorially through the grounds to the Warner house, climbed in the dining-room window, and seated themselves at a table secretly set for eleven and decorated with gay place cards sketched by Lilly Warner. At the proper time the maid announced dinner to Charles and Susan, who had been sitting as usual in front of their parlor fire, unconscious of the preparations in the dining room. They came across the hall to be greeted by the laughter of their good friends. Twichell said later the surprise was all it was meant to be. "We had a delightful time," he added, "fragrant with memory, gratitude and friendship." [19]

The strained relation between the Clemens and Hooker families has appeared in the context of Isabella's religious experience, but in her diary Mrs. Hooker leaves us a vivid impression of Mark and Livy as well as a sense of the delicacy of her social position in post-War Nook Farm. On the day after Thanksgiving 1876 she took a friend of hers to see the Clemens home. (The whole neighborhood felt free to show it to those who had not seen it.) During the tour, she and Mark had "an uncomfortable interview" which grew in importance as she thought about it, despite her realization that she might be oversensitively magnifying its significance:

> I joked him about not caring for a pretty lamp shade after he found it so very cheap — & he was vexed and said something about things going round the neighborhood & explained that he had no knowledge or taste himself & so when an established house said a thing was good & charged a good price for it he felt sure that it was worthy of Livy & and that was all he cared for. I said oh that was handsomely said but really as a matter of fact I thought one often paid a high price for a homely article under such circumstances — which he didn't seem to like & again spoke of being talked about. When I said why it was all a joke as I heard it & retailed it — & one so given to joking as himself mustnt mind it etc — but his eyes flashed & he looked really angry — though Livy coming in then & hearing only the last sentence about cheap things not being worth presenting, said most lovingly — "Why yes, dear I think they are — no matter how small the gift, the thoughtfulness & love make them valuable" — but as this helped my side he did not seem to relish it & I felt uncomfortable. Bret Harte was there (but did not hear this conversation) & I felt almost a dislike of him, which is unusual with me, & when passing thro the billiard room afterward they were there together & there were bottles of spirit near. I felt a new distrust of such companionship & ever since the thought has haunted me that perhaps I have

something to do there by way of warning—yet I dread to lose the friendship of that house which is but a slender thread already I fancy.[20]

The Clemens family and the Hookers were still friends after this incident, but interchange was infrequent when Livy's mother was not in Hartford.

The relations of the Clemens, Warner, and Twichell families with the Stowes were not so intimate as those among themselves, for though Harriet was still of competent mind when these friendships were being formed, she was so much older than the others that they approached her with courteous respect. Until shortly before Calvin's death in the summer of 1886, she and her family spent the winters in Florida, and in the summer when she was on Forest Street the other Nook Farm families were usually out of town. The Clemenses and the Twichells knew her better than did the Warners. On November 17, 1882 Harmony and Joe joined Mark and Livy and Harriet at a dinner in honor of George P. Lathrop, Hawthorne's son-in-law. Twichell, as usual, enjoyed the festivities, especially the "pleasure of hearing Mrs. Stowe talk. She was in the mood for it, and struck a reminiscent strain having much to say of the old anti-slavery days. We were conscious of a great reverence toward her." [21]

Still interested actively in the world of 1883, Harriet came to the Asylum Hill Church when a P. C. Mazoormdar of Calcutta preached the sermon as Twichell's guest, sought him out afterwards, greeted him with great cordiality, and asked him about India. In 1884 Harmony and Joe called on the Stowes directly after the Stowes' last trip to Florida to discover that Harriet had just received the letter of praise from W. E. Gladstone inspired by his reading of *The Minister's Wooing*. In 1886, when the *Critic* asked Twichell for an article on Mrs. Stowe, he went to see her for the necessary permission and assistance, both of which she granted with "the sweetest patience imaginable." Mark Twain, who shared the neighborhood's respect for the aged heroine of antislavery, sought to amuse her whenever he could, as in the famous incident in which he sent his tie by the butler when Livy reminded him he had called on Harriet without it. Once he planned a fairly elaborate "Jarley Waxworks," preparing and costuming the children of the neighborhood to assume the likeness of "historical figures." He called on Mrs. Stowe ostensibly to introduce Moncure D. Conway to her. After Harriet and Conway had talked a few minutes about their English friends, Mark introduced the characters, first of which was a knight in full armor. After saying "Bring on that tin-shop" as if aside, he recited a fictitious tale of the knight's adventures. Conway found it all charming and "never forgot the evident affection for Mark felt by his neighbors," [22] but the incident is interesting also for its demonstration of the neighborhood affection for Harriet Beecher Stowe.

In her ten years of overprotracted old age after Calvin's death, Mrs. Stowe's mind collapsed under the accumulated strain her life had placed upon it. In blissful forgetfulness, she walked about the neighborhood, thin, small, and childlike, hunting out wild flowers to carry in her hand and take home to her embarrassed spinster twin daughters. Mark's greenhouse and conservatory were for her a paradise. To the vexation of the Clemens gardener she gathered blooms there, neglecting to use the scissors hung at convenient points to remind her not to injure the plants by breaking off the stems. Grace King, when she visited the Warners in 1887, marveled at Harriet's talking to herself as she walked about and was astonished to see her running lightly, like a wild animal under the trees, her face happy and bright, her hair tied with a black ribbon.[23] Mrs. Warner assured Miss King that she would soon be accustomed to the sight. One afternoon, as Livy Clemens sat on the "Ombra" (the Clemens name for the large porch overlooking the stream) talking with Annie Price, Mrs. Stowe came in to proffer a handful of wild flowers. Harriet was glad Livy accepted them. She could not help gathering flowers as she walked; yet when she brought them home, her daughters invariably said, "Ha! What are you going to do with them; everything is full." "Mrs. Stowe," Livy added to her account of this incident in her diary, "is so gentle and lovely." [24] Often Mark and Livy heard quiet music in their drawing room. They would find Harriet at the piano singing old and melancholy songs, spirituals, and frontier melodies so deeply ingrained in the automatism of her memory that she still remembered all the words.

But as the dreamy anesthesia in which Harriet spent her last years slipped imperceptibly into a more erratic mindlessness, her behavior, to the distress of her affectionate neighbors, became occasionally grotesque. A muscular Irishwoman was assigned to accompany her, but with instinctive shrewdness Harriet daily eluded her. On her aimless expeditions through the houses of her neighbors, she would in this phase slip up behind anyone musing or reading and "fetch a war whoop that would jump that person out of his clothes." [25] Once she ran to Colonel Charles W. Burpee of the *Courant* staff, who lived down Forest Street, and threw herself upon him, calling "Fred! Fred!" confusing his identification with the Civil War with her dead son's.[26] Mark sometimes grew impatient with Harriet's daughters for allowing her to escape her guardian to play practical jokes and frighten pregnant women with her antics; in his notebook he calls the twins "Soft Soap" and "Hellfire." But he and the rest of the neighborhood usually thought Harriet more pathetic than dangerous. In her forlorn babblings, as in her wistful, childlike lucid moods, she was an object of tenderness and a reminder both to residents and to visitors of Nook Farm's historic importance as a literary shrine. Since she was in her age and greatness a symbol of the Farm's significance, she contributed to the unity of the neighborhood.

The interdependence of Nook Farm families enveloped other intimacies. From her arrival, Livy Clemens was universally loved. Lilly Warner, attractively blonde, intelligent, and highly literate,[27] wrote her often when Livy was in Europe or Elmira. Livy and Harmony Twichell were as intimate as Mark and Joe, and Livy helped her friend over domestic financial hurdles and contributed to the education of her children. The women of the neighborhood gave frequent lunch parties for each other, often inviting the wives of their husbands' friends. Through this ritual Livy came to know Mrs. Frank W. Cheney of South Manchester and many of the other social leaders of the larger Hartford social life. Without a single exception, every letter, diary, and other document I have consulted mentions Livy, whenever occasion arises, in terms of admiration that have the cumulative effect of redeeming her personality from the depressing pallidity innocently implied by Paine and triumphantly exaggerated by Brooks. The virtues appealing to her friends were those of the ideal woman of the period — unassuming beauty, limitless devotion, grace in hospitality, intellectual anonymity — and as a result she sometimes seems to us hard to characterize as an individual, so little do we know of her passions. But to her contemporaries she was not merely a paragon, but a live object of adulation. When she walked from her house to the Warners in a long red negligee, which strikingly emphasized her large dark eyes and very white forehead, or appeared in any dress in any of the other homes on the Farm, she was enthusiastically welcomed, perhaps even more unreservedly than Mark. She was in no quarter considered the colorless wife of a great man. Posterity has endowed with sinister implications her innocent acquiescence to her generation's notion of the perfect woman. Reconstruction of her role in the everyday life of Nook Farm, however, demonstrates the absurdity of these latter-day imaginings.

But beyond the extension of a highly developed family life into the larger context of a neighborhood circle, the Clemens household, and to a lesser extent the Warner, Twichell, and Stowe homes, opened out to the Boston literary circle and indeed to all of literary America. Part of the day-to-day satisfaction of life in Nook Farm was the recognition by authors from other parts of the country or from abroad that Hartford was a delightful place to stop in. After Mark opened his new house in 1874, he was seldom without visitors, especially while the extension of his acquaintance among literary figures was still an exhilarating novelty of his Eastern residence. By 1875 Hartford was considered "a half-way land of rest between New York and Boston." [28] Fields, Aldrich, Osgood, Howells, and many others rode out to Nook Farm whenever they passed through the city. These visitors tell us much about Nook Farm home life. The explicit admiration in their comments makes clear the unique success with which Mark Twain's circle applied to the passing days its conception of what life should be like.

On one memorable occasion the Howells, Osgood, and Aldrich families converged on Hartford to be entertained jointly by Clemens and Warner. Mrs. Aldrich, who describes the visit in her memoirs, was more conscious than anybody in Hartford of Mark's Western drawl and unpolished drawing-room manners, but under the influence of Hartford hospitality she finally succumbed to his charms. The first night, the group dined at the Warners', and after dinner the combined talents of Howells, Osgood, Mark, Aldrich, and Warner "produced an incomparable hilarity." On the last night, in the Clemens library, the party decided to stay up till dawn. About midnight Mark left the house to buy more ale. He found a saloon open, but during the search he lost his cap. After stories and small talk had filled many hours, Mark changed into white cowskin slippers, which contrasted startingly with his evening dress. Without warning, "with most sober and smileless face, he twisted his angular body into all the strange contortions known to the dancing darkies of the South." [29] Mrs. Aldrich was apparently a little uncomfortable during this performance, but all the other guests, their exhilaration proof against fatigue, laughed till they cried. The ale, wit, and parlor tricks captivated the company until daylight.

Mrs. James T. Fields, who visited Hartford with her husband in 1876, noted some of Mark's instability. While she was at his home, Mark apparently lost his head over the minor illness of one of the children and exhibited exaggerated contrition when in his excitement he forgot to order a carriage to take his guests to the train. She thought his apologies amusing, and somewhat condescendingly detected in him a desire for "growth" which made him attractive. Livy looked to her like an exquisite lily, white, delicate, and tender. In spite of Mark's eccentricity she felt that the household was very loving, though "Mrs. Clemens's mother, Mrs. Langdon, hardly knows what to make of him sometimes, it is quite evident." [30]

The connections of Clemens and Warner with the younger Boston group were always close. Howells, whom Mark had met in 1869, became his friend, second in intimacy only to Twichell, and was a frequent visitor through the 1870's. Howells said he would rather talk to Mark than to any other man in the world, outside his own blood.[31] Twichell came into the friendship as early as 1874; his journal records every meeting, of which there were many. Howells appealed to Twichell at once because of his "Christian savors."

> M.T. & W.D.H. walked home from church with me, and subsequently I went to Mark's and dined with them — just for love. Upon leaving H. followed me to the door and we had on the threshold quite a talk on religious subjects and I was sorry we couldn't have more. He seemed very humble and earnest, and vastly loveable.[32]

In an attempt to attract Howells permanently to Hartford, Mark urged him in 1874 to buy for sixteen or seventeen thousand dollars Mr. Hall's house, next door to him on the corner of Forest and Farmington. But though Howells wrote Warner that he was merely living in exile in Cambridge, that his true home was in Hartford, or in *Heartford* as he resolved to spell it thenceforth, he could not sever his editorial connections to come.

The Warner house was as hospitable to Howells as was Mark's. Warner had become acquainted with him in 1873 through the *Atlantic* at the time Howells was editing Warner's *Backlog Studies* for publication. If Warner felt like making a joke now and then, or saying a lively thing, Howells wrote, he should do it; it could easily be struck from the proofs. He urged Warner to get more personality into his travel writings. Later the writer-critic relation swung the other way as Warner urged Howells to fill larger canvases in his novels.[33] The professional friendship soon became personal. After a visit to Warner in 1877, Howells wrote that the exquisiteness of such occasions was very creditable to the life of their time.

Others came. Hjalmar Boyesen found Cambridge very "pale and colorless" (though he stayed with Howells and dined with Longfellow) after the stimulating gaiety of Hartford. He had entered into Nook Farm life with exceeding quickness. Not only did he barely miss the beginning of the millennium in 1876 at the Hookers', but on another occasion he met a friend of Fanny Hesse's in the Warner house, to whom Twichell soon married him. Bronson Alcott, at eighty, came down to see Warner and to talk with Twichell about common ancestors.[34] Frances Hodgson Burnett, Helen Hunt Jackson, Grace King, and many other female writers appeared regularly at Warner's house, for he entertained an awe-inspiring succession of protégées.[35] Mrs. Fields and her constant companion, Sarah Orne Jewett, came often to visit Warner or to pay homage to Mrs. Stowe. Writers from the country at large — Bret Harte, Joel Chandler Harris, George W. Cable — visited Hartford as often as Boston and New York. Celebrities from other countries sometimes appeared in Nook Farm. Thus on November 15, 1883 the following entry appears in Twichell's journal:

H. [Harmony] and I went to M.T.'s in the P.M. to meet Matthew Arnold, his wife and daughter, at tea, — a great pleasure. Mr. and Mrs. Arnold read for me a before illegible note of Dean Stanley's which Dr. Allen gave me in London last year. The Arnolds, all three, made a most favorable impression of themselves socially. Mr. Arnold, in particular, was a gentler, more sympathetic person than his writings would lead some people to expect.[36]

This procession of notables insured that the daily life of Nook Farm included besides the residents almost always an illustrious and congenial guest. The kind of dinner and conversation the families enjoyed together was also the fare offered to visitors. The stimulation that hospitality gives to host and guest alike was a constant enrichment of the neighborhood life.

Mark led the way, as always. His house was the most magnificent. His guests came more often and stayed longer. In the three seasons each year that he spent in Hartford, at least as much of his energy went into entertainment and family affairs as ever went into his books. Twichell, Warner, and most of his guests found the brilliance exhibited in his social encounters greater than that displayed in his writings. In the dancing, the singing, and the story telling with which he amused his neighbors and visitors, they saw a unique genius which they found impossible to record. Twichell naïvely reiterates his admiration, as when he added Mark's dinner for Mr. Frechette, the poet laureate of Canada, to his catalogue of delightful occasions.

M.T. *never was* so funny as this time. The perfect art of a certain kind of story telling will die with him. No one beside *can* ever equal him, I am sure.[37]

This opinion was widely shared.

And always in the Clemens house, spontaneous gatherings of neighbors filled the evenings with what passed for gaiety in the Age of Innocence. Where at a later time Hartford people would leave their homes in the evening for recreation in public places, in Nook Farm they walked over to Mark Twain's. If the family were at home, they went in. Thus on June 13, 1885 the Clemens family spent an entirely typical evening. They ate an early dinner on the Ombra. Afterwards, while it was still light, Patrick McAleer, who had been the Clemenses' coachman from the Buffalo days, drove the long carriage from the stables to the porte-cochere so that the family of five could embark for a sunset drive. The carriage went out into Farmington Avenue a little way, returning soon to deposit Jean, who at five years had to go early to bed. Then out once more until dusk. As soon as Patrick had delivered the family home again, and after Clara and Susie had been put to bed, George and Lilly Warner walked over across the grass, followed later by Annie Price. Lilly wandered off home after a bit, leaving Annie and

George to play whist with Mark and Livy. After four games, Charles and Susan Warner came in. The company talked of Charley's most recent trip until Dr. George Williamson Smith, president of Trinity College, and a Miss Corey stopped by on their way home from downtown. Since the number was now eight, two tables of whist were set up. "We had a jolly remainder of the evening," Livy winds up her diary entry, "eating ice cream, hearing and telling funny stories of which latter Mr. Clemens was full." [38] Two nights later, George and Lilly were back again. Harmony and Joe dropped in; then Mr. Dunham, with Sally and Molly, arrived from Prospect Street. Once again two tables of whist and once more a "most delightful evening." Besides spontaneous gatherings of this sort, the members of the "Friday Evening Club" assembled weekly in Mark's billiard room to play by his rules. During these stag sessions Livy went over to the Warners' house for whist.

But this conception of the home and the kind of life most satisfyingly lived in it had implications that extended beyond a diversion of creative energy into volatile expressions. Always delighted by neighborhood activities, Mark and Livy soon felt the inevitable strain of dispensing more formal hospitality on a large scale. The house itself was hard to manage, though their servants, highly paid and competent, did not give Livy much difficulty. In 1877, Mark spoke of travel abroad as escape from the responsibilities of housekeeping. By 1881, he was complaining that Livy would be stronger and happier if it were not for the wearying slavery of housekeeping and child rearing. And the incessant social activity left him little time for work. "Work? — One *can't* you know, to any purpose. I don't really get anything done worth speaking of, except during the three or four months that we are away in the summer . . . I keep three or four books on the stocks all the time, but I seldom add a satisfactory chapter to one of them at home." [39] The home life of Nook Farm, centered on enjoyment of personal contributions into which Mark threw himself with prodigal gusto, seemed more strenuous as he grew older, as repetition diminished its exhilaration, and as the demands of individual development asserted themselves. Beginning about 1880, Mark's absorption in the life of family and neighborhood and in the continuous hospitality made necessary by intimacy with a large circle lessened in proportion to the frustration of the business enterprises into which he had plunged. The expenses of his home mounted with his income. Soon he was driven to support a scale of living that seemed occasionally to be less charming than he had expected, but from which he could not retreat. The ideal of family life he had so triumphantly achieved left him in the 1880's with an impressive sense of heavy involvement and burgeoning responsibility. "A life of don't-care-a-damn in a boarding house is what I have asked for in many a secret prayer," he said in 1882.[40] Before another decade passed the prayer was to be realized, but with neither pleasure nor relief. A peak of domestic happiness never to be regained had passed. The days when the visitors from Boston and New York and the South and West came and pronounced their Nook Farm visits "the most delightful social experience in life," and when the residents of Nook Farm "tasted sweet fellowship to the full," were to end soon but not to fade in memory. The significance of this subtle shift in the equilibrium that contained Mark Twain's volatility and Hartford society will appear when we examine the books he wrote in the Hartford years.

Meanwhile Mark Twain clung to the social values that his Hartford residence helped develop. Despite the growing obviousness of its tremendous price in money, energy, and deflection from literature, he worked even harder to maintain the earlier unalloyed satisfaction as it began to slip away from him. His devotion to his home continued to be praised by those whose judgments he prized; he began to mark for preservation the bread-and-butter letters from his guests. Said effusive Mr. Stanley, the explorer: "Such a house! Such a good & perfect little wife! Such a family immeasurably excellent in quality — ! Oh my friend rejoice in your happiness." [41] Thomas K. Beecher wrote Livy, "You must know . . . that yours is one of the few *restful* homes in which intelligence, culture, luxury and company combine to the compounding of a pleasure which every visitor longs to taste again." [42] Mrs. E. J. Hamersley, neighbor, congratulated him, on his fiftieth birthday, on what Hartford considered his primary achievement in life: "I want to use my privilege as a friend to congratulate you on what I know is infinitely more dear to you [than fame], a beautiful & a happy home, in which the rarest of its ornaments are the lovely children & the gracious mother whose presence illumines the place — & pardon me if I add the self-gratulation that this home is in our own city." [43] Despite occasional irritations and a persistent weariness under the strain of social activity, such testimonies confirmed his devotion to the manner of life he had elected.

Rest and Recreation

JUST AS THE FIRESIDE LITERARY AND INTELLECTUAL CONVERSATIONS IN WHICH Nook Farm initially found its relaxation widened to include a program of home entertainments — croquet, whist, charades, theatricals, and billiards — so recreation outside the home grew more steadily varied in Hartford during the seventies and eighties.

The children of the prosperous class, who except for the Clemens girls went to the public schools, formed a social set seeking its amusement away from home. In winter they clambered aboard the horse car at the Woodland Street turntable, rode in the stove-heated trolley (seated on wooden benches, with their feet on straw which, despite a mortar of dried tobacco juice, did not keep out the drafts) down to the river for ice skating and racing, or to the Rink for roller skating. Sledding was available closer home, for the best residential sections were hilly.[44] Many of the families who maintained carriages (a sure mark of the upper brackets) also owned sleighs, and well-chaperoned sleighing parties jingled out Farmington Avenue toward West Hartford or down Wethersfield toward the Colt estate. In summer the boys concentrated on sports — hanging around the ball park, admiring the professional athletes, attending the games, or playing in sandlot contests of their own.[45] Boys and girls alike, as well as their parents, played tennis; tournaments arranged by the Tennis Club under the presidency of Joe Twichell (who was also center fielder on the Men's Club ball team) were regularly run off. Gay blades wagered money on the outcome of these amateur championships — Helen Post, Twichell's neighbor, deliberately lost a match when she heard a young man announce his bet in the words, "Post against the field," not so much because of the gambling as the omitted "Miss." The turf tennis courts were also used for dancing parties at which old and young danced outdoors, sipping a gentle punch between sets and dispersing homeward at ten o'clock. Some of the families went on excursions in their river boats, and group picnics were in the eighties the most frequent form of summer diversion, not only for adolescents but for adults. Horseback riding was popular with both sexes. Women were permitted to ride astride and yet remain modest by an ingenious riding skirt. When they mounted they folded to one side a pleated panel, which was instantly rebuttoned across the front as they dismounted. If the hand was quicker than the eye, the transformation from skirt to trousers and back again was unnoticeable. Buggy riding, of course, was forbidden to the unengaged. Horse racing, now illegal in Connecticut, was then frequent at the Charter Oak race track. Bicycling became a craze in 1884.[46] Men managed to master the awkward two-wheeler. Since the divided skirt necessary for the high two-wheeler involved a degree of exposure that was for a time considered unseemly, clumsy tricycles were in order for the girls.

But walking was the chief sport. The middle-aged and elderly walked constantly, for pleasure and health, and the boys tackled marathon distances. Mark and Warner and Twichell patrolled a regular route through the hills west of the city. John Hooker walked ten miles a day most of his life.

William Lyon Phelps, after he had moved into the Nook Farm vicinity at the age of eleven, frequently walked the thirty-seven miles between Hartford and New Haven in a day. In 1887, when he was a student at Yale, he once walked two hundred miles to the White Mountains. Twichell and Mark essayed the trip to Boston on foot in 1874, but after the first day had blistered Mark's feet and lamed him, the two turned the tour into a joke and continued by train.[47] Twichell attracted Boston newspaper attention for walking nine miles to Newton Highlands to fill a pulpit and back again after the sermon. Entire families strolled ten miles to a picnic. Hiking clubs are still occasionally discoverable in Connecticut, but the general enthusiasm for walking for the fun of it has by this time vanished — in Hartford as elsewhere.

Besides athletic and semiathletic activities, and enjoyment of sports as spectators, Hartford people of the dominant prosperous class sought rest and relaxation in travel with a frequency and persistence that testify to the social value attached to having traveled and to the fatigue arising from their home regimens. It was almost a social necessity to go to Europe every two or three years if for nothing else than to renew or add to the household bric-a-brac.[48] Those who went abroad spoke of the escape from the busy life at home, of the relief from wearying attention to "housekeeping, both national and domestic." Most of them spent at least four months on a trip. Warner and Mark might go for a year or more, and Mrs. Hooker might stay over the winter while John returned home, later to rejoin her when summer came again. The Perkinses, Robinsons, Dunhams, Trumbulls — in fact every member of Hartford society — followed the fashion, touring with planned thoroughness the European countries, branching out occasionally to the Holy Land or Egypt. Twichell journeyed several times to Europe; his travels began with a trip to Peru in 1873.

After 1875 it was a social necessity in any case to get out of the city in the summer. Between European trips, the Hartford families vacationed at minor inland resorts or along the shore. Mark and Livy, after trying Saybrook (on Long Island Sound) during their first Connecticut summer, went to Quarry Farm thereafter when they were in this country. The Hookers summered regularly at Norfolk, Connecticut. The Twichells and Warners, the Bushnells and Cheneys, usually assembled in the Adirondacks. Narragansett Pier harbored many Hartford people. The annual exodus was in part pursuit of the social ideal of relaxation via change of scene, in part a very sensible retreat before the malaria afflicting Hartford in hot weather. Charles Dudley Warner, incessant professional traveler who finally toured all the summer resorts to gather material for a combination travel book and romance, *Their Pilgrimage*, referred in another book to the summer nomadism as "nothing less than society on wheels" and with mock seriousness ascribed the summer wanderings to the "discovery of the disease called nervous prostration, which demands for its cure constant change of scene, without any occupation." [49]

But though the Eastern resorts — Cape May, Atlantic City, the Catskills, Martha's Vineyard, Bar Harbor, Newport, Saratoga, and all the rest — came into importance in the late eighties, Hartford people did not join the fashionable parade to the glittering watering places. They continued going where they had gone before the *nouveaux riches* adopted similar habits on a costlier and more glamorous scale. Their custom of changing scene was as firmly fixed in the early seventies as in the late eighties. The directions taken by this society in seeking recreation in foreign lands and in other sections of this country had the effect of enriching conversation at home by an enlargement of what could be intelligently talked about, broadening sectionally rigid opinions by exposure of hometown prejudices to Old-World or national concepts, and extending the congeniality of Hartford people for each other by more fully developing the individuals who comprised the literate, prosperous, and "cultured" strata in the city. "I find that I derived very marked physical benefit from the recreation and rest I had," wrote Twichell to Mark Twain after his 1877 trip to Bermuda (the first of four trips for Twichell and of many more for Mark), "and furnished my mind with a rich stock of new impressions as well." [50]

The quest for rest and recreation and for change of scene did not include, oddly enough, extensive patronage of the drama. The theater made its way with difficulty in Hartford. Although the conservatism of the conventions hedging the intermingling of young men and women was no more striking in Hartford than in any other stable city in America — St. Louis, Cleveland, Chicago, New Orleans — to go to the theater was more than usually improper in Hartford before or immediately after the Civil War. The judgment did not originate in logic. Outside the group of persons with whom we are immediately concerned, it persisted through the eighties. Phelps's mother was opposed to theatergoing because it was *wrong*. A Christian does not do what is wrong, but Billy finally contrived with his father's assistance the opportunity to see a Shakespearean performance.[51]

In the Nook Farm group, among the older families, this prejudice had also been strong. Mark Twain dealt it a sharp blow. In the winter of 1874, Will Gillette, brother of Lilly Warner, disappeared. He was "studying" in New York, they said. Actually he was on the stage in Mark's dramatization of *The Gilded Age*, serving as foreman of the jury in the trial scene. All he had to say, George Warner told Twichell, was "Not guilty." Mark had helped Will get the part and a little later lent him $3,000 to finance his career as actor, producer, and dramatist. When the neighborhood discovered the truth, Edward Gillette came posthaste to Twichell for the latter's judgment on the profession. Joe, who himself had never been to a professional stage show in Hartford, said he would not have chosen acting as a career for Will but he did not feel at all shocked or apprehensive.[52] In January 1875 John Raymond brought "The Gilded Age" to Hartford for an engagement at the Allyn House, then the only theater. Will Gillette had a better role now. His whole neighborhood turned out to see him. Mark rented a box for the Twichells. Joe and Harmony took Dr. Burton and Dick. The audience, thinking Mark was in the box, clamored for him until Raymond read his message: "I cannot come to the theatre on either evening, Raymond, because there is something so touching about your acting that I can't stand it." The clerical party had a pleasant time. Will's secret was out. Hartford clergymen had been seen at the theater. Nook Farm had deferred to Mark Twain's leadership; never again would it be hostile to the theater.

As the second step in the demolition of an old taboo, Mark led into the open the private theatricals that for years had been a feature of home entertainments. In 1876 he and a group of what later would be Little-Theater-minded townspeople rehearsed Peter Spuyk's "Loan of a Lover" and performed for two nights before local gentry and many out-of-town intimates of Nook Farm residents. The play did not sidestep the community prejudice against profanity. Yet no protest was raised, except by a single ironic and earnest clerk in General Franklin's insurance company, who sent a letter to Mark requesting the omission of a word of such "rectangular and severe orthodoxy as damned." Mark, furious at the impertinence, sent the letter to Franklin:[53]

Dear General:—

They say that this pilgrim (who is a stranger to me) works for you in your insurance company. Do you know him? Is he in earnest?—or is he merely ill-bred enough to venture upon facetious impertinence with people who have not the humiliation of his acquaintance, under the delusion that he is conveying a gratification? This mess of pious 'rot' was handed to Dr. Wainwright early yesterday evening with the earnest request that I should read it before going on the stage—a request which I didn't comply with, I being too wise for that.

Please return this holy idiot's letter to me—shall have literary use for it one of these days.

Thought I detected your welcome face on the back seats the other night, but couldn't discover Mrs. Franklin's.

Ys Sincerely
S. L. Clemens

Mrs. Clemens says *she* saw Mrs. Franklin & hailed her. I'm glad. Mrs. C. she holds Mr. H. B. Langdon's [the insurance clerk] views, too. That's just like a woman's logic! I haven't said a word against the man's *views* — I am only objecting to his impertinence in shoving them upon *my* notice. *I* don't care what the man's views are — it's a free country.[54]

Franklin, returning the note, promised that the clerk, son of a minister, would be reproved. With more grace than one would expect from the general, he smoothed over the reference to Mrs. Clemens and restored the incident to its proper perspective.

I think Mrs. Clemens only endorsed this man's bosh because she with a woman's intuition & mercy saw what a goose the man was, and then pitied him. I confess that I am effeminate enough to be sorry for him.[55]

Livy's disapproval of stage profanity clearly did not extend to insistence that it be omitted, and the protest of the young clerk was sufficiently noteworthy to cause Mark and Franklin to think it "pious rot" and "bosh" respectively.

Antitheater prejudices in the city at large dissipated fast thereafter. In 1877 Howells asked Warner: "Do nice people go to the theatre in Hartford?" They did. By 1880 theatergoing was generally accepted throughout the city, except by a few conservative oldsters, as a respectable and amusing form of recreation. Wallack's on Main Street regularly presented New York productions. The town saw Booth, Barrett, Irving, Terry, Jefferson, and the Daly company there, and in other houses the procession of glass-blowing exhibitions and the presentations of Mark's good friend, P. T. Barnum of Bridgeport. The Strakosch Company brought grand opera. In 1880 Will Gillette was back again, this time in the leading role of a miserable play he had written himself. Harmony and Joe went again with a great crowd of Hartford folk. Twichell still could not regard the sight of one of his boys on the stage with entire satisfaction, particularly because the play was of such a low order. He was on the whole, he said, nonetheless a sympathetic observer. "We shall see how the experiment of yoking religious principle with life on the stage works."[56] In 1885 Livy went with Susan Warner and Annie Price to see a Boucicault play. The women thought the leading actress irresistible, though once or twice "a little coarse." Many of Livy's friends were there, she wrote Mark, including an impossible single lady who kept saying "What a stick" with irritating audibility.[57]

Recreation was sought by the Nook Farm and city people in a wide variety of sources, within the home and outside it. As elsewhere in America, and probably with greater general gaiety and ease and imagination than in most places, the articulate class in Hartford pursued a usually unspoken determination (far from the single-minded accumulation of capital ordinarily imputed to these citizens) to live an agreeable, diversified, and rich as well as moral life. They accomplished much of their intent. In this milieu Mark Twain was for a long while very happy. He left it only when he was convinced that he could no longer afford the cost.

Nook Farm and Hartford Society

DESPITE THE SIZE OF HIS INCOME, MARK TWAIN WAS FREQUENTLY HARD PRESSED by his enormous household expenses. During the eighties, his business enterprises drained off the thousands of dollars his books brought in. But in the seventies, before he was committed to financing the typesetter, he was often forced to economize, to lecture, to worry about finances. In the winter of 1877, for example, his coffers were empty. The family took up temporary quarters in Europe. In June of 1878, his personal depression over, Mark could write to Howells a letter illustrating his joy in prosperity and his continuing identification of prosperity with living in Hartford.

> Privately, I have some good news to tell you. That is, I believe it will gratify you — in fact I am sure it will — though I am not acquainted with a great many people whom it would please. It is this: *we've quit feeling poor*! Isn't that splendid? You know that for two years we have been coming to want, every little while, and have straightway gone to economizing. Yesterday we fell to figuring and discovered that we have more than income enough from investments to live in Hartford on a generous scale. Well, now that we are fixed at last, of course the communists and the asinine government will go to work and smash it all. No matter, we have resolved to quit feeling poor for a little while, anyway. This thing was so gratifying to me that my first impulse was to run to you with it.[58]

The determination "to live in Hartford on a generous scale" was strong in Mark Twain. But the cost was a constant worry to him. His neighbors encountered similar difficulties, if with more resignation. Somehow Nook Farm had committed itself to a way of life almost wholly satisfactory, but unfortunately impracticable without very substantial resources.

The neighborhood was doubtless attracted beyond its economic depth by a wealthier class in Hartford with which it associated on equal terms. Mark Twain and Warner knew well the Marshall Jewells, for example, who lived in diamond-studded lavishness quite beyond the capacity of the professional people of Asylum Hill. The wedding, in October of 1875, of Jewell's daughter Josephine was an elaborate ceremony that exemplifies the social level of a class richer than the residents of Nook Farm. The Asylum Hill Church was like a hothouse — filled with a trainload of the most exotic flowers procurable in New York. The costumes, of fabrics gathered all round the world by the Cheneys (silk manufacturers), were richly elegant. Mrs. Jewell wore a robe of velvet the color of crushed strawberries and trimmed with wide Venetian point lace. Her ornaments were plain diamonds; her headdress, white and garnet feathers. The bride's dress was of very heavy white silk. The Jewell mansion, decorated for the reception with festoons of smilax, and the grounds, lighted with innumerable Japanese lanterns, were thronged by such crowds that it was hard for the *Courant* reporters to see the costumes of the guests, though they noted glimpses of long trains, velvet fluting, much silk, and many diamonds. The bridal cake was topped by a pyramidal superstructure two feet high; the wedding presents were insured for $10,000; the bride and groom left for New York on a special train. All the Nook Farm group, Mark and Livy included, were present at this most brilliant social event of the year. President Grant sent his regrets.

Besides the wealthier manufacturers who lived on Asylum Hill, near Nook Farm, a somewhat older aristocracy centered in the area on Wethersfield Avenue where, amid the heavily gilded furniture of Armsmear, the palace in which her husband had died in 1862, Mrs. Samuel Colt held court. Her fingers heavy with diamond rings, she entertained two hundred guests at a time at dinners or lawn fetes beside the artificial lake on the elaborate grounds. Mrs. Colt's wealth, though small in comparison with the private fortunes being amassed in other commercial centers, provided an income of at least $200,000 a year. Doctor Gatling, like Samuel Colt an inventor of firearms and also well endowed with worldly goods, lived less pretentiously next door. His daughter (unexpectedly the first woman in Hartford to go roller skating after the Rink was built) was an ornament of Mrs. Colt's soirees.

Hartford, in short, enjoyed at this time the highest per capita wealth of American cities. The luxury prevailing among the wealthy and the standards of expensive comfort by which the well-to-do governed their expenditures seem to have drawn Nook Farm into conspicuous consumption that it could not afford. At one time or another, every one of its residents had acute financial trouble. Harriet Beecher Stowe, poor after the Oakholm fiasco, managed at high personal cost to write herself out of debt, but before her death she was to be poor again. When her copyrights expired in the nineties, her daughters were forced to sell the Stowe home and live on charity from friends. Charles Dudley Warner, living modestly in comparison with city standards, was constantly forced to keep his eye on the amount of money each page he wrote would make available for the upkeep of his house. The Hookers and Gillettes were frequently faced with imminent disaster. Though Josephine Jewell had married in great pomp, Ned and Mattie Hooker could not even be wed in their parents' home in 1879, for Isabella and John had been forced to let the house for a year and to board with their disagreeable tenants. Lilly Warner arranged a wedding for the couple in her own house, but the bride and groom had to move in with their parents and their parents' tenants, after all. Yet John Hooker earned between $10,000 and $15,000 a year in his law practice.[59] The whole Nook Farm group, a moderate-income circle of professional people, was sorely extended to maintain the expensively comfortable way of life it preferred. Gracious living came dear.

The adoption of the standard of living set by a more prosperous class indicates how strongly Nook Farm's literary and professional people felt themselves a part of the whole Hartford community. In spite of the intramural intimacy which in one sense set it apart from the city at large, the neighborhood was permeated by the mores of the wealthy. When the writers accepted the material and secular goals of Hartford industrialists and insurance men as their own, they quickly discovered the necessity for constant effort and eternal watchfulness lest they falter in meeting the obligations that perpetuation of their standard of living laid upon them. Identical ideals united Hartford and Nook Farm. The effect of this identity on the literature emerging therefrom was enormous.

Group Intellectual Life

ONE AREA IN WHICH THE NOOK FARM NEIGHBORHOOD OPENED INTO THE LARGER community was the organized intellectual life, of which the literary men were the acknowledged leaders. The zest with which cultural development was pursued reflects again the congeniality of the society and the multiple sources of its satisfactions. In comparison with these social benefits, the intellectual advancement attained was in itself negligible.

The most important of the three clubs that deserve examination was primarily for men, though women were tolerated at its meetings if they kept silent. Horace Bushnell, Calvin Stowe, and J. Hammond Trumbull—one theologian and two scholars—founded the Monday Evening Club in the 1860's to provide members of intellectual attainment and local or national celebrity with a forum for the exchange of ideas and the exercise of intellectual curiosity. Burton, Parker, and Twichell became members, as well as Warner, the Reverend Francis Goodwin,[60] William Hamersley,[61] General William B. Franklin, Governor Robinson, Charles Perkins, Doctor Smith, General Hawley, and other city leaders. In 1871, Mark was invited to join. Meeting every two weeks from October to May in the homes of the twenty members in turn, the club listened to a short essay from the man assigned to perform. Discussion followed — ten minutes to a member. Refreshments were served, including a supper or beer and liquors.[62]

The topics discussed ranged through the varied special interests of the essayists. In the seventies, subjects included the "Eastern Question" (Warner), "Life Insurance as Related to Public Policy" (one of the businessmen), "Is This a Regenerate Age in the United States?" (Twichell),[63] "Calvinism" (Parker), "Love of Truth" (Burton), and "Modern Fiction" (Warner). In the eighties the subjects were still of this variety, Warner speaking more on social than literary subjects — "A Study in the Treatment of Criminals," for example, in 1884.

Mark Twain threw himself into the doings of the club, using it as a testing ground for his serious ideas. He coaxed guests to its meetings from out of town — Howells, Stedman, and others — with promises of a "rattling good time." His contributions included "The Facts Concerning the Recent Carnival of Crime in Connecticut," "Universal Suffrage," and "License of the Press." Usually his papers were not calculated to reflect the views of the majority. He argued for woman's suffrage, vigorously attacked the press for its harmful effect on "the stupid people — who constitute the grand overwhelming majority of this and all other nations." He read a chapter of the early version of *What is Man?* in 1881, which, unlike his other shockers, caused everyone present to "scoff at it, jeer at it, revile it, and call it a lie; a thousand times a lie!"[64] In February 1883 he further elaborated the same theme with much the same response. On two occasions he attacked the community's loyalty to the Republican Party. Mark was, then, laying before his neighbors his religious and social views, uncensored by Livy or by his friends. He incurred verbal opposition but, in no case, personal disapproval. Whatever the conservatism of some of the members or the differences discussed in the meetings, no conflict over the presentation of those ideas arose to affect Mark's personal relations with his community. Before he moved to Hartford, he was discussed with approval in a panel on American humor led by J. Hammond Trumbull;[65] all during his Hartford residence he was a welcome member and all his life thereafter his name stayed on the rolls. The atmosphere in which such ideas were expressed was anything but stuffy, and without exaggerating the intellectual caliber of the conversations one may conclude that as a group experience the club meetings were stimulating and mutually rewarding occasions in the full life of the members.

The Monday Evening Club was not explicitly an effort to achieve cultural self-improvement so much as a formalized exchange of ideas for the fun of it. About 1875, however, Mark organized the Saturday Morning Club for the young women of Asylum Hill, girls from sixteen to twenty who met weekly at his home for the formal purpose of cultural and social training. At first the program consisted of essays, but under the leadership of its only male member, essays were abandoned in favor of talk that would develop conversational "vigor and facility." The club was regaled, in addition, by an impressive list of guest speakers whom Mark pressed into service. Boyesen read an unpublished story in 1877; in the same year Howells talked about Venice. In the third-floor billiard room Bret Harte stayed up all night with a bottle of whisky to write his "Thankful Blossom" in the fall of 1876. He came downstairs in the morning, manuscript complete, bottle empty, and himself so classically drunk that his ossification was mistaken for formal sobriety, to read the story to the virgins assembled in the library. Under less picturesque conditions Fields and Warner also addressed them. Mark was the most frequent contributor, reading many of his own sketches and Robert Ingersoll's speeches, summarizing the life of Lord Macaulay, theorizing about mind reading, plagiarism, temperance, and the Knights of Labor. The club continued long after Mark left Hartford in 1891, and *A Club Corner*, its journal,[66] records the variety of fare thereafter — lectures and discussions about modern art, history, literature, religion, science, and medicine. F. Hopkinson Smith lectured on "Bohemianism," Professor Tyler of Amherst on "Daisies and Buttercups," and Henry Robinson on "Exemption from Taxation." The club as a whole tackled "The Art and Science of Advertising" a week after "Theosophy." These girls got a liberal if not a thorough education in the widely varied and at least superficially stimulating intellectual climate that characterized Hartford before the Ice Age set in during the nineties.

But Mark, indefatigable inventor of new entertainments, did not forget the older women. In the middle eighties, Livy's friends formed a Browning Society, which gathered weekly in the billiard room or in the library to hear Mark read Browning's poems. To preparation for these readings, he said he devoted three days a week — very enjoyable work for one who of his own inclination had not read a poem in his life. Livy, Susie, and Lilly Warner were the first members, but soon other ladies from the neighborhood and from Farmington, New Haven, and South Manchester were attracted by the new titillations available in the Clemens home. At their meetings nothing but the reading was talked of; conversation on mundane topics was forbidden. The ladies found Browning a beautiful experience; rendering reverence to him was even more lovely than attending High-Church exercises. A guest at one of the meetings wrote Howells:

When I took my seat first as a hearer in the library . . . I looked about the carved black oak panelling of the walls . . . and the books and little pictures which broke their dark surface, and perceived that the place was in itself a sort of revelation of poetic meanings. The fine, smooth outlines of the head of our hostess came out with wonderful clearness against the dark background, and seemed fitting and in perfect keeping with the flowers and filtered sunshine of the little conservatory.[67]

Mark's exquisite clearness and refinement, she went on, radiated high breeding. He read without drawl or marked cadence and made the text transparent by subtle emphases in the right places. The Browning class also survived Mark's departure in 1891. Richard Burton took it over, and as late as May 1893 it was still flourishing.

It was not until the nineties that the club fever swept the nation as American culture widened and deepened. *A Club Corner* pointed out in 1891 that "Club life is the order of the day . . . We are yielding to the Spirit of the Age, which demands combination, and the fusion of ideas." [68] Hartford, impelled to exercise its curiosity by the cultivated gregariousness of its educated people, had been well ahead of the club movement. The eighties left a maze of women's organizations in the city — for example, the Union for Home Work, the Friendly Visitors, the Indian Association, the Needlework Guild, and the United Workers. Men also organized for numerous purposes — in the Owl Club to study American history and in the Twentieth Century Club to look forward to the era of material marvels. Charles Dudley Warner found ridiculous the extremity to which the fad was carried; he satirized it gently in a reference to popular complaints about lack of variety in American life. He wrote that a club might have been established to study the Want of Diversity:

The members would have been obliged to set apart a stated time for it, to attend as a duty, and to be in a mood to discuss this topic at a set hour. They would have mortgaged another precious portion of the little time left us for individual life . . . It seems illogical that we could produce diversity by all doing the same thing at the same time, but we know the value of congregate effort.[69]

But Mark, at least, did not grow tired of the club work to which he devoted so much enthusiasm. It was another link between him and the society in which he was happiest. He had less time than anyone else on Nook Farm for an individual life and certainly no facility for developing himself independently of his family and friends, even though he did not always follow their ideas. He took joy from his associations with the three clubs with which he was identified in the same measure as from his relations with his Nook Farm and Asylum Hill neighbors and intimates. Whether the general level of intelligence was raised by organized culture did not really concern him.

The Ideal of Conduct

AN INTERESTING AND IMPORTANT CHARACTERISTIC OF HARTFORD SOCIETY IS the decorum that bridged the religious and secular experience of Nook Farm and uniformly glazed the community's behavior. The amusements, diversions, and interests comprising the everyday life of family and neighborhood fused into a pattern of respectability. Critics have generally seized upon the propriety of this environment and lamented at ingenious length the stultifying effects upon Mark Twain's genius. I do not intend to prolong an argument that has always resulted in the distortion of remarkably adaptable and indefinite evidence. An understanding of Mark Twain's Hartford milieu and his adjustment to it, of Mark Twain's books, cannot be complete, however, without at least a brief reference to the locally accepted code of correct behavior.

The decorum of Hartford originated in the religious heritage of its people. Propriety was originally, of course, a by-product of moral behavior. At one time in New England, presumably, a member of a social group regulated his actions according to his conscience (then a monitor to be seriously reckoned with), with less concern for appearances than for the inner conviction of rectitude. Gradually, as the character of community life changed and the primitive Calvinist conception of crime and punishment lost some of its elementary effectiveness, good taste became the standard by which an individual judged his own behavior and that of his neighbors. It was still immoral to sin, but it became also inadvisable to give the impression of being a sinner. A set of conventions arose to determine the sort of conduct universally accepted as safe and incapable of misinterpretation. Violation of these conventions made an individual subject to the disapproval originally reserved for an immoral act.

A thorough social history of the United States, if we had one, would show that in some sections of our society and at some times the rigidity and artificiality of the conventional code varied widely. In Hartford, at least, the influence of decorum was much more marked as the secularization of religious life progressed. Not until the 1890's was it glacial in its disapproval of unconventional behavior. In the seventies and eighties correctness was still not an ideal in itself. But throughout the second half of the century, as the attention of educated people shifted from a preoccupation with religion to the wide enjoyment of earthly life, as this development provoked uncertainty and a wide divergence of individual reaction, the outward forms of behavior came more and more under the government of convention. A society no longer closely regulated by a common deference to uniform religious principles that all its members could interpret alike turned, it appears, to a more superficial uniformity to preserve its integrity. The decrees of Calvinism were replaced by the pressures of gentility. The disintegrative aspects of a dissolving religious control over conduct were countered by a secular device to preserve social order. When the impossibility of fixing the world to a static conception of a fully moral universe became evident, Hartford people spontaneously turned to convention to replace the stability that in reality had gone forever.

When Mark Twain came to Hartford in 1871, he joined a society integrated, not by the hollow conventionality of a later time, but by a still-living concern for the Christian ethic. Calvinism was gone from Hartford; the new religion, almost without formal creed, consisted entirely of adherence to the Golden Rule. As it happened, Mark could, despite his disbelief in a conventional God, heartily endorse the Christian ethic. He thus was able to sympathize fully with the central morality of the Nook Farm society. At the same time he found it possible to express himself in opposition to minor community prejudices without incurring disapproval. The moral code, still practicable and uniform despite the confusion and variation in religious belief, was more important than the social conventions arising from it.

Mark's early identification with the moral point of view of Nook Farm is illustrated by an incident of 1877. In July, Mark came down to Hartford from Elmira to investigate reports of burglary. He discovered that his "burglar" was a young man surreptitiously visiting an English servant girl, whose duties in the Hartford house while the Clemenses were away obviously had not kept her busy. When he questioned the young lady, Mark was told that she was pregnant. Her visitor, she lamented, had refused to marry her. Instantly aroused to right this wrong, Mark hid a policeman and Twichell on the premises and lay in wait for the transgressor. When the latter appeared, Mark confronted him with the alternatives of imprisonment or matrimony. Keeping his temper perfectly (as Twichell notes with some surprise in his diary), Mark persuaded the miscreant to marry the girl, overruling the man's original refusal to allow anybody's bastards to be attributed to *him*. Twichell, who had become very hot in the stifling bathroom, emerged to perform the marriage with mingled feelings, which included great sympathy for the bride and groom and the impulse to offer them what advice he could. The policeman was a witness. Mark gave to each his blessing and a $100 check and sent the couple off. He had corrected a wrong, enforced the moral code, and dramatically ranged himself with the upholders of the moral order against the deteriorating forces of which Victoria Woodhull was a representative. The girl, however, was no more pregnant than he was.[70] Mark had not thought to question her story and, like the society he sometimes criticized, passed judgment before inquiring into the breach of convention he had observed. But in any case, neither Twichell nor Mark was long embarrassed by the incident, for the marriage prospered.

But though Mark subscribed to the ethical concepts of Nook Farm, he was not always willing to adopt the social prejudices comprising the code of propriety when they were further afield of the right-wrong dichotomy. He was not forced to do so. As we have seen, he disagreed with the community attitude on the theater and acted accordingly, without penalty. He did not suppress his opinions simply because he was in a minority. He did not keep the Sabbath. He did not dress conventionally. His drawing-room behavior could be "unrefined." Aroused to fury at a dull Monday Evening Club session by the references to "Holy Writ" or to the "Almighty" with which most of the speakers concluded their remarks, he protested against the "piety ending," despite his recognition that it was merely a traditional formula inherited from the personal habits of Horace Bushnell. After his protest, the formula was never used again. In more than one instance Hartford deferred to Mark Twain rather than require him to conform to its prejudices. Most of the time, therefore, he was not galled by the mores of this society. They sometimes amused him, but they never confined him against his will. They were not as strict as they have often been represented. Mark could violate them in numerous small ways without feeling the cold draft of social disapproval. In fact, his individual eccentricities, residue of his Western upbringing, were hardly noticed at all. His critics among his neighbors emphasized his refinement, his sensibility, his oneness with them in judgments; their emphasis reflects an exaggerated notion of the genteel values but certainly indicates a flexible application.

Mark had more difficulty when he violated the canons of taste in Boston, where the local brand of gentility seems to have been less adaptable to the living individual. In 1877 he delivered what turned out to be a disastrously malapropos speech at the Whittier dinner. He was cruelly punished for his indiscretion and penitently remorseful for a long time afterwards. And he had had earlier difficulties in Boston. Mrs. Aldrich thought he was drunk when she first saw him and, not catching his name, froze him out of the house. The parochial spirit in the literary gentility of Boston never rose in Hartford to smite him, though both Warner and Twichell concurred in the reality of the breach of taste at the Whittier dinner, if not in the graceless frigidity with which it was rebuffed.

The Nook Farm community, in fact, seems much more conventional than it actually was. Isabella Beecher Hooker can hardly be thought of as decorous, yet her observance of small proprieties was as impeccable as her violation of large ones was courageous. Her husband was most anxious about appearances and suffered more than anyone else for the eccentric opinions he shared with his wife. But he voiced his convictions with energy. The willing coöperation of all the residents of Nook Farm in gentility should be considered, I think, not so much a restrictive blight upon individual development as an evidence of neighborhood unity. Though decorum characterized the social activity of Nook Farm, it arose as a spontaneous uniformity in community behavior. It was neither rigid, nor hollow, nor sinister. It did not diminish the exhilaration with which Mark Twain and Twichell enjoyed life; it did not cool the warmth of the neighborhood intimacy. In no way did it complicate the gratification that Mark Twain's neighbors derived from their everyday life in Nook Farm.

4

IDEAS OF AMERICA

1871–1891

Ideas of Politics

NOOK FARM, WHICH HAD FOUNDED THE REPUBLICAN PARTY IN CONnecticut, remained, like the rest of Northern America, prevailingly Republican after the Civil War. With the Union victory in 1865, the residents of the colony, confident of the country's inevitable development through expanding manufacture to fulfillment of the democratic promise, relaxed their tense wartime interest in national political affairs. Local contests for Senate seats or for the governorship attracted now a more immediate interest than affairs in Washington, though Warner and Mrs. Stowe kept their eyes on Reconstruction and protested against the harsh treatment of the South. Twichell, after a year or two of civilian life had tempered his earlier sternness, joined them in the opinion that the country's wounds must be healed as soon as possible. Republicanism was the only political loyalty in the neighborhood, not only because of the role Nook Farm had played in establishing the party, but because membership in Democratic ranks was on two counts unthinkable. First, the party was tarred by its acceptance of slavery, and second, it catered, they assumed, to the ignorant immigrant, the uneducated workingman, and the irresponsible Irish who were moving into Hartford to man the factories. The feeling that such a membership could not produce suitable political leadership supplemented Anglo-Saxon solidarity to make the Republican Party the only choice for Nook Farm, as it was indeed for all such neighborhoods everywhere. Furthermore, the rise of theoretical communism in Europe and native distrust of rule by the uneducated persuaded the Hartford community away from the radical Republicanism of the late fifties. Without being conscious of a trend to the right, the city became in politics generally conservative.

Until 1876 little occurred in Washington to redirect Hartford's attention to national developments. The undeniable corruption under Grant was attributed neither to Grant nor to his party, but to the dishonesty of debased individuals — who constituted the chief menace to the Republic. No deep anxiety was felt for the future of Republican dominance, for national majorities in both Grant elections in 1868 and in 1872 were substantial. At home a closer contest for the state governorship was fiercely fought. The *Times*, still maintaining the Jacksonian sympathies that before the Civil War had appeared in Nook Farm's political platform, became the target of Hawley and Warner during the local elections. In April 1871 a violent contest between Marshall Jewell, the Republican *Courant* candidate, and the incumbent, J. E. English, the Democratic *Times* candidate, progressed through unrestrained charge and countercharge in a public barrage much more savage than temporary animosity demanded. The *Courant*'s assertion that English had sold the state to Boss Tweed was supported by correspondence the *Times* said was forged. After a noisome campaign, Jewell won by little more than 100 votes out of a total of 90,000. But the vigilance of the *Courant*, more clairvoyant in detecting Democratic fraud than logical in proving it, was rewarded by more Republican victories than defeats during the seventies and eighties. The day after each election conventional vituperation ceased and political life was again tranquil.

Mark Twain, though exposed to Jacksonian ideas in Hannibal when he set type for Ament's paper, had subscribed to the Whig principles of Orion's journals. Then, despite his brief service in the Confederate Army, he automatically became a Republican when he followed the Wells-Fargo route to Nevada with Orion, a Lincoln appointee. He was not particularly interested in party politics during his first five years in Hartford. Thus on the day after the congressional elections of 1874, Mark and Twichell talked their way to the Tower without mentioning the Democratic victory. Without making party distinctions, Mark attacked country-wide rottenness and Western politicians in the satiric *Gilded Age*, but, despite his personal devotion to Grant, he stayed aloof from political campaigns. In 1875 he wrote

Orion that the era of corruption was not Republican or Democratic, but national, and named a number of "moral ulcers," among whom he included Henry Ward Beecher. "*Politics* are not going to cure moral ulcers like these nor the decaying body they fester on." [1]

Mark's remedy for decay in the body politic was an adjustment of the suffrage laws. The franchise should be reapportioned among men of knowledge and accomplishment. In a sketch for the *Atlantic* called "The Curious Republic of Gondour," he anonymously suggested a system whereby every man would have at least one vote, but men of various degrees of education and industry would cast a greater number. A college graduate would be entitled to as many votes as a millionaire; each could outvote a substantial number of ordinary citizens. He told Mrs. Fields that he hoped to live long enough to see the wrong of universal suffrage overthrown, and in 1877 he wrote the daughter of Mrs. Fairbanks that republican government based on universal suffrage "ought to perish because it is founded in wrong & is weak & bad & tyrannical." [2] Mark's position, more an affectation of aristocracy than a harbinger of his future despair of human capacity, was very close to Warner's. Warner could not quite reconcile the Declaration of Independence with the corruption he saw around him — a rot he and Mark attributed to the votes of the ignorant, who elected dishonest men to political office. Since the Democratic Party was the more tainted by the effects of universal suffrage, Mark voted Republican like the rest, but he thought it little matter that he voted at all.

The Tilden-Hayes election of 1876 woke Mark and the rest of Nook Farm to intense concern over Republican fortunes. Reaction against Grant, exhibited in a Democratic Congress after 1874, made dubious the prospect of a Republican victory. Twichell had hoped that a strong man and reform candidate would be nominated by his party, and now he was afraid that the Hayes nomination meant postponement of the better day in politics Mark publicly declared himself a Hayes man, presided over a Hartfor rally, and delivered a widely quoted speech on Civil Service reform. T Howells he wrote confidently that Hayes was bound to win, even though Howells's campaign biography of his wife's cousin had sold only 2,000 copies As the campaign progressed, Mark felt that he had a stake in the result the anxiety of the whole neighborhood grew in tenseness as election da approached. When it came, all the men went soberly to the polls. Twichel took the aged Austin Dunham to mark his last ballot. The old man, prominent Hartford conservative, made a prayerful occasion of his ventur to the polling place. As he left he said fervently, "God grant that the Re publican ticket may be successful." Twichell suggested in his journal, "Heaven give the state and the country many such citizens!!" [3]

The next day brought the news of Tilden's election to the presidency. Twichell, sickened at first like the others, rallied to find some consolation in a conviction that the Republican Party sorely needed chastening. In his first bitter certainty that "the better element had been outvoted by the worse," he wrote a letter (published in the *Courant* on November 9, 1876) saying,

> Does anyone doubt that here in Connecticut the people who voted for Mr. Robinson [4] are, on the whole . . . very much pleasanter folk than the people who preferred Mr. Hubbard? . . . *New England* is beaten in this contest . . . Taking *that* view of the result I like the company I am in. I am aware that the democratic party regard New England as a benighted region, sitting always in a good deal of darkness; but I, owing perhaps to the disadvantage of my birth in New England, and my consequent comparative lack of intellectual and moral privileges, hold New England in a regard that makes me quite willing to stand with her majority in difference with the majority of the rest of the states, and on this occasion in consequent defeat . . . I had really rather be among the mourners at this funeral than be the undertaker.

Twichell regretted his haste at once, but he had expressed accurately enough the provincial loyalty to New England that persisted in his city despite all cosmopolitan modifications.

The next day's relief in the news that the election was in doubt accompanied a subordinate anxiety about new national dissension ahead. While the country proved its strength by keeping the peace, Mark, Twichell, Warner, and their friends watched anxiously the fraudulent counts and recounts and were fervently thankful and inclined to ask no questions when Hayes was installed without uprising in March of 1877. Twichell believed that the country had been delivered by God from a crisis that might have approached the Civil War in seriousness. "We have shared the political anxiety," Mrs. Stowe wrote, "and tomorrow morning will dawn on R. Hayes the newly elected President of the United States. I hope his reign will be one of *real* reconstruction . . ." [5] This experience, arousing an interest in political affairs that would not again lapse, was a maturing one for the community. Twichell's certainty that better citizens were Republicans was followed a year later by a fuller understanding; in connection with granting the South a voice in government, he asserted a greater faith in the average voter than Mark Twain felt at this time or than Warner was ever to feel. "The safety of the Republic in the long run," he said, "is in consistently carrying out its theory i.e. admitting all the people to a voice in public affairs. This course involves trying incidents as now, but is the only one allowed by the genius of our government." [6]

The uprising of 1877 to protest what in the railroad industry was the fourth ten-per-cent wage cut in seven years moved Mark Twain to a reassessment of his own attitude toward suffrage. As 100,000 men went on strike and the total of unemployed reached 4,000,000, a sympathy with militant labor superseded his earlier conviction that it should be allowed an ineffective voice at the polls. Mark was to progress from the snobbery of his 1875 views to a final questioning (after the Hartford period) of capitalism itself. Nook Farm argued about the political principles behind the labor troubles, but sympathy for the oppressed finally modified Mark's theoretical Republicanism and made him receptive to political development during succeeding years. He and Warner and Twichell came to know Hayes (Warner and Twichell and General Hawley called at the White House in 1880 [7]) and thereafter kept in close touch with events of his administration—Twichell in faith, Warner in anxious conservatism,[8] and Mark in transition toward independence.

In the meantime the nomination of Garfield in 1880 was entirely pleasing to Nook Farm and all of Hartford. Mark was an ardent Republican campaigner, despite his emergent liberalism, and addressed a local rally with Henry C. Robinson and Warner. He delighted in welcoming his old hero, U. S. Grant, to the city and helped him urge the populace to elect the Republican nominee. "Garfield suits me thoroughly and exactly," Mark said; his neighbors were as completely satisfied. When Garfield died in 1881, a stupefying gloom settled over Nook Farm to remind its residents of their grief when Lincoln was assassinated.

But in 1884, when Blaine was awarded the Republican nomination, the unanimity of the community was shattered. Albert Bigelow Paine, who errs otherwise in following Mark's reminiscence of the event, accurately places Mark, Henry C. Robinson, Charles E. Perkins, E. M. Bunce,[9] and F. G. Whitmore in the billiard room (at a regular meeting of the Friday Evening Club) when the news was announced.[10] Mark declared at once his determination never to vote for Blaine. Twichell stood with Mark, Paine adds, but actually Twichell had taken the lead in disapproval of Blaine when the latter had sponsored anti-Chinese bills in Congress.[11] Mark had probably borrowed from him the full bill of particulars against Blaine, including an ominous array of corrupt practices. Paine states mistakenly that Warner and Hawley joined Mark's rebellion against the party, that Warner resigned from the *Courant*, and that Twichell nearly lost his pulpit because of the anger of his congregation at his political apostasy. Actually the entire community was unsettled by the dilemma: should it vote for Cleveland, a Democrat with a mistress, or for Blaine, a Republican with a record of dishonesty? Most of the confirmed Republicans voted with their party and criticized the dissenters, but no action was taken to express formal disapproval of any of the rebels.

Mark, as was his custom, expressed his views vigorously and publicly and argued his point in letters to his friends. To the Monday Evening Club he delivered a paper on "Consistency" in which he said "the atrocious doctrine of allegiance to *party* plays directly into the hands of politicians of the baser sort" and ridiculed the Hartford invocation of long-range party loyalty as a justification for voting Republican. He presided at Mugwump rallies in the fall of 1884. He pleaded with Howells to withhold his vote from Blaine, even if he could not vote for Cleveland, and attacked the prejudice against Cleveland which Howells shared:

> To see grown men, apparently in their right mind, seriously arguing against a bachelor's fitness for President because he has had private intercourse with a consenting widow! Those grown men [know] what the bachelor's other alternative was — & tacitly they seem to prefer that to the widow. *Isn't* human nature the most consummate sham & lie that was ever invented? Isn't man a creature to be ashamed of in pretty much all his aspects? Is he really fit for anything but to be stood up on the street corner as a convenience for dogs? [12]

He went on to criticize Hawley and Warner (whom Paine placed with the Mugwumps) and Charles Hopkins Clark for eating crow in their paper and for planning to vote for Blaine, whom they privately despised. Warner did not resign from the *Courant*, and Hawley pushed a vigorous editorial campaign against Cleveland, the Democrats, and the Mugwumps.

Twichell records his position in his journal:

> The political campaign for the Presidency coming on, and Mr. J. G. Blaine of Maine having been made the Republican candidate, I found myself, for once, unable to go with my party. Mr. Blaine had for a good while been exceedingly offensive to me on several accounts, and I was convinced that the most desirable issue of the canvass, both for the country and the Republican Party, was his defeat.[13]

He announced his stand by signing with Mark an "Appeal to the Republican Voters of Connecticut," which asserted, after citing five charges against Blaine: "His defeat may save our party, by freeing it from the control of the camp followers and office-seekers, who have too often dictated its policy." No other member of the Nook Farm community joined the group of fifty signatories. Twichell recorded the result for himself:

The displeasure which my political action in regard of Mr. Blaine excited among my friends and parishioners was considerable as I had anticipated it would be. I received a number of letters expressing strong disapproval of my course, though nearly all of them were entirely kind in their tone.[14]

I find no mention in the journal or in the *Parish Memorabilia*, or elsewhere in the voluminous source material of the period, of any suggestion that he resign his pulpit. In an open letter to him, signed "A Republican Friend," which appeared in the *Courant* of October 17, 1884, he was asked for the evidence he had considered in doubting Blaine's good character and why, then, he was not voting for Cleveland. The tone of the letter was calm and reasonable.

When election day came, Twichell, unable to vote for Cleveland because of the latter's personal conduct, and for a Democrat because of his identification of Republicanism with patriotism, voted instead for the Prohibition candidate for President and the Republican ticket for state and town officers.[15] Mark voted for Cleveland. Twichell was glad Blaine was defeated.

The failure of Mr. Blaine to reach the presidency (though involving the accession of the Democratic Party to power — (a lamentable incident in itself as I deeply felt) was, in my view, an event of more hopeful significance to the nation, than any that had occurred since the war.[16]

Mark was triumphant. No one of the loyal supporters of the party was unduly disturbed, and the controversy, which had been more temperate than any other Hartford election quarrel, soon ended. Blaine had carried the city.

For Mark this election confirmed the political independence in which he "found a spiritual comfort and a peace of mind quite above price." [17] It defined the Hartford prejudice against sexual transgression as stronger than its considerable aversion to corrupt politicians. It showed that Twichell was capable of reëvaluating his own prejudices and that he was sufficiently courageous to risk his congregation's disapproval when he was so moved. It crystallized the community's unrest under the national record of public dishonesty. It stirred more voters to think about political affairs and revived an interest that had declined in keenness since 1876.

Politically, then, Nook Farm and Hartford were conservative, but once again Nook Farm was the source of whatever liberalism was slowly forming. Warner, always a party man, continually questioned in private the party's policy and was, like some of his neighbors, less conservative than he looked. For social and historical reasons the Democratic party was no alternative for him either. After leaving Hartford in 1891, Mark extended his independence into a sympathy with Howells's theoretical socialism. His criticism of politics in the 1890's became (when his despair enveloped him) a conviction that the "Great Republic was rotten to the heart," but he did not publish much of his political speculation. The conservatism of Hartford, then, did not force Mark Twain into silence, or chastise Joseph Twichell for speaking out. As for the political climate of Hartford, Mark was able to retain the opinion of it that he had expressed in 1876. Then, he had written a friend in St. Louis of the political situation in the allegedly "genial culture" of the West which he had cheerfully left.[18]

> I think I comprehend the position there — perfect freedom to vote just as you choose, provided you choose to vote as *other* people think — social ostracism, otherwise . . . Fortunately a good deal of experience of men enabled me to choose my residence wisely. I live in the freest corner of the country. There are no social disabilities between me and my Democratic personal friends. We break the bread and eat the salt of hospitality freely together and never dream of such a thing as offering impertinent interference in each other's political opinions.[19]

There were no disabilities between him and his Democratic or Republican friends in the election of 1884. And though Hartford was hardly a hotbed of liberal political thought, one cannot recall any American community of the time that was. In a Republican atmosphere made unoppressive by tolerance, Mark was never conscious of political alienation from his Hartford way of life. Just as he subscribed to the moral code of his neighbors, though differing from them in religious belief, he shared the sensitivity to the moral content of politics that characterized Hartford's interest in public affairs. His application of the moral issues to individuals running for office sometimes differed from that of the community majority, but his analysis of political corruption as the result of individual immorality indicates his subscription to the city's point of view. Ethical rather than ideological issues were the questions that concerned him now as later.

Ideas of Business

PRIMARILY A BUSINESS COMMUNITY, HARTFORD PRIDED ITSELF UPON THE intelligence and integrity allegedly accompanying development from the eighteenth-century pinchpenny shrewdness to the mature commerce of nineteenth-century Connecticut. "The keen jockey way of whittling out a living by small bargains sharply turned," Bushnell wrote in 1851 when

Hooker was thinking about the purchase of Nook Farm, ". . . is no proper inbred distinction but only a casual result . . . that pertains to the transition period between the small, stringent way of life in the previous times of home-production, and the new age of trade."[20] The Civil War had ripened the new age into comfortable prosperity in Hartford, but not into sensational wealth. Harriet Beecher Stowe said upon her move to the city: ". . . old Hartford seems fat, rich, and cosy,—stocks higher than ever, business plenty,—everything as tranquil as possible."[21] The city's fatness was less the mushrooming of wartime profiteering than the culmination of steady, cautious progress reflecting the self-respecting solidity of Hartford's businessmen. As I have noted, the expression of this spirit and this medium prosperity in the streets and houses of Hartford was for Mark Twain the first attraction of the city. Soon after, he was to be as deep in commercial enterprises as any citizen of Hartford. He was to conduct himself less cautiously than his friends, the tradesmen. They were far more experienced in restraining the speculative passion that inspired more predatory promoters elsewhere in the country.

Hartford's development included the rise of manufacturing industry and the establishment of the insurance companies which then (as now) far overshadowed all other business interests. The insurance business was particularly well adapted to the community climate. Moral integrity, once essential to salvation, became in less exact form just as necessary for long-run profits. Caution in investment was mandatory; a high rate of return could be easily justified as a cushion for regular disasters. The first Hartford insurance company was founded in 1810. Nine years later, J. P. Morgan's grandfather Joseph, proprietor of Morgan's Exchange Coffee House, rounded up 137 partners to petition the legislature for the charter of the Ætna Insurance Company, with capital stock of $150,000, and to begin the development that was soon to place Hartford insurance money in much of the country's business. The complex pattern of investment was a far cry from the direct dealings of the Yankee trader. The Phoenix Mutual Life, Connecticut Mutual, and many other stock and mutual companies were soon organized. Most prospered, for the incidence of canny, substantial, cautious, and hardheaded executive ability was very high in Hartford. In 1863 James G. Batterson,[22] enterprising proprietor of a monument works, founded the first accident insurance company (The Travelers) in America in 1863, and before long expanded his charter to include other types of policies. By 1886, twenty large insurance companies were flourishing in convenient proximity.

The first major test of Hartford's chief commercial enterprise was the Chicago fire of 1871. Every insurance company in Chicago was wiped out, many firms in New York were ruined, but in Hartford all but one or two weak companies managed to pay their obligations and survive. Local panic was averted when Marshall Jewell of the Phoenix and an agent of the Ætna rushed to Chicago to pay the first claims over a barrelhead while the fire still burned. Ætna paid out $3,750,000; its stock went from 231 to 50, but it soon rallied. Orion Clemens, who watched Hartford business meet the test, recognized the great benefits of the disaster to the Hartford companies. The surviving firms, he noted, would double their rates and attract an enormous amount of business because of their demonstrated soundness and the demise of much of the competition. So quick was the recovery, in fact, that the fire of 1872 in Boston, in which the Hartford insurance men were more deeply involved than in Chicago, caused hardly a ripple, except another increase in rates and a further fattening of unexpended reserves. Premium payments poured into Hartford; the dollars fanned out into nation-wide investment, the returns from which flowed back again in a swelling stream. It was, of course, the determination of insurance executives to protect the prosperity of their companies, by fixing rates not only to regulate competition and to prevent government interference, but to support the expansion of all private business in which their millions were invested. The administrative officers and directors of the companies were well known to Mark Twain. Batterson, the Dunham family, Jewell, and many others were his friends. Mark himself was a director of the Hartford Fire Insurance Company.[23]

The eyes of the professional businessmen were watchfully on the nation's industrial progress, alert to the safety of old investments and quick to note promising new ventures. The investing executives avoided the more erratic forms of speculation and refrained from the shadier varieties of gambling. They protected their businesses from outside manipulators who recognized fertile fields there, and they quietly propagandized for laissez faire in order to exclude those whose better intentions made them no more welcome. "Unskilled hands should be commanded by enlightened public sentiment to leave the delicate mechanism severely alone," they argued; rate-cutting competition was fatal to sound insurance; the entire nation could trust to their "native intelligence, sharpened to a keen edge in frequent adversities" and to their "scrupulous integrity in dealings with the public."[24] These arguments prevailed. No consumer protests had yet forced impartial inquiry into whether prudent preparation for the next holocaust required all fire-insurance companies, allegedly in competition, to charge identical high rates.

Hartford manufacturing, based on the same ideology, was, though comparatively a minor activity, similarly prosperous. In the old days, the chief products had been manufactured woolens and gin.[25] During the seventies and eighties, firearms, silk textiles, leather belting, and machine tools were the principal commodities. Capital invested in manufactures doubled between 1860 and 1870 to reach $21,260,000. Slower growth during the seventies brought the figure to $27,691,000. In 1880, $8,457,000 was paid in wages to 20,951 employees in 880 factories — an average annual earnings for executive and skilled laborer alike of $403.17. The next ten years showed little change. Though the Irish workingmen remained poor without protest, their employers flourished.

The four principal manufacturing firms were Colt's Patent Fire Arms Manufacturing Company, the Jewell Belting Company, Pratt & Whitney, and the Cheney Silk Mills across the river in Manchester. By later standards these were very small businesses, family owned and based on the original patent of the founder. Marshall Jewell, who had learned in Russia how to scent leather, made his belting company the largest plant in the world for that specialty, yet in 1889 his factory employed only 153 men and girls. Pratt & Whitney, who built Mark's typesetter, employed 700 men in the same year to make thousands of products — all machinery or machine parts. The Colt plant, a foreman from which became the Connecticut Yankee at King Arthur's court, employed 500 mechanics in its plant and arsenal. The Cheney mills flourished after Colonel Frank W. Cheney investigated silk culture in China and Japan. The Nook Farm colony knew the chief executives of these plants, who all held insurance-company directorships and whose prosperity was not based on one enterprise alone.

The businessmen of Hartford were constantly aware of industrial developments outside New England and abroad. They combined business trips with their travels for pleasure and supplemented their native shrewdness with wide observations, all of which confirmed their conservatism and caution. Commerce they intended to dignify by winning for it the status of a profession. To maintain that dignity they sought education and community prestige and participated tirelessly in local affairs. Their way of life has already been described in other areas; their business activities cannot be detached from the whole pattern of their behavior.

Commerce and culture were united on a corporate as well as a personal plane. Hartford was the center of the subscription book trade. Oliver D. Cooke and Son, the pioneers, had circulated the *Family Encyclopedia* in door-to-door sales in 1822 with much success, and by the time of the Civil War, Hartford, with a population of only 30,000 in 1860, had twenty publishing houses. Just as the insurance companies pushed their agents and claims adjusters into every state of the union, so the publishers sent their agents into every rural byway. They discovered a gold mine untapped by the city bookstores. In pursuit of profits, they contributed to the broadening, if not the deepening, of American culture after the Civil War by distributing bulky and popular books on every subject to corners of the country where only the Bible had previously penetrated. At an enormous discount books were farmed out to general agents who hired on commission the canvassers, mostly "maiden ladies and widows, who supplemented their specious arguments with private tales of woe" [26] and moved from house to house with gold-emblazoned sample volumes accumulating tremendous advance sales. Mark thought the promotion of a subscription book required "a deal of genuine generalship in order to maneuvre a publication whose line of battle stretches from end to end of a great continent, & whose foragers & skirmishers invest every hamlet & beseige every village hidden away in all the vast space between." [27]

Most aggressive and successful of these houses was the American Publishing Company, which for some years published the books of Mark Twain. Elisha Bliss, Jr., was its president; its directors were Hartford proprietors of bookbinderies and presses, most notable of which was Case, Lockwood and Brainard, long printers and binders of the dictionary of that Hartford lexicographer, Noah Webster. When the success of *Innocents Abroad* had been demonstrated, Mark bought some stock at the high price for which his book was responsible and became himself a director of the American Publishing Company. Bliss was a particularly shrewd judge of his public and was little concerned with the literary pretensions of the wares he sold, though acutely interested in the profitable dissemination of his cultural wares in all directions. His 1871 letterhead carried a list typical of the fat collections of facts selling widely in rural areas all over the country:

Sights and Sensations............Browne [Junius H.]
Agriculture ....Hyde
Overland through Asia ....Knox [T. W.]
Uncivilized Races, or Natural History of Man............Wood [Rev. J. G.]
Innocents Abroad ....Twain [Mark]
Beyond the Mississippi............Richardson [A. D.]
The Great Rebellion............Headley [J. T.]
Pebbles and Pearls............Abby Sage

Quarto Family Bibles
AND OUR
Illustrated $1.00 Paper, "The American Publisher"

The Hartford Publishing Company and Worthington, Dustin offered the same sort of fare.

Vast markets, opened up by an efficient distribution system, tempted serious writers living on meager royalties from trade publishers. When Mark and Warner each drew $18,000 for *The Gilded Age*, their friends began to think of the fortunes they too might win. Howells wrote Warner that he was willing to let Bliss publish his Venice sketches. Mark constantly recommended his friends to Bliss — Aldrich, Bret Harte,[28] Joel Chandler Harris. Boyesen asked Mark in 1885 if an illustrated history of Norway would pay as a subscription book. Calvin and Harriet Beecher Stowe had each published in the sixties a book "by subscription only." Calvin cleared an unexpected $10,000 on his *Origin and History of the Books of the Bible*, and Harriet a like sum on a collection of potboiling biographical sketches called *Men of Our Times*.

But the prejudice against subscription books was firm. To Helen Hunt Jackson, Warner wrote in 1874 of the feeling general among professional authors: "I think if you were to see your dainty literature in such ill conditioned volumes, you would just die. There is no doubt, however, that 'by subscription' is the only way for the author to make any money." [29] The press contributed to the prejudice by snubbing subscription books because their publishers took no advertising. But much more important than the ungainly shape in which subscription books were cast and the lack of newspaper criticism was the fact that "mighty few books that were strictly under the head of *literature* will sell by subscription." [30] Only Mark could write as he pleased and find a market among the people who did not visit bookstores. The custom of the subscription book trade was not to elevate the public taste, but to match it with either Mark's humor or the compendia that identically adorned the parlor tables of the nonliterary. Mark withdrew his books from the American Publishing Company after Elisha Bliss's death in 1880. For a time he financed his books under J. R. Osgood's imprint. Finally he established his own publishing house in New York. When he found himself a "general" with a battle line of books strung across the continent, he published the same sort of subliterature and subscribed to the criteria developed originally in Hartford.

Nook Farm was intimately aware of the community's business interests and followed, like the men of commerce, the relationship of Hartford investment to the nation's economy. The lawyers in the neighborhood depended on suits arising out of business for their living, and the writers were concerned not only about their own livelihoods but about the place of business in the future of the democratic experiment. Fascinated by the subscription publishing business, Mark was in 1870 full of admiration for the shrewdness of Bliss, which he later tried unsuccessfully to emulate. Bliss?

One of the smartest businessmen in America! And as part of his adoption of the Hartford way of life Mark became the most enthusiastic, erratic, and feckless businessman in the city.

Despite the detailed letters published in *Mark Twain, Business Man* (1946), the full story of Mark's career in business has not yet been told; very little of what should be a full-length study can be incorporated here. In the twenty years of his Hartford residence, he was engrossed by its dominant commercial interests; the damage he sustained in his ill-starred encounters with the profit motive has a bearing on his art not yet fully understood. The high enthusiasms with which he plunged into speculations of almost every variety, duplicating in a more sophisticated environment the quest for gold that he had given himself to in the West, were to be turned into frantic desperation as he scrambled for the wherewithal to pay his bills, before he moved away from Hartford, no longer able to afford his house. He was revolted by the details of business and impatient with its demands on his time, but the fascinations of the gamble led him deeper and deeper into speculation.

Early in the seventies his first enthusiasm for Bliss turned into doubt whether the firm was being run intelligently and then into the certainty that he was being swindled. In 1876, Bliss was moved to protest against Mark's public criticism of his management. Even his drunken illustrator was taunting him with Mark's choicest vilifications. Mark alternated between rage and contrition, but it was by no means a soothing solution to establish his own publishing firm — C. L. Webster and Company — with his nephew in charge, for Mark could not delegate authority and was lacerated continually with irritating details, ending by thinking Webster the most "assful" man he had ever met. The well-meaning Fred J. Hall, who succeeded Webster when the latter's health understandably broke, performed no more satisfactorily. The publishing house scored a tremendous triumph with General Grant's *Memoirs*, but because Mark drained capital from the overextended business for his investment in other interests, it went down in bankruptcy in 1894.

Mark had first brought Webster to New York to run a company promoting the Kaolotype, an impracticable engraving process. This was only one of a hundred inventions which he sponsored. He took all of them very seriously, whether it was the hinged pants button [31] or the pregummed scrapbook, which all in all occupied as much time as he spent writing *Huckleberry Finn*. He also invented a method for stropping a razor, meditated on a steam-railway brake, and listened to all the members of the inventing fraternity in Hartford. By 1878, before he had really got deep in the complex harass-ments of the eighties he was already victim of an intermittent "badgered, harassed feeling . . . It comes mainly of business responsibilties and annoyances . . ."[32]

In 1880 a Hartford jeweler sold him a $2,000 interest in the Paige typesetter, nearing completion at the Colt plant. As Paige tinkered, William Hamersley and Mark nursed their secret for four years. Mark saw millions in the invention. But though Hamersley, epitomizing Hartford's cautious interest in new developments and avoidance of large risk, withdrew from the sponsorship, Mark Twain in 1885 bought a half interest in the machine and began subsidizing its development at the rate of $3,000 a month. He announced his discovery to his Hartford friends, but they looked over the machine carefully and refused to get excited. By 1887 he was so short of money that he could send his sister Pamela only fifteen dollars for Christmas; in 1889 he began to peddle stock in order to put the finishing touches on the machine. By this time a dozen expensive master mechanics had been completing the machine (now transferred to the Pratt & Whitney shops) for nearly a decade. Mark offered William Gillette 1/2500 of the stock for $1,000, but, like Dean Sage, Ned Bunce, and Henry C. Robinson, Will declined. In the fall he enlisted Joseph T. Goodman to sell $100,000 worth of stock to Senator John P. Jones. But though in his eyes the Paige machine marched alone and far in the lead of human inventions, capitalists in the country at large were no more interested in the machine as a canny investment than were his Hartford friends. Mark was convinced that the compositor would be worth $55,000,000 a year — to be realized from world-wide rentals — but at the end of the eighties he was deeply in debt and always maddeningly a hand's breadth away from the riches he sought. In February of 1891 he made a final desperate attempt to solicit Batterson's intervention, promising himself that this was his last appearance in the character of promoter of commercial enterprises. He could not convince Batterson that the glitter of the Paige machine represented real gold. The fascination and torment had at length come to nothing.

The great machine tragedy was his most absorbing interest during the eighties, but Mark found time to inquire of Leland Stanford in 1885 the feasibility of obtaining a charter for a railroad from Constantinople to the Persian Gulf.[33] On April 22, 1890 Henry Green, of Sisson Street, Hartford, wrote to Mark asking for help in financing a new kind of mechanical organ; Mark wrote on the envelope a reminder to call upon him. It is difficult to imagine how much time his enterprises required. In Hartford most of his days were cluttered with business affairs. He wrote less and less, and mostly while at Elmira. The rebuffs he suffered from his friends as he tried to finance the completion of the typesetter undermined his pleasure in Hartford society. He had soared above it in the daring and imagination of his speculative vision, and its earthbound attitudes were galling to him. His own self-deceptions were eventually to result in a deep dissatisfaction with himself and a sense of failure which, combined with the inclination to remorse, led him into self-condemnation and despair. It was not only his satisfaction with Hartford life that vanished with his hopes of riches; his whole happiness went with them. After his departure from Hartford in defeat, he came to hate the ways of business, himself for his disastrous involvement, and all his business associates, upon whom he heaped in vituperative relief the fluent maledictions preserved in his private papers.

A further symptom of personal disturbance can be seen in the ambivalence of Mark's attitude toward his city. His loyalty to Hartford came to be paralleled by violent, if temporary, exasperation with the city's management. In the late eighties he found himself recording his loathing of the stench of the city water, which probably was no worse in 1886 than it had been in 1871, for in every spring freshet fish died in the mains. In 1888, the city, at the instigation of a prominent citizen and "skunk," moved a street light from Mark's gates to the corner of Forest Street, and Mark spitefully contracted for his own light and police protection and planned to refuse taxes except on his house and land. He phrased a satiric open letter to burglars and undertakers, pointing out that Hartford's opportunities were matchless — lights out at two in the morning and an open malarial sewer running through the city. In an unsent letter to the *Courant* he suggested that even low-grade honesty required that a black flag with skull and crossbones be flown from the Capitol dome to warn the public that the city was a death trap. And to the gas company he wrote on February 12, 1891:

Dear Sirs:

Some day you will move me almost to the verge of irritation by your chuckleheaded Goddamned fashion of shutting your Goddamned gas off without giving any notice to your Goddamned parishioners. Several times you have come within an ace of smothering half of this household in their beds and blowing up the other half by this idiotic, not to say criminal, custom of yours. And it has happened again today. Haven't you a telephone?

Ys
S L Clemens[34]

It is possible to overemphasize the importance of these protests and to neglect their humor, but examination of the Mark Twain Papers supports the conclusion that alienation of Mark Twain from Hartford and indeed from the world was gradual. It began in his happiest years. His malady centered in an unbalanced and immature response to experience; it manifests itself in Mark's business experience as certainly as elsewhere.

Other members of Nook Farm had difficulty in preserving their balance in the business whirligig, though none involved himself with the same fatal thoroughness. Mrs. Stowe could not keep hold of the large sums of money coming her way. Her investments were not as sensationally maladroit as some of Mark's, but they were frequently profitless before she fully learned the folly of raising frost-sensitive oranges in northern Florida. John Hooker, Edward Gillette, and George Warner were partners in difficulty. John's livelihood was curtailed by his unpopular advocacy of feminism and spiritualism, and, despite a lifelong ambition to be a justice of the Supreme Court of Connecticut, he could not be chosen for the post so long as his judicial decisions might originate in the spirit world. He had to content himself with thirty-six years as the Court's recorder. Charles Dudley Warner was never tempted as Mrs. Stowe and Mark were by speculative ventures, for he belonged by inheritance to the steady stock that manned Hartford's business. But he had a very sharp eye for an honestly turned dollar, whether it came from the *Courant* or from his publishers.[35] Beginning in the 1880's he began to sense a deep suspicion, which was to find expression in his novels, of the effects of American business on personal development and on American culture. Mrs. Stowe early condemned the materialism of her age on moral grounds; the others of Nook Farm, all affected eventually by the implications of an industrial civilization, were to find their optimism much modified by events before 1890.

But during the early years of the two decades with which we are concerned, the Nook Farm writers had not attained the interrogatory disquiet that eventually segregated them from the rest of the business community. With the professional businessmen they acquiesced in the ideals of an expanding America. As they acquired experience in an industrial culture, they attacked abuses but continued to assume that the good of the whole nation was being served by expanding capitalism. Warner and Mark in *The Gilded Age* said nothing in their satire on political corruption and speculative exploitation that the entire Hartford community could not agree with. The American system was sound. The excesses in its exploitation by the unscrupulous were controllable. Industrial democracy was a successful experiment, with incredible promise for the future.

The writers and the businessmen were in accord, then, up to about 1885. Both groups were far from provincial in their view of the national economy. Both were advocates of honest business practices. Hartford's insurance companies and allied banks were financing the national expansion. None of their leaders participated in the fraudulent acquisition of national resources or in the stock waterings flagrantly manipulated by the operating officials of the railroads they helped capitalize. But the business group was partly aware, I think, of the uses to which their money was put; and although they refrained from personal dishonesty — of which they had a horror — they must have been forced often to remain silent partners in corrupt practices and to grow uncomfortable under a sense of responsibility they could not altogether avoid. In a sense they were spectators of piracy. They did not name their fears, but beneath their confidence they sensed danger and immanent immorality.

Sometimes dishonesty came close home. In 1877 a deacon of the Asylum Hill Congregational Church, a nephew of Harriet Beecher Stowe by marriage, was arrested for embezzling $15,000 from the deposits of the Farmers and Mechanics Bank, of which he was cashier. The president of the bank was charged with a somewhat larger larceny. The two together had apparently falsified books to cover the loss of $220,000. The news came to Twichell during a dinner party at Doctor Burton's where the clerical triumvirate were assembled with their wives. John Hooker, messenger of disaster, came anxious with the rumor that a great breach of trust had been committed and that the deacon was involved. For Twichell the news had a sickening credibility, for during the past year he had been secretly ministering to his leading parishioner to cure him of alcoholism. He went immediately to the deacon's home to be assured but not convinced that the crime was wholly the bank president's. The news was as shocking to the whole congregation. Of the first church service after the rumor was confirmed in the press, Twichell wrote, "Sunday morning beheld the most troubled and cast down congregation that ever assembled in our church — more than grief. It was consternation — a kind of fear" [36] — fear that the code of business ethics was close to disintegration, that the temptations one day might be too strong for them as they had been for one very like themselves, fear perhaps that their technical innocence might cease to distract them from the possibility of real guilt. The deacon attended the services but left during the closing hymn.[37]

The standards of business morality survived the shock, as those of personal morality had survived the alleged adultery of Henry Ward Beecher. There were few such incidents between 1871 and 1891, but increasingly the gusto of commercial pursuits was less evident than a defensive shoring up of a system vaguely incompatible with the Connecticut conscience — an instrument of personal integrity more easily muted than entirely silenced. The laws of Hartford society required not only decorous behavior in investment but a rigid abstention from grand larceny. The parishioners of Twichell's prosperous church were by present-day standards unpleasantly eager to avoid the moral implications of many of their business dealings and to disclaim responsibility for the national scandals in the industries they helped finance. But there is nothing really sinister in their lack of perception. The intellectual temper of the times did not permit or even suggest thorough investigation of the contemporary shortsighted public policy toward private business or re-evaluation of the rights and privileges of property. Hartford housed no ruthless exploiters; it did not contribute directly to the national degradation. Optimistic and somewhat gullible, Hartford was, like most of America, satisfied with the mushrooming benefits of material progress, which inevitably hid for a time the menace behind the rampant industrialism. The Nook Farm writers eventually saw dimly through the screen; their community knew an even vaguer disquiet.

Ideas of Humanity

THE CONFIDENT IF DEFENSIVE CAPITALISTS IN HARTFORD ASSUMED THAT AN unregulated economy would result in an equitable and just distribution of opportunity for wealth. Their own city was prosperous; its wealth was distributed in many hands. But at the bottom of the ladder was poverty, often acute. It had to be dealt with, of course; in pity and patience the citizens tirelessly applied in poultice form the generous charity which relieved the patient without curing the social infection that repeatedly brought him down. It is easy to condemn charitable medications of the nineteenth-century type dispensed in Hartford. But so long as the citizens believed, as they did, in the social justice of the American system, their ideas of social welfare were bound to a contingent superficiality. Under the leadership of the churches, the community fought a continuous fight against poverty and its consequences. It wondered now and then why the campaign had to be so unremitting, but reform in the economic system to get at the cause did not occur to the city as a whole until the twentieth century.

Nook Farm, inhabited by serious citizens with a strong sense of community responsibility, contemplated the city's poor with compassion. Nevertheless, Harriet Beecher Stowe, with a theoretic coldness unlike her, attributed pauperism to the influx of the pauper population from Europe.[38] Charles Dudley Warner said, "In the United States . . . the labouring class is better actually and in possibility than it ever was in history, and . . . there is little poverty except that which is inevitably the accompaniment of human weakness and crime." [39] Hartford almost unanimously endorsed these views and used them sometimes to criticize charity as responsible for the poverty it attempted to treat. Anyone who was healthy, honest, dependable, temperate, virtuous, and energetic could make a good living, for the bounty of the land was so plenteous and the need for labor so great. But generosity conquered logic, and at the risk of encouraging shiftlessness, Nook Farm led the city in contributions of money and effort to finance the charities.

The city government doled out relief to chronic paupers; organizations of citizens like the Union for Home Work sponsored charity bazaars, fairs, and general entertainments during the crises caused by depression or hard winters. Calico sociables at which ladies wore calico dresses and men ceremonially carried a piece of the same material over their arms persisted into the seventies. Amateur plays were presented. Larger efforts were periodically organized; these were usually the "Grand Bazars." During the first week of June 1880, for example, the Union, announcing that society exists for relief of the needy, put on a fair under the leadership of a committee of gentlemen including S. L. Clemens, C. D. Warner, General W. B. Franklin, General Hawley, William Hamersley, H. C. Robinson, A. E. Burr, and Morgan Bulkeley [40] and a committee of executive ladies — their wives. The roller-skating rink was divided into richly furnished booths, and during the evenings men admired the miniature exhibition of world progress and walked on ladies' trains. Nathaniel J. Burton thought the splendors on display would strike the founders of Hartford like "an original dream."

> The innumerable articles of beauty and use, the aesthetic cultivation displayed, the profusions and splendors of dress drawn from all the looms of the world, the music, and the multitudes moving to its time-beat, the ladies holding forth the fascinations of their several booths . . . while countless gentlemen worship around and joyfully squander their substance, the great buildings, the most shining illumination — what would those grave and strenuous and rather strict fathers manage to say to all this? [41]

The community leaders then alive had much to say. Bishop Clark announced in the fair's paper his discovery that the purpose of the fair was honorable, but that charity should be carefully systematized and that "our generosity must always be tempered by discretion." Henry C. Robinson, as a Hartford businessman, voiced the same warning:

> But capital is cautious, and a true man, who has caught this infection from his capital, is occasionally so skeptical of organized charities as almost to avoid them.[42]

Rather than the encouragement of vice, he suggested that donations be made to three really worthy causes — a chapel at Cedar Hill cemetery, a new museum for curiosities, and a department of journalism in every university, "necessary for the education of our public."

Other citizens used the opportunity for self-congratulation. Although, one writer wrote, the new sewers and the post office would apparently never be completed, Hartford could boast of "the permanent stability of our homes and institutions . . . broad, generous culture . . . Few cities are more deserving of honor than ours." Poems on contemporary manners were contributed from all directions. Affirmations of the soundness of paternalism included praise of the Cheney Silk Mills, where 1,500 workers lived happily in a model village in which "Capital and Labor walk hand in hand, the one trying to elevate and benefit the other."

The literary members contributed more readably to the festivities. Warner sent an essay on "English and American Manners" praising the kind of hospitality practiced in Nook Farm.[43] Harriet Beecher Stowe looked around for something to celebrate and decided on the climate. New England's springs were better than Florida's; they were more noticeable.[44] Twichell sent in a story of the 71st Regiment's taking unto itself black servants to the discomfiture of Marylanders. Mark Twain fittingly published in a Hartford paper the chapter of *The Prince and the Pauper* that Hartford insisted be omitted from the book — "The Boy's Adventure." [45] He sent in also a comment on decorum in two answers to an unspecified conundrum:

> Conventional people are those delegations that are accepted; unconventional people are those delegations that are shut out.

and:

> Conventional people are always anxious to say and do what is perfectly proper; unconventional people only aim to say and do what is really right.[46]

The fair, a great success, was in microcosm Hartford at one of its most representative moments. Other fairs were arranged by the same committees. In the bitter winter of 1883, Mark Twain and Mrs. Stowe autographed books and led a costume march at a "Carnival of Authors" sponsored by Mrs. Colt, Mrs. Robinson, and Harriet to net $5,000 for the Union.

When Mark Twain came to Hartford, the city missionary, the single full-time social worker of the community, was Father Hawley. His ministrations were heartily supported by the Nook Farm residents. Indefatigable in his distribution of "soup-pieces" (baskets of food for eight wretched meals) and old clothing, he epitomized the earnest, generous, but ultimately ineffective efforts to relieve the suffering by the waterfront. He never assisted those who used whisky. "How little," he said to his office assistant, "one side of the world knows how the other side live! . . . Oh, who can tell the sorrows and the sufferings of the poor children living in a drunkard's cheerless home."[47] When he encountered an alcoholic breath among the alms seekers crowding his office, he took the man aside, talked to him, extracted a pledge from him, and chalked him up as provisionally saved. His generous selflessness attracted Mark Twain, who praised him in one of his unpublished autobiographical dictations as a man whose tireless zeal was unique among his fellows, except where the object was the acquisition of somebody else's money on gratifyingly harsh terms.

In 1875 sixteen of Hartford's citizens asked Mark to lecture again, as he had in 1873, for Hawley's fund. Mark replied with a letter written in Twichell's study:

Hartford, Feb. 20th, 1875.

GENTLEMEN: — I accede to your request with pleasure. Many months ago I permanently quitted the lecture field, and said I would not appear upon a platform unless driven there by lack of bread. By the *spirit* of that remark I am debarred from delivering this proposed lecture, and so I fall back upon the *letter* of it and emerge upon the platform for this last and final time because I *am* confronted by a lack of bread — among Father Hawley's flock. Most people lie by the spirit and the letter too, but I am not one of that kind; for I have been very carefully brought up. I wish to impose upon you the condition that the expenses of this enterprise shall be paid out of four or five pockets (mine to be one of them), to the end that *all* of the money that comes in at the door shall go to Father Hawley's needy ones, unimpaired by taxes on its journey. I am glad to know that you are going to put the tickets at one dollar; for what we are after, now, is *money* for people who stand sorely in need of bread and meat, and so the object justifies the price. As this will probably be the last time I shall ever have the opportunity of hearing sound wisdom and pure truth delivered from the platform, I wish to buy a ticket to this lecture, and I herewith send money for the purchase. I am aware that I could get in for nothing, and still be acting in a measure honorably; but when I run my lecture over in my mind and realize what a very *bonanza* of priceless information it is, I find I cannot conscientiously accept of a free pass.

Respectfully,
Mark Twain.

To Messrs. Joseph H. Sprague, George G. Sill, H. C. Robinson, and others.[48]

Twichell had earlier investigated Hawley's work before recommending it to his businessman congregation. In December of 1873, he described from the pulpit the two days he had spent with the city missionary. He emphasized Hawley's ability to distribute largess without the demoralizing effects his parishioners feared. "I asked him," Twichell said,

> to show me some of those that might be called the *worthy* poor, that is, whose poverty was innocent, in distinction from those whose poverty was the fruit of their own improvidence or vice, — a discrimination, by the way, which the Gospel of Christ does not seem to say much about; a discrimination, at any rate, which Christ in *His* charity, has not made with respect to *me*.[49]

He urged his flock to consider that the needy families are "American," that most of them need help only because of the panic. He had visited with Hawley a Negro family of six. The father was immobilized by rheumatism, and the mother, afflicted with fever sores, lay on three chairs with a pillow in "as comfortless an abode as I ever saw." When she could, the mother washed clothes, standing on one foot with her lame leg on a chair behind her. "It doesn't put a premium on laziness to help *that* family a little." [50]

Most of the residents of Nook Farm were as active as Mark Twain and Twichell in support of charitable works. When Hawley died in 1876, John Hooker was proposed as city missionary, and though he wanted to accept, he could not. Isabella was as much interested in local charity as her husband, contributing to the Union for Home Work, which she "longed to help always." In planning her reign over the world, in fact, she had not forgotten to include a project for a charity center in the Gillette woods — a sort of Nook Farm Foundation. She was pleased when a young friend, the very one she was training to administer the Nook Farm benevolences in the New World, was appointed city missionary. The colony was not restrained by the business community's reservations about the harmful effects of charity. Even Warner, who believed that unsystematic charity increased pauperism and that poverty was attributable largely to indolence, thought even shiftlessness demanded abundant pity.

The general attitude toward the working classes, whether they lived in acute distress or not, was in Hartford allied to the business community's reluctance to foster laziness. So far as I know, only Mark Twain came eventually to sympathize with the labor movement — at a time, after he had left Hartford, when his despair of any good in the human race made it pointless for him to publicize his enlightenment. Twichell, who fought against what he considered the coldly unchristian reluctance to relieve suffering, did not connect his pity for the poor with his political convictions. In Elmira, Thomas K. Beecher came closest to the ill-defined battle lines and most explicitly took up arms in the still unorganized reform movement. He ran for Congress on the Greenback ticket in 1880. Twichell had lightly chided him for his political irregularity. Thomas replied in a protesting letter that illustrates the kind of response to economic injustice unknown in Nook Farm. "I wish," Beecher wrote Twichell, you had any social convictions as to the welfare of the masses . . . I enclose the green-back platform — which with trifling exceptions I cannot gainsay. Read it and think, that's all. Dear Joe Twichell whom I loved from the word go — as the healthiest & heartiest minister that lets me call him friend — this very mail brings me two letters, one from a widow — the other from a man of fifty in Idaho — whose struggles I have known for 20 years. Whatever you and I have felt in days by gone as the scared fugitives from slavery came shivering to us by night showing cracked pit scars, & in rags, until we could endure *slavery* no longer — the same I feel daily & hourly as the unending procession of my neighbors files by me — anxious, heartbroken, or worse, with eyes of hate & envy, as they know themselves the bleeding grist of our great financial mill — that in defiance of Scripture & the testimony of the ages insists that to lend money — exact interest . . . & grow rich while brother men & partners are *cleaned out* — is honest christian enterprise.

No — Joe — praise me for my patience. These twenty five years I have been of intenser convictions than Garrison ever was . . . You know I am not a party man — nor a blasphemous Kearney — nor a . . . communist. I am only Jeremiah *redivivus*.

— There, I love you & so I write as I never wrote other.[51]

Twichell incorporated this letter in his journal without comment. His own optimism was proof against the evidence of ill heaped up around him. The excesses of an acquisitive society must be curbed in accordance with the Christian ideal of humanity, but the unfettered operation of capitalism, coupled with the prevailingly humanitarian instincts of human beings, would eventually result in the extinction of poverty.

The Nook Farm colony never wavered in its support of the ideal of humanitarian brotherhood. Mark Twain was never to forsake it, despite his alienation from the religion which in New England sponsored that ideal. His generosity was quick, hot, and inexhaustible. But though he did not express the community's hesitation to provide alms, he did not feel that such an attitude was a derivative of greedy self-interest, nor did he make this point of view the object of satire. Mark's insight into his generation may have been keener than ours. Actually, the prosperity of Hartford was characterized less by greed than by satisfaction with a democratic system providing the golden opportunity that enterprise and energy could convert into the good and comfortable life. Except for the possession of an education and an income as a distinguishing characteristic, Hartford was classless, and the undifferentiated prosperous would welcome any of the working class who made good. Those who were incapacitated for one reason or another were the objects of charity. The others held their futures in their own hands.

That the paternalistic attitude of Hartford's dominant class toward the foreign-born and native workers was adequate for the period is pragmatically demonstrated by the acquiescence of the victims. Never in the seventies and eighties did the laboring class strike or make any other audible protest. Just as no one in Hartford spoke out for reform in the time of Mark Twain's residence, and as those of the Nook Farm colony who finally rebelled against the ideas of their generation responded to disturbances outside the peaceful city, so also was the local working class inclined to await the fruition of the dream. The combination of ethical capitalism and humanitarian assistance to its casualties preserved something of the community integrity of old New England — where the villagers looked after their poor and diligently avoided being among their number. Brotherhood, it was believed, would cure the excesses of predatory business elsewhere. That it would have helped cannot be doubted.

In any case, anarchy, as exhibited by the "dastardly revolutionists" who threw bombs among Chicago policemen at Haymarket, was unthinkable. John Hooker wrote to the papers that his sympathies were with the laboring class,

> who, I think, do not get a fair share of the product of their labor . . . I have watched with much interest the progress of socialism in Europe . . . Karl Marx, their greatest thinker . . . laid it down as a fundamental principle of socialism that it was to reach its ends by *evolution* and not by *revolution*.

The remedy for the workingman's depressed lot was properly not violence, but the ballot and self-improvement.

> There is not a man, however humble in life, who, if he will be temperate, virtuous, and industrious, cannot, with ordinary health, secure to himself and his family reasonable comforts.[52]

Ideas of Feminism and Reform

IN THE EXTERNALLY STABLE, CONSERVATIVE, TOLERANT, AND ETHICAL SOCIETY of Hartford, the citizens deplored the departure elsewhere from the ideals illuminating their own prosperity. But despite the distance between the actual and the ideal in America they saw no need for drastic change. Ostensibly the gap was being filled by progress, which became almost a commodity with nonrelative, positive value. From Nook Farm came the only demand for a fundamental broadening of equality: a clamor from Isabella Beecher Hooker for the liberation and enfranchisement of women.

Shortly after Isabella married John Hooker in 1841, she fell into the habit of bringing her knitting to his law office and helping him pass the lonely hours between clients. During the days he read law to her, and at night — since his eyes were too weak for artificial light — she read literature to him. One day John came to Blackstone's chapter on "Domestic Relations and the Reciprocal Duties of Husband and Wife" and read the passage, familiar and acceptable to him but new and shocking to Isabella, in which Blackstone pointed out that husband and wife are one person in law, that "the very being or legal existence of the woman is suspended" during her marriage, and that the husband was entitled to beat his wife (in moderation) to correct the creature under his wing. Isabella surprised John with her consternation. "And this is your code," she cried, "that is to bring peace on earth, good will to man, and harmonize the universe!" John puzzled over her outburst. He and Isabella discussed the topic endlessly; they finally dropped it as a "hopeless mystery." Not until she read John Stuart Mill on "Liberty and the Subjection of Woman" did Isabella begin to ponder action. When Anna Dickinson, who at nineteen was touring the country for Lincoln, came to Hartford in 1861, Isabella feared lest harm should come to Anna's arguments and to the new party in her "conservative and prejudiced city"; no woman had spoken in public in Hartford before. John and Isabella, charmed by her talk, took her home for the night. After the family went to bed, Isabella and Anna talked heart to heart. The girl told the woman, whose energy longed for a cause to espouse, of Susan B. Anthony and Elizabeth Cady Stanton. But it was three years before Isabella could bring herself to meet these notorious women. When she did, she asked humbly to share "their work and obloquy." The two leaders of the suffrage movement, who had been tirelessly fighting a hopeless battle for fifteen years, were glad to accept her assistance. After three days of the "most intense soul-searching debate" at the home of Paulina Wright Davis in Providence, Isabella became a professional advocate of women's rights.[53]

She abandoned the anonymity of her "A Mother's Letter to a Daughter on Woman's Suffrage," published in *Putnam's Magazine* (1868),[54] when in 1869 she called in Hartford the first women's rights convention. The assembly organized the Connecticut Woman Suffrage Association and Society for the Study of Political Science. Influential Hartford people, mostly from Nook Farm, joined with Isabella to summon the convention — Doctor Burton, Francis Gillette, Frances E. Burr,[55] Catharine Beecher, Calvin and Harriet Stowe, Mrs. Marshall Jewell, and Ward and Susan Cheney. Mrs. Hooker's aspirations to immediate leadership were satisfied for a time with the chairmanship of the Executive Committee. Burton, elected its president, said on the stage of the Opera House after Isabella had finished speaking: "If such women don't vote before I die—well . . . I won't die till they do."[56] Despite every effort, however, he did.

Isabella considered crucial from the beginning the criticism of women suffragists as unladylike. To the list of sponsors she persuaded to sign the call, she attracted people who, though opposed to the movement, like her sisters and Francis Gillette, agreed that it was proper to discuss the subject in public and thus breach the battlements of decorum. Upon the speakers she invited from out of town, she urged a cautious, rather than a militant, approach. Elizabeth Cady Stanton, tough-minded from years in the fight, wrote of Isabella's strategy:

> Mrs. Hooker wrote each a letter of instructions re dress, manners, and general display of all the Christian graces. I did my best to obey orders, and appeared in a black velvet dress with real lace, and the most inoffensive speech I could produce; all those passages that would shock the most conservative were ruled out, while pathetic and aesthetic passages were substituted in their place. From what my friends said, I believe I succeeded in charming everyone but myself and Susan who said it was the weakest speech I ever made. I told her that was what it was intended to be.[57]

The Hartford convention was a success in endowing the idea of equality for women with more respectability than it had earlier enjoyed; the vehemence with which the movement had been considered immoral was considerably mollified. But Henry Ward Beecher, lion of the convention, was soon to go down in the wrangle over adultery, which (because suffrage leaders, as we have seen, had made public his alleged transgression) undid Isabella's spadework to make the women's rights crusade entirely proper.

After her temporarily successful convention, Isabella plunged into the national contest. She tried to take Harriet and Catharine with her. Susan B. Anthony's suffragist paper, the *Revolution*, was near failure in 1870; its sponsor, the eccentric George Francis Train, was running out of mad money. Isabella induced Harriet to join her as its associate editor, but Catharine protested against its title and persuaded her two sisters to request a change to something less violent. While this question was being debated, Susan alienated the Beecher sisters (Isabella temporarily; Harriet and Catharine for good) by calling a mass meeting in behalf of the woman in the triangular Richardson-McFarland murder case—the sensation of New York in 1870. Isabella and Harriet withdrew from the paper. Hoping to attract attention away from Mrs. Anthony's fatal involvement in scandal, Isabella began to ponder political maneuvers to win the franchise. Harriet and Catharine, not so much concerned with the vote, anyhow, as with cultural development of women, lost interest in Isabella's campaign and pursued independently their own labors in behalf of female education.

In 1871 Isabella saw her chance to assume the leadership of the National Woman Suffrage Association and to direct its activities with a propriety that had hitherto been lacking. She decided to hold a convention in Washington, close to the halls of Congress. Mrs. Stanton, amused, sent a hundred dollars (as a contribution to expenses) and her determination to stay away, both of which Isabella welcomed.[58] Susan Anthony decided to go to Washington to rescue the convention if it faltered under Isabella's inexperienced direction. The meeting, intended to be a model of decorum and to repeat on a national scale the moral rehabilitation accomplished by Isabella's Hartford assembly, took a dramatic turn toward the sensational when Victoria Woodhull took the audience by storm. Isabella experienced again, this time in more acute form, the emotional thrill of her meeting in Providence. Isabella and Victoria began to pursue a course of political action that ended in a third-party convention later in the same year in New York. After a farcical stage battle, during which Mrs. Anthony, who objected strenuously to premature political action, had the lights of the hall turned out, Isabella became reconciled to Mrs. Anthony's leadership, but her heart was with Victoria, now running flamboyantly for the national presidency. The involvement of the suffrage movement with the Beecher-Tilton scandal, already discussed, occupied most of the next five years. Isabella's efforts to keep a moral veil about the suffragists had come to grief with the entrance of Victoria Woodhull, but such was her devotion to her friend and her cause that Isabella ceased to concern herself primarily with the maintenance of a respectable reputation. At any rate she never enjoyed one again.

At home, Isabella secured the passage in 1877, after a seven years' fight, of a Connecticut bill to establish the legal right of women to hold property. Succeeding Burton as president of the Connecticut association in 1871, she presided over the biennial conventions for the next twenty years. She rejoiced in the notoriety of the two old maids of suburban Glastonbury, Abigail and Julia Smith, whose protest in 1876 against taxation without representation caught the imagination of the country, when their cows were seized by the town in lieu of taxes. Isabella attended all the national conventions. In 1878 she proposed reconstruction of the police force to incorporate women. If she were police chief, she would install matrons in all the station houses. These female constables would wash, feed, and clothe all male vagrants; teach them to sew, wash, and iron; record their history; and then turn them out as skilled laborers ready for housework.[59] She would balance the scarcity of house servants with the abundance of tramps and thus bring society into convenient equilibrium.

Later she developed her most important idea — that women could grow in stature only if responsibility were placed upon them. A speech first given at the National Convention of 1887, "The Constitutional Rights of the Women of the United States" and later widely circulated through the country, closed with this peroration, which I include here to summarize Isabella's intellectual contribution to the suffrage movement, to provide a sample of her voluminous occasional writing, and to exhibit the kind of thinking Nook Farm gave to the position of women and to other political questions.

There are those who say we have too many votes already. No, we have not too many. On the contrary, to take away the ballot even from the ignorant and perverse is to invite discontent, social disturbance, and crime. The restraints and benedictions of this little white symbol are so silent and so gentle, so atmospheric, so like the snowflakes that come down to guard the slumbering forces of the earth and prepare them for springing into bud, blossom, and fruit in due season, that few recognize the divine alchemy, and many impatient souls are saying we are on the wrong path — the old World was right — the government of the few is safe; the wise, the rich should rule; the ignorant, the poor, should serve. But God, sitting between the eternities, has said otherwise, and we of this land are foreordained to prove His word just and true. And we will prove it by inviting every newcomer to our shore to share our liberties so dearly bought and our responsibilities now grown so heavy that the shoulders which bear them are staggering under their weight; that by the joys of freedom and the burdens of responsibility they, with us, may grow into the stature of perfect men, and our country realize at last the dreams of the great souls who, "appealing to the Supreme Judge of the world for the rectitude of their intentions" did "ordain and establish the Constitution for the United States of America" — the grandest charter of human rights that the world has yet conceived.[60]

She held in other writings that in politics and law a combination of man's and woman's natures was essential; she was ready at every convention with a fresh speech. "If all the advocates," the Washington *Post* said after observing a number of her Washington appearances, "were as cultivated, refined, and convincing as Mrs. Hooker, one might almost be tempted to surrender. She certainly possesses that rare magnetic influence which seems to say, 'Lend me your ears and I shall take your heart.'"[61]

But she was constantly forced to fight. In 1871 Francis Gillette argued with Isabella in long front-page articles in the *Courant*, temperately considering her proposition that women should occupy public office because "governments, as administered by men, are too rigorous or punitive, and need to be permeated and softened by what is called 'The Mother-Spirit and Christlike Soul.' "[62] In 1878 Isabella returned to the argument that female suffrage was not immoral, using as her evidence chiefly the authority of her husband's impressive ancestry.[63]

Catharine and Harriet became her active opponents on the question of political rights. Catharine announced in the *Courant* of February 1, 1871:

> I am informed that my name has appeared in some of the public prints as an advocate for woman suffrage. This is not true either of myself or of a large majority of my family and personal friends, most of whom would regard such a measure as an *act of injustice and oppression*, forcing conscientious women to assume the responsibilities of the civil state, when they can so imperfectly meet the many and more important duties of the family state, and the connected ministries of instruction and benevolence.

For her and Harriet the agitation for suffrage seemed to oppose their own campaign to dignify as a profession woman's role in the home. The drudgery of work in kitchen and nursery was used by suffragists as an argument for extending the sphere of woman, but that sphere could most fruitfully be enlarged by educating women to manage more perfectly their own domains. Yet, they admitted:

> The sphere of woman is properly to be enlarged. Every woman has rights as a human being which belong to no sex, and ought to be as freely conceded to her as if she were a man, — and first and foremost, the great right of doing anything which God and nature evidently have fitted her to excel in. If she be made a natural orator, like Miss Dickinson, or an astronomer, like Mrs. Somerville . . . let not the technical rules of womanhood be thrown in the way of the free use of her powers.[64]

And of course if she were gifted in writing books, she should be allowed to develop in the literary direction. But the vote was not necessary to this freedom.

The most persistent and difficult opposition Isabella faced was rooted in the strength of the ideal of womanhood prevailing in Hartford and in nineteenth-century America. Those who were not willing to give it up resisted stubbornly the logic of Isabella and her cohorts. Horace Bushnell said that woman suffrage was "a reform against nature — an attempt to make trumpets out of flutes, and sun-flowers out of violets." No right of suffrage is absolute in man or woman; woman was not created equal nor called to govern; scriptural doctrine supports these conclusions. Suffrage would coarsen her, transform her womanly face and expression. No exposure to politics can make her a "force-element and . . . a self-centered, governing, driving engine character . . ." Women, after all, are "relatively frail and delicate, in a finer type of grace and color, a less coarse, stormy voice, a different innervating quality which is distinctively feminine." The true direction of development is in the education of children so that the great public evil of drink would be eradicated. Woman can sing, and promote charities, and dwell in religion, and write poetry. Of the latter:

> Is it not a matter of fair expectation that, when the women of an age not far off, find where the inspirations are, and set their nimble, fine-strung harps in play, they will give us modes of thought and sentiment and wonders of perception, more ethereal and closer to the living fiber of souls than we have hitherto known? The very fact that women are in a smaller and more delicate key, will permit their wings to carry them higher, and will let us hear them empty their music into the sky, clear above where our male larks and eagles have been able in the past times to go.[65]

Bushnell's emphasis on the fragile delicacy and the cloistered ethereal femininity of the gracious woman singing in her home, administering refinement to her naturally coarse husband, and teaching her children to abhor alcohol was the chivalric idea in Hartford clothing. To it his generation subscribed; its violation by the suffragists was the most serious of their sins. "Woman" was synonymous with grace and purity and virtue; she was not for the world of commerce and politics and the vulgar compromises of reality.

John Hooker, who, until Isabella amended his attitude on this as on other questions, believed in womanhood as Bushnell outlined it, took issue with his neighbor in *The Bible and Woman Suffrage* (1870). The whole burden of Christ's teaching was the law of liberty and personal responsibility,

> which can find its full application only in the perfect equality of man and woman in the home and in the state. When it receives this application society will have taken the greatest step ever taken since Christ came, toward a perfect Christian civilization, and the reign of Christ, which his followers have worked for and waited for so long, will be near at hand.[66]

He used to think, he said elsewhere, that woman's "essential qualities in youth were sweetness, delicacy, and modesty, and in after life, a home-loving wifeliness and madonna-like motherliness."[67] But retaining his satisfaction in her faithful and loving attention to her family, he believed that the ideal woman should be informed on public affairs, aware of her responsibility for social progress, and ready to be a power for good in the community. He knew it was possible to be such a citizen without losing a "particle" of wifeliness and motherliness, or sweetness or delicacy, for Isabella was the embodiment of such virtues, and he was glad to announce the fact to the world. Mary Hooker Burton seconded her father by arguing that the ideal of womanhood need not be sacrificed with the entrance of women into public affairs. No one would believe otherwise if he could see Mrs. Hooker in her role as tender mother and devoted wife, of housekeeper and hostess among the "greenery of her petted plants." [68]

But despite the Hooker family's insistence that reform of woman's role in society would not soil her essential purity, Hartford withheld endorsement because of the reform in sex customs implicit in the suffrage movement. Isabella had been frank enough in the early seventies when she tried to envisage free love as an acceptable doctrine and when, after she repudiated that possibility (loathsome but not unthinkable), she discussed the sexual role of woman in her book *Womanhood: Its Sanctities and Fidelities*. In a discussion of such subjects as maternity, sexual passion, sex education, and prostitution she announced fearlessly that

> the best welfare of our race, both moral and physical, requires that they be understood; and if so, the truths that need to be stated should be stated with delicacy, but in language that can plainly be understood; and language that plainly conveys its meaning is far better in its moral effect than that which deals with its subject in covert and ambiguous expression; and thus suggests concealed indelicacy and stimulates unwholesome curiosity.[69]

Her investigation of the relative sexuality of man and woman demonstrated that women are feebly endowed with passion and men are overstocked. Maternity lessens the power of physical enjoyment, she said, speaking for all "thoughtful married women." Since this is true, women must teach the truth frankly to their sons so that they will understand the physical and moral nature of woman and control their passions accordingly.[70] The size of families will thus be restricted by self-restraint, and women will be free for greater happiness and self-development. Her argument is in part testimony either to sexual frigidity in her and in her intimates or to the ineptitude of their husbands. While Victoria Woodhull, full-blooded and passionate, was demanding in her lectures that men learn the considerate skill necessary to satisfy the aroused passions of women and insisting with a modern accent that unsatisfied desire led to frustration, Isabella was feeling a holy joy in the idea of Christ's conception without male intervention. The recommendations of both women consisted of an open consideration of sexual practices, for which society was not ready. Preserving the ideal of purity was easier than discussing the furtive clumsiness and ugliness of ignorant sexual passion. In so far as suffrage ultimately involved reassessment of all relations between the sexes, it was repugnant to many, in Hartford, again, exactly as elsewhere.

Nook Farm was very close to the radiant energy of Isabella Beecher Hooker. The residents encountered there the other national leaders of the suffrage movement, who came to Isabella's house as often as the literary great came to Warner's and Mark's. Isabella made sure that her neighbors were exposed to each new turn of her thought. She would spot a susceptible guest at the Warners' and attack him vigorously. The only quick conversion on record, however, is that of Grace King in 1887. Mark Twain sympathized with Isabella's crusading energy, though he restrained himself from publishing his comments on it.[71] He believed that the influence of women in politics would be to reduce corruption and to increase the caliber of elected officeholders. Isabella regarded him as an ally, asked him to speak at rallies, and counted on his contributions to help finance her meetings.[72]

The sexual implications of feminism may have a critical bearing on Mark Twain's literature, not only for their importance in the climate in which his most creative years were lived, but for their relevance to the lack of sexual motives in his fiction. As Bernard DeVoto has pointed out,[73] nowhere in Mark's gallery of characters is there a convincing white woman of marriageable age, and nowhere is sex treated with anything but mawkishness. The taboo restricting Mark from an enormous territory is the same that enforced the decorum of his generation. It may have risen from a personal deficiency, though Mark's delayed marriage was obviously happy and normally passionate. Censorship outside himself was not responsible; no one was more careful than he, even in his earliest writing, to avoid suggestive language and the vocabulary and motivation of desire. But whether its sources be personal or social or both, his characterization is asexual even when he recreates the girl who is the object of endlessly repeated love dreams.[74] And the extent to which he carried unconsciously the sterilization of all suggestion in his art that passion is any part of life testifies to a stronger impulsion than merely the preservation of polite reticence.

In some very vital sense, then, Mark shared the ideal of womanhood announced by Bushnell. He exhibited his deference to it in his public and private adoration of Livy, who was, as I have earlier indicated, the perfect example of such a woman. But his worship of his wife was not bloodless; neither was she. In his adulation of Livy, Mark Twain was endorsing the qualities in women celebrated in his generation. But his unpublished writings demonstrate that his attitude was formed in a context of sexuality — which Isabella Beecher Hooker would have been glad to legislate out of life via the education of man in continence.

At any rate, feminism — now of little more vital interest than mohair furniture — was a crucial issue in Mark Twain's Hartford, absorbing all the reformist energies in the city. The feminists thought emancipation of women fully as important as the liberation of the Negro. In the years of which I write, more persons were active in this reform than in the extension of economic justice. That the latter, in the twentieth century, came into gradual operation before the passage of the suffrage amendment in 1919 is significant of the strength of American insistence on the elevation of womanhood above worldly taint and on the integrity of society as preserved by the trappings of propriety. In Hartford lived an eccentric but effective leader of this movement, in interesting proximity to the chief writer of the time, who said of her and of her work, after her death in 1907, that her splendid energies had helped achieve the only revolution for the emancipation of half a nation that cost no blood. With her powerful colleagues, Anthony and Stanton, Isabella Beecher Hooker had broken the chains of her sex and set it free.[75]

5

LITERATURE IN HARTFORD

1871–1891

Hartford as a Literary Community

A LONG TRADITION, STRETCHING BACK TO THOMAS HOOKER'S ARRIVAL in 1636, lay behind the ideas and experience we have noted in Hartford during Mark Twain's residence. The ideals of the business community, for example, had crystallized out of the cautious commercial dealings that for two and a half centuries had been accompanied by unbroken prosperity. The city's political conservatism was rooted in the militant Federalism of the state during the formative years of the nation. This Federalism was associated with the Calvinist disinclination to yield political power to the masses, who were demonstrably not among the Elect. In Connecticut, substantial property holdings had become prima-facie evidence of Grace. Progress toward a less grudging acceptance of the democratic idea had been steady, but slow, for in Hartford it was never the practice to rush into innovation or to accept change at all unless it could be made a sound brick in the stable social structure. The traditions of the city gave its culture the depth, dignity, and authority of long experience.

The literary tradition discernible in Hartford's history, not primarily esthetic in emphasis, is nevertheless abundantly specific in its record of ideas and tastes. Hartford's educated articulateness produced a competent written expression to parallel the city's activities. Literature was not considered an endeavor set apart for special individuals; it was widely indulged in by amateurs and professionals together. Most of the books produced in Hartford are not readable today, but the impetus to write has proved continuous among the citizenry from Thomas Hooker's sermons of the early seventeenth century to Odell Shepard's historical novel (*Holdfast Gaines*) of 1946.

After a long list of sermons published by the seventeenth- and eighteenth-century divines (most notable of whom was Jonathan Edwards [1]) and a much less voluminous secular literature,[2] Hartford finally rose to literary and political eminence with the assembly of the Hartford Wits, who settled in the city during the 1780's. John Trumbull, Lemuel Hopkins, and Theodore Dwight — prolific poets and conservative satirists — made their community for the subsequent two decades the Tory headquarters of the embattled Federalists. Trumbull, the first Hartford author to discover the merits of subscription publishing,[3] joined his contemporaries, including Richard Alsop (bookstore proprietor), in the contribution of serial verse satires to community ventures like the *Anarchiad*, *Political Greenhouse*, and *Echo.* Joel Barlow, whose sympathies became more equalitarian than those of his Hartford friends, completed *The Vision of Columbus* in the city in 1786, but after establishing *The American Mercury* he wandered away the next year. Theodore Dwight founded *The Connecticut Mirror* a little later and between 1809 and 1819 edited it for the Federalist cause. The conservative influence of the Hartford Wits culminated in and passed with the failure of the Hartford Convention, called in 1814 to effect the secession of the New England states during Mr. Madison's war. Dwight was secretary to the convention.

The second notable literary group of Hartford's history was the Knights of the Round Table, an informal club organized in 1819 at the home of Samuel G. Goodrich. The membership included young men later to become locally famous lawyers like Samuel H. Huntington, Jonathan Law, and Isaac Toucey, or editors like William L. Stone and divines like Jonathan M. Wainwright, later an Episcopal bishop. The club issued irregularly until 1833 small publications, often in series — highly miscellaneous in content and now very rare. *The Round Table* by "George Bickerstaffe and others," *The Square Table* ("or the meditations of four secluded maidens seated around it"), and *The Stand* were the principal serials.[4] These men hoped, in a dull time, to keep alive the literary glory of the preceding generation.

Goodrich, a Hartford publisher and bookseller, was the best writer of the group. He, in particular, was sure at the time of his residence in Hartford between 1811 and 1822 that American literature was at low ebb; it was positively injurious to the commercial credit of a bookseller to undertake American works. He sought greener fields in Boston in 1826, where under the pseudonym "Peter Parley" he wrote two hundred children's books of which he sold 7,000,000 copies. In an interesting autobiography, *Recollections of a Lifetime* (1856), he contrasted Hartford's later development with the town as he had known it.

> The city of Hartford, ever noted for its fine situation, in one of the fertile and beautiful vales of the Connecticut, is now distinguished for its wealth — the fruit of extraordinary sagacity and enterprise on the part of its inhabitants — as well as for its interesting institutions — literary, charitable, and philanthropic.

But in 1810, he had found it

> a small commercial town, of four thousand inhabitants, dealing in lumber, and smelling of molasses and Old Jamaica — for it still had some trade with the West Indies. Though the semicapital of the state — the yearly sessions of the legislature being held there and at New Haven alternately — it was strongly impressed with a plodding, mercantile, and mechanical character. There was a high tone of general intelligence and social respectability about the place, but it had not a single institution, a single monument, that marked it as even a provincial metropolis of taste, in literature or refinement.[5]

A third group of writers, who similarly found Hartford a depressing marketplace, gathered in the 1820's around a female poet of enormous fame in her own time — the vaporous Lydia H. Sigourney. She had come to Hartford in 1814; before she died, she published there sixty-four volumes of obituary poetry.[6] As sociable as she was sentimental, she brought to her salon the young men of the city who were interested in belles-lettres. James Gates Percival, a sort of minor Poe and interesting eccentric, looked in while he was in Hartford editing the 1827 edition of Webster's unabridged dictionary, but the lilac and lavender of Mrs. Sigourney's circle did not compensate for the rum and molasses elsewhere. He soon moved to New Haven to live in seclusion, paying his respects to Hartford in solemn valedictory verses:

> Ismir! Fare thee well forever!
> From thy walls with joy I go
> Every tie I freely sever
> Flying from thy dens of woe.

Ismir! Land of cursed deceivers
Where the sons of darkness dwell
Hope, the cherub's base bereavers,—
Hateful city! Fare thee well.[7]

George Denison Prentice, later famous as editor of the Louisville *Journal*, began his career in Hartford editing the *New England Review*, in which he printed many of his own poems. After he brought John Greenleaf Whittier to town in 1830 to succeed him on the *Review*, Prentice introduced him into the Sigourney set. Whittier's closest Hartford friend became John Gardner Calkins Brainard, editor of the *Mirror* and author of three books of uneven but not impossible verse. Although Prentice, Whittier, and Brainard did not revere Mrs. Sigourney's saccharine elegance or adopt it in their own works, they found in her society a literary atmosphere lacking in the city at large. After his departure, Whittier wrote Mrs. Sigourney that Hartford was by "no means a *literary* place, and it has been remarked that were it not for yourself it would be only known as the place where a certain Convention once assembled."[8] Yet his brief residence in Hartford, during which he published his first book of poems, proposed unsuccessfully by mail to Miss Cornelia Russ, and debated with Mrs. Sigourney his conflicting inclinations to devote himself to poetry and to Abolition, was full of pleasant associations for him—particularly as he thought of his friendship there with the Mrs. Hemans of America.

Mrs. Sigourney outlasted this coterie to dominate Hartford's subliterature until 1865. Though her own international fame established her supremacy, dozens of Hartford housewives competed with her during the sentimental forties and fifties in the manufacture of pathos out of weddings, funerals, train wrecks, early deaths, widows in distress, and little babies, dead or alive, whose tiny shoes were never put away. Emily Foote, the wife of a Hartford minister, published in 1879 a collection of poems representative of the later days of an unbroken tradition. Most notable of her work is "The Undertaker's Last Ride," of which I furnish one stanza:

He lived to do good
In all ways that he could,
And one form his benevolence took,
Was to dress human clay,
Before laying away,
And retain its most natural look.[9]

A Hattie Howard was prolific in doggerel, and little Lucy Cotton Bull, ten years old, produced *A Child's Poems* in 1872 to astonish the community by her early emulation of her older contemporaries. She wrote:

> 'Tis poetry, poetry everywhere—
> It nestles in the violets fair,
> It peeps out in the first spring grass.
> Things without poetry are very scarce! [10]

William Cullen Bryant contributed a very cautious introduction to Lucy's book, saying at polite length that he had never seen exactly comparable poems from the pen of so young a young person. Of the many female writers of prose in Hartford, Mrs. Julia P. Smith was the most successful. Her *Widow Goldsmith's Daughter*, a domestic novel, sold 50,000 copies in the seventies, and for a time her fame qualified her for inclusion in the many newspaper articles on the Nook Farm colony. The colony was not acquainted with her.

The best serious writing between the Hartford work of Brainard, Percival, and Whittier and the appearance of the Nook Farm writers came from Rose Terry Cooke, born in Hartford in 1827. She began her delicate and observant exploration of Connecticut local color in the first issue of the *Atlantic*, which led off in 1857 with her "Sally Parson's Duty." [11] She wrote often for the *Courant* and the Springfield *Republican* and in 1860 published her own poems, infinitely superior to those of her Hartford female contemporaries. In her short stories she perfected the sketch of New England character and dialect, blending realistic observation with sympathetic coloring. An especially good friend of the Twichell family, she was well known to the Nook Farm colony, but her residence in Winsted during the seventies and eighties kept her apart. The only other notable poet of Hartford in her time was Henry Howard Brownell,[12] whose promise, exhibited in poems of naval warfare, was never fulfilled. He died in 1872.

But at all times during the nineteenth century, nonliterary citizens of Hartford wrote interminably, either to amuse themselves or to offer the results of their professional labors to a wide audience. Physicians, senators,[13] bishops, inventors,[14] and machinists wrote and published poems for the pleasure of it. Many scholars and antiquarians—in a lineage extending back beyond Noah Webster—wrote hundreds of books on their specialties. Some of the most prolific professors of Yale, Brown, and Amherst had grown up in Hartford, where the number of articulate educators at Trinity College, the Asylum for the Deaf and Dumb, and the Hartford Theological Seminary was impressive. Besides Catharine Beecher and J. Hammond

Trumbull of the Nook Farm environs, Emma Willard was well known. Her works, a series of books that sold more than a million copies, ranged from a *Treatise on the Motive Powers Which Produce the Circulation of the Blood* to "Rocked in the Cradle of the Deep."

By 1871, then, Hartford had accumulated a literary heritage that insured at least a sympathetic environment for the Nook Farm group. In Hartford, literary aspiration was an ambition familiar to all sorts of people. Despite the commercial character of the community from the rum-and-molasses days to those of actuarial calculation, the literary impulse was strong, even among those who lived by business, like James G. Batterson. Those who did not themselves write were at least untiring readers. The literate city was accustomed to the presence of writers. It is not surprising then to see the Nook Farm colony form there as an integral part of the community and to watch it thrive in an appropriate climate of community interest. Insurance men would read Mark Twain's books and consider themselves competent and welcome to proffer their advice. If the writers who enjoyed this attention felt qualified, in turn, to enter into business — as Mark Twain did — they were merely confirming the community attitude that literary pursuits are not divorced from the rest of life. If the standards of literary taste in Nook Farm were close to those of the city, the identity is again testimony to Hartford's recognition of the continuity between artistic and mundane activities. In the twentieth century one finds little interchange and less sympathy between the business world and the literary profession. Wallace Stevens, vice-president of a Hartford accident-insurance company, is a major American poet, but few people in Hartford know his work. The literature of Hartford in the seventies and eighties, however, was closely interwoven with the whole life of the community, deriving relevance and variety from the context and contributing richness to it.

The Professionalism of the Nook Farm Writers

PRINTING AND BINDING WERE IN HARTFORD A PROMINENT BUSINESS; THE SALE of books by subscription, as we have seen, was developed with extraordinary success there. It is no accident that the city possessed in 1870 facilities for covering the nation with the production of the Hartford writers. A long tradition of book writing accompanied an equally extensive history of bookmaking as the articulateness of the city found convenient outlet through its own publishing houses. The writing of books was a profession in Hartford, recognized by the community as such, rather than merely the expression of a cultivated city. For the Nook Farm writers literature was an occupation, as law was for their neighbors or the ministry for their religious leaders. They planned their careers in their profession with eyes more upon their immediate audience than upon the uncertain attention of posterity, and looked longer at the commercial than at the artistic possibilities of each book they contemplated. Their dependence on their pens for status in the community and for support of their families is important in the evaluation of their literary achievement. Their relation to the public, and their development of an instrument of style to reach that public, must be understood before we can estimate the limitations of their work as a contribution to the cultural achievement of their times. It is necessary to read the millions of words produced by these writers to feel something of the weight of their labors, but the conclusions resulting from such a discipline must be summarized before we can see their best work in perspective.

In 1871 Harriet Beecher Stowe's potboiling days were practically over, for she was entering then the long afternoon of her career. She no longer found it necessary to keep two books going at once, or to maintain the flood of magazine articles with which she had kept pace with her family's expenditures. She did not begin a serial now in the *Christian Union* without knowing whether she would end it in a happy Christian marriage or in death by consumption. She no longer committed herself to editorial obligations which in earlier days had forced her to write on the kitchen table, surrounded by clamoring children. On three occasions in the seventies, however, she bestirred herself to publish material for a motive no more important than the restoration of faltering income. The more complicated genesis of five other books written in this period of diminishing activity makes consideration below more appropriate.[15] In 1872 Harriet transferred *Men of Our Times*, which the Hartford Publishing Company had circulated in 1868, to the Worthington, Dustin subscription house, also of Hartford, for another try by a fresh set of agents. The book was peddled at least tacitly as a new one, under the title *The Lives and Deeds of Our Self-Made Men*. Harriet did not revise the sketches or add to them. Except for the pages on the childhood of Henry Ward Beecher, for which she had experience and memory to enliven her otherwise dreary biography, her development of the thesis that "America has been a great smelting furnace in which tribes and nations have been melted together," is almost completely uninspired, though she had been in her novels compellingly fervent about the human product of "Christian democracy." In 1874 she produced a similar compilation for distaff celebrities — *Women of Sacred History* — for the New York publishing house of J. B. Ford, which she and her prolific brothers and sisters were trying to make prosperous for their own benefit.

And in 1873 Harriet collected some essays on Florida under the title *Palmetto Leaves.* In this early boost for Florida she increased the growing national curiosity about the place by celebrating its healthfulness of climate for the aged and infirm, the problems and promise of its real estate, and its commercial suitability for raising profitable citrus crops. Her continuing faith in the potentiality of the colored race appears in her argument that the Negro labor force needed only training and education to be as efficient as it was inexpensive. In total, her attempt at economic analysis is remarkably like the even more commercial efforts of Warner to publicize California. Her motive, not particularly to increase the value of her Florida holdings, was simply to make a book of her observations there. Her orange-growing experiences provided grist to her mill, the wheels of which still ground purposefully, though with slackening momentum, in the seventies. She, like Warner, shared the interest of Nook Farm and Hartford in the economic development of the country.

Harriet's twenty-year-old habit of capitalizing her experience in every direction — in books for children, novels, short stories, poems, texts for educational purposes, and essays to promote the Christian perceptions of her public — though not merely pecuniary in inspiration, was nevertheless sustained by the pressure of necessity. Her facility for total conversion of her experience and thinking to salable forms in the face of burdensome debts had been inexhaustible. Her output had been Gargantuan for so tiny and so busy a woman. Relaxing now in the face of advancing years and declining vigor, she could look back upon a professional career of authorship that had made her a success by Hartford's standards. She had been willing to make use of every subject at hand. Under discipline to maintain the station she had unexpectedly attained with the success of *Uncle Tom's Cabin,* she finally wrote her way through to the retirement she had sought when she moved to Hartford in 1862 to settle down among the gentlefolk. In 1878, her seventieth year, she attained that retirement.

But though Harriet's labors were almost over in 1870 and her literary yeomanry inconsequential thereafter, Charles Dudley Warner, whose productive career began then, wrote nine or ten potboilers during the subsequent two decades. These volumes — mostly travel books — can be dismissed as hack work in order to simplify the consideration later of the better books less justly forgotten. Warner came to Hartford as a journalist, under no more illusions of being an artist for art's sake than his neighbors were. He adopted the Nook Farm standard of living with its pressures for continuous prosperity. Until a series of gardening sketches he wrote for the *Courant* were published in book form in 1870, he did not dream of trusting even part of his livelihood to authorship. The sensational success of *My Summer in a Garden*[16] changed his mind. Thereafter he did not pause between manuscripts. Warner had no real inventive facility to justify the continuous authorship which a professional writer found inescapable if he would sustain the market value of his reputation and the regularity of his royalty checks. Accordingly, the staple product of his professionalism became the travel book. He chose his medium shrewdly. He could maintain his responsibilities in the *Courant* by having his books prepublished there as travel letters; he could pay for the trips he liked to take anyway; and he could push into new territory to add a new title with only a geographical alteration of the basic formula.

In 1872 Warner published *Saunterings*, the result of his first trip to Europe. His method was simple and casual; rather than guidebook statistics, he professed to offer only his personal impressions as a traveler. His account of climbing Vesuvius is very different from the extravaganza Mark Twain makes of the same outing in *Innocents Abroad*. Though Warner finds opportunity for very quiet pleasantries, he usually plies the reader with sober details of scenery. For the charm of Sorrento he was prepared by Mrs. Stowe's romantic *Agnes of Sorrento*; all the Nook Farm writers had traveled widely in Europe and recorded their experiences in their own ways. The distance between Warner and Mark Twain is illustrated by the low-toned whimsy Warner cultivated in sentences like this:

> There are three places where I should like to live; naming them in the inverse order of preference, — the Isle of Wight, Sorrento, and Heaven.[17]

Warner, like Mark, found a great hunger in this country for accounts of foreign lands, both among the hundreds of thousands who had been tourists and liked to relive their experiences and among the many more who aspired to go abroad but could not. He complied with the demand as fast as he could.

In 1874 Warner took Twichell with him on the kind of excursion both enjoyed. The professional traveler recorded a summer tour of Nova Scotia in *Baddeck, and That Sort of Thing*,[18] a popular and familiar little book which, though it aims at informality, tells us nothing about Twichell, little about Warner (except implied amiability), and a great deal about the pedestrian details of traveling the northern country — the characters encountered, the places visited, the conveyances ridden, and the church services attended. Warner returned to Europe for a long sojourn in 1874–75. Out of his excursions into the Near East came *My Winter on the Nile* and its sequel *In the Levant*.[19] These are the dullest but the most ambitious of his travel books. His attempt was to analyze the "Oriental atmosphere" and to examine the temper of Egypt and the Levantine countries for the impact of Occidental influence. He concluded that conditions in the Near East were "the result of social, moral, and religious conditions, totally foreign to our experience, and not to be estimated by it." He demonstrated his point by failing utterly to predict the political disturbances that swept the region even before his books were off the press. However undiscerning, his observations of surface conditions again found a wide audience.

The third of his five long European tours, in 1881–82, was recorded in *A Roundabout Journey*, which added Spain and Moroccan Africa to his earlier itineraries. At a bullfight he found the ceremonies boring and the slaughter of horses disgusting. He fled from the arena before the bull was killed to retire into an old church where he discovered "some visible evidence that the Christian religion has still a foothold in Spain." For many reasons, including the open caresses of newlyweds traveling in trains, he concluded that Spain was the least attractive country in Europe. It was safe, he said, to generalize thus about the nations he visited so briefly, for the experienced traveler learns to catch very soon "the moral atmosphere of a strange land, and knows whether it is agreeable or otherwise, whether the people seem pleasant or the reverse."[20]

Finally, in the usual order, Warner turned from European to American explorations in *On Horseback: A Tour in Virginia, North Carolina and Tennessee* (1888) and *Studies in the South and West* (1889). The first book, a journal of a summer trip with T. R. Lounsbury of Yale, is less wearisome than the accounts of foreign travel because of its lighter tone, its lesser bulk, its inclusion of small talk, its partial characterization of the travelers, and its avoidance of the travel-is-broadening motif. To round out the volume, Warner included "Mexican Notes," magazine articles he wrote after a two-month visit south of the border in February and March 1887, and "The Golden Hesperides," his first reference to California, in which he compared the later migration in pursuit of climate to the earlier quest for gold. *Studies in the South and West* was sponsored by *Harper's* (with which, after 1886, Warner was associated editorially) in an effort to promote understanding among various sections of the country. The prosperous life of the Union, he said, depended upon the "life and dignity of the individual States." But of the individual states he reconstructs only enough of the local manners to justify the observation that each has a promising future. Though Henry Harper believed that the expedition did much to advance national unity, it is difficult for us, now that we know our country better, to see in these essays anything more than a laborious coverage of an extensive geography. To be sure, this tour, like all his others, served to enlarge Warner's observations of the nation and the world and to fill the reservoirs upon which he drew more successfully in his relatively important books. The West, which privately he did not like,[21] he called definitely American, materialistic in spirit, dedicated to practical education, but open-minded, hospitable, and sagacious in handling new problems. "Comments on Canada" completed this volume and Warner's coverage of the continent.

Through all this pedestrian journalism, Warner's reputation as a sage guide to foreign countries and to his own steadily grew. His income from these ventures was substantially increased in 1890 when the Atchison, Topeka, and Sante Fe Railroad offered him $10,000 cash and the use of a private car in return for four laudatory articles about southern California. Harper was to publish the pieces in his magazine and pay him better than usual rates as compensation for the reduced royalties he was to earn with the subsequent book, which was to be distributed widely at a low price. The contract, preserved in the Warner papers, does not make explicit the railroad's motive, but it is clear that the railroad expected the articles to increase settlement along its route and to accelerate the development of southern California, into which it had pushed its tracks before need for them had grown up naturally. No scruples deterred Warner from accepting, though the arrangement was, of course, concealed from everyone but the signatories of the contract and presumably Harper's associates. Warner's devotion to his trade was so much a custom to him now, his habit of looking for ways to make money with his pen so deeply ingrained, and his point of view toward the railroad exploitation of the western country so much more favorable than that of a later generation, that he did not hesitate to complete this assignment and to write the articles later published as *Our Italy* (1891). Precedent was available to justify a very dubious transaction. Henry Ward Beecher, for example, had accepted from Jay Cooke and Company stock in the Northern Pacific Railway worth $15,000 to influence the public in its favor in the *Christian Union*.[22] Warner, in short, thought of himself as a literary workman; this opportunity provided only a more than usually lucrative return for his professional services.

Our Italy, handsomely printed, was sold very widely, probably at a slight loss made up by the railroad. All over the East it persuasively praised California's climate, in which everything imported from the Mediterranean countries could be profitably grown at home and, via the railroad serving the region, easily shipped to market. An Eastern horse transferred to California improves in size, configuration, wind, and endurance; man is as much benefited as the horse by the change. Californian Indians live to be 130, 140, and up.[23] Land is cheap, water by irrigation is more dependable than unpredictable rainfall elsewhere, and wages are high enough to attract the laborer without repelling the prospective employer. California has an especially fine future as the fairest field for the experiment of a contented community. Proud of the book's enormous circulation, Henry Harper said that *Our Italy* sprang from an idea of his own for his magazine. Originally Howells was to accompany Warner, but he withdrew. Warner at first feared that the "crudity of the West was such that he could not find in it the necessary stimulus . . . to inspire him to produce the sort of thing that we desired from his pen," but "enthusiasm came over him." [24] On his return he is alleged to have slapped Harper on the back, saying, "Harry, I was entirely mistaken; a man has not lived until he has been over our Western Country." [25] Warner's book was delightful, Harper added, "and a more characteristic and inspiring American story was never more delightfully told." [26] In actual fact, Warner disliked the whole business and the book he wrote about it is by long odds his worst. But Harper's reminiscences are valuable in reconstructing Warner's vanished importance as a professional interpreter of America to Americans growing increasingly as curious about their own country as about foreign lands.

Warner's professionalism exhibited itself also in his lifelong devotion to other journalistic enterprises. During the seventies and eighties, as one of the owners of the *Courant*, his proprietary interest in journalism as a vocation was continuous. In the last fifteen years of his life his main energy was no longer devoted to the *Courant*, for the neighbor he trained, Charles Hopkins Clark, was in that period growing rapidly into his place. *Harper's* magazine absorbed his interest; he edited "The Editor's Drawer" and "The Editor's Study" as successor to Howells. In a speech to the American Social Science Association in 1881,[27] he expressed his businessman's attitude toward the conduct of a newspaper as well as the sense of moral responsibility he combined with it. He pointed out that the object of a newspaper was to make money for the owner. He was glad to note that the most successful journal financially was always the best journal. The editor's claim on the public is exactly that of the manufacturer. And the subscriber and the advertiser have only the rights in the newspaper that they pay for. For both commercial and ethical reasons, however, the level of newspaper fare should be raised by improving reportorial accuracy and by decreasing the length of editorials and the size of advertisements. All in all, Warner concluded, the moral tone of the American newspaper is already higher than that of the community in which it is published. Warner wanted a responsible press, but he was not likely to forget that its conduct is a business.

Besides his editorial participation in the management of the Hartford *Courant* and of *Harper's*, Warner was indefatigable in seeking out other journalistic opportunities. Although his nominal editorship of the *Library of the World's Best Literature* at a yearly salary of $10,000 was to be an activity of the nineties, he prepared earlier a life of Captain John Smith for an abortive "Lives of American Worthies" series, contemplated by Henry Holt, which was to deal without "historic gravity" with notables of American history who could easily be made fun of.[28] Pedestrian rather than humorous, Warner's book is unexpectedly thorough biography, but one of his bread-and-butter books nonetheless. *Washington Irving*, the careful life that Warner wrote also in 1880 for the American Men of Letters series, of which he was general editor, fares better. The variety and volume of Warner's vocational activity extends further into scores of uncollected magazine articles which I have not attempted to locate. Warner did not chafe under the pressures forcing his busy engagement in so many labors. He had what Mrs. Stowe called "faculty"—the organizing ability she herself exhibited to prevent suffocation by work. He ordered his occupations so as to leave time for the amenities of the life he preferred. Though his profession exacted continuous effort, he never complained of the amount of work he had to do. Indeed, his labors cannot have been so wearisome in the performance as some of his books are in the reading. Throughout his career he was probably borne up by the two good reasons for writing books that J. R. Osgood pointed out to him in a letter of 1874: to do good and to make money.

Mark Twain, of course, was very much a member of this guild. It is not appropriate to include much of his work with the outright potboilers of his neighbors, for during his residence in Nook Farm his creative strength lifted most of the dozen books belonging to his greatest period into an accidental artistry more important than their commercial origin. He had conceived of *Innocents Abroad* and *Roughing It* primarily as money-makers. In the years immediately before and after his marriage he had resolved never to touch a book with no money in it, but he had also promised himself as early as 1868 that he would leave off chasing phantoms after he married, abandon literature "and all other bosh,—that is, literature wherewith to please the general public," and write only to please himself.[29] Much later, looking back, he liked to think that only *Following the Equator*, with which he regained solvency after his bankruptcy in the nineties, was written for cash. In one sense he was right, but in another, every book he ever wrote, except *The Prince and the Pauper* and *Joan of Arc*, was constructed with its prospective sale as the important condition of its composition. If the recorded evidence is fair, Mark Twain devoted more conscious attention to the distribution, publication, and cash value of his books than to their success as art. He felt the same pressures compelling high production that affected his neighbors. The royalties from *Innocents Abroad* would have supported him for life had he chosen to live like a Concord philosopher. But he lived in an expensive neighborhood with Hartford standards to spur him to make money—a purpose he had known before he came but one he had one day expected to abandon. He engaged in business enterprises that devoured money faster than his books could supply it. The more money he made, the more he needed. At the peak of his success he earned and spent in one year (1881) a hundred thousand dollars.

Travel was a more lucrative subject for Mark than for Warner. His first two books had covered territory that became familiar to Warner—Europe, the Near East, and the American West. In 1879, Mark published *A Tramp Abroad* after the year in Europe including the walking tour with Twichell, who appears in the book as Harris. Mark's purpose was obviously the manufacture of another fat volume for the subscription trade. He filled the book with mock legends, digressions like the burlesque ascent of the Riffelberg, and tag ends of improvisation of all degrees of quality from the excellence of the bluejay story crystallized from the oral humor of the West to the dullness of his history of Alpine glaciers. The personality he assumes is more sophisticated than his guise in *Innocents Abroad*, and his satire includes more precisely the tourist American. But his book, designed as a basketful of travel notes and associated entertainments for five dollars, is of no permanent consequence.

Two other minor works, sometimes still read, belong to this period. *Sketches New and Old* (1875) and *The American Claimant* (the latter published in 1892 but written before Mark's departure from Hartford) consist of seventy-six sketches, only one of which—"The Private History of a Campaign That Failed"—belongs with his first-rate work. The others, mostly the routine product of the professional jokesmith, comprise a commodity readily salable but highly perishable. Many are pieces written in the sixties for newspaper columns and resurrected after his fame made them valuable. *Sketches New and Old* is of some academic interest in tracing the origin of Mark's total achievement in the humorous tradition of the Southwest and in marking a stage in the evolution of his satire from chance ridicule of accidental features of society, like Sunday School books and the abuses of the jury system, through to the wholesale contempt characteristic of his old age. "The American Claimant," the title sketch of the second collection, is a farcical extension of *The Gilded Age*, running Colonel Sellers through a series of preposterous enterprises that use him not so much as the instrument for dissecting the speculative impulse as the object of burlesque.[30] As in the dramatic version of the earlier novel, the Sellers myth is mechanically perpetuated to capitalize its earlier popularity.[31] The other sketches in the volume are scrap material originally cut out of *A Tramp Abroad* and utilized profitably now to achieve essential poundage. But it is not so much the hack work of this period that establishes Mark Twain's involvement in the professional pursuit of literature as his whole biography. Riches to him were always a dream; maintenance of a high standard of living was an urgent purpose behind his whole literary accomplishment.

The Nook Farm writers were, of course, acutely interested in the behavior of their publishers and in the profitable exploitation of the market for which they wrote. Mrs. Stowe, who interfered least with her publishers' business, watched her sales figures and her statements carefully and in 1872, for example, wrote Fields that he ought to advertise how many copies of *My Wife and I* had been sold. "I like people to know it for very many reasons," she said,[32] one being pride that she could write a novel of contemporary life and another her conviction that nothing succeeds like success. In addition to skillful handling by the publishers, profitable promotion demanded favorable critical reception. Mark and Warner were particularly adroit in making sure that the expectations of the audience should be whetted rather than dulled by critical reviews. Howells was of inestimable assistance to both because of his commanding position of influence in setting the degree of enthusiasm that lesser critics would copy from him. If he could not conscientiously praise one of their books, like *The Gilded Age*, he offered to withhold his comment to prevent damage. Warner and Mark both wrote Whitelaw Reid of the New York *Tribune* before the publication of the same book to suggest an early favorable review there, and Warner asked E. C. Stedman, Hartford writer then member of the New York Stock Exchange, to review it for *Scribner's*. Mark became insistent that no book of his be published until Howells had written a review of it from the proofs. Thus Howells promised to get the "sheep jumping in the right places" to facilitate the success of *Tom Sawyer*, and he offered to allay the unexpectedness of *The Prince and the Pauper* by unrolling a carpet of critical praise just ahead of its arrival. Other professional arrangements attesting the determination to leave success as little as possible to chance included prepublication at the best possible rates[33] in a reputable journal (if possible "simultaning" with an English magazine), the zealous protection of copyright, and the establishment of property rights abroad as well as at home.[34] Accumulated experience taught them all the devices for realizing and protecting the maximum returns from their ventures.

If a writer is to attain professional success in his own time, he must come immediately to terms with his audience. The Nook Farm writers succeeded in doing so with a minimum of conscious deference. Howells was again helpful in enabling them to avoid offense, but his censorship did not extend beyond the excision of details which he thought might offend the feminine reading public. Mrs. Stowe, Warner, and Mark Twain, sharing the same concern for keeping their enormous clienteles, adopted rather different attitudes toward the publics upon which their professional success depended. Since each had achieved great success from the start, he was able to extend the relation established in his first book without marked alteration in subsequent works. Brief reference to the attitude of Nook Farm writers toward the national audience may define further the nature of their work.

Warner and Mrs. Stowe, naturally enough, differed more from Mark Twain than from each other in estimating the demands of their publics. They assumed that the growing literate class was comprised of educable citizens who desired to increase the fullness of their lives by reading, to add to their stock of information about the world, to improve themselves in the direction of a moral culture, and to seek relief from their own surroundings in literary recreation. Harriet adopted from the start the assumption that her readers would welcome a moral lesson, if it was informally preached and suitably illustrated. *Uncle Tom's Cabin* was frankly a fervent appeal to conscience, and its readability — now its most important quality — was intended to make effective and universal its great message to her countrymen. The subsequent professional career launched by its success did not include a suppression of her moral teachings, for her wish to elaborate them was supported by the willingness of her following to listen. She continued to write under the compulsion of the most elementary, vivid, and powerful missionary spirit of all New England's ethical tradition. No respect for money as the attractive object of continuous production altered her intention to use fiction as a power for moral good; no conflict arose between her ethical and her commercial intentions. Her inclination to preach was by far the stronger of her motives. Integral in her own temperament, it was supported by the New England history at her back (which she reached out to recreate as a lesson for modern times) and strengthened by her upbringing, education, and involvement in the great religious questions of her era. The literate public permitted her devotion to religious themes by continuing to read her works even after they became, in the seventies, something of an anachronism amid growing secular interests. This changing temper, incidentally, Harriet recognized by turning to contemporary society in three novels we will come to in which she kept her theme but changed the setting of its narrative illustration.

The ethical direction of Warner's work was much more subtle, and more appropriate for a man beginning to write after the Civil War. In his travel books he included little comment explicitly hortatory, but in his essays and in his serious fiction he followed the New England line. Art, he felt, required an idealization of nature that would beckon people entangled in reality to a higher growth. "Yet the main object of the novel," he wrote in 1883, deferring to a demand Mrs. Stowe did not recognize but fortunately complied with instinctively, "is to entertain." But in that entertainment there is an elevating force.

> The best entertainment is that which lifts the imagination and quickens the spirit . . . by taking us for a time out of our humdrum and perhaps sordid conditions, so that we can see familiar life somewhat idealized, and probably see it all the more truly from an artistic point of view.[35]

The influence of his heredity was strong upon him, but the instinct primary in his older neighbor to make books count for good was in him less obvious. Abreast of the secularization of old New England attitudes, he was more a humanist than a primitive moralist. At any rate he sensed that his audience was with him, and he too felt it necessary to pay no special deference to the public supporting his enterprises. He clothed his theses in urbane exposition, but he did not relinquish the intention to point out the advantages for everybody of the good life.

Mrs. Stowe and Warner assumed, after all, that they were addressing audiences of people much like themselves. They spoke to them in their own persons. But Mark Twain adopted, not only a pseudonym, but a literary personality that became a guise in which he could more easily make people laugh. He aimed at the "submerged masses" and said he was content if he reached them, regardless of the critical evaluation by cultivated people who passed judgment on his work. In 1889 he wrote to Andrew Lang:

> I have never tried, in even one single little instance to help cultivate the cultivated classes. I was not equipped for it either by native gifts or training, and I never had any ambition in that direction, but always hunted for bigger game — the masses. I have seldom tried deliberately to instruct them, but have done my best to entertain them, for they could get instruction elsewhere. . . My audience is dumb, it has no voice in print, and so I cannot know whether I have won its approbation or only got its censure.[36]

He did not add that he could find out whether his most recent book had found approval by noting the advance sale of his next book, and his statement of intention is too precise to be entirely accurate. But in any case the frontier literature, of which Mark Twain's work in the seventies and eighties is the culmination, was not preoccupied with the moral nature of man. He was himself not inclined to preach as he entertained, and he conceived of his audience as wanting laughter rather than uplift. He too was sufficiently correct in the assumptions natural to him to be able to write as he liked. All three Nook Farm writers were fortunate to be publishing in a time when the appetite for books of all sorts was rapidly increasing. Their commitments to find and keep a substantial public could be discharged without more serious compromise than deference to literary etiquette and the minor requirements of taste.

Each writer of the Nook Farm community, then, wrote to a dimly perceived audience which he considered receptive to the kind of book he felt fitted to write. The most important effect of his dependence on popularity, probably, was to prolong each writer's exploitation of a vein that had proved successful. Since Mrs. Stowe found, in this period, one novel of contemporary society successful, she wrote two more. Warner multiplied his travel books (when he might have been extending his study of American manners), and Mark his humorous sketches, more as a commercially sensible maintenance of inventory than as the expression of an irrepressible creative urge. The choice of subject matter was certainly influenced by the proved success of their first ventures. Any inclination to experiment with technique or materials was modified by the professional caution advising against desertion of the sure thing for the questionable innovation. Thus the pressure of the public, as imagined by the writer committed to keeping his name alive in its mind, tended to confirm other drives to write prolifically as well as to confine the product largely to the staple items of proved market value.

The audience was therefore an important determinant of the volume and the character of the large majority of books issuing from Hartford. Breathing different air, we still read some of these books and try to recapture their social origins. Of crucial importance in such a grasp at history is the influence of the now dispersed readers of these first printings on the prose styles of the Nook Farm writers. Style intangibly resides in the reciprocal relation between the sensibility of the artist and the responsiveness of the audience. The more we know of one pole, the more we learn about the other and about the current running between. Without pausing long on the stylistic accomplishments of the Nook Farm writers, we may note in passing toward a summary of their total literary achievement that they developed their individual use of the language, at least in part, according to their evaluation of their audiences' receptiveness. The prose of each artist (on a higher level) was, of course, also appropriate to his interpretation of the life he recorded and to the achievement of greatness rather than of popularity, but it began simply in the effort not to be literary, but to be intelligible.

As a stylist, Mrs. Stowe was the least conscious craftsman of the group. In her maturity she read very little. She wrote with an instinctive awareness that if she said what needed to be said in the most natural way, her message would go straight to the hearts of her readers. She denied thinking about form as such and contested the charges of professional critics that her work did not always have literary value.[37] Similarly, she paid no attention to syntax. She poured out her books on paper and shipped her manuscript at once to editors who well knew what to expect. They disentangled her sentences as well as they could — rewriting her text on the margins of the proofs, changing diction, correcting solecisms, and transposing phrases. Such was the overriding power of her fluency that the natural flow of her prose was not damaged, and such was the tact of experienced editors like Howells that she was patient and grateful (but not really teachable) under correction. Constant among temporal variables in her style, and perhaps its most influential characteristic, is the chatty informality, ingenuous and friendly, which not only made lucid the frequent shifts of scene and highlighted the amateur ease of a born storyteller but brought the reader into easy sympathy with her purpose.[38] She talked down to no one, in spite of her missionary motives, and with more sincerity than art appealed to the understanding of her great public by taking it into her confidence. Her manner was down-to-earth, her informality was enlivened and extended by her humor, and her style, quaint as it seems now, is still attractive in its very lack of art.

Warner's simple style is similarly keyed to what he had to say and to whom —rather than to the literary tradition of which he was much more conscious than Mrs. Stowe. He, too, was not highly skilled in the technical niceties of syntax and sentence construction, in spite of his academic training at Hamilton.[39] But more deliberately than Mrs. Stowe, he formulated a principle of style already in use by all the writers of Nook Farm. In an essay, "Simplicity,"[40] he canonizes lucidity as the basic objective of all language and the most important criterion of enduring literature. He suspected any prose that called attention to itself. In his reviews he constantly deplored elaborate writing and praised simple phrasing; in his own works he avoided ornamental figurativeness altogether. Warner's style is the instrument of utility, then, rather than of verbal beauty. He lent his authority as critic and creator to support the development of an Amercian prose style which since the eighteenth century had moved from relatively elaborate circular sentences toward the linear spareness now approved. It is difficult to measure Warner's influence in a modernization that would have taken place without him, but in his time he adapted the vehicle of his ideas to what he considered a demand for intelligibility by his reading public. Informality as well as simplicity was also his habit, particularly in the personal essays in which he was at his best.

The unpretentiousness of Mrs. Stowe's and Warner's prose — its utilitarian, simple clarity serving as a tool for intelligibility — was well adapted to the necessity for reaching effortlessly an audience schooled in a democratically literate rather than aristocratically specialized interest in literature. Their plainness was also keyed to the element of instruction in their works. Just as the seventeenth-century divines, who wrote an elegantly obscure prose in works addressed to their colleagues and to the connoisseur, preached in the pulpit in words of few syllables and sentences of one simple idea, so Harriet Beecher Stowe, aiming at the susceptibilities of a mass of readers, knew that people do not heed a teaching they do not understand. The effective plea for moral behavior requires a style that permits instant comprehension.

With lucidity as the basic requirement, Harriet's purpose is manifested in two developments, each adapted to a particular sensibility. Her emotional fervency was in her slavery novels expressed in a set of stylistic devices and religious images that presumed a reader-responsiveness to direct and passionate exhortation. As religious belief proliferated into varieties of creeds obscuring the ironclad morality of Calvinism, Harriet responded by adopting gradually a style more casual, less fervent, and even more transparently plain. It was during this transition to exhortation by implication rather than by fervent imperatives that Warner began to write. His prose is almost without Biblical reference. Informality, desirable also in the effective communication of a didactic message, found different expressions in Mrs. Stowe and in Warner. Harriet, in her later as in her earlier style, maintained always the cozy intimacy of the next-door neighbor. Warner's informality was always somewhat more impersonal, as if it would be an effrontery, for example, to imply that a reader needed the correction recommended for offenders at large. His informality carefully refrained from presuming too much, for the audience of post-Civil War years was perhaps more sophisticated than it had been and less susceptible to obviously moral appeals.

Ethical instruction had nothing to do with the clarity of Mark Twain's style. The lucidity and the vigor of his prose stemmed from his use of the vernacular. Since his style was roughly an adaptation to authorship of the speech of American people, its simplicity is perhaps more the actual language of the public than a condescending adaptation of a literary style to that public. Whatever the implications in its origin, Mark's style was clear as water. His point of view toward exactness of diction and preciseness of meaning was highly conscious. His criticism of himself and of other writers always began and usually ended in considering the quality of the English. He sought perfection in the attainment of complete intelligibility. His style developed from the tumbled mediocrity of his early sketches, through the supple swiftness he developed in the Hartford period, to an epigrammatic precision in his later years. In the period that we are now examining, he constantly guarded against slovenliness and tried to make his prose economical, his choice of words exact, and his sentences short. He wrote Howells in 1875:

> In spite of myself, how awkwardly I do jumble words together; and how often I do use three words when one would answer — a thing I am always trying to guard against. I shall become as slovenly a writer as Charles Francis Adams, if I don't look out. (That is said in jest; because of course I do not seriously fear getting so bad as that. I never shall drop so far toward his and Bret Harte's level as to catch myself saying "It must have been wiser to have believed that he might have accomplished it if he could have felt that he would have been supported by those who should have &c. &c. &c.") [41]

In 1890 he contributed to a manual for beginning writers another characteristic comment:

> One notices, for instance, that long, involved sentences confuse him, and that he is obliged to reread them to get the sense. Unconsciously he accustoms himself to writing short sentences as a rule. At times he may indulge himself with a long one, but he will make sure that there are no folds in it, no vaguenesses, no parenthetical interruptions of its view as a whole; when he is done with it, it won't be a sea-serpent, with half of its arches under the water, it will be a torch-light procession.
>
> Well, also he will notice in the course of time, as his reading goes on, that the difference between the *almost right* and the *right* word is really a large matter — 'tis the difference between the lightning bug and the lightning. After that, of course, that exceedingly important brick the *exact* word — however, this is running into an essay, and I beg pardon. So I have seemed to have arrived at this, doubtless I have methods, but they begot themselves, in which case I am only their proprietor, not their father.[42]

Developing his incisive lucidity with his audience in mind, Mark recognized that clarity was essential to reach the "submerged masses." It was not to inculcate a moral teaching that he tried to make them instantly aware of everything he was saying. But just as Mrs. Stowe knew that an uncomprehending sinner was not likely to be reformed, so Mark was sure that a confused reader could not be entertained.

Mark Twain's style, designed also as a practical instrument to reach his audience, is a far greater artistic achievement than that of his neighbors. Its strength and brilliant informality, its concreteness and particularity, and beyond those qualities a less tangible energy which frequently makes his prose as atmospherically emotional as literally accurate, make his prose one of the great styles of our literature. Shaped by a diversity of influences, more of them from life than from books, it matured under Mark Twain's determination that it be inconspicuous, transparent, and precise in the reproduction of ideas or of American speech. The impetus behind his verbal perfectionism was the pressing need to be fully understood by a nation of ordinary people, whose sensibility he shared and whose attention he wished to engage. Like his neighbors, he enlarged the "literary" notion of style to make it a vehicle suitable for carrying the substance of his books everywhere to everyone, but among the Nook Farm writers, he alone achieved a style that would in a later generation be at its best entirely effective. The prose of Mrs. Stowe's New England novels has now only a historic relevance to their subject, effective as it remains in spite of its archaic rhythms. Warner's prose is not read at all, as it happens, though for reasons that do not discredit his contribution to the evolution of the written language.

Evaluation of the professionalism of the Nook Farm writers, it is clear, involves more than the simple assumption that writing books for money is entirely separate from the creation of permanent art. It would be absurd to say that these artists composed only to accumulate cash. The obligations of the Nook Farm colony for constant production are important not as the *only* conditions of their literary activity, but as the surest guide to a fuller understanding of the virtues and defects of books in which we remain interested. Their preoccupation with the necessities of literary success in their own time did not prevent free utterance of what was in them, but it quite obviously affected their literary product as a whole. It determined habits of work as relevant to the creation of their good books as to the construction of the inferior commodity we have examined so far.

The far reaches to which the guildsmen of Nook Farm carried their professionalism were mapped not only by an age in which the dissemination of books approached the dimensions of mass production but by the commercial culture of Hartford. The subscription publishing business had much to do with enlarging the reading public. The impact of the world of business—whether manifested in insurance, firearms manufacture, or bookmaking—had important effects on the artists who had allied themselves closely to their own place and adapted themselves more or less competently to their own climate. The necessity for making a prosperous living made the final creative achievement of these writers in many ways accidental. In such an environment, their important work could not be the culmination of a long, conscientious development toward consciously perceived goals attainable only after abstemious conservation of creative power. Constant writing, necessary for a dependable income, must involve a blunting of critical self-perception. Otherwise much that is written cannot be allowed to appear in print. The Nook Farm writers must have had to believe that what they were writing was better than it usually was, or their efficiency would have fallen and much of what was published would have been uneconomically suppressed. At any rate, neither Mrs. Stowe, nor Warner, nor Mark Twain developed discrimination with which to separate good work from trash and, actually, had little occasion to do so. It seems chiefly a lucky chance that so much (rather than so little) of their product is good enough to remain alive. And it is no longer surprising that the few good books are marred with otherwise puzzling defects.

Perhaps even more important than the overtolerant self-criticism that professionalism of this variety requires and thus may encourage is the dissipation of time and energy in books written under economic and social pressures. The shortcomings of the major works that we will eventually consider accrue from strength wasted on inferior manuscripts. Mark Twain's best books are victims of his inclination to write what came most easily and most rapidly. If a *Huckleberry Finn* ceased to grow by itself after four hundred manuscript pages, Mark laid it aside to write *A Tramp Abroad*, unaware not only that he was trifling with immortality but that his abandoned novel had any merit at all. As a result of a lack of discipline that may be associated with a compulsion to write the most in the least time, his work is imperfect in form. Rather than thinking his materials through to inevitable structure, he turned, without knowing he was compromising final success, to another idea which he would develop furiously until again, as he said, the tank ran dry. All the Nook Farm writers made exorbitant demands on their talents to produce dozens of books rather than conserving their gifts for the completion and the revision of a few.

That the Nook Farm colony consisted of professional writers rather than deliberate artists is a simple fact, then, that expands on examination to explain much. Their professionalism is not to be deplored so much as understood. It contributed to the development of an effective style. It permitted Harriet Beecher Stowe and Charles Dudley Warner to conform to the New England literary tradition; it allowed Mark Twain to develop independently in different genres. It did not smother the individuality or the genius of these writers. On the other hand, it makes the emergence of *Huckleberry Finn* or *Oldtown Folks* a complicated phenomenon occurring in spite of the mediocrity that usually attended Mark Twain and Mrs. Stowe as they plied their trade. Whatever its importance in the criticism of the total product of Nook Farm, it illustrates the appropriateness of the product to the time and place in which it was produced. The interdependence of these artists and their community is most clearly demonstrated, perhaps, in the adaptation of their literary skill to the maintenance of their status as prosperous citizens of Hartford.

The Nook Farm Writers as Commentators on Contemporary Society

THE PROFESSIONALISM OF THE HARTFORD WRITERS INEVITABLY IMPLIES A SUBscription to the ideals of their own generation. Its source in their identification of literary success with Hartford's social standards suggests an intimate involvement in the complexity of their time which would impair their ability to discern its pattern. The Nook Farm writers had little inclination to assume an intellectually detached attitude toward their generation. But their detailed experience with disintegrative multiplicity precipitated ideas about their own era that comprise the interesting if not particularly profound criticism of society preserved in their books of the seventies and eighties.

After Harriet Beecher Stowe published *Oldtown Folks*, her most significant evaluation of ancient New England, she turned her attention immediately from past to present. She poured her opinions of the latter into three novels—*Pink and White Tyranny* and *My Wife and I* (both published in 1871) and *We and Our Neighbors* of 1873. The cast of all three books was generally the New York "smart set," to which Harriet apparently had no exposure except in her visits to friends and relatives in the city. Her opinions may not have been based on extensive experience, but they did not lack positiveness on that account.

Pink and White Tyranny is the story of Lillie Ellis, petted, beautiful, brainless, and ultimately unworthy — the specimen of the kind of woman, Harriet said, that current social ideals were producing.

> She was the daughter and flower of the Christian civilization of the nineteenth century and the kind of woman, that, on the whole, men of quite distinguished sense have been fond of choosing for wives, and will go on seeking to the end of the chapter.[43]

After Lillie marries John Seymour for his money, she commits every modern sin. She redecorates her husband's comfortable old house according to the French taste. She escapes from his respectable village to Newport, where she revels in idleness, flirtation, and sly cigarette smoking. In New York, where she comes under the influence of Civil War profiteers, she is entangled in high society. Back in her village, she undermines its stability by poisoning the minds of young folk with a glamorous reception. Because she does not assist her husband in his benevolent direction of its affairs, his mill fails and his business is ruined. John Seymour, discovering even that his wife has lied about her age, finally realizes her shallowness. He faces his disillusion like a man and devotes himself to her regeneration. Lillie gradually responds, produces three children (more or less by the way), and becomes a chronic invalid. As she sinks slowly she learns of her selfishness, discovers at last the meaning of love, and dies beautifully. The new Lillie, her eldest daughter, is all that the mother might have been.

Among the hundreds of similar books written at this time, it would be hard, though not impossible, to find a more elaborate *non sequitur*. But as a record of Harriet's opinions in the seventies, *Pink and White Tyranny* is the fascinating vehicle of her miscellaneous reactions to social developments after the Civil War. It provides her with the opportunity to point out that love, my dear ladies, is *self-sacrifice*, that happiness cannot result from selfishness, and that fascination by the shallow glitter of high society must be resisted. In choosing a life mate, a man must ignore superficial beauty and examine his prospective bride for plainer virtues and genuine compatibility. To smoke cigarettes is as unwise as to feed babies from a bottle; both practices, furthermore, are immoral. To maintain a paternalistic interest in one's employees is sounder business than to exploit them impersonally. To live in a quiet, conservative village surrounded by hospitality, affection, and community loyalty is fundamentally more rewarding than to pine for city excitements. But once one has made a marital mistake, one must make the best of it.

"We informed our readers in the beginning," Harriet points out at the end, that *Pink and White Tyranny* is not a novel, but a story with a moral; and, as people pick all sorts of strange morals out of stories, we intend to put conspicuously into our story exactly what the moral of it is.[44]

The chief moral (she had provided material for so many that it was well to emphasize her main point) is that divorce, morally wrong, is never an alternative a man or woman may adopt, no matter how grievous his plight or how permanent the incompatibility.[45]

If the sacredness of the marriage-contract did not hold, if the Church and all good men and all good women did not uphold it with their might and main, it is easy to see where the career of many women like Lillie would end. Men have the power to reflect before the choice is made; and that is the only proper time foı reflection.[46]

Those who suffer must do so for the public good. Harriet had recorded her protest against dissolution of the pre-War stability of family, against the worldliness of the wealthy, against feminine selfishness and male stupidity, and had asserted her persevering determination to check, if she possibly could, the mistaken course of society. It was producing too many women like Lillie Ellis.

After this instructive picture of the consequences of yielding to modern temptations, Harriet turned her attention in *My Wife and I* and its sequel, *We and Our Neighbors*, to the happier adventures of young people of good breeding and intentions. *My Wife and I* rose out of the women's rights controversy to mark Harriet's opposition to the crusade to which her sister Isabella had lately committed herself. In the preface she says that the purpose of the book is to "show the embarrassment of the young champion of progressive principles, in meeting the excesses of modern reformers." The latter group will be represented by a modern young woman of "advanced ideas and behavior." Harriet makes her male narrator say,

I trust that Miss Anthony and Mrs. Stanton, and all the prophetesses of our day, will remark the humility and propriety of my title. It is not I and My Wife — oh no! It is My Wife and I. What am I, and what is my father's house, that I should go before my wife in anything?

The story is simply the record of a high-minded young journalist named Harry, who is attempting to establish himself in New York City and to win the hand of the equally high-minded Eva, daughter of a fine old family. But, as Harry points out, "it is not so much the story, as the things it gives the author a chance to say." His courtship gives Harriet ample opportunity to expound further her doctrine of womanhood and its responsibilities. Eva has a sister named Ida, who is the Harriet Beecher Stowe type of feminist — a girl who has educated herself widely and seriously and who dislikes the simpering role that modern society has assigned to women. Ida takes Harry and Eva to "a sort of New-Dispensation Salon" held weekly by Mrs. Stella Cerulean, a brilliant and charming woman who

> felt herself called to the modern work of society regeneration, and went into it with all the enthusiasm of her nature, and with all that certainty of success which comes from an utter want of practical experience.[47]

Mrs. Cerulean led a set inspired by the spirit of martyrdom but without a precise idea of how to get martyred effectively. Its members daily indulged in spiritual communications and maintained that marriage relations ought to be terminated whenever either husband or wife grew tired of the routine. Audacia Dangereyes, a hussy who storms into Harry's room one night, paws him familiarly, calls him "Bub," and invites him to drop by her room sometime for a smoke, is introduced as the bold female promised in the preface. Mrs. Cerulean, a respectable woman, welcomes Audacia as a valuable recruit for her campaign to establish the superiority of women.[48] This alliance shocks Ida, who withdraws from her tentative participation in feminism and dedicates herself to further study; before women qualify for the ballot they must attain a superior education and culture. Suffrage, she thinks, is to be the result of gradual evolution rather than destructive revolution. And no impulse to reform can justify handling with coarse fingers "every holy secret of human nature, all those subjects of which the grace and the Power consist in their exquisite delicacy and tender refinement." [49] Organized feminists picture society as a pack of breeding animals and wish to eliminate all laws and institutions.

My Wife and I, besides expressing the point of view on feminism and the development of woman through education that Harriet worked out in Nook Farm, reflects also her attitude toward spiritualism. Although she disapproves (without much elaboration) of Mrs. Cerulean's séances, she is not surprised when Harry dreams that his childhood sweetheart comes to him from heaven and says she still lives.

> Right along side of this troublous life, that is seen and temporal, may be the green pastures and the still waters of the unseen and eternal, and they who know us better than we know them, can at any time step across that little rill that we call Death, to minister to our comfort.[50]

In her comments on some of the developments of American life after the Civil War, she does not deny possibility for change in current ideas about the spiritual world and the enlargement of woman's sphere. But the organized spiritualists and feminists are pushing too precipitately toward their goals in too violent an upheaval of the moral order.

We and Our Neighbors follows Harry and Eva through their domestic bliss with a minuteness we need not emulate. The book is again an omnibus of social comment — this time not against feminism but in favor of happy marriages, hospitable, sensible, enlightened homemaking, charity for servants and for fallen women, friendly relations with one's neighbors, kindness to animals, and, once again, faithful adherence to the Christian religion. She elaborates her comment on divorce beyond the dogma of *Pink and White Tyranny* to find that the problem is connected with the "fact" that human beings are more different one from the other than they used to be.

> In times when the human being was little developed, the elements of agreement and disagreement were simpler, and marriages were proportionately more tranquil. But modern civilized man has a thousand points of possible discord in an immutable near relation where there was one in the primitive ages. The wail, and woe, and struggle to undo marriage bonds in our day, comes from this dissonance of more developed and more widely varying natures . . .[51]

Eva and Harry are a perfectly matched couple. Their life together is a model of what modern matrimony should be.

For the first time in these sprightly novels, Harriet has a good deal to say of religion in the modern world. She makes fun of the decorous observance of religious ceremonies in New York's best churches:

> The responses of the worshipers were given in decorous whispers that scarcely disturbed the solemn stillness; for when a congregation of the best-fed and best-bred people of New York on their knees declare themselves "miserable sinners," it is a matter of delicacy to make as little disturbance about it as possible.

But since religion is primarily a personal application of the teachings of Christ to everyday life, the disappearance of public fervency is not alarming. Church services provide the opportunity, if the preacher is effective, for auxiliary inspiration and for a retreat from the hurly-burly of the streets. In this connection, not even the most stringent Protestant, Harriet tolerantly points out, can

> fail to honor that rich and grand treasury of the experience of devout spirits of which the Romish church has been the custodian. The hymns and prayers and pious meditations which come to us through this channel are particularly worthy of a cherishing remembrance in this dusty, materialistic age.

And the Episcopal church has a good deal of the Catholic devoutness, for Episcopacy is the half-way house to Rome. She carries this flowering tolerance, paralleled in her own religious experience, to her view of the alleged gulf between Christianity and everyday life. Though it is said, she told herself, that the Christian religion is losing its hold on society, actually

> there never was a time when faith in Christianity was so deep and all-pervading, and when it was working in so many minds as a disturbing force. The main thing which is now perplexing modern society is the effect which is making to reduce the teachings of the New Testament to actual practice in life, and to regulate society by them. There is no scepticism as to the ends sought by Jesus in human life. Nobody doubts that love is the fulfilling of the law, and that to do as we would be done by, applied universally, would bring back the Golden Age, if ever such ages were . . . In a world where is always ruin and misery, where the inexperienced are ensnared and the blind misled, and where fatal and inexpiable penalties follow every false step, there must be a band of redeemers, seekers, and savers of the lost . . . and here is just the problem that our own age and day present to the thoughtful person who, having professed in whatever church or creed, to be a Christian, wishes to make a reality of that profession.[52]

Eva joins the redeeming band by rescuing a prostitute. Presumably we should all do the same.

So Harriet's novels of contemporary manners in urban America, after a detailed record of modern domesticity and shifting social backgrounds, return to her central concern with religion. The love of Christ becomes the lodestar in the confusion of materialism, and following the gleam is the course recommended to those who find themselves drifting into the errors of modern times. Mrs. Stowe's social criticism is confined to divergences from Christian behavior, which she saw multiplying far too rapidly. She recognized that the world of her maturity was not the "simple state of society" of her childhood, that the age of steam brought with it "individual peculiarities which are the result of the stimulated brains and nervous systems of modern society," and that the "throng and rush of modern society" provoked "a thousand stimulants to excitement,"[53] but calm faith in the love of the Redeemer, persisting through the furor, could enable anyone to achieve victory over the perplexities besetting him in the clangorous world of the 1870's.

The work of Charles Dudley Warner comprising his comment on his own time consists of a trilogy of thoughtful novels and two sets of essays — one a personal and uncritical reproduction of the life of his own neighborhood and the other a more formal evaluation of national developments. It is interesting that the life of Nook Farm provided the materials for his best work, three books ripening out of his personal compatibility with his neighbors and secondarily from his literary admiration of Charles Lamb and Washington Irving.

In the late sixties, most of the residents of Nook Farm installed on their property small kitchen gardens, the tending of which for a few years was a pleasant hobby. As Warner hoed in his own little plot, his thoughts must have turned automatically to the literary usefulness of his recreation, and soon he was printing a weekly light essay in the *Courant*. The comparison of his contest with frost, fertilizers, birds, snakes, cows, chickens, and insects with the struggles of other amateur horticulturists grew into a neighborhood joke and a subject for table talk and afternoon conferences in the quiet summer months. Warner's record was an almost literal account of his season's gardening, treated with the lightness and humor that characterized the conversation of the neighborhood. He made gardening a mock allegory of Calvinism. The principal value of a private garden is not to provide vegetables and fruits, but to teach the higher virtues, hope deferred, and expectations blighted. "The garden thus becomes a moral agent, as it was in the beginning." Total depravity is represented by snake-grass and pusley. The stern man of Geneva appears as the black cat given the Warners by the Stowes. He was named Calvin for the gravity, morality, and uprightness with which he kept the birds away from the peas. The moral qualities of vegetables and their relative social rank provide material for making fun of the social peccadilloes of cultivated society. "The cucumber . . . is a low comedian in a company where the melon is a minor gentleman." Lettuce resembles conversation. Like most talkers, it runs quickly to seed but sometimes comes to a head, "growing more solid and satisfying and tender at the same time, and whiter at the center, and crisp in . . . maturity." Vegetables, like people, must avoid the appearance of evil, or they will be rooted out with the weeds. Warner brings the Darwinian principle of natural selection to bear on gardening problems and refers to feminism and to his opinion of the ballot for women in his affectionate portrait of his wife's helplessness with the hoe. Two clergymen (they would be Twichell and Burton) come to watch him in the moral contest with vegetable depravity, but the educated clergy seem to lack the disposition to hoe. President Grant arrived in Nook Farm to visit Hawley. Warner asked him

> if he wouldn't like to come down our way Sunday afternoon, and take a plain, simple look at my garden, eat a little lemon ice-cream and jelly-cake, and drink a glass of native lager-bier.[54]

Grant came. Warner reports the slow but witty conversation in the garden and records that Grant found the visit an unexpected pleasure and would remember it as his choicest memory of New England. Many other neighborhood events found their way into his papers. Perhaps the best essay is the last, in which the gardener clears the vegetation in October, mulches the strawberries, and turns away, writing *Resurgam* on the gatepost. And Calvin also leaves the garden for the house. It is time to light a wood fire on the hearth. A mouse in the kitchen is worth two birds gone south.

Henry Ward Beecher, who also visited the garden and later read the *Courant* pieces it prompted, wrote J. R. Osgood in 1870 to suggest publication in book form. He prepared an arch introduction which effectively, though unintentionally, heightens the cool lightness and the absence of coyness in Warner's unpretentious papers. In the use of his personal experience against the background of informality and affectionate congeniality in his own neighborhood, Warner discovered his most appropriate genre — the small essay that depends for its charm on humor and personality. His slightest work was not only his most popular, but his best. *My Summer in a Garden* had a tremendous success. Its popularity lay in the attractiveness of the life he was living, the humor with which he understated the large topics of the day as he plied his hoe, and the charm of leisurely and satisfying living he evoked in "the play of color and bloom [not only among the vegetables but throughout the neighborhood] which is called among the Alps the afterglow." [55] The afterglow was vastly important in the more memorable work of the Hartford writers, whose experience acquired a deep meaning only when mellowed by the emotion that accompanies reminiscence.

So successful and so effortless was Warner's first book that he began almost at once to record the hearth-side winter conversation of Nook Farm in a further series of essays published a year later as *Backlog Studies*.[56] In it he attempts to capture the "unwearying flow of argument, quaint remark, humorous color, and sprightly interchange of sentiments and opinions called conversation" and to present in no special order the substance of that conversation. The fire on the hearth, dying out in New England in favor of graceless gas logs and suffocating hot-air heating, provides well-being to kindle the domestic virtues and the powers of conversation. In Boston being well dressed provides a satisfaction that religion cannot give; the equivalent in Nook Farm is being warmed by a wood fire. The talk picks up on the subject of the current generation's ingenuity in excluding air from assembly places and houses — an intention foiled only by the "ill-fitting, insincere work of the builders, who build for a day, and charge for all time." From topic to topic the talk rambles, from the Concord school of philosophy —

You know that in Concord the latest news, except a remark or two by Thoreau or Emerson, is the Vedas. I believe the Rig-Veda is read at the breakfast-table instead of the Boston journals

—to New England weather—

I wish I could fitly celebrate the joyousness of the New England winter. Perhaps I could if I more thoroughly believed in it . . . We are made provident and sagacious by the fickleness of our climate . . . Our literature, politics, religion, show the effect of unsettled weather.[57]

The people who are quoted in the book can be identified. Warner is the Fire Tender, Susan is the Mistress, the Parson is presumably Twichell, with the slightly querulous humor of Bushnell merged into the characterization. The Next-Door Neighbor, whose opinions are the most unconventional, is quite clearly Mark Twain, who speaks on one occasion as follows:

I tried a Sunday School book once; but I made the good boy end in the poorhouse, and the bad boy go to Congress; and the publisher said it wouldn't do. The public wouldn't stand that sort of thing. Nobody but the good go to Congress.[58]

The characters called Mandeville and Herbert I do not recognize, but they are undoubtedly drawn also from life. The conservatism of Francis Gillette is reflected in a remark the Fire Tender makes: "A witty conservative once said to me, that we never shall have peace in this country until we elect a colored woman president." Warner's predilection for honest rather than predatory business appears in these remarks:

I confess I have a soft place in my heart for that rare character in our New England life who is content with the world as he finds it, and who does not attempt to appropriate any more of it to himself than he absolutely needs from day to day.

And his optimistic conviction prompts him to observe:

The longer I live the more I am impressed with the excess of human kindness over human hatred, and the greater willingness to oblige than to disoblige that one meets at every turn.[59]

Backlog Studies is good reading for one interested in exploring the day-to-day life that Mark Twain reveled in, but as literature it suffers from the defect that Warner clearly realized. The impermanence and extemporary fitness of fireside talk, which owes its attractiveness to an intangible combination of each person's mood, his appreciation of his friends, and the interaction of personal qualities, cannot be fully recorded in print. It represents development for Warner from the bucolic simplicity of *My Summer in a Garden* to a more complex kind of essay (in which appears the influence of Oliver Wendell Holmes), but the results are not as continuously interesting as the earlier book. There is, however, a life in *Backlog Studies* that has departed forever from his travel books.

It was some time before Warner's participation in the experience of his neighborhood reappeared between covers. *In the Wilderness* (1878) grew out of the summer life in the Adirondacks in which he and Bushnell and Twichell took such great pleasure. More miscellaneous and uneven than its two predecessors, this book is in places funnier than either. "How I Killed a Bear," in which Warner fully realized the ludicrousness of his encounter with a wild animal, is an amusing sketch. That an amiable and peaceful man like himself should be eaten by a bear was no less absurd than that he should succeed, as he did, in killing one. Summer experiences of being lost in the woods, of hunting the deer (here he becomes sentimental about the doe's sacrifice in leading the dogs away from her fawn and indignant about the heartlessness of civilization, which aims to tame or kill), and of camping outdoors are mildly interesting as description of the summer recreation of Nook Farm folk. Warner did not return again to the informal essay until he wrote *As We Go* and *As We Were Saying*.

Warner's comments on life outside his immediate circle make less attractive books than his noncritical essays, but, as embodied in another half-dozen books of the seventies and eighties, they turn to more serious use his observation of what he thought the world was coming to. Like Mrs Stowe, he accepted equably the universe in which he found himself, but like her he was impelled to point out what he considered imperfect. With an urbane sincerity quite different from Mrs. Stowe's naïveté, he urged individual self-cultivation and adherence to personal integrity in a world which he felt was being distracted from the ideal by the practical. The central message of his comment on a materialistic age was this:

> Whatever the greatness of the nation, whatever the accumulation of wealth the worth of the world to us is exactly the worth of our individual lives.[60]

The most worthy pursuit a person can engage in is attainment of the good life. Success in that endeavor involves not only good intentions but keen perception of ideals of conduct persisting through distracting social change. The democratic idea has limitations. Its basic doctrine, equality of opportunity, prompts men to devote their lives to getting ahead in the world. The struggle for material success reduces individuality to mediocrity, cancels individual differences, and sterilizes cultural inclinations. Just as it was more subtle than Mrs. Stowe's, Warner's criticism of society was probably more perceptive.

It is appropriate that Warner should approach the evaluation of his own times through the medium of literary criticism and that as a literary critic he should consider literature not so much as esthetic experience as an opportunity to understand society. He said in the title essay of *The Relation of Literature to Life*:

> All genuine, enduring literature is the outcome of the time that produces it, is responsive to the general sentiment of its time; this close relation to human life insures its welcome ever after as a true representation of human nature . . . consequently the most remunerative method of studying a literature is to study the people for whom it was produced.[61]

The test of any piece of literature is the universality of its appeal to human nature. In order for modern fiction to appeal permanently, Warner wrote again in 1883, literature must idealize nature. The failure of contemporary novels, he was convinced, was that their unidealized view of society made no allowance for the existence of high principles of which everyone must recognize the validity even if he has difficulty seeing evidence of them in the practical world. Beneath all literary fads and the social flux producing them, an imperishable artistic standard persists. Certain immutable principles have developed during the history of literary criticism. The artist's job is to ascertain these principles and apply them to our changing life; the critic's task is to mark whether the artist's performance conforms to the eternal qualities. These are simplicity (including clarity of expression), knowledge of human nature, and charm of personality. The last of these gives the final value to any work of art. Study of the classics of literature enables a man to see more clearly the permanent values which must not be submerged in the temporal confusion of society. Warner believed that the age in which he wrote — "completely adrift in regard to the relations of the supernatural and the material, the ideal and the real" — was too harassed for the production of pure literature, but a citizen attempting to understand life and come to terms with it could turn to the undying literature written in an age before writers began to address their works fruitlessly to the mood "of unrest, of questioning, to the scientific spirit and to the shifting attitudes of social change and reform."[62]

But though Warner recognized the uncertainty of his time and its effect on individuals attempting to adjust themselves to it, he was, of course, not really pessimistic about the future. In the early 1870's he was somewhat more optimistic than he was to be in his old age. Immediately after finishing *The Gilded Age*, in which he had helped Mark satirize the behavior of speculators and the dishonesty of politicians, he asserted his confidence that in every *essential* the America of 1874 was far advanced over that of fifty years earlier:

> I have no doubt that this [age] is better than that, in manners, in morality, in charity and toleration, in education and religion. I know the standard of morality is higher. I know the churches are purer.[63]

In 1974 Americans will look back a century to say that the era after the Civil War was crude, disorderly, and fermenting with new projects, but that sound progress was under way. Warner prophesied the growth of a more universal faith in humanity and a firmer belief in life beyond the grave.

As time matured Warner's own faith in humanity and in progress, he was never to relinquish this view, but increasingly he emphasized the defections of his generation from the progress he thought possible. Though he believed material progress was being accompanied by intellectual advance, he was disconcerted by the more obvious evidence for the former than the latter. For one thing he became concerned with the social consequences of equality. The dogmas of the Declaration of Independence were being applied without taking account of their shortcomings. The principle that fifty-one ignorant men can legislate for forty-nine intelligent men is false. The opinions of the majority are binding only if they conform to the principles of justice. Attaining the ideal society, he asserted, requires taking into account the differing intellectual capacities of men and women. The distinctions between sexes, between races, should be retained.[64] The disastrous effect of the notion of equality has been a growing discontent among the mass of mankind. Though the laboring classes are better off than ever before in the history of the world, never have they been so restive, so inclined to strike. The unrest comes from their notion that they, like the successful men who rise to riches in an industrial age, should be able to attain wealth. The essential problem in the capital-labor agitation is to find a way to cultivate in employers a sympathy for their workers as men and to foster in laborers an interest in their work beyond the money they receive.[65]

Warner found the urge to make money even more discouraging among the rich than among the laboring classes. The conservatism of his Federalist position toward labor did not blind him to the excesses of capital. The desire to accumulate money by manipulation and the debilitating effect on society of greed began to be the whole theme of his serious discourse toward

HARRIET BEECHER STOWE

THE HARRIET BEECHER STOWE HOUSE

CHARLES DUDLEY WARNER AT ABOUT 40

THE CHARLES DUDLEY WARNER HOUSE

the end of the eighties. But he carried on at the same time a related study of manners which appears in three lighter books — *Their Pilgrimage* (1887), *As We Go* (1891), and *As We Were Saying* (1894). The first of these was commissioned by J. H. Harper as a text for the drawings of Reinhart. The artist and a fictional narrator in pursuit of fashionable recreation combined with courtship make a tour of all the summer resorts. The improbable framework enables Warner to comment on the well-to-do classes at play and on the conflict of the newly rich with the established aristocracy. The snobbery of Newport, the idiosyncrasies of American vacationers, and the vanity everywhere are illustrated in great detail. Warner is amused by a rich woman who says "I'm provincial. It is the most difficult thing to be in these levelling days," by a wealthy Midwesterner who sits on one hotel piazza after another talking real estate ("It's about all there is to talk of"), and by the row of millionaires sunning themselves in black broadcloth and white hats on the porch of the United States Hotel at Saratoga, saying little but looking rich.[66] The detail of this book is interesting, the story as a whole absurd. Henry James, seeing a promising attempt to examine American manners, was interested in it as in nothing else coming out of Nook Farm.[67]

As We Were Saying and *As We Go* are collections of Warner's contributions to "The Editor's Drawer" of *Harper's* magazine. They combine the manner of his personal essays about the life of Nook Farm with the kind of observation recorded in *Their Pilgrimage*. Civilization is too heavy a topic for the Drawer, he said, but even there some of its characteristics claim his attention. He finds that the individuality lost in a society demanding devotion to material objectives, for example, is also threatened by refinement, for it is always easier to persist in the "subordination of one's personality to the strictly conventional life" than to strike out on an independent course. *As We Go* is a further compilation of miscellaneous comment on life in the United States. The fact that

> culture in this country is full of surprises, and so doubles and feints and comes back upon itself that the most diligent recorder can scarcely note its changes [68]

does not really limit the cheerfulness with which he records one set of cultural characteristics after another. The only addition he makes to ideas already cited from his earlier books is the assumption by women of intellectual development while men devote themselves to business. Women congregate in esoteric societies to dig up all sorts of literature and history for final judgment.

> In every little village there is this intellectual stir and excitement; why, even in New York, readings interfere with the german; and Boston! Boston is no longer divided into wards, but into Browning sections.[69]

Women may be taking the virility out of literature, since all the novels are written by, for, and about women, but in their interest in the arts there is something more hopeful than the blind instinct of young men for preserving themselves in the world. These struggling youths are unable to take advantage of the good they might derive from the prevailing culture of the female leisure class.

But though this pair of little books is readable and the comments on nineteenth-century life in their longer predecessors interesting, Warner's closest and most effective study of American life is *A Little Journey in the World*. In the first full-fledged novel he wrote by himself, Warner summed up in 1889 the results of twenty years of observation. *A Little Journey* is the first volume of a trilogy tracing the accumulation and dissipation of a great fortune. The events he imagined provide opportunity for analysis of deterioration in those succumbing to the ideals of the plutocracy — wealth, power, and social position.[70] Harry Henderson, an intelligent young man without scruples, becomes one of the three or four great capitalists of the country. He is married to Margaret DeBree, who had been brought up in the New England ethical tradition. Margaret adopts the principles of her husband, is converted to the gay whirl of the very rich, and, without having found happiness, dies in childbirth. Such is the simple story. Like the narrative in Mrs. Stowe's society novels, it was designed as the vehicle of ideas.

The story opens in a New England city named Brandon (clearly Hartford) where the life and the ideals of a small neighborhood (Nook Farm) are described to serve as a contrast to the world Margaret is soon to enter. The ideas floating about this friendly community are among those we have already examined. The change in religious observance is illustrated by the role of the neighborhood church as a headquarters for charity, sewing circles, sociability, and good feeling rather than worship.[71] The women's rights movement wanders in and out of the dialogue. Thus Margaret wants to be neither a sheriff nor a locomotive engineer, but she does desire "the freedom of my own being, to be interested in everything in the world, to feel its life as men do," and to do good in the world. In their comfortable libraries, the Brandon neighbors discuss spiritualism and religious cultism.

The scene shifts from the leisurely and mellow life of Nook Farm to the relentlessly busy social life of New York. In an extension of his studies in manners, Warner describes the fascination for Margaret of the operas, teas, dinners, and "four o'clocks" (devoted, for example, to the plight of the unmarried women of India), of the gallantry, mutual admiration, and gaiety of high society. For a time Margaret is bothered by a feeling that somehow New York is really smaller than Brandon. She remembers with disquiet the opinions of her neighbors that the rich are vulgar, that manipulators deliberately ruin the small businesses such as thrived in Brandon, and that no large fortune is honestly come by. But soon after her marriage to Henderson she begins to lose her Brandon integrity and to share the amorality of her husband.

Henderson's career, sensationally successful after his alliance with a low-brow tycoon, includes manipulations in railroad stocks that bring ruin to thousands of small investors. His partner "reasons" with Congressmen who would interfere with new enterprises and "induces" them to take an interest in what was "demonstrably for the public good." [72] Margaret learns even to accept this procedure as natural and necessary. Her husband buys a steam yacht, indulges in public charities, and travels in a special train to a colored college to dedicate a building he had donated to house studies in the reconciliation of science and religion.[73] He grows more and more hard. Margaret decorates an enormous palace with incredible extravagance and devotes herself to the duties of hostess at monster receptions. By this time she is lost to Brandon and, insensible to the public criticism of her husband's piracy, is wholly consumed by the triviality and shallowness of the wealthy. She dies unaware of her own degeneration.

A Little Journey is the complete expression of Warner's point of view toward the developments of his time. As a book it brings together the threads of his career as a critic — the utilization of Nook Farm materials (*Backlog Studies*), the observation of manners (*Their Pilgrimage*), and the central thesis of his serious essays. Warner intended his trilogy to be his supreme effort. The attempt he made to knit together the ideas growing out of his reflection in Nook Farm on the things he saw in the rest of the world is interesting as illumination of the intellectual environment in which Mark Twain lived. As a novel, however, Warner's book is less successful than as a concentration of his ideas. His intent to examine the ethical culture of cities like Hartford in contrast to the vicious acquisitiveness of those in control of financial manipulation was most promising. But Warner could not realize the dramatic possibilities in the deterioration of Margaret DeBree. The gradual and credible change in her becomes, toward the end of the book, a sudden capitulation which must remain inexplicable in view of her character in Brandon. The kind of society in which a person lives may determine the kind of person he becomes, as Warner implies. But the mature product of an ethical training does not credibly become a deluded puppet in a less desirable environment without considerable explanation.

To judge *A Little Journey* by his own standards, Warner's style has the lucidity he postulated as the first criterion of enduring literature. The ruminative, ironic, witty, and calm narrator has the charm of personality that he established, in accord with the taste of his generation, as the third requisite. But in the second (knowledge of human nature), Warner fails to translate the knowledge he may have had into convincing characterization. Nevertheless, the finality with which he has been forgotten, even by professional students of American literature, is unjust. That we have so greatly exaggerated the complacence of his era is in part owing to our failure to read its commentators. Warner had considerable insight into the ills of his time. He tended to confine his analysis to rather limited groups of symptoms and did not repudiate utterly the society in which he lived, but his detailed testimony to its peculiarities deserves serious attention. Warner was alarmed by the behavior of the plutocracy, but confident that the middle-class ideals of his own community would survive. It is possible that those who are relatively well adjusted to their environment may be able to tell us as much about it as those who retreat from it in disgust.

Hartford provided Charles Dudley Warner with a point of view toward modern America that in its day had a wide influence — all the more because it was phrased as a partial criticism rather than wholesale condemnation. In the correction of abuses to which the country finally turned in the progressive movement of the early twentieth century, critics like Warner played important preparatory roles. Praises of *A Little Journey* came to him from his wide acquaintance among American writers and from the public at large. The aged father of William Dean Howells wrote from Ohio to his son: "I have been reading Warner's story of A Little Journey in the World. I am very glad to see him take so just a view of the plutocracy that is fastening its grasp upon the country. I am glad so many good writers are waking up to see and expose the abomination — which is terrible to contemplate." [74] And in Nook Farm, defensive in protection of its way of life, the chorus of approval was unanimous.

A look at the uniformity of social criticism from Nook Farm does not justify assertion that Harriet Beecher Stowe and Warner were always systematic analysts of the complexity of their times, or that their intuitive recognition of a fundamental unrest constitutes an articulate perception of the real nature of their age. The experience from which they drew the conclusions amplified in their works was broader than most people think and their interests in the world less provincial. Even so, their assertion of the moral goodness of human nature and the educability of errant individuals was based more on faith than on observation. Given the instinctive point of view of their New England inheritance, it was inevitable that they should consider the development of American democracy as fundamentally sound, and the manifestations of materialism as correctible not by government regulation of business, for example, but by a recall to moral principles. They did not go deep into the problems of industrialism or realize the development of a fundamental conflict between political democracy and the authoritarian and irresponsible conduct of business. But they recognized that great changes were taking place and made an earnest effort to interpret them.

During the seventies and eighties, Mark Twain had less interest in trying to disentangle social forces. His experience with people, much more intimate than that of his neighbors, was also so much more detailed that he was not conscious of human beings as living in interdependence in social groups. He did not possess the patience or the inclination to make prolonged studies of the manners marking off one social class from another. The individual act rather than the pattern of behavior caught his attention. He was very much aware of cruelty, stupidity, generosity, and occasional insight in people, but he was relatively oblivious to the social ideals which in his own time affected their behavior. He knew what was laughable in men; he could love and hate humanity at once and bring its specimens to life on paper. But since he was without the impulses of Mrs. Stowe and Warner to guide the reading public toward their conception of an ideal society, his social criticism is much less than theirs a conscious effort to correct deviation from orderly and moral behavior.

Two of his books — *The Gilded Age* and *A Connecticut Yankee* — may be considered here, however, because of their family resemblance to the work of his neighbors. Both tell us something of his attitude toward his own time and his involvement in its contradictions. Mark's observations of corrupt politicians in Washington and his first-hand experience in the frenzied hunt for riches in Nevada formed a cluster of experience which in 1873, in collaboration with Warner, he embodied in the social satire of *The Gilded Age*. "In a state where there is no fever of speculation, no inflamed desire for sudden wealth," Warner and Mark wrote in the ironic preface to their jumbled and exuberant attack on the excesses of the decade after the Civil War,

where the poor are all simple-minded and contented, and the rich are all honest and generous, where society is in a condition of primitive purity, and politics is the occupation of only the capable and the patriotic, there are necessarily no details for such a history as we have constructed out of an ideal commonwealth.[75]

The book has nothing to say against the ideology of an expansionist economy and satirizes not the system so much as the self-delusion, the dishonesty, or the frontier crudity of individuals taking advantage of it. Corruption in politics, bribery of Congressmen and Senators, vulgarity in the parvenu stratum of society are pilloried from the Nook Farm point of view. The abuses are traced to the occupancy of positions of power by individuals who are not among the best people. The cautious and ethical attitude of Hartford's businessmen and Nook Farm's professional people is the point of view implicit in the satire, which thus approximated Warner's later disapproval, in the name of the cultivated middle class, of the plutocracy.

In a very real sense (unexplored in Mark Twain criticism) *The Gilded Age* is a reactionary book. It exhibits the reservations about political democracy that its authors formulated in the seventies. Warner and Mark Twain imply that with universal suffrage corruption in high places is inevitable. The mass of citizens, at best ignorant, at worst stupid and self-seeking, votes for mountebanks or demagogues whose motive in seeking office is lust for plunder.[76] Examination of the context in which the book was written makes quite clear the distrust of its authors in the voting citizenry. Elsewhere Warner and Mark stated the cure — Mark in the "Curious Republic of Gondour," which suggests limiting effective suffrage to men of education and property, and Warner in "Equality," which defines the true nature of liberty as a freedom limited to persons of education, ability, and a sense of moral responsibility.

But *The Gilded Age* is sufficiently effective to name for posterity a fantastic period of our history, not because of any deep insight into the pollution of the body politic, but because of one characterization — Colonel Sellers.[77] The plot is impossible — an imperfect amalgam of Mark's unsureness in structure and Warner's early deference to the sentimentalism of Mrs. Stowe.[78] But among its disordered events and wooden characters, Colonel Sellers comes to life as the climax of Mark's burlesque achievement. In an atmosphere of fabulous opportunity, where for the American "the paths to fortune are innumerable and all open," where there is "invitation in the air and success in all his wide horizon," Sellers is the visionary who can look at a trickle of muddy water in Missouri and see that it needs only widening, deepening, straightening, and lengthening to make it, after a hypothetical railroad is brought in, the finest river in the Western country and the scene of a perfect speculative enterprise. None of his schemes succeeds, but his resilience is inexhaustible. After every disaster, Sellers is ready with a new project in which he sees millions. "That's the way I block it out, sir—and it's as clear as day—clear as the rosy morn!" [79]

The life-giving power that Mark exercised in the animation of this fabulous clown depends in part upon his own participation in the frenzied speculation of his day. He had himself known the fever overtaking men in search of pots of gold and had seen with his own eyes the hallucinatory rainbows leading to untold riches. Even after moving into the unspeculative, canny business culture of Hartford, he continued to dream. If his typesetter had proved practicable, he would have become himself the proprietor of one of the country's great fortunes. Just as his temporarily Tory attitude, reinforced by the conservatism of Warner, blunted his satire of rampant, political abuses which could have destroyed the republic, so his own susceptibility to the lure of sudden wealth complicates his satire of the speculative spirit. But out of the confusion of a most uneven book, a comic character emerged to testify to Mark's ambivalent understanding of the excesses he burlesques and to his stronger interest in the individual than in the ills of society.

Sixteen years later, after most of his Hartford life had become history, and after the hold of its culture on his attitudes had loosened, Mark published in 1889 *A Connecticut Yankee in King Arthur's Court*, a triumphant celebration of nineteenth-century democracy. In response to a number of interests, including his study of history, his conviction of the inhumanity and ignorance of the Middle Ages, his growing humanitarian sympathy with the masses he had earlier distrusted, and perhaps specifically his anger at Matthew Arnold's criticism of General Grant's memoirs and of American civilization in general,[80] he wrote a defense of American democracy that is markedly more Jacksonian and affirmatively equalitarian than *The Gilded Age*. The difference between these books reflects less specifically a political development in Mark Twain than a growth in his emotional sympathy for the downtrodden.

The years between December 1884 and December 1889—the longest period between 1867 and 1910 in which Mark published no books—are those of his greatest involvement in business enterprises. During that period he was thinking of himself as a captain of industry and only intermittently working on the manuscript of *A Connecticut Yankee*. He intended to make it his swan song, his master work. In 1886, he did not even plan to publish the book, for he expected that with the completion of the typesetter he would not be dependent on royalties. As he prepared his analysis of Arthurian times, he thought of it not primarily as a satire, but as a contrast between two civilizations that would throw light on both. In a letter to Webster, he described his approach to the subject:

> I have begun a book whose scene is laid far back in the twilight of tradition; I have saturated myself with the atmosphere of the day and the subject and got myself into the swing of the work. If I peg away for some weeks without a break I am safe.[81]

But the tank soon went dry and did not refill until late in 1888. By that time, Mark's abhorrence of the "sterile ignorance" of King Arthur's time had crystallized his admiration for "the vast and many-sided knowledge" of his own age and prompted him to his chief tribute to the miraculous achievements of an industrial civilization.

The story of the head foreman of Colt's arms factory, who finds himself in medieval Camelot after being stunned by a crowbar, takes Mark back to the democracy of the Western plains and away from some of the hesitations of Hartford. The Yankee is fervently opposed to aristocratic privilege:

> The blunting effects of slavery upon the slaveholder's moral perceptions are known and conceded, the world over; and a privileged class, an aristocracy, is but a band of slaveholders under another name.

And in praise of universal suffrage, which once Mark hoped would be abolished, he writes:

> Men write many fine and plausible arguments in support of monarchy, but the fact remains that where every man in a state has a vote, brutal laws are impossible.[82]

His confidence in the instinctive justice of ordinary people is symbolized by anachronistic recollections of life in the Mississippi valley. The Yankee sees suckling in the mud of Camelot's main thoroughfare the same hog that Huck Finn saw in Bricksville, Arkansas. The Yankee speaks unaccountably of the sunsets and displays of northern lights along the upper Mississippi, of Arkansas proofreading, and of steamboat explosions. When Mark Twain's mind compared modern America with medieval England, his loyalty to the former appears as a deeper sympathy with the Jacksonian sentiments of parts of the West than with the Federalist fears of the East.

In any event, the mechanic of the nineteenth century proves himself a giant among pigmies and an intellectual among moles as he transforms England into an industrial democracy. He is not without some of the pessimism that developed in Mark Twain along with passionate concern for social justice.[83] In 1889 Mark was still convinced of the glory of an industrial civilization, but he was beginning to suspect its inequities. He was always to believe that permanent progress in humanity and justice had taken place since the Middle Ages, even though he was to assert later the worthlessness of the human race in all periods. He was attracted and repelled simultaneously by the behavior of human beings and by the society of his time, but in *A Connecticut Yankee* he asserted his approval, unmistakably and enthusiastically.

The disorder that characterizes his entire literary performance jumbles all Mark's social criticism. *A Connecticut Yankee*, despite its burlesque, is alive with his vitality as an artist and full of his contradictions and shortcomings as a thinker. But whatever *A Connecticut Yankee* may be, it is not, as some critics have argued, an inverted satire on the nineteenth century. Mark makes repeated incidental references to ridiculous business practices like sandwich-sign advertising and leaves forever unsettled the actual benefit to medieval England of the Yankee's installation of nineteenth-century civilization (he blows it up to end the book). But as his notes and letters indicate, we may take his praise of modern times at face value. Its political implications — which Mark again does not elaborate [84] — are more liberal than Mark's views in 1873. His enthusiasm for the material progress of his time does not mean that he did not share his neighbor's misgivings, for Mark Twain's opinions were not necessarily consistent.

The climate of Nook Farm encouraged examination of American life. Its citizens accepted the course of national development in their own day as progress toward the universal application of the Golden Rule. At the same time they recognized cracks in the moral foundation under American civilization as its materialistic superstructure rose higher and higher. They detected in themselves and in society a confusion of immediate self-interest with long-range community objectives. They judged their times by their own moral standards and traced the errors of their generation to individual defection. Their religious training begot their social criticism; their rebellion against the religion into which they were born had not loosened the grip of conscience or completely secularized their attitudes toward the world around them. They sensed a conflict between careering industrialism and allegedly Christian democracy. But since their own religious faith had suffered complicated modification in answer to the developments of the life about them and since their own moral standards had undergone adaptation to permit their participation in that life, their attitudes toward their times were also far from simple. They were so much entwined in the contradictions and confusion of their period that they could not formulate clearly the questions which stirred in them an inchoate disturbance. Nook Farm was a colony of citizens recording its own experience under social influences that it could not disentangle. As writers in a complicated age very different from the kind of life into which they had been born, they demonstrate in their books about their own times that their geometry could not quite span its opposites.

The Nook Farm Writers and the Genteel Tradition

THE RELEVANCE OF HARTFORD'S SOCIETY TO THE BOOKS WRITTEN THERE IS APparent everywhere. Of the writers of Nook Farm, only Warner made specific use of neighborhood events and experience. But the general stimulus and the particular satisfactions in the hearth-side amenities memorialized in *Backlog Studies* were fully as germinal in the literature of Mrs. Stowe and Mark Twain. The community felicity recorded in Mrs. Stowe's letters and in the second volume of Mark Twain's *Autobiography* was probably for all three writers an environmental encouragement to literary activity providing day-by-day satisfactions more pleasant than those originating in the solitude of composition. But if thus intangibly the congeniality of the neighborhood permitted free development, the society of Nook Farm, in a different and more easily defined context, was to be mildly directive. Mark Twain was to be encouraged toward refinement.

It has often been said that the gentility of Hartford, supposedly hostile to the burgeoning of Mark Twain's satiric power, helped warp him away from his mission as a satirist of his own times and imposed upon him a mediocre conventionality that emasculated his work and frustrated his spirit. The obvious untruth of such a judgment does not mean that Mark was unaffected by the standards of taste operative in Hartford and in Elmira. His conformity to those standards was for the most part an eager adaptation to the customs of Eastern culture. During the seventies and eighties he was very much a member of his own generation. Its ideals were his own. And we have not seen here any conflict complicating his adjustment to the gentility of Hartford. But he was most certainly the object of well-meaning advice that he go beyond the burlesque and realism (his stock in trade) and attempt the kind of book most highly regarded by gentlefolk.

Mark's encounter with practitioners of good taste outside his immediate family began in a meeting with Anson Burlingame, who urged him in Hawaii in 1866 to improve himself socially and culturally by associating only with his betters. Mrs. Fairbanks, who represented cultivated Cleveland, continued the course of instruction aboard the *Quaker City* in 1867. Olivia Langdon assumed responsibility for his tutelage upon their marriage in

1870 and thereafter welcomed the assistance of William Dean Howells. All four of these advocates of good breeding, accepting more of Mark Twain's eccentricity and relative uncouthness than they attempted to modify, recommended chiefly that he discipline his inclination to burlesque in the direction of a graceful diction, a dignified literary personality, and a conscious regard for the polite conventions.

A full realization of how much was accomplished, despite Mark's successful defense of his own individuality, requires the reading of his early sketches, which are frequently crude even by post-Victorian standards. A comparison of the *Alta* letters with *Innocents Abroad*, and of the Sacramento *Union* accounts of his Hawaiian trip with the relevant sections of *Roughing It*, shows many thoroughly sound revisions in favor of taste without a substantial dilution of vigor.[85] A Mr. Brown, fictitious traveling companion who enabled Mark to be vulgar in his early travel letters without implicating himself, was eliminated altogether when the letters were revised for book publication.[86] As Mark was settling into polite society, he excised much vulgarity, but by no means abandoned burlesque. In Hartford he could write and publish in spite of the disapproval of Livy and Howells "The Invalid's Story," a sketch in which the aroma of Limburger cheese, waxing potent in a heated baggage car, is mistaken for the smell of a corpse in a near-by coffin. Burlesque of this sort — the decay of corpses is a frequent reference in Mark's humor — became a permanent defect of his entire work. Its publication is evidence at least that whatever censorship he was subjected to was not really strict. From the perspective of our own time it often seems excessively tolerant.

Mark Twain's humor, even in its earlier and cruder form, had, in fact, been enthusiastically received in Hartford. Before he moved to Nook Farm, his work had been discussed in the Monday Evening Club, and praise of him in the *Courant* had been warm. As early as 1866 a newspaper of near-by Springfield, edited then by Samuel Bowles (the nationally respected liberal editor and close friend of John Hooker), had reprinted an estimate by a Western critic which represents Eastern opinion of his early writing.

> His humor is peculiar to himself; if of any type, it is rather of the western character of ludicrous exaggeration and audacious statement, which perhaps is more thoroughly national and American than even the Yankee delineations of Lowell. His humor has more motive than that of Artemus Ward; he is something of a satirist, although his satire is not always subtle or refined. He has shrewdness and a certain hearty abhorrence of shams which will make his faculty serviceable to mankind. His talent is so well based that he can write seriously and well when he chooses, which is perhaps the best test of true humor. His

faults are crudeness, coarseness, and an occasional Panurge-like plainness of statement.[87]

Bret Harte wrote this early comment. Like later Hartford criticism, it dignified Mark's buffoonery with seriousness of purpose.

But though Mark's friends in Hartford shared the general delight in *Innocents Abroad* and *Roughing It*, they began to request more and more explicitly that he rise above the limitations of humor to attempt a really serious book. They did not suggest a higher aspiration because they discredited his accomplishment in his native medium; they simply thought him capable of orthodox greatness in the classical tradition.

Mrs. Fairbanks, of course, urged Mark onward and upward continually. She wrote him about 1880:

Now, I want you to write another book, in an entirely different style — I can see just what you could do, with some manuscript that you have, and more that you might make, that would give you the fresh enjoyment of *surprising* the public. Won't you do [it] right away? The time has come for your *best book*. I do not mean your most taking book, with the most money in it, I mean your best contribution to American literature. I have thought of it a great deal of late and wished the thought & wish would inspire you my boy.[88]

Edwin Pond Parker, the preacher who made a hobby of literature, spoke for Mark's well-wishers at home.

Your rank as a writer of humorous things is high enough — but, do you know — Clemens — that it is in you to do some first-class serious or sober work.

Now let me say *to* you what I have repeatedly said *of* you — that I know no American writer of your generation, who is capable of writing such forcible, sinewy, racy English as you.[89] You are abundantly capable of turning out some work that shall bear the stamp of your individuality plainly enough, and at the same time have a sober character and a solid worth & a permanent value. It might not pay in "shekels," but it would do you vast honor, and give your friends vast pleasure.[90]

This letter was delivered to Mark at a time when he was completing a new novel.

In the summer of 1877, Mark began to think seriously about a book to satisfy his wife, his neighbors, and the friends elsewhere who hoped to elevate his literary aspirations. Mrs. Theodore Crane, Livy's sister, had in the library at Quarry Farm a copy of Charlotte M. Yonge's *The Prince and the Page*. It focused Mark's attention upon Edward VI. He had been reading English history extensively.[91] During the winter in Hartford, he recorded in fifty words the central theme of *The Prince and the Pauper*. Around the accidental interchange of Edward VI and a guttersnipe he began carefully to construct a picture of sixteenth-century England, drawing heavily on a half-dozen sources.[92] In February 1878 Mark wrote Mrs. Fairbanks that he was writing a historical tale of three hundred years ago

> simply for the love of it — for it will appear without my name — such grave & stately work being considered by the world to be above my proper level. I have been studying for it, off & on, for a year & a half. I swear the Young Girls' Club to secresy & read the MS to them, half a dozen chapters at a time, at their meetings. They profess to be very much fascinated with it; so do Livy & Susie Warner.[93]

Mark was writing rapidly at this time. Since the tale was ostensibly for children, he read the chapters to his daughters and to the girls of the Saturday Morning Club. At one family audience, Susie and Clara perched on the arms of his chair, while Livy listened from across the fire and Mrs. Fairbanks beamed in the background. The adults glowed in the book's "loveliness"; the children were entranced. But by summer, composition had halted in the face of plot difficulties. A long trip to Europe and its record (*A Tramp Abroad*) were completed before he picked up the manuscript again in the fall of 1880. This time he finished the book and began to circulate the manuscript among friends who had not heard him read it aloud. *The Prince and the Pauper* was in a way more theirs than his; he was anxious not to publish it without corroboration from those who had urged him to write it. On Christmas Eve, then, of 1880, he could answer Parker's letter:

> I thank you most sincerely for those pleasant words. They come most opportunely, too, at a time when I was wavering between launching a book of the sort you mention, with my name to it, and smuggling it into publicity with my name suppressed. Well, I'll put my name to it, and let it help me or hurt me as the fates shall direct.
>
> It is not a large book, so I have not scrupled to ask Howells and Twichell to run over the manuscript and advise me what to modify and what to knock out. I must go warily seeing this is such a wide departure from my accustomed line.
>
> Howells has read it and he winds up his four pages (mainly of vigorous approval) with the remark — "I think the book will be a great success unless some marauding ass who does not snuff his wonted pasturage there should prevail on all the other asses to turn up their noses in pure ignorance. It is such a book as I would expect from you, knowing what a bottom of substance there is to your fun, but the public at large ought to be led to expect it, and must be."
>
> Howells found fault with two things, some descriptions of English court ceremonials which he wants shortened, and a story of a boy, a bull, and some

bees, which he won't have in the book at all, because he says it lowers its dignity, so I guess I'll have to scratch that out.

But what I'm coming to is this: — Will you, too, take the manuscript and read it, either to yourself, or, still better, aloud to your family? Twichell has promised me a similar service. I hoped to get criticisms from Howells's children but evidently he spared them, which was carrying charity too far!

Merry Christmas!
Yours truly,
S. L. Clemens[94]

With Parker, Twichell, Susie and Lilly Warner, the Saturday Morning Club, and the neighborhood children participating in the criticism of *The Prince and the Pauper*, it became, more than any other book of Mark's, the product of community collaboration. In concession to his friends, he made many changes, excised the extended burlesque of the whipping boy's story, but insisted on retaining some of the phrases his critics objected to, refusing in particular to strike out one "blot" Twichell and Parker caviled at.[95] The book was gradually made ready for the press during 1881 while the community waited eagerly to learn the reaction of the critics and of the public.

Only one uneasy voice was raised to question the fitness of Mark Twain's dabbling in romance. Joseph T. Goodman, the editor who had recognized Mark's gifts in Nevada and helped him map out his literary territory, learned what was going on in Hartford. He wrote in October, 1881:

I see mention of your forthcoming, "Prince and Pauper," stating that it is a story of remote English life. I'm very impatient to see it, for of all things I have been anxious that you try your hand at another novel. But what could have sent you groping among the driftwood of the Deluge for a topic when you would have been so much more at home in the wash of today?[96]

It was a good question. Goodman anticipated the opinion of posterity by preferring the disorderly representation of contemporary American life in *Roughing It* (written with Goodman's assistance) to the ingenious, pleasant, but superficial *Prince*. He was too far away to interfere effectively with the influences which in this single instance turned Mark from his proper materials to the only consciously "literary" book he wrote during his Hartford residence.

Nook Farm was charmed, of course, when the book appeared during the Christmas season of 1881 in the gaudiest format Osgood could contrive.[97] A December 28, 1881 *Courant* editorial written by Warner or Parker welcomed Mark to the company of great and serious writers:

> Mark Twain has finally fulfilled the earnest hope of many of his best friends, in writing a book which has other and higher merits than can possibly belong to the most artistic expression of mere humor.

Of course, the humorist should not be undervalued, the reviewer said; he has a mission higher than provoking the "guffaws of the gaping crowd."

> There is a humorous aspect of human life and of human affairs, the successful presentation of which not only excites mirth but dispels many an illusion, pricks many a bubbled conceit, and exposes many a cheap fallacy and thin sentiment as could be done by no other means so well.
>
> Nevertheless the functions and office of the humorist in literature are somewhat limited. His honor is not likely to be durable.

With this new book Mark Twain revealed himself a diligent and thoughtful student of English classical literature and strengthened his claim to the most vigorous style of his age. The excellences and charms of the romance

> are such as only a man of genius, writing with a sober if not serious purpose and with utmost literary sincerity, could furnish. The conception of the story is unique and original, the intricate plot is developed with admirable clearness, and the inherent improbability at the base of the story is so artistically treated that one quite forgets it till the end is reached.

A few blemishes of slang and a few inappropriate humorous exaggerations should have been expunged in judicious revision, but the book is nevertheless occasion for congratulations on the attainment of a new honor in literature. "May he soon try again!"

Mark's other friends concurred. Mrs. Fairbanks was rapturous. Her husband wept over the book, except when he came upon some "Munchausen element."[98] The book, she said, was his "masterpiece in fineness." When would he do another? There was time for another. And since he was fortunate to breathe the inspiring air of Hartford, he would find there occasion for a second masterpiece. Mrs. Stowe, similarly susceptible, was to read the book over and over with childlike delight. In April of 1887, Harriet encountered Mark on the sidewalk, took both his hands, and told him with a fervency which brought tears to his eyes: "I am reading your Prince and Pauper for the fourth time, and I *know* it is the best book for young folks ever written."[99] Six weeks later she came upon the Ombra to announce completion of her sixth reading.

Outside Nook Farm, the professional critics whose reviews I have read were unanimous in high praise and pleased by Mark's achievement as a serious writer. They praised his talent for description, plot construction, and character creation, and admired his philosophical inclination and his achievement of a subdued refinement of expression, an ennobling moral, and a pleasant treatment of a far-away epoch. *The Prince and the Pauper* was thought the climax of his craftsmanship.

At the midpoint of his Hartford residence, then, Mark wrote a book precisely gauged to the taste of Hartford. The delight of his refined friends turned to mild disappointment in the backsliding apparent in his next two works, *Life on the Mississippi* and *Huckleberry Finn*. Eager, in all friendliness, to excuse Mark for abandoning the kind of book it liked most, Hartford sadly attributed his retrogression to the cold reception the salesmen of *The Prince* encountered on all the back roads. Mark's neighbors recognized his professional necessity to please his audience and professed to understand his deference to vulgar taste, but they manufactured and rather enjoyed for a long time the sad irony that America would not let its best writer fully develop his talents. Charles Hopkins Clark spoke at Mark Twain's death in 1910 of Hartford's long-lived regrets:

> If we are not mistaken, the readers of this paragraph will generally agree that his finest book was "The Prince and the Pauper," but it sold the least, and he has been quoted as giving that fact as his reason for not following that line any further.[100]

Speaking somewhat earlier for the critical fraternity at large, Henry Vedder, a sort of weathervane for literary opinion in the nineties, referred to what he considered the ironic likelihood that a humorist can never be taken seriously. Readers failed to enjoy *The Prince and the Pauper* because they looked for a joke and could not find it.

> It is only when, as "Mark Twain," he writes some such trash as "The Adventures of Huckleberry Finn" that this really capable writer can make sure of an appreciative hearing.[101]

The commercial failure of the book was doubtless a strong motive for returning to the Mississippi materials, and it was an excellent reason to furnish to the community. But for all kinds of reasons, Mark could not be completely at home when he was not writing out of his own personal experience. Whatever the motive, Mark abandoned the historical past until he came to complete *A Connecticut Yankee,* chiefly significant in what it says about the present. And in that book the burlesque he had suppressed in *The Prince and the Pauper* ran riot, to disappoint again those who thought it ultimately unworthy of his gifts.

But again, Hartford's disappointment involved no real disapproval of

Mark Twain. Supported by a tendency to see a moral seriousness in his humor, his neighbors accepted him as he was. The pressure they exerted was exceedingly mild. Though Parker might long for a tender tale with a moral, Twichell would supply the suggestion for *Old Times on the Mississippi*. And if the community was thrilled by *The Prince* as by no other book, it was enthusiastic about all of Mark's work and felt no active distaste for his relatively rowdy humor. They loved the man. No reservations about the nobility of his literature could diminish their affection for him.

In connection with the community's recognition of Mark's compulsion to please the taste of the masses, it is significant that the one book he wrote in Hartford in experimental obliviousness to its commercial success and in deference to the genteel tradition is without many of his faults as a writer. Anyone who reads *The Prince and the Pauper* can see in it the most nearly perfect structure of his collected works, the greatest number of consecutive pages unmarred by flagrant burlesque digression, and the clearest realization of consistent tone — a unique achievement in form applied to artificial materials. Restraint, care, and economy accompanied a conscious effort to prove his literary competence outside the area of his professional activity. For the technical excellence, we may credit the amateur and professional critics of Hartford — since he contrived his book with their criticisms in mind — with a partially accurate perception of Mark's faults. The error of people like Edwin Pond Parker was not their insistence on polished technique, but their underestimation of American materials. They preferred charm to realism, the past to the present, the exotic to the homely. The critical intuitions of Nook Farm were not entirely faulty; in no case did they do Mark Twain serious harm. If, in responding to them, Mark had given the same attention to the form of his Mississippi books that he gave to *The Prince and the Pauper*, his great books would have been greater. But he thought of the carefully constructed book as art and of his improvisatory river volumes as business. For art he had little time.

Yet even *The Prince and the Pauper* has upon it the signs of Mark Twain's authorship. Just as he refused to delete a reference to Henry VIII's corpse, so he did not altogether yield in other directions. The gentility of his period is refracted, even in this most genteel book, through his own vigor of style and his own individuality. He attempted to have his characters speak in an idiom laboriously constructed out of lists of archaic words and phrases gleaned from his source books. But though he tried seriously to make all the conversation in his costume-piece appropriate, he could not resist a mixture of modern and sixteenth-century idiom.[102] Within the archaic medium, he often managed considerable vigor.[103] The connective passages, monosyllabic and concise, sometimes return to the Mississippi for their imagery.[104] The description of the rogues who torment the prince is built upon the vivid concreteness and particularity of Mark's most characteristic work. But despite unmistakable signs of his authorship, the subordination of his usual manner to conventional treatment of a charming and instructive tale was almost complete. Mark kept himself out of the book;[105] the personages he substituted for his normal cast of characters have little life. He had not met them on the river.

The soft persuasions of the neighborhood shaping *The Prince and the Pauper* into the book it preferred to all his other works were, as we have seen, the characteristic expression of the cultural tradition nourishing the cultivated folk of Hartford. A member of the younger generation, son of Doctor Burton, grew up on Forest Street to absorb the literary attitudes dominant in the neighborhood and to join Charles Dudley Warner as the second professional literary critic of his group. Richard Burton's career is not important except as indication of the strength and variety of the ideas affecting the books written in Nook Farm. The inclination to gentility was not only strong enough to modify Mark Twain's robustness; it was also sufficiently fecund to reproduce itself into the next generation.

Young Richard Burton, child of Nook Farm, knew its graciousness and conformed to its limited attitudes. The activity of the older writers in whose presence he grew up bent his inclination toward literature, and after his education at Yale, he began a lifetime as a literary academic, a minor poet, a now almost inaudible essayist, and a critic whose standards never changed from those he learned in his own backyard. In his *Literary Leaders of America*, long used as a text in the colleges, he entered Emerson, Hawthorne, Longfellow, and Lowell into the catalogue of literary saints. Compelled to consider Whitman, he offered the evidence of F. B. Sanborn of Concord that Whitman radiated essential health and goodness. "It is important to realize this of Whitman the man," Burton continued, "since so much in Whitman the writer might mislead the reader to another conclusion."[106] Whitman "hymned animality," used maddening cadences, and punctuated his prose eccentrically. The first charge, Burton pointed out, was most serious. Asserting the prejudices not only of Nook Farm, but of the culturally squeamish America of which the Farm was only an extraordinarily well-developed microcosm, he concluded after all that manifestations of flesh link us ignobly with the lower orders. In print, the connection is not to be referred to.

Burton's attitude toward Mark Twain was exactly that of the entire neighborhood. To a national audience he pointed out that though Mark Twain was intensely democratic and typically American he was worlds removed from the newspaper funny man. He showed his city's inclination to see nobility in Mark's humorous work.

> [The] prose poet in daily converse . . . was no mountebank in motley wear, shaking the fool's zany for the momentary, thoughtless merriment of the crowd, but a wise, sane, deep-souled man teaching us the lesson of life.[107]

Mark was personally as delicate as a maid, tender as a lover. In his mirth there is never any bitterness. Huck and Tom keep a morning freshness in the quaint English speech in which they are "embalmed," and the beautiful little masterpiece, *The Prince and the Pauper*, eloquently demonstrates the mellowness and sweetness which grew steadily sweeter and more mellow toward the end. Of course, the surroundings of such books as *Huckleberry Finn* and *Tom Sawyer* might seem to a gentler training harsh and homely. And much of Mark's seriousness is obscured, "more's the pity," in horseplay and broad Rabelaisian fun. But what matter that the speech of his characters be rustic, that the setting of his books be crude, and that the incidents smack of the soil when the total impression is ennobling? Burton saw in Mark the gentility he was looking for and managed to bring his older neighbor farther into the territory occupied by polite authors than the evidence justifies. In his typical accommodation of Mark's personality and writings, he represented perfectly the attitude of his townsfolk toward literature and life and preserved that attitude far into the twentieth century.

For Mrs. Stowe and Charles Dudley Warner, the literary implications of the decorum of Nook Farm life suggested no conflict, for they had grown up among the traditions that brought gentility to flower in the eighties. Never conscious of its censorship, they were seldom tempted to write a word or record an idea that would cause specific offense or leave even a diffused impression that propriety had been violated. Their books are permeated with the prevailing taste of the people among whom they were written. Warner, earlier than Burton, made explicit the point of view of the thoroughbred critic in his summary of Washington Irving's career. Irving epitomized for Warner the ideal literary man; his attractive qualities were his sweet humor, his sentiment, his simplicity, his gentle effectiveness (chiefly in producing the quiet musing mood in the reader), his tenderness for tradition, and his equable temperament. That Irving's works are rarely stimulating or suggestive is set down as important evidence for their worth, along with his creation of a local romance and his "moral quality."[108] The characteristics Warner admired in Irving were mostly those he sought in his own writing, and those he and his neighbors preferred to see in Mark Twain.

Mark accepted in his personal life the basic gentility of Nook Farm. But rather than a lifelong habit, his acceptance of the social ideals of his time was an adaptation to a culture into which he had not been born. The possibilities of conflict were present, but they did not materialize to prevent his expression of what he had to say. By rationalizing his independent development of his own genres as basically serious and noble, Nook Farm's people made Mark one of them, rather than by materially changing his course. The gentility of Hartford thus was more flexible, amiable, and genial than sinister. The narrowness, complacence, sterility, and Grundyism sometimes thought to have vitiated the literature of the post-War decades and to have prevented Mark Twain from attaining his full greatness do not appear decisive in Nook Farm. Mark Twain and his neighbors were not so different in sensibility as has occasionally been supposed. His minor deviations from the genteel tradition in the performance of his profession were minimized with the benignity characteristic of Nook Farm's total attitude toward him.

The Nook Farm Writers: Nostalgic Recollection and Literary Greatness

IF THE HARTFORD WRITERS HAD PRODUCED ONLY THEIR HACK WORK AND THEIR comment on modern times, their books would illuminate the researches of a historian but would not as literature compel the attention of the non-specialist. Their lesser books do not rise conspicuously above the contemporary welter of second-rate works, and they have no unique merit as instruments of present-day insight into their period. But the record of the world in which Mrs. Stowe, Warner, and Mark Twain had once lived, when they were young before the Civil War, is incontestably literature of a much higher order. The greater power of their historical fiction is an accident of their emotional adjustment as adults to contemporary reality. Nostalgia attending remembrance of times gone by was the emotion that germinated in Nook Farm a permanently useful evocation of the American past and a literature of very great intrinsic importance.

Mrs. Stowe had turned back to New England as early as 1834. In Cincinnati, far from the Litchfield and Hartford of her girlhood, she wrote "A New England Tale" and made of it the first genuine piece of "local color." She began with the amiable informality that was always to mark her style:

> And so I am to write a story — but of what, and where? . . . [not of England, France, Greece, Italy, etc.] No, no; these are all too old, too romance-like, too obviously picturesque for me. No, let me turn to my own land — my own New England; the land of bright fires and strong hearts; the land of *deeds* and not of words; the land often spoken against, yet always respected . . . Now . . . this heroic apostrophe . . . is merely a little introductory breeze of patriotism, such as occasionally brushes over every mind, bearing on its wings the remembrance of all we ever loved or cherished in the land of our early years.[109]

This early, simple wish for the home she had moved away from became after Harriet's slavery novels (*Uncle Tom's Cabin* and *Dred*) the emotional source of *The Minister's Wooing* (1859), *The Pearl of Orr's Island* (1862), *Oldtown Folks* (1869), *Oldtown Fireside Stories* (1872), and *Poganuc People* (1878).

The Minister's Wooing, which bridges her antislavery and New England novels,[110] contained most of the themes Harriet was to elaborate later. In it she announced the thoroughness, the realism, and the sobriety with which she intended to recreate the New England of the past:

> It is impossible to write a story of New England life and manners for a thoughtless, shallow-minded person. If we represent things as they are, their intensity, their depth, their unworldly gravity and earnestness must inevitably repel lighter spirits, as the reverse pole of the magnet drives off sticks and straws.[111]

Harriet's story of Mary Scudder — who is loved by the high-minded divine, Dr. Samuel Hopkins, and who loves James Marvyn, a sailor reported dead at sea without experiencing grace,[112] — is set against a background of capable housekeeping. The rigors of Calvinist theology and its impact upon human beings, the delicacy of the Puritan maiden of sensitive "organization," the varieties of New England character, and the tragedy of death without redemption are the topics of all her regional books. As a bonus she brings in also the polished and immoral cosmopolitanism of the outside world. Sophistication is represented by Aaron Burr, the one degenerate grandson of Jonathan Edwards, whose mischief resembles that of another, Ellery Davenport, in *Oldtown Folks*. *The Minister's Wooing* defines the themes and establishes the method for picturing a region, but the pallor of the romance and the obtrusiveness of the melodrama make it less effective than her later invocations of the same purpose.

The Pearl of Orr's Island reflects increased skill in the delineation of character, particularly of the weather-beaten oldsters of the Maine coast, who like "last year's mullein stalks, upright, dry and seedy [are] warranted to last for any length of time." The central figure is the child Mara, who ascends toward a pure adulthood beside the sea and worships Moses, the foundling of exotic inheritance. She is doomed, like so many of Harriet's females (and so many New England women in real life) to burn "with the intensity of lighted phosphorus" and to die early of consumption, smiling at the vision of paradise that never failed to enliven the last rising of the hectic flush. The story suffers chiefly from a failure of inspiration in mid-passage; the energy of the first pages fades as the children grow up. But chestnut burrs like the Toothacre sisters, kindly souls like seafaring Captain Pennell and his wife, and tough-minded, combative matrons like Dame Kittredge,[113] comprise a vivid gallery of New England originals of which Harriet is still the chief custodian. The women ply their skillful, frugal ways in ample kitchens and look out to sea from their kitchen doors in the afternoon to watch for ships and breathe salt air. The book in which they are brought to life is no doubt artless and naïve, but it is also authentic and fresh.

Just as *The Minister's Wooing* is chiefly the history of a phase of Calvinism, *The Pearl of Orr's Island* is a study of character. Late in the sixties, Harriet brought her experience in both subjects to the composition of *Oldtown Folks*, the masterpiece of her long career. From the beginning this book "boiled and bubbled daily and nightly." She wrote James Fields in 1869:

> It is more to me than a story; it is my résumé of the whole spirit and body of New England, a country that is now exerting such an influence on the civilized world that to know it truly becomes an object.[114]

Everything Mrs. Stowe wrote, to be sure, was more than a story, but here more than anywhere else improbabilities of plot are happily inundated by a flood of actual incident and credible characterization which has behind it the full authority of Calvin Stowe's experience and Harriet's genius for evoking the life of the age in which her heart's deepest sympathies lay. Her announced object was

> to interpret to the world the New England life and character in that particular time of its history which may be called the seminal period . . . The seed bed of New England was the seed bed of this great American Republic, and of all that is likely to come of it.[115]

She achieved a monumental study of character under the influence of Calvinism. All shades of religious belief from the aggressive rational asperity of Grandmother Badger, the Arminian liberalism of her husband, and the Anglicanism of Boston's Tory remnant (represented by Lady Lothrop) to the worldly agnosticism of Ellery Davenport are shown in dramatic integration with the whole life of Oldtown. All New England's character types are prodigally illustrated. Among the company are personages whose fidelity to life goes beyond regional peculiarity. The loafer and ne'er-do-well philosopher, Sam Lawson, for example, is not only a symbol of the obdurate handful who refused to accept the community fetish of unremitting industry, but a delightful gratuity as an individual. Members of an enormous company like Miss Asphyxia Smith, the workhorse maiden who ran her own farm (and who, she said, would no more get married than put her nose in hot swill), and like Crab Smith, cruel, mean, and arid, constitute an earthy counterbalance to the less apparent lifelikeness of Harry, the boy who perfects the religion of love, and of Esther, the pure still maiden whom Harry marries. In her resurrection of Oldtown, Harriet goes deeper than the picturesque to explore shrewdly the psychological degeneration of old families like the Rossiters, of whose peculiarities she writes:

> There was in them a sort of intellectual vigor, a ceaseless activity of thought, a passion for reading and study, and a quiet brooding on the very deepest problems of mental and moral philosophy. The characteristic of such families is the greatly disproportioned force of the internal, intellectual, and spiritual life to the external one. Hence come often morbid and diseased forms of manifestation. The threads which connect such persons with the real life of the outer world are so fine and so weak, that they are constantly breaking and giving way here and there, so that, in such races, oddities and eccentricities are come to be accepted only as badges of family character. Yet from stock of this character have come some of the most brilliant minds in New England.[116]

And she traced the formation of the American government to the strength of mind and will developed by the hardier people of New England who were brought up to think and struggle and suffer.

Harriet's purpose to show how the life of Massachusetts determined American growth and character involved, as she was aware,

> many personages, many subjects, many accessories, for no human being grows up who does not intertwist in his growth the whole idea and spirit of his day.[117]

But in these New England books, Harriet's thesis is no longer really the principal motivation of her achievement. Much of the integrity of New England could be recaptured, to be sure, but no one knew better than she that a day had passed. She was not really requiring her readers to *do* anything, to reform, or to turn back. She had helped to destroy, in her own rebellious rejection, the Calvinism of her youth; she knew that times and tempers must change. Her concern with the stable society that flourished under arbitrary religious certainties still includes a tremendously powerful sympathy and a deep affection. Her revival, then, of the historical past was more centrally nostalgic than didactic. In *Oldtown Folks* she recognizes explicitly the emotion behind *The Minister's Wooing* and *The Pearl of Orr's Island*. As Harry and Tina and Horace Holyoke approached adulthood, she wrote,

> We cannot always remain in the pleasant valley of childhood. I myself, good reader, have dwelt on its scenes longer, because, looking back on it from the extreme end of life, it seems to my weary eyes so fresh and beautiful; the dew of the morning lies on it; — that dew which no coming day will restore.[118]

A yearning for the morning land, which logically contradicts Harriet's acceptance of a later and less sure society, is the emotion that makes unimportant all the faults of *Oldtown Folks* — the difficulties of plot, the disordered combination of narrative and expository analysis, the quaintness of style — and transforms the book from unexciting literalness as history to far-reaching power as mythology. That *Oldtown Folks* still is alive to contribute to our understanding of the national past is a tribute less to its historical accuracy than to the atmospheric truth enveloping its evocation of times gone by. It tells us something about the world in which she wrote and her relation to it as well as about the past which she could not dismiss. Her emotional involvement with two different chapters in our civilization is the complication in the life of Harriet Beecher Stowe that made articulate her great intuitive gifts.

In 1872, Harriet, never one to throw out the leftovers, gathered up some stories that she could not squeeze into *Oldtown Folks* and published them as *Oldtown Fireside Stories*. Calvin had furnished these tales to her from his bottomless memory of chimney-corner folklore. Harriet retells them without a moral thesis of any kind, aiming only to preserve examples of "traditions and narratives which had all the uncertain glow and shifting mystery of the firelit hearth upon them." The stories are not singly of great interest, but in total they are an amusing reference to the chief recreation of New England children and to the suspension of belief mellowing the crustiest adults when they sat down before the fire. People like Aunt Lois ("the very impersonation of obstinate rationalism") held also the most "undoubting faith" in the supernatural. She said of ghost stories, an important genre in the New England oral tradition:

"I don't believe such things," at last she snapped out, "and I don't disbelieve them. I just let 'em alone." [119]

When Harriet was seventy, her susceptibility to nostalgic remembrance (which is, of course, partly a function of increasing age) produced *Poganuc People* (1878), the last of her New England series and the most directly autobiographical. It is a simple recollection of her childhood in Litchfield, where the passing of the seasons, each with its own pleasures, brings Dolly Cushing to virtuous young womanhood. The parsonage of Lyman Beecher is the scene of the busy domesticity so fully explored in the earlier novels, with details now from Harriet's own life—her discovery of a copy of *Arabian Nights*, for example, in the bottom of a barrel of sermons. The old house was "a silent influence, every day fashioning the sensitive, imaginative little soul that was growing up in its own sphere of loneliness there." [120] Outside in the village, the inroads of Episcopalianism and of Democratic politics were weakening Congregational solidarity, and, since the time is 1818, Harriet's book becomes a significant chapter in the passing of the society of which she is the historian. Dolly's father comes to see that the old régime has crumbled and adopts her cheerful religion of love, which in spite of its assumption that the pastor no longer has a crucial role in the guidance of his parishioners gives him more to do. Salvation is no longer limited to the predestined Elect.

He saw that intemperance and profanity and immorality could be subdued by the power of religious motive working in the hearts of individual men, taking away the desire to do evil, and that the gospel of Christ is to-day, as it was of old and ever will be, the power of God and the wisdom of God to the salvation of every one that believeth.[121]

Without the other books as earlier volumes in a series, *Poganuc People* would be too slight to deserve much attention. But it is the strongest book Harriet wrote after *Oldtown Folks*. Its simplicity of story and paucity of events are animated still more obviously than in the preceding volumes by nostalgic sympathy. With this picture of her own childhood, Harriet brings a century of New England history to a close, feeling the full poignance of its ending:

As to Poganuc, all whom we knew there have passed away; all the Town-Hill aristocracy and the laboring farmers of the outskirts are gone, one by one, to the peaceful sleep of the Poganuc graveyard. A village of white stone stands the only witness of the persons of our story. Even the old meeting-house is dissolved and gone.

Only the natural beauty of her native village remained in 1878 to remind her of everything gone:

> Generation passeth, generation cometh, saith the wise man, but the earth abideth forever. The hills of Poganuc are still beautiful in their summer woodland dress. The Poganuc river still winds at their feet with gentle murmur. The lake, in its steel-blue girdle of pines, still reflects the heavens as a mirror; its silent forest shores are full of life and wooded beauty. The elms that over-arch the streets of the central village have spread their branches wider, and form a beautiful walk where other feet than those we wot of are treading. As other daisies have sprung in the meadows, and other bobolinks and bluebirds sing in the treetops, so other men and women have replaced those here written of, and the story of life still goes on from day to day among the POGANUC PEOPLE.[122]

Harriet Beecher Stowe's most important books grew out of an emotion uniting her New England tetralogy as a continuous evocation of a past that she knew better than the world of her maturity. Her nostalgia was not merely for the specific scenes of her own childhood — its happiness and loneliness and tranquility — but for the whole history of her homeland. Her understanding of its people and of the religious society in which they lived was converted into literary greatness by instinctive sympathy with its ideals. Thus her materialization of the New England past became a passionate utterance. The depth of feeling with which she turned from her own time to one she could better understand made her work highly influential in its day in the literary movement which after the Civil War turned writers everywhere to the exploration of particular regions of America. And the strength of man's concern with the past, with the traditions of his own region, and with the culture of his own country means that these books of Harriet Beecher Stowe's, written in a time when change was effacing the contours of a preindustrial democracy, will probably be permanently interesting.

Charles Dudley Warner had known a corner of New England which in its remoteness still retained in his formative years much of the rock-founded stability and external austerity of the eighteenth century. When Harriet Beecher Stowe was writing of her girlhood in Litchfield, and shortly after Mark Twain had indelibly recorded in *Tom Sawyer* his boyhood on the Mississippi, Warner wrote *Being a Boy*,[123] the recollection of his childhood on a farm in the Berkshires. Although this book was considered a novel at the time of its publication,[124] it is actually a series of simple essays, telling in words of one syllable the experiences of a boy growing up in the rural

New England of the early nineteenth century. The delights and drudgeries of the farm, the trials of Sabbath keeping, the joys of nutting, herb gathering, birch swinging, snowfighting, and all the little pleasures attending the life bounded by farm, meetinghouse, and school are recalled in an atmosphere of quiet humor and tender memory. It is probably Warner's most representative book — unpretentious, undramatic, but authentic in detail.

The New England heritage was to Warner a genial tradition; his memory of it included nothing of its provincial austerity and all of its charm.

> It is a wonder that every New England boy does not turn out a poet, or a missionary, or a peddler. Most of them used to. There is everything in the New England hills to feed the imagination of the boy, and excite his longing for strange countries. I scarcely know what the subtle influence is that forms him and attracts him in the most fascinating and aromatic of all lands, and yet urges him away from all the sweet delights of his home to become a roamer in literature and the world, — a poet and a wanderer. There is something in the soil and the pure air, I suspect, that promises more romance than is forthcoming, that excites the imagination without satisfying it, and begets the desire of adventure. And the prosaic life of the sweet home does not at all correspond to the boy's dreams of the world. In the good old days, I am told, the boys on the coast ran away and became sailors; the country boys waited till they grew big enough to be missionaries, and then they sailed away, and met the coast boys in foreign ports.[125]

Warner had himself wandered far, both in foreign lands and in the literature that he made of them. In his maturity he joined his Nook Farm neighbors in the attempt to go home again.

There was for the boy John — Warner's name for himself — a considerable solitude spent in studying the view available from the top of a tree, in happily searching for rare plants, and in rounding up the cows (which he named *Unus*, *Duo*, up to *Decem*) in the far pasture. His experience with religion was complicated slightly by his inability, despite the promptings of his elders and contemporaries, to feel a conviction of sin. But his only wound was an uneasy apprehension that by being insensitive to sin he was somehow different from other people. This was a passing difficulty. In no other way was the idyl disturbed. Warner's fondness for the memory of his upbringing apparently obliterates all the pain (no reference to the death of his father or his separation from his mother) and all the tumult of childhood. His boy is perhaps not quite alive, but the mellowness of Warner's remembrance makes his book an attractive allusion to old-fashioned New England country life, in the passing of which he felt more than a twinge of regret.

But in Warner, as in Mrs. Stowe, we may note a more general nostalgic tendency than that which many people feel for their own lost youth. The tenor of all his serious work was in a sense not only a summons, but a recall to the good life — as if that life had once been a reality in the earlier days of the nation before the immigration of poverty-stricken masses from Europe had diluted the Puritan stock and before the idealization of material success had superseded the attainment of individual culture. Warner's literary life was a dwelling in the past, whether what had departed was last year's vegetable garden, yesterday's fireside conversation, or the ideals of a preindustrial age. Whenever his voice is still audible and whenever what he is saying still holds one's attention, he is speaking of a way of life already left behind or one that he knows soon will go. He was emotionally as well as logically a conservative. His vision of the dissolution of the middle class by a corrupt plutocracy rises to intensity when his emotional loyalties transcend his documentation of change to dignify a vanishing order with the attractiveness of good and golden days. Perhaps his general nostalgia is merely resistance to change. Perhaps it is peculiar to himself, entirely a personal matter rather than an indication of a social unrest. In any event, seldom has a single recognizable emotion accompanied the production of so much lasting literature as in the tiny community of Nook Farm. Seldom has nostalgia been the one uniformity in such diverse work, and only here, so far as I know, has it appeared to be the one sure characteristic dominant in all the good books of a literary community and absent from all the bad.

For the best work of Mark Twain — the only work clearly imperishable — is similarly the record of a vanished world. Only the books distilled out of his own experience on the Mississippi River and recorded much later in Hartford and Elmira are now generally regarded as among our great books. Nostalgia for his childhood began early in Mark and expressed itself significantly as he began his life in the East. On February 6, 1870, happy, prosperous, and four days married, he wrote Will Bowen, his friend in Hannibal, that the old life had just swept before him like a panorama.

Heavens what eternities have swung their hoary cycles about us since those days were new! — Since we tore down Dick Hardy's stable; since you had the measles & I went to your house purposely to catch them. . . since Jimmy Finn was town drunkard & we stole his dinner while he slept in the vat & fed it to the hogs in order to keep them still till we could mount them and have a ride . . . since we used to undress & play Robin Hood in our shirt-tails, with lath swords, in the woods on Halliday's Hill on those long summer days . . . since I jumped overboard from the ferry boat in the middle of the river that stormy day to get my hat, & swam two or three miles after it (& got it,) while all the town collected on the wharf & for an hour or so looked out across the angry waste of whitecaps toward where people said Sam. Clemens was last seen before he went down . . . since we accidentally burned up that poor fellow in the calaboose; since Laura Hawkins was my sweetheart — . . .[126]

But this feeling was not yet strong or deep enough to give power to a novel about his boyhood. At the time of this letter, Mark tried to construct out of his recollections his first fiction. The *Boy's Manuscript*[127] is an unlucky effort to use the river materials. Cast in the first person, the sketch concerns Billy Rogers's puppy love for a girl named Amy; full of burlesque, it ends in estrangement over Billy's determination to be a pirate. Though the manuscript contains an episode in which Bill Bowen and Billy Rogers stir up a louse with a pin (the tick episode in *Tom Sawyer*), the vision of striding into church as a successful pirate, the wart cure involving burial of a bean at the crossroads, and other specific materials later to appear in *Tom Sawyer*, it foreshadows generally only the Tom and Becky story. The Muff-Potter, Jackson's Island, and Injun Joe sequences, all of which overshadow the boy and girl romance in the story as we know it, do not appear in the first version. More important, the early sketch contains only a very meager characterization of the children and is atmospherically deficient in the more genuinely nostalgic poetry of *Tom Sawyer*.

The composition of the later book, belonging to the Hartford years, was scattered perhaps between 1872 and 1875, with most of the manuscript completed in the fall of 1874. The book — second only to *Huckleberry Finn* — has many faults. Its improvisatory progress skips past psychological anachronism and improbabilities of time to arrive at the perfection of an idyl that has engaged the mature imagination of many people in three generations. The power it still possesses has little to do with its realism or its particularity as a more or less accurate picture of childhood in a given place. Nostalgia elevates the book to a universality including most men's rearward vision of childhood's excitement. The lives of Tom Sawyer, Huckleberry Finn, Joe Harper, and Becky Thatcher are in an ideal way full of adventure, joy and terror, and the beauty of the whole outdoors. The book they live in has power to evoke the meaning of childhood, not as it is, but as it is looked back upon from a geographical, cultural, or psychic distance — a power which Mark achieved between his fumbling beginning in the *Boy's Manuscript* in 1870 and his successful transformation of its materials into his novel of 1875. The achievement of cultural and psychic distance in the first five years of his identification with Hartford has been detailed in earlier chapters.

The conscious attention that Mark gave his manuscript indicates the accidental nature of its success. In the method of patchwork creation soon to be typical of all his composition, he was not sustained by the conviction that he was at work on something of great importance. On July 5, 1875, he wrote to Howells that *Tom Sawyer* was a book only for adults. But in January 1876 his story was "professedly and confessedly" for boys and girls. This change of direction affected the text of *Tom Sawyer* very little (although the adults of St. Petersburg may once have had more importance in the plot), but it reflects the uncertainty of Mark's own point of view toward his work and his unconsciousness of the influence his residence in the East was working upon it. Beneath his waverings about the purpose of the book and its proper audience is a central emotional certainty that makes *Tom Sawyer* a reproduction of the beauty of a Hannibal childhood as perceived from maturity in Hartford. So directive was that emotion that Mark could develop his theme without indulgence in the burlesque which always intrudes when he is uncertain about what to do with his materials. Much later, the real meaning of his book became clear to him. "*Tom Sawyer*," he said, "is simply a hymn, put into prose form to give it a worldly air." [128]

Mark's return to the experience of his Mississippi days was in the beginning instinctive and intermittent. In the middle seventies, nostalgia did not dominate his writing to lead him back, without other stimulus, to the river. It is probable that *Tom Sawyer* arose partly out of the success that children's books were enjoying in the seventies and specifically out of Mark's admiration for his friend Aldrich's *Story of a Bad Boy*.[129] An external suggestion, anyhow, prompted Mark to write in 1874 the series of papers comprising *Old Times on the Mississippi*. Howells had asked him for something for the *Atlantic*; Mark had nothing ready. But soon he was writing his editor,

> I take back the remark that I can't write for the Jan. number. For Twichell and I have had a long walk in the woods, and I got to telling him about old Mississippi days of steamboating glory and grandeur as I saw them (during 5 years) from the pilot-house. He said "What a virgin subject to hurl into a magazine!" I hadn't thought of that before. Would you like a series of papers to run through 3 months or 6 or 9? — or about 4 months, say? [130]

Twichell's delight, then, in the river experience sent Mark into his proper territory to recreate, again with permanent success, the vanished steamboat age. Under the stimulus of Howells's praise, Mark plunged ahead with these papers in late 1874 simultaneously with *Tom Sawyer*, pleased with the newness of his subject. The result is a brilliant picture of the romance of piloting, full of the river's beauty and excitement and of love for his first profession —

both more meaningful in the remembrance than they had been in actuality.

Mark did not return to the *Atlantic* papers until 1882, when in order to inflate them for a subscription book he revisited the river with a stenographer. The resulting book, *Life on the Mississippi*, published in 1883, is a striking demonstration that not merely the use of Mississippi materials determines the greatness of Mark's work. Those materials had to come from early experience remembered in middle age. The forty chapters he added to the original sketches are a dreary compilation of burlesque yarns, essays on the economics of cotton planting, comments on scenery, and references to such diverse subjects as burial above ground in New Orleans and statistics on churchgoing in St. Louis. The catalogue of contemporary observation along the river, extremely interesting from time to time as social history (as in his description of the "House Beautiful") does not coalesce into the unity of the first twenty chapters. Yet the structure of the *Atlantic* papers is hardly more formal and no more consciously contrived. Their unity is emotional. *Life on the Mississippi* is one-third magnificence and two-thirds the hack work of a professional traveler. The genius of Mark Twain is in this volume exhibited side by side with the dead stuff of his trade. He did not know them apart.

Mark's return to the river, intended only to provide padding for an almost perfect earlier achievement, made more vivid in his own mind the finality with which the world of his youth had disappeared. On the silent levee at St. Louis he was hurt by the desolation that had replaced the steamboatman, once a hero in a glorious age:

> His occupation is gone, his power has passed away, he is absorbed into the common herd; he grinds at the mill, a shorn Samson and inconspicuous. Half a dozen lifeless steamboats, a mile of empty wharves, a negro, fatigued with whiskey, stretched asleep in a wide and soundless vacancy, where the serried hosts of commerce used to contend.[131]

His account of Hannibal springs to life in the midst of the dead chapters because of the reminders he sees there of the past and his sense of subsequent alteration. He recalls the stimulus thunderstorms gave to the conviction of sin and the violence that always relieved the sweetness of his recollections. He remembers the tramp who burned to death in the calaboose after he had given him matches and his own feeling of responsibility for the death. In the emotion prompted by all the still extant signposts to his childhood, he wrote his wife,

> That world which I knew in its blossoming youth is old and bowed and melancholy now; its soft cheeks are leathery and wrinkled, the fire has gone

out in its eyes, and the spring from its step. It will be dust and ashes when I come again. I have been clasping hands with the moribund — and usually they said, "It is for the last time." [132]

The visit to the river in the 1880's was a powerful stimulus to the seminal emotion that had already produced two great books. Experience in review not only gave him the impetus to complete *Huckleberry Finn*, long in a pigeonhole, but fixed his mind permanently on the life of his youth which, despite the variety of his published works, was to become the theme of many of his unpublished manuscripts, as nostalgia for his homeland became intertwined with the bitterness of his maturity.

In the summer of 1883, with the Mississippi country still vivid in his mind, Mark was writing happily and easily. He picked up the manuscript of "Huck Finn's Autobiography," which he had started in July of 1876 "more to be at work than anything else," [133] and carried it nearly to completion. "I'm booming, these days — got health and spirits to waste . . ." he said; "this summer it is no more trouble to me to write than it is to lie." [134] After holding it back until Webster could amass a tremendous advance sale, Mark published his most popular book in February of 1885. Amid a critical silence almost unbroken, *Huckleberry Finn* came into a world which did not for several decades recognize it as a masterwork in our native literature. To the cultivated classes who had loved *The Prince and the Pauper*, *Huckleberry Finn* was a disappointment; [135] but for ordinary people its vulgarity was not repulsive and its truth and humor were instantly apparent.

Huckleberry Finn is a much more complex book than *Tom Sawyer* — more extensive in its materials and more sober in its implications. At first glance, its structure appears carelessly linear; an anecdotal series of adventures is unified chiefly by the continuing presence of Huck Finn or Nigger Jim or both. A score of episodes begins in the absurd forays of Tom's raiding band, skips down the river, and winds up in the mock-romantic delivery of Jim from captivity. The characteristic transition between incidents is as easy as the Mississippi's current; the raft is carried downstream from the completed adventure to the new one around the bend. In contrast to the three carefully interwoven plot strands of *Tom Sawyer*, the nineteen adventures of Huck and Nigger Jim have persuaded many readers that as a novel *Huckleberry Finn* has the organization of a freight train.

But when Mark Twain was riding the crest of remembrance, he achieved, without trying, a more fundamental unity than plotted formality could ever give his work. The experiences of the wily boy and the naïve slave

MARK TWAIN IN 1875

OLIVIA CLEMENS, ABOUT 1875

THE MARK TWAIN HOUSE

HARTFORD, MAIN STREET, ABOUT 1870

HARTFORD, OLD STATE HOUSE SQUARE, ABOUT 1870

undergo continuous fourfold intensification. Beginning with the boarding of the *Walter Scott*, tension accrues steadily through more and more involved incidents up to final release in the burlesque ending. The naturally climactic course of the narrative through raids by the Duke of Bridgewater and the rightful King of France on Pokeville (scene of the revival meeting), on Bricksville (where the Royal Nonesuch was performed), and on Peter Wilks's village is paralleled by an increasingly revealing description of riverbank culture.[136] And as the book pursues its major purpose of dissecting the unelevated humanity of midcontinental villagers, it grows gradually toward a complete characterization of Huck and Nigger Jim. The documentary novel thus comes alive as a masterpiece of imagination. Finally all the picaresque themes are ingested into an authoritative atmospheric wholeness more informing than that in Mark's other river works. The Mississippi is the ribbon of the plot, river life is its single subject, and superstition, chicanery, gullibility, innocence, naïveté, and shrewdness are among its distillates.

If *Tom Sawyer* is the idyl of boyhood, then *Huckleberry Finn*, ostensibly only a sequel, is the careful anatomy of an alluvial civilization. Mark Twain's observations are refracted through the unshockable resilience of his almost neutral observer. Unaffected by the violence he sees, Huck brushes off his contacts with the meanness of river life as all in a day's drifting. To him his father's drunkenness and ignorant cruelty are evils to be outwitted, not deplored. If he is moved at all by the bawdyhouse tumbling down the flooded river with a corpse aboard or by the plight of the cutthroats marooned in a wrecked ship, he does not, at any rate, change expression. When he is entangled in a feud between rival clans of river nobility, he puts a swift period to his perception of tragedy:

> When I got down out of the tree I crept along down the river bank a piece, and found the two bodies laying in the edge of the water, and tugged at them till I got them ashore; then I covered up their faces and got away as quick as I could. I cried a little when I was covering up Buck's face, for he was mighty good to me.[137]

Huck takes panoramic rascality for granted. When (in the persons of the Duke and the King) particularly aggressive knavery crowds onto the little raft, Huck adjusts his native wiliness to accommodate rather than defeat it. For if he had "never learnt nothing else out of pap, [he had] learnt that the best way to get along with his kind of people is to let them have their own way." He never has time for sentimentering, but he is sorry to see the impostors tarred and feathered in Pikesville. But though the aggressors get a little of his pity, their stupid victims in the sordid villages rate none. Huck's account of the gullibility and cowardice of the classically decadent town of Bricksville — climax of the book's description of decrepit Arkansas — is so completely impartial that the reader attempting to abstract heroism from Colonel Sherburn's defeat of the mob is thwarted by his prior cold-blooded murder of Boggs in the presence of the latter's daughter. An incident ripe for moral judgment by observer, author, and reader is thus left aseptically clean.

But when the wheel of Mississippi life turns again and the royal impostors begin the robbery of the Wilks daughters, Huck takes his stand with the innocent, for here there is something nobler to defend than greedy stupidity and human hoggishness. After the flight from the graveyard and the sale of Jim's liberty, the gentler life of Hannibal is reintroduced and the book finds again on a farm 1,100 miles down the continent the simple plainness of Tom Sawyer's village. The gathering of the farmers in the Phelps living room, in awkward ambush for Jim's deliverers, is the last sharp vignette of river people. *Huckleberry Finn* puts to canvas a single picture of the Mississippi valley and of the defective progeny of Adam who ingloriously inhabit it.

The teeming variety of loafers, deadbeats, cowards, raftsmen, robbers, revivalists, and drunks is balanced by a reasonable number of better people — Mrs. Loftus, the Phelps and Wilks families, the Grangerfords, and, above all, Nigger Jim. The runaway slave develops from merely superstitious chuckleheadedness as Miss Watson's slave to selfless heroism as Tom Sawyer's nurse. His simplicity, innocence, patience, and purity of character, in contrast to the villainy on the raft and the spiritual starvation ashore, justify hope for the human race. It is the slave, not the slaveholder, who is finally vindicated. To add an ironic bite to the contrast between Jim and lesser whites, Mark Twain preserves even in Huck the condescension of white to black and revives again and again the moral struggle flaring within Huck whenever he must face himself as a nigger stealer. This theme achieves its climax in Huck's famous battle with his conscience, but on the road to his final capitulation he more than once is forced to humble his racial superiority before the Negro's surer generosity. After Huck had duped Jim into believing that their separation in the fog was a dream and Jim in simple dignity reproached his tormentor, Huck thought a while:

> It was fifteen minutes before I could work myself up to go and humble myself to a nigger — but I done it and I warn't ever sorry for it afterward, neither.[138]

Huck's defensive refusal to admit Jim's superiority, except in specific instances of unkindness repented, is a vertebra of the book's realism.

Huck Finn and Mark Twain both looked without abhorrence upon the valley civilization and the people trapped in its mud and meanness. In contrast to the smallness of the river settlers is the natural loveliness that had bathed *Tom Sawyer* and *Life on the Mississippi* with pastoral warmth. Jackson's Island is still as beautiful and its thunderstorms are as lurid. Huck is articulate about the pleasures permitted by climate — lounging naked on a raft, swimming in warm river water, and watching stars at night. "It's lovely to live on a raft" and "the sky looks ever so deep when you lay down on your back in the moonshine" are his pastoral refrains. The still heat, characteristic of the Mississippi valley through all climatic variations, mutes the noises on the Phelps farm:

> When I got there it was all still and Sunday-like, and hot and sunshiny; the hands was gone to the fields; and there was them kind of faint dronings of bugs and flies in the air that makes it seem so lonesome and like everybody's dead and gone; and if a breeze fans along and quivers the leaves it makes you feel mournful, because you feel like it's spirits whispering — spirits that's been dead ever so many years — and you always think they're talking about *you.* As a general thing it makes a body wish *he* were dead, too, and done with it all.[139]

Huck's susceptibility to superstition afflicted him thus mournfully not only at the Phelps place but throughout his long voyage; fright before supernatural signs is as essential to the atmospheric uniqueness achieved in *Huckleberry Finn* as is the Mississippi summer. Huck and Jim connect in their own minds the disparate events of their downstream voyage as inevitable consequences of such mad acts as handling a snakeskin. Jim with his hair-ball had foretold the return of Huck's father. The early pages of the book, full of incantations, are recalled at the end when Jim's Negro guardian turns out to be more naïvely superstitious even than he. Huck observed that "niggers is aways telling about witches in the dark by the kitchen fire," but even he "always reckoned that looking at the new moon over your left shoulder is one of the carelessest and foolishest things a body can do." No recollection of life on the Mississippi came to Mark Twain unattended by a sense of the present poetry of what had once been the shiver of midnight dread in the recognition of evil omens.

The narrative excitement, social description, definitive characterization, and atmospheric poetry of *Huckleberry Finn* are suspended in a perfect medium. In his earlier Mississippi books, which though less complete as evocation are nevertheless successful, Mark Twain had written in his own person. Now Huck's first utterance,

> You don't know about me without you have read a book by the name of *The Adventures of Tom Sawyer*, but that ain't no matter,

announced the undertaking, for the first time, of a major novel in the American vernacular. Because it is unlikely that in life Huck could be such a virtuoso even in his own idiom, the book becomes an extended tour de force, but the brilliance with which the spoken language is made to embrace its large subject dispels the fundamental unrealism in Huck's fluency. His natural speech, recorded with seldom-interrupted fidelity, is competent to describe unforgettably a vertical cross section of American interior civilization. The correspondence between style and substance contributes to the uniqueness of *Huckleberry Finn* as a chronicle yielding more insight into American experience each time it is read.

Yet the structure of this strong book, as we know from Mark Twain's biography, took shape in a series of improvisatory spurts inspired finally by a lucky visit to the river. Its greatness cannot be attributed to conscious skill and its success testifies not to art but to instinct. The detachment which in this instance disciplined Mark Twain's mercurial gifts is plainly an accident of his own equilibrium in the middle eighties. For Mark had reached, in the years between 1880 and 1885, his own brief maturity. His youthfully exuberant acceptance of everything in life had been tempered by experience but not yet transformed into the acrid bitterness that was soon to deflate his natural buoyancy. This five-year period was probably the most satisfying half decade of Mark's life—the harvest time of fame, riches, and family happiness. His pleasure in Nook Farm was at its peak, and his subscription to its values attained the near perfection of which *The Prince and the Pauper* had been the fitting celebration.

But Mark Twain was at least partly aware also that at fifty years of age he had reached the summit of his felicity. He knew by this time the limitations of human nature and stood on the circumference of his own aspirations. He was looking back to a simpler time with a greater insight and resignation than he had known before. His nostalgia was more complicated than the simple homesickness of 1875, the year of *Tom Sawyer*, and he no longer was inclined to paint the Mississippi in entirely charming imagery. The first intimations of disillusion extended backward to deepen into realistic colors (but not blacken into despair) the romantic hues of his earlier recollections. If *Tom Sawyer* implied wishfulness that life should continue to be what Mark imagined it to have been when he was a child, *Huckle-*

berry Finn is the more experienced realization that the vanished life of the river was no more genuinely idyllic than human life ever is. To imagine it more beautiful than it was, was no longer necessary. The adult willing to live in a world of many values and deal with each situation as it comes need not impose his own morality on the world's disorder and then lament its deafness to his philosophizing.

At any rate, *Huckleberry Finn* is an objective portrayal of a society neither virtuous nor vicious, neither hateful nor attractive. Since the qualities of humanity impartially reported are topics upon which Mark Twain was later to editorialize violently, his unique restraint during the composition of this novel seems a facet of his own brief equable arrangement with life. For a time he could take baseness and indecency in stride and accept their role even in the enchantment of the river. Later he not only abandoned the balanced point of view but threw out the scales.

Yet in spite of his tolerant adjustment to human imperfections, Mark was still, like his friends about him, looking backward. At the peak of his happiness, he was impelled in Hartford to remember Hannibal and put it on paper. In Nook Farm, imagination grew fertile only when it turned to the environment that had first put its mark upon the writer. Mark's books, like Warner's and Mrs. Stowe's, derive their power from evocation of a pre-industrial society. All the Nook Farm writers — different in many other ways — were rebels against the Calvinist certainties of their childhood. Their rebellion may have left them free, but it could not erase what they first had learned or replace the emotional security that intellect had shattered. Their generation bridged the gulf between a socially stable and a patternless America. Their conflict with confusion made good books. The classics emerging from the environmental uneasiness beneath the surface placidity of Nook Farm stem more directly from the pain of changing worlds than from all the literary gifts lavished on trash and truth alike. Beautiful in the distance beyond the Civil War and peaceful in contrast to the kaleidoscopic present, youth remembered is the emotional source of Nook Farm's literature.

6

THE DISSOLUTION OF NOOK FARM

1891–1918

The Death of Harriet Beecher Stowe

IN 1891 MARK TWAIN CLOSED THE GREAT HOUSE HE COULD NO LONGER maintain and moved his family to Europe. No ceremony attended his going; the farewells were casual. The absence would be brief — a year, perhaps. Neither Mark nor Livy, nor any of those who remained behind in Nook Farm, suspected that the Clemens family would never live again in the house that had been the brightest, the gayest, and the most celebrated in the city. And those in Hartford who saw Patrick McAleer drive the Clemenses down Asylum Hill to the railroad station had no idea that this June departure meant the passing of Nook Farm's ascendancy as a literary colony, its greatest writer gone for good.

Harriet Beecher Stowe still lived in Nook Farm, it is true, and after the Clemens house was shuttered she continued to roam its grounds and play with the neighborhood children there. She clambered up and down the wooded bank and sailed improvised boats in the dirty water of the Little River. But, despite her physical presence, she had withdrawn from the adult community years before. Even when awareness of herself occasionally returned, she was almost oblivious to her surroundings. She hardly remembered having been an author.

Harriet was waiting. With a crowded life behind her, a life stretching over most of the nineteenth century, she was conscious only that she had known sorrow and that soon she would know joy. In the meantime she was at peace. All the fame she had attained, the great people she had met, the books she had written, all the causes she had championed and attacked meant nothing to her now. The turmoil, the trouble, the passions that had moved her had faded before the bright vision of heaven that made her last days a time of calm expectancy. No failure of her mind could efface the religious certainty in her heart's fiber. The experiences of her life, except the always vivid childhood, she could forget. The world in which she lived became vague as the eternity toward which she made her way came nearer and nearer. Whenever she became aware of her neighbors and others who had been her friends, she spoke only of heaven and the peace its nearness gave her old age. When Livy Clemens sent her roses on Christmas Day of 1890, Harriet returned thanks and consoled Livy for the death of Mrs. Langdon. "She will no more come to us," Harriet wrote, "but we shall go to her in that beautiful land where there is no more sickness, sorrow nor death, forever, & where God shall wipe away all tears."[1] And three years later, in almost her last letter, she wrote to Oliver Wendell Holmes of the thoughts filling her mind in intervals of lucidity:

> I make no mental effort of any sort; my brain is tired out. It was a woman's brain and not a man's, and finally from sheer fatigue and exhaustion in the march and strife of life it gave out before the end was reached. And now I rest me, like a moored boat, rising and falling on the water, with loosened cordage and flapping sail. . .
>
> Blessed I have been in many ways, in seeing many of the desires of my heart fulfilled, and in having the love of many people, as has been made manifest to me in these my declining years. Sorrows also I have had, which have left their mark on my heart and brain.
>
> But they are all passed now. I have come to the land of Beulah, which is heaven's borderland, from whence we can see into the gates of the celestial city; and even *now* all tears are wiped from my eyes.[2]

After another three years, Mrs. Stowe's long rest in Beulahland came quickly to an end on June 28, 1896. Simple funeral services were held a few days later at 73 Forest Street. The house was filled with the kind of flowers Harriet had gathered in her rambles about the neighborhood— ferns, lilies of the valley, white lilies, and roses. Twichell read briefly from the Bible; Francis Goodwin read Episcopal prayers. No eulogy sped Harriet's soul to heaven. It would have been an impertinence to comment on the credentials of the person who was credited with reopening the Celestial

City to all those who loved God. She had, in her eighty-five years, demonstrated beyond question her own eligibility.

The citizens of Hartford and the old friends from other cities who gathered in the little gray house in Nook Farm for Harriet's funeral knew that the death of Mrs. Stowe had the finality of a historic moment. The Forest Street home had been a shrine to which they had come quietly to pay their respects — long after the world, which once she had shaken to the heart, had forgotten that Harriet Beecher Stowe still lived. The community had lost its saint. With her death the American past — the domination of New England, the struggle to end slavery, the Civil War — had suddenly become history; her funeral was occasion for recalling not only the changes that had taken place in America but the departed glory of Nook Farm. Those who still survived looked at each other, remembering when they were young and reviewing the events of the years that had made them old. Mrs. Henry Ward Beecher was there. Isabella Beecher Hooker sat apart from her. Both were old and tremulous, but, since the quarrels during the Beecher-Tilton trial a quarter century earlier, neither had forgiven the other. Susie Clemens, visiting Hartford while her father was lecturing around the world, prompted the mourners to think of Mark Twain and Livy and of the better days when the Clemenses had lived next door. Annie Fields and Sarah Orne Jewett made their last pilgrimage to Nook Farm. Mrs. Fields laid purple flowers on the coffin. Miss Jewett, whose admiration of Mrs. Stowe begot her own study of New England character, mourned that none present could "really know and feel the greatness of the moment," but its significance as a symbol of the earth's turning grew steadily in her mind after her return to South Berwick.[3]

It was a great moment. Harriet Beecher Stowe had been — besides a central figure in the events and thoughts and emotions of her day — a genius in the recreation of an important period in American history and in the animation of a host of characters in the time and place she understood best. Her greatest work, complicated by contemporary and accidental characteristics and circumscribed by its very appropriateness to her own temperament and to her environment, rises above the circumstances of her life and times to be permanently delightful. She was an originator in literature. The reader of this day may find in her work the satisfaction that literature exists to furnish and the interplay of temperament and society that brings it into existence.

Among the friends who came from New York was J. B. Pond, who had managed the lecture tours of Mrs. Stowe and more often those of Mark Twain. He was well known in Nook Farm. Like the others who came to bury Mrs. Stowe, he renewed his acquaintance with the living. For him the absence of Mark Twain caused an even greater vacancy than Harriet's death. His letter to Mark describing his visit must have moved Mark also to recall the days when all his neighbors and he were young.

My Dear Friend:—

I have just returned from Hartford with Mrs. [Henry Ward] Beecher. We attended Mrs. Stowe's funeral yesterday. Mr. Twichell conducted the service. It was a pathetic incident, and I might almost say, event. There were present most of the distinguished people of Hartford, and all of your old neighbors. Within a few minutes walk lay Mrs. [Mary Beecher] Perkins. In her ninety-second year,—a physical invalid with an intellect as brilliant and sparkling as ever. She is quite deaf. I called on her and she seemed quite delighted to see me. She had not seen Mrs. Stowe for eight years, although she has been stopping in Hartford for two years. She said she preferred to remember her sister as she saw her eight years ago. Mr. and Mrs. Warner and Susie [Clemens] [4] were present. Charley Stowe [Harriet's son] was there with his family. I received a gracious reception from everybody, having known Mrs. Stowe so long and she having been my friend for twenty years. It was a pleasure to hear so many kind expressions from everybody. I called at Mr. Warner's and Mrs. Warner went with me to your house where we found Susie in possession of the old place. She, and her faithful Katie, spend their days at the house. She seemed very glad to see me. She told me that she had heard from you about two weeks ago; that you had decided to spend the winter in England (near London), and that she and Jean [Mark's third daughter] expected to sail in September. She seems quite happy where she is. She says it seems very much like home to her, and she wished you would come back. The place is beautiful, but there is a terrible atmosphere of lonesomeness there. The last time I visited the place you and Mrs. Clemens and a party of Hartford friends were there, and it was delightful. Mr. and Mrs. Twitchell had many kind inquiries and expressions for you and of you and are very very anxious that you come back sometime to live. I wonder if your ears burned yesterday. Everybody seems to think you fail to give them any information about yourself. Mr. Warner said, "Mark never tells any of us anything about his movements, or even his address." I replied that I thought you were uncertain as to that yourself. We have all come to the conclusion, however, that you will be in South Africa during August, so I send you letters and papers there.

I started to write you about Mrs. Stowe, but it seems to me my thoughts are of the living more than on the dead. Susie told me that she (Mrs. Stowe) was in the habit of coming over nearly every day to your place for a chat, and was pleasant and childish. Hattie Stowe [Harriet's daughter, one of the twins] told me that her Mother had played with the children and seemed more like a child for the last four years than a woman. Her memory seemed to have failed, and she seldom referred to the past. She was in good physical health until she was strikken last Friday. There are none of her old friends left to write of her. The familiar poet-friends, and men of letters, she has outlived; even Mrs. Gov. Claflin, of Boston, died on the 13th of May last. Mrs. Beecher, in her eighty-fifth year, accompanied me. She is quite feeble. Mrs. Hooker was at the funeral, but she and Mrs. Beecher did not meet, — a very pathetic condition of affairs.

P.S.: — I had a delightful visit with Mr. and Mrs. Twitchell, who are about the most substantial friends you have in the world. J. B. P.[5]

Nook Farm was still an integrated community after 1896, but without Mrs. Stowe and without the Clemens family life to its aging inhabitants seemed to be without the brilliance once so meaningful.

The Last Years of John and Isabella Beecher Hooker

JOHN HOOKER WAS TO LIVE ON IN HARTFORD UNTIL 1901 AND HIS WIFE UNTIL 1907. Their old age was a prolongation of the interests in feminism and spiritualism that dominated their lives during the seventies and eighties. In 1891, their golden wedding anniversary was an elaborate affair of great public interest. The influx of Beechers, feminists, and other admirers of Isabella into Hartford to pay tribute to the couple was a heartening indication to the old warriors that their lives had been worth the heartaches. The ceremony underlines the importance of Nook Farm's nonliterary activities.

The unconventionality of the Hookers' religious and political opinions apparently did not diminish the fervor with which their fiftieth anniversary was honored. The press of Hartford and of surrounding cities, not yet bringing itself to mention Isabella with much enthusiasm, praised John all the more eagerly to compensate for its omission of his wife. On August 5, 1891, the *Post* called him "the best-loved member of his profession in the state to-day"; the *Courant* of the same date announced, "Few come to his years who are so universally valued and beloved of their fellow-men, whose influence has made so unswervingly for righteousness." The neighbors helped John and Isabella plan a large reception in the City Mission building. Lilly Warner took charge of the elaborate decorations. Portraits of most of the Hookers' ancestors and collateral relatives were hung about the platform. The whole city was invited to the day-long festivities via public notice.[6] The hall was thronged all afternoon and evening. Side by side on a dais draped in evergreens, John and Isabella looked happily over their courtiers. William Lloyd Garrison came down from Boston, and Thomas K. Beecher from Elmira. Susan B. Anthony and a large company of suffragists circulated among Hartford's society women, chief of whom was Mrs. Samuel Colt. In the evening Senator Hawley presided over appropriate ceremonies. At their close, the whole company sang hymns and Dr. Edward Beecher, 87, pronounced a shaky benediction. The reception was the climactic event of the Hookers' last years; the applause of their friends and the effusive letters from absent celebrities were most pleasant.

But the golden wedding celebration did not mark the Hookers' retirement from public life or mean that their remaining years were happily free from hostilities. John lived more quietly than Isabella. His long association with the Supreme Court as reporter continued until 1897, and now, no longer ambitious to be appointed one of the judges, he enjoyed his work thoroughly. His chief amusement during the droning of the lawyers was the composition of doggerel. He and the judges dozed frequently. If one of them woke up to find another asleep, he composed a poem humorously critical of such unjudicial behavior. This simple pastime never palled. After his retirement from the court, John wrote miscellaneous essays and letters to the press and finally his patchwork *Reminiscences*, published in 1899. His miscellaneous papers were comments on morality, religion, and politics. Their exhortation ranged from appeals to young men designed to keep them pure until marriage and to the public to restrain the abandon of bicyclists, whose recklessness endangered human life.[7] His last years were leisurely, simple, and, in a way, scholarly. In February 1901 death did not take John Hooker unaware. If the Hartford *Courant* is accurate, he had ample time for his fitting final remarks: "*Oh praeclarum illum diem, cum ad illum divinum concilium coctumque profiscam, atque ex hac turba et coltuviae discedam.*" In epitaph, he was named the embodiment of "good old Colonial stock and of old Colonial stuff." [8] But his withdrawal from the toil and trouble actually had been accomplished some years before his death, and like his sister-in-law, Mrs. Stowe, he had been able to contemplate heaven in a long period of peace before he set out to find the land of which he had felt compelling intimations.

Isabella pursued her two main interests, feminism and spiritualism, with undiminished vigor until her death. The great comfort of her old age was that woman suffrage was much closer than it had been in 1869, but the likelihood of her death before women were finally enfranchised made her furious. "The degradation of my political classification with minors, criminals, and idiots is harder to bear than ever before," she wrote in 1905, "and rouses within me a storm of indignation that shakes my very soul of souls." [9] Her anger sustained her crusading energy. In 1892 she petitioned the Connecticut Constitutional Convention to adopt state suffrage, but the gentlemen who had been so kind the preceding year refused even to hear her now. She remained active in the National Suffrage Association, and in the nineties was a venerable celebrity at its meetings. At the 1898 convention she took the stage as usual, a handsome figure in silver gray, and began to read her speech. She could not be heard by the audience; it became audibly restless. Susan Anthony interrupted to chide the gathering and to observe that it ought to be perfectly satisfied to sit still and look at Mrs. Hooker—"a picture to delight the artist." Isabella then said, "I never could give a written speech, but Susan insisted that I must this time." She put her manuscript down and spoke thereafter with her customary force. When she was done, the hall rang with applause. Susan Anthony threw her arms about Isabella; the resulting tableau brought all the audience to tears. Mrs. Anthony then said:

> To think that such a woman, belonging by birth and marriage to the most distinguished families in our country's history, should be held as a subject and have set over her all classes of men, with the prospect of there being added to her rulers the Cubans and the Sandwich Island Kanakas. Shame on a government that permits such an outrage! [10]

Isabella said later that she would be glad to join her husband-lover in the Great Beyond, if only she could first shake off her earthly disfranchisement. The respect she commanded as a stunning old lady, the procession of suffrage strategists who came to her home for counsel, the satisfactions of a long and courageous career of leadership could not compensate for her inability to mark a ballot and place it in a ballot box. Until she won the privilege unjustly denied her, heaven could wait.

Isabella remained constantly in touch, late in life as well as early, with the next world. In her last years she was still developing mediums and perfecting her own sensitivity. In 1905 she took a Mrs. Lazarro from Hartford to her Norfolk summer home, and with her newest friend had long communication with her dead husband. Since Clara Clemens was then in a sanatorium near by, Isabella asked Mark to come in for a conversation, but later withdrew her invitation in a fit of the querulousness with which she now treated all nonbelievers, no matter how long they had been her friends. "Dear Friend Clemens," she wrote,

> I find I must recall my invitation to you to meet my friend Mrs. Lussarro [Lazarro] in my cottage for friendly converse on the great questions of life & immortality. My thought was that being a psychic yourself & understanding in part the laws of spirit intercourse you were ready to enter the whole realm under the guidance of competent teachers such as Mr. Hooker & myself. So I sent you

his book of Reminiscences & waited to hear from you . . . I find that you are still in the attitude of most so called *"investigators."* You know it all — but you demand through these public mediums an elucidation of the wisdom & justice of the omniscient Creator of the Universe. You have certain tests in your mind & till these are satisfied you decline to listen to evidence.

Well dear friend it will be a long and wearisome journey that way, so I thought of inviting you to meet the little woman who stands by the little wicket gate to immortality & quietly opens it to every traveler that has the countersign — it is closed to all others. But we were admitted, my beloved & I, long years ago as I told you — & have almost walked the heavenly streets *together* for years & years — till he entered in, & *still we are together.* So I meant to invite you to talk with *us* in a friendly way through our good friend who holds the key to the wicket gate.

But I see you are not ready for such humble entrance, so I must withdraw my invitation for this afternoon but am most cordially & affectionately your old friend

Isabella Beecher Hooker [11]

As in the seventies and eighties, then, Isabella's eccentricity about the future world complicated her present relationships. The old alignments in Nook Farm held to the end. The Twichells had no use for the Hookers; the Warners remained the Hookers' closest friends.[12] Twichell kept Mark informed of the Hartford gossip about Isabella, and through him Mark gathered that everybody in Hartford hated her. Twichell wrote in December of 1897 of his consternation in unexpectedly finding Isabella at the Warners' and again, in October 1898, of his amazement at the Warners' spending the whole summer with Isabella. Once more in April of 1899 he wrote Mark of his sorrow that the Warners were deeper in Isabella's toils than ever. Mark Twain stayed neutral, for though he heard little good of Isabella he respected her courageous defiance of Hartford prejudices and recognized her brilliance.

Meanwhile Isabella recorded in page after page her transactions with the spirit world. As she came closer to the end she returned to the obsessive certainty that she would be called upon to govern the earth.[13] But most of all her spirit messages were a solace to her unhappiness and a substitute for defective adjustment to a callous world unjust to women of distinguished heritage. Isabella took heart each morning; she began the day by receiving the greetings of all her relatives and friends in heaven. One such rendezvous was recorded in the *Courant* of March 20, 1908, as follows:

Lots of your family want to say good morning. Lots of Footes [Lyman Beecher's in-laws] and Beechers, quite a little army come to make a morning call and wish you all a happy day, but your father leads the procession and he brings some Footes with him, and Beechers and Hookers join hand in hand and Days with John Hooker and all make a circle, and Mr. Day [husband of her daughter Alice], wants to say he knows he's welcome, though not as deserving as he might be. No ill feeling but stubbornness.

In 1907 Isabella died at eighty-five. Those who hated her were silent for a time; her admirers praised her courage, her devotion to her view of truth, her brilliance, and her leadership in the suffrage fight. Mark Twain was an honorary pallbearer at the funeral. But no sooner were the services over than her granddaughter, Katherine Burton Powers (the girl who Isabella was sure would not live past New Year's Day of 1877) brought suit to break Isabella's will.[14] During the litigation Isabella's traffic with spirits became evidence and the city of Hartford grew widely familiar with her neurotic imaginings. All the old quarrels were recalled. The career of Isabella Beecher Hooker was reviewed more in malice than in pity.

Isabella's long residence in Nook Farm extended from the years when it was woodland and pasture to the time when it was no longer distinguishable as an urban neighborhood. The flash of her eccentricity gave life to the colony. Her contagious interests in some of the great social questions of her day were exhilarating. The controversies she provoked were certainly never dull. Her contributions to the ideas and experience of her circle were lavish. Her deranged aspirations, which took form in courageous and nonconformist behavior, appear at first to have no literary importance. In their context, however, they assume a surprising relevance to an understanding of Mark Twain's milieu. Isabella Beecher Hooker was never mad. Her troubled life reveals in convenient magnification the partial conflict that forced into form the greatest books of her neighbors.

Charles Dudley Warner: The Last Decade

WARNER'S LAST NINE YEARS WERE BUSY ONES, BUT HE DID NOT WRITE AS RElentlessly as during the previous twenty years, nor did he contribute anything new. Aside from the collections of magazine articles which we have already noted, he published three books after Mark Twain's departure from Hartford. *The People for Whom Shakespeare Wrote* is a simple and pleasant book asserting that if we would comprehend Shakespeare we must understand the history and popular mind of his time. It outlines customs in food, dress, and travel in Elizabethan England. As soon as convenient, Warner returns to his argument that realism is nonliterary and that the drama of

Shakespeare's time was not merely expressive of the nobler qualities of its own period but "faithful to the emotions and feeling of universal human nature."[15] Warner still believed that only the admirable qualities of man were really universal. His "social" approach to literature, largely a review of interesting but trivial detail, is adapted to prove the thesis that the great writer chooses from the experience of his era those signs of healthfulness that are alone recognizable from generation to generation.

Yet when Warner completed the trilogy beginning in *A Little Journey in the World* with *The Golden House* and *That Fortune*, he described in great detail the deterioration of the best in "universal human nature" amidst a society devoted to the acquisition of wealth. His purpose, of course, was to recall mankind from its headlong abandonment of ethical ideals. He justified his long look at the sordid events attending the loss of Henderson's fortune by his noble purpose, which the naturalists, reveling in tawdriness for its own sake, did not share. "The comfort is," he was careful to say at the end of *That Fortune*, in almost the last pages he wrote,

> in all this struggle of the evil powers masked as justice, that the Almighty Ruler of the world does not forget his own, and shows them a smiling face in the midst of disaster. There is no mystery in this. For the noble part in man cannot be touched in its integrity by such vulgar disasters as we are considering.[16]

Despite the grip of the plutocracy on the financial world, poor people are kind to each other and believe in something. In New York the bankrupts in fortune and affection are nothing in comparison with the "great body of moderately contented, moderately successful, and on the whole happy households."

But it is not Warner's avowed purpose that makes *The Golden House* and *That Fortune* interesting, but the apparently accurate application of his knowledge of contemporary manners. In spite of himself, the realism he kept under too close a control gives his books their only surviving interest; his scoundrels have more life than the vapid good people who are their foils. But though his characters command little attention as persons, their activity reveals the imperfections of democracy, arising, Warner said, from individual greed. Against evidence to the contrary — by which he was sufficiently disturbed to embody it in three novels — he asserted his faith that human nature is inevitably moral. But his manner suggested that he was not entirely satisfied with so threadbare an assumption.

The Golden House continues Warner's description of the dishonesty, cruelty, greed, and ultimate unhappiness of the very rich. At another level, Warner pursues the dangerous attractiveness their way of life has for the well-meaning but unwary young men who is ruined by his betters but redeemed by his faithful wife. At a third stratum Warner shows the attempt of social workers to relieve the sufferings of the poor — sufferings increased by the manipulations of the financiers. Around the three stories an impressive documentation accumulates not only to convince us all that it is better to do good than to be rich and unworthy but to give us numberless glimpses of society. As source books for social history, *The Golden House* and its companion volumes are more valuable than their obscurity would indicate.

In *That Fortune* Warner brings to maturity a young man, Philip, who like himself was fortunately born and brought up in New England and prepared to withstand temptations after he goes to New York to make his way in journalism. Philip had the right equipment for living in the modern world.

> Somehow the old books, and the family life, and the sedate ways of the community he knew, had given him a fundamental and not unarmed faith in the things that were and had been.[17]

He went out from his village with considerable cultivation, candor, common sense, patience, and simplicity of faith, and he used his New England patrimony to "make himself rather than to make money." Like Warner, he went into a law office but left it when he found that he could not sacrifice his ideal of justice to legalistic connivings. Philip then tries to establish himself as a writer, encounters the temptations of meretricious journalism,[18] and decides to stake his all on a serious novel. In the meantime he meets the daughter of Carmen Henderson-Mavick, who has been brought up by her Scotch governess on only the best literature and is consequently, despite the sins of her parents, a maiden of incredible wisdom, virtue, and beauty.[19] After protracted maneuvers Phil wins her and scores a triumph with his idealistic novel. *That Fortune* is continuously interesting, but as Warner's observations of New York society run out, the romance becomes interminable. Eventually, Warner is able to make his major point. The poisonous fortune, dishonestly come by and corrupt in its influence on the human beings enslaved in its spell, is finally lost for good. The inadequacy of the criminal code is compensated for by the inexorableness of the moral law. Legal precepts may not allow indictment of the practices by which such wealth is amassed, but the rightness of things, the balance of crime and punishment preserved by the universe, insures that the transgressors are appropriately destroyed. In Wall Street, the wages of sin is death.[20]

Warner went far in the correction of social ill by moral suasion, but his insight into conditions, keen enough to record the manifestations of evil, did not recognize that the moral code in which he had been trained could never be operative in an unregulated Wall Street. His observations are interesting; his analysis of manners is detailed and precise; but the argument was in its own time ineffective and in ours seems naïve. In the last decade of the nineteenth century, Warner was still applying an old set of standards to a world no longer behaving as if the appeal of the Golden Rule were irresistible. It was anachronistic to recognize the oppressiveness of the plutocracy and to neglect amendment of the laws creating it. Warner, with his faith in the predominance of moral good apparently unshaken, was willing to protect *laissez faire*, to wait until all the robber barons met with poetic justice. He viewed the plutocratic ascendancy as a menace to individual Christian development. His emphasis was ultimately more religious than political. But though he did not accept the need for destroying dictatorship by legislation, he called the attention of a considerable public to what in his eyes was evil. He did not hesitate to speak out.

Warner was not a reformer. In his conservatism he could not second the innocuous socialism of Howells any more than in his loyalty to Hartford attitudes he could sanction acceptance of Wall Street's domination of business. In specific reform movements, however, Warner was very much interested. His last years found him, for example, a tireless advocate of prison reform. The emphasis on individual moral responsibility dominating his novels of manners appears again in his interest in the reclamation of prisoners — all of whom, he believed, came to grief because of remediable personal weakness rather than from environmental compulsion. Every prison should be made a reformatory; the length of every sentence should depend on the progress of rehabilitation in the penitentiary.[21] Rather than amend the conditions permitting lawlessness, Warner focused upon the derelict himself. His allies in this work were Mrs. Fields and Miss Jewett. The former once sent this typical message to Warner: "Our generation has much to do yet to save the country before it can lie down to sleep with quiet mind";[22] the reform of the prison system was apparently at the top of the list.

Warner was busy also campaigning for the education of the Negro in practical trades, working with Hamlin Garland to form the National Institute of Arts, Science, and Letters, and holding the presidency of the American Social Science Association. He continued to travel widely and typically spent his winters in New Orleans. He maintained his interest in his old occupations; he dropped into the *Courant* office to preside over the tickers bringing in the news. He denounced imperialism at the outbreak of the Spanish War and was much displeased when his old friend, Joseph Twichell, mentioned in the pulpit the "incidental benefits" of the conflict.

He felt like rising in meeting to move that "in consonance with the views just presented, we postpone the Christian religion to a more convenient season." [23] In his last year he suffered two attacks of pneumonia; the second forced his retirement from all activities except long walks and reading.

From 1891 on, Warner had been in Nook Farm less and less frequently. His editorial association with *Harper's* magazine, his nominal editorship of the *Library of the World's Best Literature*, as well as his other interests kept him much of the time in New York. The community life of Nook Farm was extremely quiet; his associations were now almost all outside it. Even the Monday Evening Club was no longer a distinguished company. Moreover, both politics and religion were barred as subjects. The men seldom met at each other's houses as in the old days. But on October 20, 1900, a company gathered at A. C. Dunham's on Prospect Street for lunch to say good-by to Twichell and Dunham, who were to sail for Europe on the twenty-second. General Hawley, Colonel Cheney, Charles Hopkins Clark, Twichell, and Warner were all there. The hour, Twichell recalled later, was "full of talk and mirth" and "bright with cheerful spirits." After the lunch was over, Warner set out alone on his daily walk, this time toward the river slums where, as everywhere in Hartford, his erect figure, slow pace, and long white beard made him instantly recognizable to all who saw him. As he passed the gate of a ramshackle house on Windsor Street, he became aware of pain. He made his way to the door of the house and asked the Negro woman who answered his knock whether he might lie down for a moment. She helped him to a cot in a small bedroom. Warner asked her to close the door. When the woman looked in ten minutes later, she saw that he was dead.

"A sad, sad day — the saddest we have known in a long time," Twichell wrote in his Journal,

> Our dear, dear friend — one of the very dearest God has given us in life, is suddenly parted from us . . . Seldom in all past years has so hard a duty been laid upon me as go with Charley Clark and Dr. Porter to the house bearing the terrible news to Susie that she was a widow. She was, of course, completely overcome at first, but sustained the shock with as much fortitude as any woman could . . . Of late Charley had been often at our house, stopping in in the course of his rambles, with which, being unable to work, he had beguiled his time, and had had many long talks with Harmony who was also more or less of an invalid — talks which she had greatly enjoyed and which are inexpressibly precious to her in memory. It was a grief to her that she could not go at once to Susie and remain with her, but the Doctor forbade. She was not permitted even to attend the funeral.[24]

Twichell and Parker conducted the services. Mark Twain and Clara Clemens came up from New York,[25] without Livy for she was not strong enough to make the trip. All Warner's surviving friends gathered in the Asylum Hill Congregational Church. There were no writers now in Nook Farm.

Warner's was a household name; his career was widely reviewed in the press.[26] He was memorialized everywhere for his kindness, humor, charm, and idealism, for his influence in his own lifetime was derived more directly from his personality than from his books. His memory was safe, Howells wrote to Mrs. Warner on October 29, 1900, "because he was both fine and kind." Charles Hopkins Clark reasserted the permanence of his fame in the *Courant* on October 20, 1910:

> Ten years ago today, men and women were saying to each other in Hartford — and in a thousand towns beside — "Charles Dudley Warner is dead." In that sudden and numbing sorrow we forgot how much there is in such a man over which death has no power and the grave no victory . . .
>
> Once, we remember, he spoke delightedly of the "afterglow" in the Alps; and a beautiful sight it must always be to the nature-lover. Incomparably softer, more lasting and more beautiful is the afterglow of such a life as Mr. Warner's.

And Professor William M. Sloane of Columbia reminded the Social Science Association that Warner would long be remembered, for

> Throughout the trying epoch of the great rebellion, throughout the still more trying epoch of ill-starred reconstruction he was a leader of New England thought, an accepted councillor, sage and conservative . . . He came to see the unity of the United States with large vision, as if from a mountain top . . . The expansive power of New England character was never represented in greater brilliancy than in him.[27]

But despite these predictions, memory of Charles Dudley Warner soon faded. By 1914 only those who had known him during the brilliant day of the Nook Farm colony still remembered him, and they were all about to die. Twichell wrote of him:

> For more than thirty years Charles Dudley Warner was my neighbor and friend. The humor, softly radiant, refined, winsome, dewy, mixed with wisdom, that was so distinctive a feature of his mind and utterance, was memorably to me one of the refinements that went with his dear company for all that time . . . His beloved shade haunts the places long gladdened by his presence, the echo of his voice seems there to linger in kindly benediction, the unfailing delight yielded by the affluent felicities of his discourse comes fondly back to memory; but the words in which they were clothed are mostly escaped and gone.[28]

And just as Warner's spoken words were being forgotten even by his closest friends, his books were soon ignored by the reading public. The man who had so earnestly labored in behalf of the ideals dominating his community was remembered after the first World War only as the person who had contributed insipidity to Mark Twain's *The Gilded Age.*

If Warner deserves more attention than he has received in the literary histories of America, it is as a notable and influential writer of his own generation and as a late nineteenth-century representative of its conservative culture. He wrote too much (and not too well), but all his work is, by virtue even of its mediocrity, relevant to an understanding of the taste, the sensibility, and the insight of his contemporaries. Throughout his pleasant essays and his amateur novels he was constantly the stubborn defender of moral integrity and individual responsibility; he brought to bear on the early problems of a crude industrial civilization the point of view of the community in which he lived and of the ethical tradition into which he had been born. Although his criticism of his times is limited by his insistence on individual morality as the salvation of the republic, the political conservatism accompanying his optimism does not obscure the accuracy and interest of his record of contemporary manners.

Warner's rebellion against the religion of his childhood was less violent than Mrs. Stowe's and Mrs. Hooker's; he suffered less in coming to terms with his environment. He may have deceived himself in order to be able to accept with equanimity a world cut adrift, as he said, from certainty. Like his neighbors, he wrote best when he recalled his experiences in a life not complicated by multiplicity. If he accepted equably the disturbances of his time, he was also instinctively and more exactly attuned to an earlier age. The placidity and integrity of his native New England village powerfully attracted him; its influence on him persisted through all his activities. Warner did not escape entirely the conflict invading Nook Farm; his reservations about his own time were the impetus behind his novels. If he had felt more acutely the gulf between what he wanted life to be and what, in his own time, it was, his novels might be more intense, more vivid, and more nearly alive. At any rate, Mark Twain had as a friend and neighbor for twenty years a man who was really not the nonentity he is often considered. Warner was a writer so much of his own century and so close to its ferment that his books contain important testimony. Knowledge of him is indispensable to an understanding of the Nook Farm community in which Mark Twain lived and wrote.

Mark Twain and Joseph Hopkins Twichell

WHEN MARK TWAIN ATTENDED WARNER'S FUNERAL, IT WAS STILL THE HOPE of his friends that he and Livy would come back to Hartford. Their intimates had been eagerly expectant and persuasive all during the nineties. But the culmination of financial difficulty in the collapse of the typesetter and the bankruptcy of the publishing house (both in 1894) delayed their homecoming. Twichell spoke to Livy for the community on April 18, 1893:

> "When are the Clemenses coming home?" is a question raised hereabouts with a frequency, a tone and an accent, which, could they be statistically and phonographically reported to you, would leave you in no doubt of the welcome that awaits your reappearance among us. Indeed, Livy, you *are* missed very sorely by ever as many people whose hunger for you I am sure you would — though humbly — own to be a tribute to your worth.[29]

Mark still hoped an upsurge of fortune would make it possible to resume life in Hartford. At the end of 1894, bankrupt, he despaired of ever being able to return,[30] but despite his need for money he would not consider selling the house and thus severing finally his ties with Nook Farm. A year later, Livy compiled "acres of figures" to demonstrate that the family could reopen the house for the winter of 1895–96 and live within the thousand dollars a month they were spending in Paris. She and her friends were again disappointed when these plans did not prove feasible. After Susie's tragic death in 1896, Mark and Livy wanted to come back as much as ever; at the same time they dreaded trying to live where Susie had died. The neighbors did not, even then, abandon their pleas. Lilly Warner wrote in June of 1899, hoping that Livy might at least revisit Nook Farm:

> I have so long missed you. Surely you will come up here before very long and *visit me*. Livy, dear, I can think how hard it will be the first time, but there must be a first time, and does putting it off lessen the pang? I think not — and when once you have let yourself come I believe you will begin to take comfort in the feeling that you are doing what your darling wanted, and wants, you to do. And then you will find how you are loved, how warmly you will be welcomed by so many dear old friends.[31]

Livy did not come, but still she could not sell the house and she could not say for sure she would not live again in Nook Farm.

Twichell remained importunate, in spite of Mark's recurrent statement that Nook Farm was no longer in Hartford but in the city of heartbreak. In June of 1900, Twichell was downcast after Livy's apparently final report to Susan Warner that she and Mark were not ever coming home. "I wish you could know," he said again,

> how fondly and fervently your return to the old friends that are left here is longed for. I feel sure that, did you return, in a little while you would be thankful that you were here and not elsewhere, — that the associations of your familiar places which are sweet and inspiring would prevail over those that are saddening . . . To miss you there [in the Clemens home] *for good and all* will be a cloud over the rest of our lives.[32]

But his gentle persistence was ineffective. Mark's visit to see Warner buried sealed the decision. He studied the outside of his house and said at last that if he and Livy ever again entered the house to live, their hearts would break at the threshold.

But not until 1902, when F. G. Whitmore, Mark's local business agent, offered the house for sale,[33] did the community finally realize that Mark and Livy would not live in Hartford again. More than a decade had elapsed before Mark Twain could formally renounce residence in the city where he lived longer and more happily than in any other place. "To us," he wrote to Twichell on January 19, 1897,

> our house was not unsentient matter — it had a heart, and a soul, and eyes to see us with; and approvals, and solicitudes and deep sympathies; it was of us, and we were in its confidence, and lived in its grace and in the peace of its benediction . . . We could not enter it unmoved.[34]

It was hard to abandon such a house, but it would have been more difficult to move back into it and face the grief inescapable even in places where Susie had not been.

The long hesitation preceding Mark's decision not to return to Hartford indicates at least that his removal was not inspired by estrangement from the community. In his last years, his stature as a world figure made residence in European capitals and in New York particularly fitting, and all his life his restlessness made frequent moves inevitable. But no evidence indicates that he thought of Hartford as too remote and small a provincial capital to be a suitable residence. His despair, swollen by personal tragedy, susceptibilty to remorse, and disproportionate sensitivity to the accidents of life, made life a mockery in any place. His exaggerated grief over Susie's death[35] convinced him that his misery would be deepened if he were to live again in Nook Farm where life once, in bitter contrast, had been full and pleasant. The rage with which he now contemplated the baseness of humanity was not turned against Hartford people. And except for the villains of the

American Publishing Company, who he thought had swindled him, he never wrote of any person there without affection. Until his death he returned frequently for brief visits and looked up his surviving cronies, all of whom he remembered with more than ordinary pleasure and mourned when they died. No matter how bleak a view he took of the world, he never turned against his old friends or severed his relations with them.

With Twichell, Mark, of course, maintained a continuous correspondence, all of which is preserved in his papers. The chief subject, besides the exchange of mutual affection and news, was Mark's bitterness. The full expression of his anger Twichell welcomed, though he frequently disputed its justice. As their views of life became widely divergent, the old friends did not grow apart. To all Mark's griefs — the death of Susie, the illness of Jean,[36] the death of Livy in 1904 — Twichell brought sympathy sanctioned by his love for Mark. On November 2, 1897, he wrote:

> We have been reading . . . your "In Memoriam" [memorial to Susie Clemens published in 1897] with the accompaniment of a gray autumn sky and the falling leaves to blend with its unspeakable heart-breaking sadness; its aching, choking pathos. It sets all the chords of memory and of love a tremble. It renews the pain of the sense of Life's inscrutable mystery, and of the mystery of human experience. It renews, also, (may I say?) the deep and solemn gladness of the faith that God in whose awful Hand we all are held, is, when you get to the end of things, Love.
>
> But I will not talk about it: in fact it seems to impose hurt and silence upon me. This, however, I could say: if there be those who are thinking "Can this be Mark Twain!" I am not one of them. I have long known that it was in you to chant the music of the hidden soul conversing with the Fathomless Elements, and as I followed your yearning, throbbing song of grief and inextinguishable regret, my inward comment was "It is he; none other than *my* Mark Twain." Mark, it made me love you so that it hurt; and, of course, I felt Livy and the girls behind you; the whole dear group was there; with the beloved shadow in the midst; and, bending over all, the angel of Tears and Sorrow. "Weeping may endure for a night, but joy cometh in the morning," says the old Book. God send you the dawn of that fulfillment soon. But I think he is already sending it.[37]

Twichell's gentle implication that the world would right itself and his persistence in referring Mark to his own faith appear in letter after letter. After Livy's death, when Mark's rage against Twichell's God reached a frenetic climax in long unpublished letters, Twichell asserted the therapeutic value of such release, invited Mark to expend his wrath freely, and at the same time cautioned him to be content with communicating the blasphemies only to his closest friend. On July 3, 1905, Twichell replied to a particularly corrosive outburst on the rotten nation and despicable human race:

All right, Mark, go ahead, I give you free leave to syphon out to me all such secretions whenever they accumulate to the pitch of discomfort. And I think it better, on various accounts, that I should catch them in my pail than that you should . . . empty them into the N. A. [*North American*] Review, or Mr. Rodgers or Mr. Howells, who might not as you suggest be able, for one reason or another, to accommodate as conveniently as I can. 'Tis an old saying that "some men's oaths are more worshipful than some men's prayers." The *motive* of your automatic curses, is, I allow, pure, though the *object* of them might, in my opinion, be more judiciously selected. But I will not argue that point with you.[38]

But sometimes he did argue:

Mark, the way you throw your rotten eggs at the human race doth greatly arride me. We preachers are extensively accused of vilifying human nature, as you are aware; but I must own that for enthusiasm of misanthropy you beat us out of sight. A favorable remark you let fall about Livy in one of your last letters was due no doubt to momentary weakness. Bless her for the kind word to Harmony she postscribed to that which has just come! For my part I think that those two girls are a credit to our race and suggest that something may yet be made of it.[39]

And in another letter:

Hence I do not despair of the Republic, or of the Human Race, for that matter. Dig down in history anywhere you like five hundred years, and take a look around you there, and then go down on your knees and ask forgiveness for being such a doggoned pessimist at the opening of the twentieth century. At the same time felicitate me on its being given me to see . . . that coming in this world in a steady progress from age to age is the kingdom of God — of righteousness . . . Oh! There's an eddy now and then, here and there but the *stream* flows in that direction. Climb out of your hole, Mark; get up where you can see a distance; drop your cursing and shout Glory . . . The *war* isn't ended yet, nor will be for more millenniums. But the parsons are winners, I tell you.

Twichell was always fascinated by Mark's tirades, and when they were not directly associated with a personal grief, he refused to take them seriously:

To me Mark's eulogy of the Human Race was like the strain of an Aeolian harp; such was my affection for the speaker. Of course, I didn't believe a word of it — any more than he did — but I was a charmed listener, and would like to hear it again. As for Harmony — she thought she had never seen him so *gentle*! Ha! Ha!!

Often he finished his replies to Mark's letters with sentences like this:

Your abominable heresies, of which you are now sporting such a menagerie, I will not delay to execrate at this time, but will return to later.

and always with affectionate messages, like this:

I love you, old fellow, in spite of all your bad behavior, very, very dearly.[40]

Mark and his friend met often after 1891. In the summer of 1896, Twichell came down from Keene Valley to be with Susie Clemens in her illness and meet Livy in New York. Mark came to Hartford on almost all of his brief, futile business trips from Europe to the United States in the early nineties. Twichell and Harmony visited Mark and Livy often during their residence in this country between 1900 and 1903. In 1904 Twichell went to Elmira to bury Livy and thereafter — until Mark's death in 1910 —spent many week ends with him in New York.

Mark returned the affection. Despite his impatience with Twichell's optimistic affirmations and his occasional resentment of Twichell's support of Livy in suppressing vehement manuscripts he wished to publish,[41] he welcomed the letters Twichell wrote to him. "You have the touch that heals, not lacerates. And you know the secret places of our hearts," Mark wrote in January 1897. He valued Twichell's skill and knowledge for the rest of his life. Never did the despair that made everything else repugnant alter his relation to Twichell, whose instinctive sympathy and affection were adequate to contain Mark's violence against all Twichell's items of faith. Like everyone Mark loved, Twichell was exempt from the execrations earned by the rest of humanity and from the contempt Mark lavished on himself. Except his own family, Mark valued Twichell more highly than anyone else alive. After Livy's death Twichell could approach more closely than anyone else an intimate statement of her influence:

Dear Mark, dear old Friend:

It is but a week since I parted from you; yet somehow the time seems long — for the reason, I suppose, that I have had so many, many thoughts of you — mostly guessing at *your* thoughts, trying to imagine them, though knowing that I could not. But I have wondered how the days were passing with you — how life and the world — the past and the future — were looking to you.

Of course, as I say, it is consciously quite out of my power to imagine anything about it. I seem to be beholding you, as it were, from a great distance. Yet I cannot get you out of my mind. One thing I am sure of: that I love you inexpressibly. In fact, I never knew till now how deep and how large your room in my affection is. The thought of Livy has a revealing effect upon me that way.

You and she have been and are, so bound up together in my heart's experience, have been so inseparable there, that all my feeling toward Livy carries over to you. And ought not the love — the kind of love — she inspired, now by her passing from us made to know itself, as, alas, it could not before, to quicken in its quickening, the love all round that lived and grew in its sweet light? — as yours and mine did. Harmony and I, reviewing in our talk the memorable years in which we were favored to taste so many pleasures within your doors now see, how clearly, that Livy was the centre of it all. Without her, without her atmosphere, everything would have been different. In her native modesty she was quite unaware of this; but it was so. Oh dear Mark, I keep thinking of things I wish I had said to her. And there are *looks* of hers that come back to me — as, for instance the face with which she used to greet and welcome us when we rejoined her during our Switzerland journey — I sharing the benediction of it because I was with you — a face shining like an angel's. Harmony hardly ever speaks of her without saying, "How she did love Mark!" [42]

The expectation lingering in Mark's mind until 1900 that he might return to Nook Farm meant that emotionally Mark Twain remained closer to Nook Farm than the direction of his ideas in the 1890's would indicate. The events of his last twenty years and his complicated response to them swept him into disillusion unlike that any of his old neighbors ever experienced. Yet a detailed study of his later life would show many of its developments as mere continuations of tendencies exhibited in his Nook Farm period and as erratic extensions, out of context, of uncertainties experienced there. His condemnations of his century, of his country, of the human race — in *Mark Twain in Eruption*, in *The Man That Corrupted Hadleyburg*, in dozens of unpublished manuscripts, and climactically in *The Mysterious Stranger* — continued to be expressed in essentially religious terms, just as *The Gilded Age* had been more an attack on personal immorality in high places than a rounded satire of a new economic order. The determinism developed in *What Is Man?* indicates its author's involvement in the religious preoccupation of the neighborhood. His despair is the extension of the volatility of temperament and the imperfect adjustment to circumstance that he demonstrated even in those days when he was most at home in the world. The sense of failure, particularly acute after he failed as a businessman and always allied to his acceptance of Hartford's standards of material success, was only the remorse which he had known earlier for lesser reasons. Humanitarian sympathy for the oppressed — evidenced in *A Connecticut Yankee* and later the motivation of his violent attacks on missionary and political imperialism — coexisted with his contempt for humanity, just as his furious defense of the Christian ethic and the Golden

Rule continued despite repudiation of Christianity. The contradictions of his later life were exaggerations of those apparent in his life in Hartford.

It is not possible to dispose of Mark Twain's pessimism by naming its "causes" or by disentangling the contradictions in his emotional disturbance. Although Mark tried to justify logically his visceral despair, he was not a logician and not an intellectual. He did not feel obliged to reconcile the inconsistencies in his opinions or to think through his ambivalent sympathies and repulsions. His responses to the events of his later life were wholly impulsive. The alternation of hostility and acceptance even in his darkest years is not reducible to simple explanation.

But the contradictions defying the appraisal of students of Mark Twain who have been inclined to attribute his pessimism to this characteristic or that circumstance seem to me to fit together in the familiar configuration of his incomplete adaptation to late nineteenth-century life. Mark's despair represents the increasing inadequacy of his adjustment as demands upon it multiplied in severity through his personal disasters. The nostalgia that turned him away from the unsatisfactory present to the relatively secure past and germinated his greatest books persisted as part of his preoccupation with the eternal hopelessness of attaining lasting happiness. Time and again he returned to the river — not only in *Pudd'nhead Wilson, Tom Sawyer Abroad,* and *Tom Sawyer, Detective,* but in many unpublished manuscripts. As his bitterness developed, it embraced the Mississippi valley. The early balanced and realistic acceptance of the life there as remembered in *Huckleberry Finn* became the darker representations of innumerable fragments culminating in *The Mysterious Stranger,* the first version of which was laid in Hannibal.

Yet the life of his childhood still remained infinitely preferable to the sordid spectacle furnished by the United States in the last years of the nineteenth century. Toward the end of the nineties, he could retreat from an environment with which he was then irrevocably at odds "to the seclusion of Jackson's island & give up the futilities of life. I suppose we all have a Jackson's island somewhere, & dream of it when we are tired." [43] He knew now, he thought, what repelled him in American life; it was the lust for money, originating in the Gold Rush of 1849. In an unpublished, but very important, set of notes, "Villagers of 1840–43," in which Mark recalls all the names of Hannibal people he could remember with comments on their characters and the events of their lives, he speaks generally of the contrast between the 1840's and the 1890's. Listing the books then read (Byron, Scott, Cooper) and the songs then sung ("Oft in the Stilly Night," "The Last Rose of Summer," "The Last Link"), Mark concluded that their sentimentality seemed puerile to a later age. But if the melancholy was soft, at least money had no place in the ambitions of young people. Their heroes underwent enormous hardships to rescue the helpless, to defend honor, to marry for love — not to accumulate a fortune. The intense sentimentality of the 1840's took no sordid shape. California changed the spirit of a whole people and corrupted their naïve innocence into hard cynicism.

As Mark thought on these things, he made notes for a social history of the United States from 1850 to 1900. He planned to expose the predations of the robber barons, plot the course of the "Californian sudden-riches disease," and blame the Civil War and Jay Gould for a century's "moral rot." In another incomplete manuscript, Mark catalogued the meretricious discoveries of a gaudy civilization. He ended an ironic celebration of financial, industrial, and mechanical miracles with this comment:

> It is a civilization which has destroyed the simplicity and repose of life; replaced its contentment, its poetry, its soft romance-dreams and visions with the money-fever, sordid ideals, vulgar ambitions, and the sleep which does not refresh; it has invented a thousand useless luxuries, and turned them into necessities, it has created a thousand vicious appetites and satisfies none of them; it has dethroned God and set up a shekel in His place.[44]

The future that Mark saw for a commercialized America was dictatorship by the financiers, followed by complete collapse of the rotten republic. America had once shown promise of moral development toward millennial democracy, but the changes taking place in the nineteenth century destroyed all hope. His death in 1910 put a peaceful period to his desolation.

Meanwhile Joseph Hopkins Twichell, whose staunch optimism and obvious normality did not falter throughout his old age, continued in the years after 1891 the parochial activities that had filled his earlier life. He preached from the pulpit of the Asylum Hill Congregational Church until 1912; he was pastor emeritus until his death in 1918. He served as a member of the Yale Corporation and, as its senior member, installed President Hadley in 1899 and addressed the University's celebration of its bicentennial in 1901. He remained always the widely popular and successful community leader he had become in the seventies and eighties, and the passage of the years accumulated local affection and honors which partially compensated for the disintegration of the Nook Farm community.

Twichell wrote much, more in his later years than earlier. Besides his sermons and his journal, which he continued to maintain until April 13, 1915, when "incapacitated by the infirmities of age" he relinquished the care of it "to other hands," he wrote many magazine articles. In 1891 he published his most ambitious book, *John Winthrop*, which, with *Some Old Puritan Love-Letters — John and Margaret Winthrop* (1893), marked his interest in New England history and his sympathy with the Puritan stock from which he came. Neither book is important. Twichell's written style is extremely awkward. His admiration for the Puritan Age and his hostility toward Roger Williams, whose expulsion from Massachusetts he defends as ridding the Old Colony of its most cantankerous and belligerent citizen, are mildly interesting. His respect for the original Puritans was in fact so great that he could find in the autocratic Winthrop a prototype of Abraham Lincoln and in Winthrop's defense of the Colony's charter the resolution and fierce insistence on liberty behind the Declaration of Independence. "For of the American spirit of Liberty through which American Independence was finally achieved, is it aught less than true to say that it was the spirit of John Winthrop risen from the dead?" [45]

His other writings were likely to be articles on the literary members of the neighborhood, on other Hartford celebrities like Horace Bushnell, or on his particular heroes, the foreign missionaries, whose achievement he delighted in and whose vigorous contest with the powers of darkness he would have loved to engage in had his family responsibilities not kept him at home. The most interesting of his occasional pieces is the article on Mark Twain which *Harper's* asked him to write in 1896.[46] He praises Mark as a man of letters, as a friend, as a humanitarian, and as a family man, quoting extensively, but judiciously, from personal letters. Twichell's reputation as an artist in anecdote and as an inexhaustibly fascinating talker is seldom substantiated in his written prose.

In Twichell's late years, as during his entire residence in Hartford, his "fellowship" rather than his intellectual attainments attracted praise. His sympathy with people, his tolerance, his ready laughter, and his bluff high spirits were little diminished by age. He was entirely impervious to the depression which even Charles Dudley Warner felt in his last years; and his attitude toward the developments of his times was always a hearty enthusiasm. The advance of civilization fascinated him. His prayer on Thanksgiving Day of 1899 was thanks that the war with Spain was spreading the benefits of American democracy throughout the world; and his farewell to his youngest son, leaving for France in 1917, reflected the same faith in the justice of the cause that he himself had taken to the Civil War.

Twichell was the most healthy-minded member of the community he survived. He knew little sorrow (death first touched his immediate family only when Harmony died four days after Mark Twain in 1910), but his well-being was due not so much to an absence of calamity as to his resilient optimism and his unquestioning faith in the rightness of things, in the power of good, and in the wisdom of God. He was as simple as his friends in Nook Farm were complex. His influence was that of a man whose confidence in simple axioms overrode all doubt. When he retired in 1912, the end of his active career was treated as an event of national importance, though little could be said of what he had done. His death in December of 1918 was almost unnoticed because of its insignificance beside the termination of World War I, but even then memory of him had not entirely lapsed. Howells said at his death, "I loved this simple, manly, unassuming clergyman." Twichell's friendship remained among the "precious legacies" of his life.[47]

The affection everyone felt for Twichell had been one of the important unifying threads of the old Nook Farm community. From 1870 to 1890 the neighborhood had seen a flowering of personal compatibilities among people so different as Mark Twain and Warner; Twichell's personal gifts were as valuable as anyone's in the neighborhood's congeniality. The man is important now only as Mark Twain's personal friend, but while he lived he was a central figure in the life of the colony.

Twichell was the last of the important members of the Nook Farm neighborhood to die. He had seen all the others to their graves and had commended their souls to the immortality of which he had no doubt. His residence in Hartford extended from the end of the Civil War to the Armistice. His experience spanned the modernization of America; his point of view was representative of the optimism of his age. Though his complete acceptance of the developments of his time is relatively undramatic, it is enlightening as a facet of Mark Twain's environment and as a characteristic of an important period in our cultural history. His death, occurring at a time when widespread disenchantment was undermining the faith for which Twichell stood and making it repugnant to the coming generation, marked the final dissolution of the Hartford colony. As an event, it ended the history of Nook Farm. As a symbol, it signalized the disappearance of the ideas and experience that had comprised Nook Farm's way of life.

Appendix

APPENDIX

A Boy's Adventure

[Suppressed chapter of *The Prince and the Pauper*, printed in the *Bazar Budget* (Hartford, Connecticut), No. 4 (Friday, June 4, 1880), pp. 1–2.]

(As I haven't a miscellaneous article at hand, nor a subject to make one of, nor time to write the article if I had a subject, I beg to offer the following as a substitute. I take it from the twenty-second chapter of a tale for boys which I have been engaged upon, at intervals during the past three years, and which I hope to finish, yet, before all the boys grow up. I will explain, for the reader's benefit, as follows: The lad who is talking is a slim, gentle, smileless creature, void of all sense of humor, and given over to melancholy from his birth. He is speaking to little Edward VI., King of England, in a room in the palace; the two are by themselves; the speaker was "whipping-boy" to the king when the latter was Prince of Wales. James I. and Charles II. had whipping boys when they were little fellows, to take their punishments for them when they fell short in their lessons, so I have ventured to furnish my small prince with one, for my own purposes. The time of this scene is early in the year 1548, consequently Edward VI. is about ten years of age; the other lad is fourteen or fifteen.)

I will tell it, my liege, seeing thou hast so commanded (said the whipping-boy, with a sigh which was manifestly well freighted with painful recollections), though it will open the sore afresh, and I shall suffer again the miseries of that misbegotten day.

It was last midsummer — Sunday, in the afternoon — and drowsy, hot and breathless; all the green country-side gasped and panted with the heat. I was at home, alone; alone, and burdened with the solitude. But first it is best that I say somewhat of the old knight my father — Sir Humphrey. He has just turned of forty, in the time of the Field of the Cloth of Gold, and was a brave and gallant subject. He was rich, too, albeit he grew poor enough before he died. At the Field he was in the great cardinal's suite, and shone with the best. In a famous Masque, there, he clothed himself in a marvelous dress of most outlandish sort, imaginary raiment of some fabled prince of goblins, or spirits, or I know not what; but this I know, that it was a nine-days' wonder, even there, where the art of the broad world had been taxed in the invention of things gorgeous, strange and memorable. Even the king their father said it was a triumph, and swore it with his great oath, "By the Splendor of God!" What a king hath praised is precious, though it were dirt before; so my father brought home this dress to England, and kept it always laid up in herbs to guard it from injurious insects and decay. When his wealth vanished, he clung to it still.

Age crept upon him, trouble wrought strangenesses in him, delusions ate into his mind. He was of so uncomfortable a piety, and so hot-spirited withal, that when he prayed, one wished he might give over, he so filled the heart with glooms of hell and the nose with the stink of brimstone; yet when he was done, his weather straightway changed, and he so raged and swore and laid about him, right and left, that one's thought was, "Would God he would pray again."

In time was he affected with a fancy that he could cast out devils — wo worth the day! This very Sunday, whereof I have spoken to your grace, he was gone, with the household, on this sort of godly mission, to Hengist's Wood, a mile and more away, where all the gaping fools in Bilton parish were gathered to hear him pray a most notorious and pestilent devil out of the carcase of Gammer Hooker, an evil-minded beldame that had been long and grievously oppressed with that devil's presence, and in truth a legion more, God pardon me if I wrong the poor old ash-cat in so charging her.

As I did advertise your grace in the beginning, the afternoon was come, and I was sore wearied with the loneliness. Being scarce out of my thirteenth year, I was ill stocked with love for solitude, or patience to endure it. I cast about me for a pastime, and in an evil hour my thought fell upon that old gala-suit my father had brought from the Field of the Cloth of Gold near thirty years bygone. It was sacred; one might not touch it and live, an my father found him in the act. But I said within myself, 'tis a stubborn devil that bides in Gammer Hooker, my father cannot harry him forth with one prayer, nor yet a hundred — there is time enow — I will have a look, though I perish for the trespass.

I dragged the marvel out from its hiding, and fed my soul with the sight. O, thou shouldst have seen it flame and flash in the sun, my liege! It had all colors, and none were dull. The hose of shining green, — lovely, silken things; the high buskins, red-heeled, and great golden spurs, jeweled, and armed with rowels a whole span long, and the strangest trunks, the strangest old-fashioned doublet man ever saw, and so many-colored, so rich of fabric and so bespangled; and then the robe! It was crimson satin, banded and barred from top to hem with a webbed glory of precious gems, if haply they were not false — and mark ye, my lord, this robe was all of a piece, and covered the head, with holes to breath and spy through; and it had long, wide sleeves, of a most curious pattern; then there was a belt and a great sword, and a shining golden helmet, full three spans high, out of whose top sprung a mighty spray of plumes, dyed red as fire. A most gallant and barbaric dress — evil befall the day I saw it!

When I was sated with gazing at it, and would have hid it in its place again, the devil of misfortune prompted me to put it on. It was there that my sorrow and my shame began. I clothed myself in it, and girt on the sword, and fixed on the great spurs. Naught fitted — all was a world too large — yet was I content, and filled with windy vanity. The helmet sunk down and promised to smother me, like to a cat with its head fast in a flagon, but I stuffed it out with rags, and so mended the defect. The robe dragged the ground, wherefore was I forced to hold it up when I desired to walk with freedom. Marching hither and yonder before the mirror, the grand plumes gladdened my heart and the crimson splendors of the robe made my foolish soul to sing for joy, albeit, to speak plain truth, my first glimpse of mine array did well nigh fright the breath out of my lank body, so like a moving conflagration did I seem.

Now, forsooth, could I not be content with private and secluded happiness, but must go forth from the house, and see the full sun flash upon my majesty. I looked warily abroad on every side; no human creature was in sight; I passed down the stairs and stepped upon the greensward.

I beheld a something, then, that in one little fleeting instant whisked all thought of the finery out of my head, and brimmed it with a hot new interest. It was our bull, — a brisk young creature that I had tried to mount a hundred times, and failed; now was he grazing, all peacefully and quiet, with his back to me. I crept toward him, stealthily and slow, and O, so eager and so anxiously, scarce breathing lest I should betray myself — then with one master bound I lit astride his back! Ah, dear my liege, it was but a woful triumph. He ran, he bellowed, he plunged here and there and yonder, and flung his heels aloft in so mad a fashion that I was sore put to it to stick where I was, and fain to forget it was a jaunt of pleasure, and busy my mind with expedients to the saving of my neck. Wherefore, to this end, I did take a so deadly grip upon his sides with those galling spurs that the pain of it banished the slim remnant of his reason that was left, and so forsook he all semblance of reserve, and set himself the task of tearing the general world to rags, if so be, in the good providence of God, his heels might last out the evil purpose of his heart. Being thus resolved, he fell to raging in wide circles round and round the place, bowing his head and tossing it, with bellowings that froze my blood, lashing the air with his tail, and plunging and prancing, and launching his accursed heels, full freighted with destruction, at each perishable thing his fortune gave him for a prey, till in the end he erred, to his own hurt no less than mine, delivering a random kick that did stave a beehive to shreds and tatters, and empty its embittered host upon us.

In good sooth, my liege, all that went before was but a holiday pastime to that that followed after. In briefer time than a burdened man might take to breath a sigh, the fierce insects did clothe us like a garment, whilst their mates, a singing swarm, encompassed us as with a cloud, and waited for any vacancy that might appear upon our bodies. An I had been cast naked into a hedge of nettles, it had been a blessed compromise, forasmuch as nettle-stings grow not so near together as did these bee-stings compact themselves. Now, being moved by the anguish of this new impulse, the bull did surpass himself. He raged thrice around the circuit in the time he had consumed to do it once, before, and wrought final wreck and desolation upon such scattering matters as he had aforetime overlooked and spared; then, perceiving that the swarm still clouded the air about us, he was minded to fly the place, and leave the creatures behind — wherefore, uplifting his tail, and bowing his head, he went storming down the road, praising God with a loud voice, and in a shorter space than a wholesome pulse might take to beat a hundred was a mile upon his way — but alack, so also were the bees. I noted not whither he tended, I was dead to all things but the bees and the miserable torment; the first admonishment I had that my true trouble was but now at hand, was a wild, affrighted murmur that broke upon my ear, then through those satin eye-holes I shot a glance, and beheld my father's devout multitude of fools scrambling and skurrying to right and left with the terrors of perdition in their souls; and one little instant after, I, helmeted, sworded, plumed, and blazing in that strange unearthly panoply of red-hot satin, tore into the midst, on my roaring bull, — and my father and his ancient witch being in the way, we struck them, full and fair, and all the four went down together, Sir Humphrey crying out, in the joy of his heart, "See, 'tis the master devil himself, and 'twas I that haled him forth!"

I marvel your majesty should laugh; I see naught in it of a merry sort, but only bitterness. Lord, it was pitiful to see how the wrathful bees did assault the holy congregation and harry them, turning their meek and godly prayers into profane cursings and blasphemous execrations, whilst the whole multitude, even down to the aged mothers in Israel and frosty-headed patriarchs did wildly skip and prance in the buzzing air, and thrash their arms about, and tumble and sprawl over one another in mad endeavor to flee the horrid place. And there, in the grass, my good father rolled and tossed, hither and thither, and everywhere,—being sore beset with the bees—delivering a howl of rage with every prod he got,—ah, good my liege, thou shouldst have heard him curse and pray!—and yet, amidst all his woes, still found his immortal vanity room and opportunity to vent itself; and so, from time to time shouted he with a glad voice, saying, "I wrought to bring forth one devil, and lo, have I emptied the courts of hell!"

I was found out, my prince—ah, prithee spare me the telling what happened to me then; I smart with the bare hint of it. My tale is done, my lord. When thou didst ask me yesterday, what I could mean by the strange reply I made to the lady Elizabeth, I humbly begged thee to await another time, and privacy. The thing I said to her grace was this—a maxim which I did build out of mine own head: "All superfluity is not wealth; if bee-stings were farthings, there was a day when Bilton parrish had been rich."

MARK TWAIN

Hartford, June, 1880.

Notes

NOTES

CHAPTER 1: THE COLONIZATION OF NOOK FARM · 1851–1871

1. Lounsbury, *Biographical Sketch of Charles Dudley Warner* (Hartford, 1905), p. v.

2. City population in 1840: 12,793; 1850: 17,966; 1860: 29,152; 1870: 37,743. *Hartford, Conn. as a Manufacturing, Business, and Commercial Center* (Hartford: Board of Trade, 1889), p. 153.

3. Isabella Beecher Hooker, "The Last of the Beechers: Memories on My Eighty-Third Birthday," *Connecticut Magazine*, IX, 289 (Spring 1905).

4. Hooker, *Reminiscences*, pp. 170–171. (Hooker was not a notable prose stylist.)

5. August 5, 1891. Quoted in Hooker's *Reminiscences*, p. 172.

6. See Carroll John Noonan, *Nativism in Connecticut* (Washington, 1938), for decay of the Whigs, strength of the Democrats, and temporary supremacy of Know-Nothingism in the fifties.

7. Joseph R. Hawley, "Charles Dudley Warner," *Connecticut Magazine*, VI, 428 (September–October 1900).

8. *My Father: Mark Twain* (New York, 1931), p. 188.

9. Mrs. James T. Fields says (in *Charles Dudley Warner*, Contemporary Men of Letters Series, New York, 1904), "He would have gone to war himself except for his extreme short-sightedness," but she is apparently commenting more on physical than on intellectual shortcomings.

10. Hawley and the other Nook Farm radicals were more interested in the eradication of slavery than in economic reforms.

11. "Every bond, in letter and in spirit, must be as sacred as a soldier's grave," was his remark as president of the 1868 Republican National Convention. Quoted by Ralph H. Gabriel, "Joseph Roswell Hawley," *Dictionary of American Biography*.

12. Annie Fields, *Authors and Friends* (Boston, 1896), p. 183.

13. *Ibid.*, and Forrest Wilson, *Crusader in Crinoline* (New York, 1941), p. 497.

14. Between 1862 and 1871, Mrs. Stowe wrote her domestic series of books: *House and Home Papers*, in book form (1865), *Little Foxes* (1866), *The Chimney-Corner* (1868), and the encyclopedic *The American Woman's Home, or, Principles of Domestic Science*, with Catharine (1869); a very profitable series of children's books: *Queer Little People* (1867), *Daisy's First Winter* (1867), *Little Pussy Willow* (1870); two society novels: *My Wife and I* (1871), *Pink and White Tyranny* (1871); two of her New England novels: *The Pearl of Orr's Island* (1862), *Oldtown Folks* (1869); her *Religious Poems* (1867); a novel of Italian legend, *Agnes of Sorrento* (1862); a biographical collection for the subscription-book trade, *Men of Our Times* (1868); and *Lady Byron Vindicated* (1869). In addition she wrote a large number of articles not collected.

15. *Authors and Friends*, p. 168.

16. Of all places. Fields, then editor, was in Europe; Osgood, left in charge, was not inclined to turn down anything from this distinguished contributor. Circulation fell alarmingly.

17. The only extended accounts by Mark Twain students of Twichell's life and his influence on Mark Twain are the unsearching remarks of Paine in his biography and the references in Edward Wagenknecht's *Mark Twain: The Man and His Work* (New Haven, 1935). Because of this inadequacy, my account of him will be fuller at every point than a strict symmetry would require.

18. Clipping, n.d., no source, in vol. O of the unpublished Twichell Journal on restricted deposit at the Yale University Library.

19. More than a hundred carefully written letters, lengthily composed under difficult conditions and intended to inform his family and

to serve as source pieces for a history of his war experiences, are preserved on deposit at the Yale University Library.

20. Twichell, Civil War Letters, April 22, 1861.

21. They remained close friends until O'Hagan, president of the College of the Holy Cross after the War, died at 48 on December 15, 1878. Twichell paid tribute to him in the *Courant*. Mark Twain became O'Hagan's friend also. He wrote to C. W. Stoddard, February 1, 1875, that he was going with Joe Twichell to Worcester "to have a 'time' with a most jolly and delightful Jesuit priest who was all through the war with Joe . . . I sent the Padre word that I knew all about the Jesuits, from the Sunday-school books and that I was well aware that he wanted to get Joe and me into his den and skin us and make religious parchment out of us after the ancient style of his communion since the days of good Loyola, but that I was willing to chance it and trust to Providence." This passage is omitted from the version of this letter in Albert Bigelow Paine's *Mark Twain's Letters* (2 vols., New York, 1917), vol. I, pp. 248–249. I quote from the copy of the letter in the Mark Twain Papers.

22. Civil War Letters, May 15, 1861.

23. *Ibid.*, June 9, 1861.

24. *Ibid.*, August 4, 1861.

25. *Ibid.*, August 25, 1861.

26. *Ibid.*, April 8, 1862.

27. *Ibid.*, April 21, 1862.

28. Twichell, Journal, vol. X, p. 5. Twichell named his youngest son after this general.

29. Twichell, "Personal Reminiscences," *Bushnell Centenary* (Hartford, 1902), pp. 70–85.

30. Reminiscences of Deacon Atwood Collins, Hartford *Courant*, March 24, 1915.

31. "It was no longer a misfortune for a young minister to enjoy the favor of Dr. Bushnell; nor a detriment to be known as his disciple." E. P. Parker, quoted in the *Courant*, March 24, 1915.

32. Hawes was a member of the rational rather than the intuitive school and therefore conservative. Though his congregation finally forced him to admit music to a place in the church exercises, he used to say after each performance by the choir, "We will now resume divine service."

33. Letter in Parish Memorabilia, vol. I.

34. Keep to Twichell, June 17, 1865, *ibid.*

35. Deacon Atwood Collins, Hartford *Courant*, March 24, 1915, quotes from Twichell's letter of acceptance.

36. H. C. Vedder, *American Writers of Today* (New York, 1895), p. 125.

37. See particularly Van Wyck Brooks, *The Ordeal of Mark Twain* (New York, 1920; rev. ed., New York, 1933), the most brilliant and most misleading book on Mark Twain, and the violent answer by Bernard DeVoto in *Mark Twain's America* (New York, 1932), the best account of the culture of the West from which Mark Twain came.

38. For text see *Mark Twain's Letters*, Albert Bigelow Paine, ed. (2 vols., New York, 1917), vol. I, p. 140 (referred to hereafter as *Letters*). A "subscription" book was one sold, largely in advance, by agents moving from house to house, rather than through bookstores.

39. Isabella's brother, Thomas K. Beecher, had been principal of the Hartford High School. In 1854 he accepted the invitation of Jervis Langdon to assume the pulpit of the Park Church of Elmira, which had been founded in 1846 by forty-nine abolitionist seceders from the proslavery Presbyterian Church. Because of the close friendship between Isabella and Thomas K. Beecher, her daughter Alice and Olivia Langdon were close friends; Isabella and Olivia's mother were intimates. The ties between Nook Farm and Elmira were very close.

40. Mark Twain to Jane Clemens, January 8, 1868, *Letters*, vol. I, p. 143.

41. Albert Bigelow Paine, *Mark Twain: A Biography* (3 vols., New York, 1912), vol. I, p. 357 (referred to hereafter as Paine, *Biography*).

42. This letter, appearing in the *Alta* of February 1, 1868, has not been republished. It can be found in vol. II of Mark Twain Memorabilia, a collection of photostats of the *Alta* letters and other writings in the Connecticut State Library; I know of no *Alta* file in the East.

43. Mark Twain to Mrs. Fairbanks, January 24, 1868, published in *Mark Twain to Mrs. Fairbanks*, Dixon Wecter, ed. (San Ma-

rino, 1949), pp. 15–16. Mark's desire for Hartford's approval reflects the lesson Mother Fairbanks had been teaching him aboard the *Quaker City*. The tone of this letter implies their previous relationship; its point is lost if it is considered a literal statement only, rather than a partly jocular reference to Mrs. Fairbanks's genteel tutelage. In all these passages, the institutional properties of "Mark Twain," of the pseudonymous guise, the persona, later so important in the Mark Twain legend, are already evident. The promise to Mrs. Hooker was to keep her informed on details of development there in feminist legislation.

44. Mark Twain to Mrs. Fairbanks, August 3, [1868], *ibid.*, p. 35.

45. Morse, Mark Twain Memorabilia, Connecticut State Library, vol. II, p. 122.

46. *Ibid.*, p. 122.

47. Later Mark was to assert that this postponement (referred to in a letter to Mrs. Fairbanks, October 5, 1868) was part of Bliss's skill as a swindler — a talent Mark splenetically improvised later.

48. Paine, *Biography*, vol. I, p. 370. Paine's information was not complete on these early Hartford visits. He errs in details and does not use the *Alta* letters. His intention, of course, was not the special one of this study.

49. Hartford *Courant*, April 22, 1910.

50. Mark Twain Memorabilia, Connecticut State Library, vol. II, p. 126.

51. The *Courant* noted on July 31, 1869, that the book would soon be generally distributed. It would doubtless have a big sale, "for the story is told in a graphic manner and is in Mr. Clemmens' raciest style."

52. This would be Charles Dudley Warner, still abroad on his first long trip to Europe.

53. *Mark Twain to Mrs. Fairbanks*, p. 92 (April 15, 1869). Paine does not allude to the negotiations with the *Courant.*

54. *Ibid.*, p. 74.

55. Elisha Bliss to Mark Twain, endorsed to Orion Clemens, November 18, 1870, Samuel C. Webster Collection.

56. In an undated (1870) letter to his family, Samuel C. Webster Collection, Mark said he expected to be in Hartford himself "in a couple of years."

57. Fragmentary letter, no date or place, Webster Collection. Mark had not found making friends in New England a slow business, but he was a little anxious lest eccentric Orion and social-climbing Molly should blunder among his correct friends. Mark does not appear to have considered settling in Boston himself. Using the Boston symbol, at that time potent in the West, he may have been trying to impress Orion with the attractiveness of what he had done for him. Orion did not last long in Hartford. He objected to the high proportion of clerical tasks, finally quit, tried to get a job with one of the Hartford papers, but failed. Mark finally installed him on a chicken farm in Keokuk, Iowa.

58. His agent in the ill-starred venture of a book on the diamond fields. Mark Twain to J. H. Riley, March 3, 1871, Berg Collection, New York Public Library.

59. Mark Twain to Orion Clemens, March 10, 1871, Berg Collection.

60. During the time they rented their home to Mark, the Hookers, some or all, traveled in Europe and visited the Gillettes. The rent Mark paid was $300 a quarter (John Hooker's Cash Book, Connecticut State Library), an interesting indication, considering the value of the dollar in those times, of the sort of house it was.

CHAPTER 2: THE VARIETIES OF RELIGIOUS EXPERIENCE · 1871–1891

1. A good summary of Bushnell's position appears in Daniel D. Addison's *Clergy in American Life and Letters* (New York, 1900), pp. 268–303.

2. According to Twichell, "Personal Reminiscences," *Bushnell Centenary*, p. 82.

3. See Horace Bushnell, *Woman's Suffrage: The Reform Against Nature* (New York, 1869).

4. Bushnell to Mark Twain, December 20, 1872, Mark Twain Papers.

5. "Down the Rhone," *Europe and Elsewhere*, p. 143. All references to Mark Twain's writings not otherwise identified are to the Stormfield Edition, 37 vols., New York, 1929.

6. *Bushnell Centenary*, p. 93.

7. First published in book form in 1859 immediately after *Atlantic* serialization.

8. The Lyman Beecher household in Litchfield included a Negro woman named Candace who may have had similar trouble with Lyman's tough judgments.

9. *Oldtown Folks* (Boston, 1897), p. 598.

10. *Poganuc People* (Boston, 1894), p. 308.

11. See *Poganuc People*, p. 63, for example, where the Federalists in Connecticut are Presbyterians and the Democrats ("rag tag and bobtail") are Episcopalians.

12. "Firstly, if underived virtue be peculiar to the Deity, can it be the duty of a creature to have it?" *The Minister's Wooing*, p. 45.

13. "New England was one vast sea, ranging from depths to heights with thought and discussion on the most insoluble of mysteries." *Ibid.*, p. 243. The doctrines of Calvinism had "the effect of a slow poison, producing life habits of morbid action very different from any which ever followed the simple reading of the Bible." *Ibid.*, p. 247.

14. *Pearl of Orr's Island* (Boston, 1896), p. 366.

15. Annie Fields, *Life and Letters of Harriet Beecher Stowe*, pp. 243–244.

16. Warner to Fanny C. Hesse, his sister-in-law, March 11, 1870, Warner Papers, Watkinson Library of Reference, Hartford.

17. Wilson, *Crusader in Crinoline*, p. 495.

18. "That organ of sharp adventurers"—Hartford *Courant*, March 4, 1871.

19. The full history of the case may be examined in *Theodore Tilton against Henry Ward Beecher, Verbatim Report by the Official Stenographer* (3 vols., New York, 1875).

20. For a full biography of this fantastic and capable woman, see Emanie Sachs, *"The Terrible Siren": Victoria Woodhull* (New York, 1928).

21. The New York *Sun*, August 22, 1874.

22. Tilton, "Legend of Good Women," quoted in Sachs, *"The Terrible Siren"*, p. 104. At one point Tilton was infatuated with Victoria.

23. John Hooker survived not only this European trip, but the experience of reading this and subsequent letters in print in the New York *Sun*, August 22, 1874.

24. Isabella Beecher Hooker to Thomas K. Beecher, November 3, 1872, published in the New York *Sun*, August 22, 1874.

25. Beecher's reply, November 5, 1872, *ibid.*

26. *Verbatim Testimony*, vol. I, p. 301.

27. New York *Sun*, August 22, 1874.

28. Molly Clemens to Jane Clemens, November 26, 1872, Webster Collection.

29. Hartford *Courant*, June 19, 1869.

30. Twichell, Journal, vol. I (entry for October 21, 1874).

31. *Ibid.* (entry for December 23, 1874).

32. *Ibid.* (later entry, undated).

33. *Ibid.*, vol. II (entry for February 15, 1876).

34. Reported in *The Beecher Trial: A Review of the Evidence* (New York, 1875), p. 34.

35. Which admittedly characterized the relation of Beecher and Mrs. Tilton, though overt adultery was not proved.

36. Richard Burton, minor poet and genteel critic, who died in 1940, taught literature at the University of Minnesota.

37. An amusing incident of the Clemens-Webster relation is recorded in a solemn ballot on acceptance of the book dated October 30, 1887 (Webster Collection) which is inscribed with Mark's *yes* and Webster's *no*, as if the matter had attained some importance. The aye had it. *Yale Lectures on Preaching, and Other Writings*, by Nathaniel J. Burton (1888), was successful. A new edition was published by Macmillan in 1925 as *In Pulpit and Parish.* See Richard Burton, "Mark Twain in the Hartford Days," *Mark Twain Quarterly*, I, 5 (Summer 1937).

38. Hooker, *Reminiscences*, p. 93.

39. *Mark Twain's Autobiography*, Albert Bigelow Paine, ed. (2 vols., New York, 1924), vol. I, p. 350.

40. Hooker, *Reminiscences*, pp. 92–93.

41. Burton to Mark Twain, September 29, 1879, Mark Twain Papers. (Mark had been abroad.)

42. *Memories of Yale Life and Men 1845–1899* (New York, 1903), pp. 434, 441, 438.

43. Hooker, *Reminiscences*, p. 98. Much of this quotation I have abridged.

44. Edwin Pond Parker, *History of the Second Church of Christ in Hartford* (Hartford, 1892), p. 232.

45. The Yale man's sense of relative values appears in an unpublished letter, Parker to

Mark Twain, October 15, 1901, Mark Twain Papers, which notifies Mark that Yale is to make him a Doctor of Letters. "Permit me to add an expression of my own gratification in the sure hope of your receiving this honor from Yale — an honor, however, of which you have shown yourself most deserving & worthy — this long while."

46. Parker, *History of the Second Church*, pp. 232, 259.

47. Twichell to Mark Twain, December 29, 1897, and February 9, 1897, Mark Twain Papers.

48. Twichell to Mark Twain, May 6, 1879, Mark Twain Papers.

49. Twichell to Mark Twain, September 5, 1901 (original owned by C. W. Force), Mark Twain Papers.

50. Twichell, Journal, vol. IV, p. 39 (entry for June 26, 1880).

51. Preserved, with 1885 as the only date, in Parish Memorabilia, vol. I.

52. Twichell to Mark Twain, September 1882, Mark Twain Papers.

53. Of Case, Lockwood and Brainard, printers, and a director of the American Publishing Company.

54. *Mark Twain in Eruption*, Bernard DeVoto, ed. (New York, 1940), pp. 207–208. I have followed the punctuation of the original typescript autobiography, Paine No. 108, p. 995 (Dictation of July 31, 1906), Mark Twain Papers.

55. Hartford *Courant*, December 14, 1905.

56. Undated *Courant* clipping, Twichell, Parish Memorabilia, vol. I. This speech has not been collected.

57. Notebook No. 12 (1877–78), entry for March 20, 1878, Mark Twain Papers. Mark wrote on the envelope of Moody's appeal for funds for Mount Hermon School that Moody was the revivalist and that he had no sympathy with the movement.

58. Twichell, Journal, vol. V, pp. 66–67 (entry for July 13–15, 1885).

59. *Ibid.*, vol. V, p. 115 (entry for March 8, 1887).

60. Hartford *Courant*, March 14, 1887.

61. The original of this letter is pasted in Twichell's Journal, vol. V, p. 121.

62. Twichell, Journal, vol. V, p. 142 (entry for October 13, 1887).

63. *Ibid.*, p. 141 (entry for October 4–7, 1887).

64. *A Little Journey in the World* (New York, 1889), p. 49.

65. *First Unitarian Congregational Society, Hartford, Conn. 1844–1944* (pamphlet, n.d.), p. 5.

66. *Ibid.*, p. 9.

67. Among the earliest and most demonstrably fraudulent had been Victoria Woodhull and her sister Tennie C. Claflin.

68. Henry Mann, *Features of Society in Old and New England* (Providence, 1885), pp. 100–101.

69. Sachs, "*The Terrible Siren*", p. 147.

70. Written to be read only "by my husband & children in case of my death" and discovered in the waste of an old barn in 1934, this volume is now in the Connecticut Historical Society Library.

71. It will not suffice to dismiss Isabella as insane. Her hallucinations, though altering her judgment of things and events, do not interfere with her literal accuracy in reporting occurrences of the external world. In every instance where events of the neighborhood to which she refers can be cross checked in the other source materials of the period, her diary is confirmed. Though the extent of her neurosis reached classical proportions, it was not based on a disability that extended beyond her obsession to render her incapable. To call her insane, as Henry Ward Beecher and Forrest Wilson did, is to miss much of the social upheaval of this period. That her religious experience is highly neurotic is, of course, inescapable.

72. Quotations from Mrs. Hooker's Diary, pp. 15–16, 134, 13–14.

73. *Ibid.*, p. 52.

74. *Ibid.*, p. 52.

75. *Ibid.*, p. 135.

76. *Ibid.*, pp. 205, 161–162.

77. Later Mark Twain's business agent.

78. This passage, as well as every detail of the party I have recorded, comes from Isabella Beecher Hooker's Diary, pp. 245–257.

79. For John's eventual credulity before the phenomena of levitation, the gyrations of an Indian girl named Minnie, and the most flagrant and irrelevant manifestations, see his

public statement in his *Reminiscences*, pp. 247–262.

80. Hooker, Diary, p. 139.

81. These passages are from *Oldtown Folks*, pp. 182, 184, 256, respectively.

82. Florine McCray, *The Life-Work of the Author of Uncle Tom's Cabin* (New York, 1889), p. 379.

83. Nor will I, though the manifestations, and particularly the indecision, are strikingly similar to some of the cases described as "obsessive" in Pierre Janet's *Les Névrosés* (Paris, 1919). If Stowe was obsessive in the Janet sense, his visions would be evidence of an unsatisfactory social adjustment to the external world beginning in childhood, rather than proof of organic lesions characteristic in the true "hysteric."

84. The passages quoted are from Fields, *Life and Letters of Harriet Beecher Stowe*, pp. 336–337, 253–254, 336–337, respectively. See also Harriet Beecher Stowe, "The Ministration of Our Departed Friends," in *The May Flower* (Boston, 1869), pp. 197–203.

85. Wilson, *Crusader in Crinoline*, p. 598. In *The Minister's Wooing*, p. 181, Harriet speaks of the time when witches were "unceremoniously helped out of the world, instead of being, as nowadays, helped to make their fortune in it by table-turning."

86. Letter to her children, date omitted, in Fields, *Life and Letters of Harriet Beecher Stowe*, pp. 308–310.

87. Mark attacks spiritualism in passing in Chapter 48 of *Life on the Mississippi*.

88. See *In Defense of Harriet Shelley*, pp. 111–147.

89. Paine, *Biography*, vol. II, p. 627.

90. *Following the Equator*, vol. II, p. 18.

91. The recollection of the farm comprises the most beautiful pages of the Mark Twain autobiography.

92. Minnie M. Brashear, in *Mark Twain, Son of Missouri* (Chapel Hill, 1934), attempts to establish an eighteenth-century provenience for Mark Twain's ideas, citing his reading of Paine's *Age of Reason* and supposing that he read the books available in the library at Hannibal which John Clemens helped to found. DeVoto answers her in "Mark Twain and the Limits of Criticism," *Forays and Rebuttals*, (Boston, 1936), pp. 373–403. Evidence is not available to settle the question.

93. Mark Twain to Orion Clemens, March 18, 1860, *Letters*, vol. I, p. 45.

94. William Dean Howells, "Editor's Easy Chair," *Harper's*, CXXXVI, 602–605 (March 1918).

95. Quotations from Clara Clemens, *My Father: Mark Twain*, pp. 22, 20–21, respectively.

96. Paine, *Biography*, vol. I, p. 412.

97. "Hitherto Unprinted Pages from Mark Twain's Notebook," Hartford *Courant*, February 20, 1916. Twichell included this passage in the material he culled from the notebook Mark had given him.

Twichell records his English experience in a letter to Mark of July 13, 1908 (Mark Twain Papers), adding that he needs "a treatise on the Rules of Proper Manners for a Satellite — or is it Sattelite as I wrote it first? Harmony and I can't agree on the point, but I am about sure I am right."

98. Mark Twain to Jane Clemens, December 4, *Letters*, inaccurately published in vol. I, p. 122; corrected text for first five sentences published in *Mark Twain to Mrs. Fairbanks*, Dixon Wecter, ed., p. 29, n. 1.

99. *Mark Twain's Travels with Mr. Brown*, Franklin Walker and G. Ezra Dane, eds. (New York, 1940), p. 166.

100. Dixon Wecter, "Mark Twain and the West," *Huntington Library Quarterly*, VIII, 359–377 (August 1945).

101. Moncure D. Conway, *Autobiography, Memories and Experiences* (2 vols., Boston, 1904), vol. II, p. 144, wrote: "In no country have I met a more delightful man in conversation than Twichell, and his ministerial adventures if printed would add a rich volume to the library of American humor." Mark wrote Howells that it was ironic that Twichell could so well detect the thing before his eyes and so well describe it by word of mouth and yet be so inept with a pen. (Unpublished portion of letter of December 1881, *Letters*, vol. I, p. 140). Twichell himself referred to this deficiency in a letter to T. R. Lounsbury on December 30, 1884 (Lounsbury Papers, Yale University Library): "I talk like a gazelle for ease and swiftness i.e. *small* talk, but when it comes to composing I'm a lead mud-turtle,

I do suffer so. It's like having a baby." Twichell wrote to Mark Twain from Vermont, August 1, 1885, about Grant's death (Mark Twain Papers): "My notion is that between us we could get ourselves expressed. I have never known anyone who could help me read my own thoughts, in such a case as you can, and have done many a time, dear old fellow."

102. Paine, *Biography*, vol. II, p. 632.

103. Twichell to Mark Twain, August 17, 1904, Mark Twain Papers.

104. Quoted passages from Twichell's letter of August 17, 1902; undated note included in unpublished portion of Mark Twain's autobiography (Paine No. 108, p. 2317, Dictation of October 7, 1907); and Twichell's letter of October 2, 1881. All Mark Twain Papers.

105. Twichell to Mark Twain, n.d. [1875], Mark Twain Papers.

106. *Mark Twain: The Man and His Works, passim.*

107. See Mark Twain's letter to Orion Clemens, March 23, 1878, *Letters*, vol. I, p. 323.

108. Mark Twain to the Gordons, January 24, 1906, *Letters*, vol. II, p. 788.

109. *Mark Twain to Mrs. Fairbanks*, p. 200 (June 3, 1876).

110. Mark Twain to W. D. Howells, December 12, 1886, Howells Collection, Harvard University Library.

111. Howells, "Editor's Easy Chair," *Harper's*, CXXXVI, 603 (March 1918).

112. Hartford *Courant*, April 22, 1910, and Paine, *Biography*, vol. II, p. 630.

113. Twichell had written after receiving Mark's invitation, which came at the time Twichell's third son was born: "I am almost too joyful for pleasure. I labor with my felicities. They load me . . . To walk with you, and talk with you, and sleep with you, and say my prayers with you for weeks together, — why it's my dream of luxury . . . Imagine me turning handsprings as I make my exit." (Twichell to Mark Twain, June 8, 1878, Mark Twain Papers.)

114. Mark Twain to Twichell, n.d., *Letters*, vol. I, p. 338. I quote from the original in Twichell's Journal, vol. III, p. 99.

115. Twichell to Mark Twain, October 22, 1878, Mark Twain Papers. Here is indication that Mark had not confessed his unorthodoxy to Twichell on the trip. Twichell would certainly have thought of it as a reason for Mark's supposing that he had hurt Twichell, even if only to rule it out. The last part of this letter is the story of an encounter typical of Twichell. He cultivated aboard ship a red-headed butcher, J. F. Beilstein. "There were plenty of highly civilized people on board, clergymen and such like, but none of them gave me half the pleasure he did with his talk of butchering."

CHAPTER 3: THE VARIETIES OF SECULAR EXPERIENCE · 1871–1891

1. With lumber at $4 per hundred feet and carpenters at $3 per day. See Chapter II of *The American Woman's Home, or Principles of Domestic Science; Being a Guide to the Formation and Maintenance of Economical, Healthful, Beautiful, and Christian Homes* (New York, 1869).

2. One of Hartford's most interesting industries was the Earth-Closet Company, manufacturers of a simple but tremendous indoor commode, which in the de luxe models automatically squirted dirt into the vault after each use. Harriet was enthusiastic about the invention but urged that the housewife build her own by plans provided in her book. Stowe, *The American Woman's Home*, p. 404.

3. *The Relation of Literature to Life* (New York, 1895), p. 97.

4. "The conservatory . . . was a midsummer out-of-doors garden, with its tangle of vines and flowers. The plants were set in the ground, the vines climbed up and overhung the roof and the fountain, with lilies at the base, made fairy music." Lilian Woodman Aldrich, *Crowding Memories* (Boston, 1920), pp. 144–145.

5. Warner to Fanny C. Hesse, March 11, 1870, Warner Papers.

6. Isabella Beecher Hooker, Diary, p. 5. Frank Fuller, once governor of Nevada, had arranged Mark's first Eastern lecture at Cooper Union.

7. March 23, 1874. The designer, Edward

T. Potter of New York, attempted to create variety in the brick exterior by varying the color of the brick and mortar and by altering the angles at which the bricks were set.

8. Mark Twain to Dr. John Brown, quoted without date by Paine, *Biography*, vol. I, p. 505.

9. Mrs. A. W. Fairbanks to Mark Twain, n.d., Mark Twain Papers.

10. Mrs. A. W. Fairbanks to Mark Twain, November 6, 1876, *Mark Twain to Mrs. Fairbanks*, Dixon Wecter, ed., p. 203.

11. Noted historian, bibliographer, philologist, and prolific author of monographs on Indian language and culture. Mark thought of him as "the richest man in America in the matter of knowledge — knowledge of all values, from copper up to government bonds" (Letter in the *Century*, LV, 154–155, November 1897).

12. Mark Twain to Howells, September 14, 1876, Berg Collection, New York Public Library.

13. Warner to Mark Twain, April 30, 1874, Mark Twain Papers.

14. Mark Twain to Mrs. James T. Fields, n.d., published in her *Charles Dudley Warner*, p. 40.

15. An illustration for Warner's *Backlog Studies* (Boston, 1873), p. 51, a series of fireside conversations, shows one andiron in the likeness of Mark Twain, the other of Warner.

16. Autobiography, Paine No. 108, p. 1354, Mark Twain Papers. Published in the November 1907 *North American Review* but not in the book version.

17. Twichell, Journal, vol. III, pp. 2–3 (entry for July 10–13, 1876).

18. *Ibid.*, vol. V, p. 80 (entry for December 15, 1885).

19. *Ibid.*, vol. V (entry for October 8, 1886).

20. Isabella Beecher Hooker, Diary, pp. 193–195.

21. Twichell, Journal, vol. V, p. 14 (entry for November 17, 1882).

22. Moncure D. Conway, *Autobiography*, vol. II, p. 145.

23. Grace King, *Memories of a Southern Woman of Letters* (New York, 1932), p. 76.

24. Olivia Clemens, Diary, Mark Twain Papers.

25. *Mark Twain's Autobiography*, vol. II, pp. 242–243.

26. Wilson, *Crusader in Crinoline*, p. 637.

27. She wrote professionally for *St. Nicholas*, but apparently for no adult journal. Her interest in children's stories was an outgrowth of the full attention she, in common with other mothers of the neighborhood, gave to the education and entertainment of children.

28. Fields, *Charles Dudley Warner*, pp. 46–47.

29. Lilian Woodman Aldrich, *Crowding Memories*, p. 160.

30. *Memories of a Hostess: A Chronicle of Eminent Friendships*, M. A. DeWolfe Howe, ed. (Boston, 1922), p. 346.

31. Howells to Mark Twain, July 21, 1889, *Life in Letters of William Dean Howells*, Mildred Howells, ed. (2 vols., Garden City, 1928), vol. I, p. 427.

32. Twichell, Journal, vol. I (entry for June 13, 1875).

33. Howells replied that the only justification he could invent for writing novels at all was on the ground used by a girl in extenuation of her illegitimate child: it was such a *little* baby. Howells to Warner, June 4, 1875, Warner Papers.

34. He gave a "general account of the various phases of religious opinion he had passed through, and seemed to take great satisfaction in having fetched out at last in something like evangelical faith." Twichell, Journal, vol. III, p. 157 (entry for October 24, 1879).

35. Warner was indefatigable in the encouragement of young woman authors. His friend E. C. Stedman wrote him in July of 1894, in care of Sarah Orne Jewett whom Warner was visiting in South Berwick, Maine: "And what a fellow you are for seeking out the most elect Naiads & the pleasantest waters." (Warner Papers)

36. Twichell, Journal, vol. V, p. 27 (entry for November 15, 1883).

37. Twichell, Journal, vol. II, p. 137 (entry for January 12, 1879).

38. Olivia Clemens, Diary (entry for June 13, 1885), Mark Twain Papers.

39. Mark Twain to Charles Warren Stoddard, October 25, 1881, *Letters*, vol. I, p. 405.

40. Mark Twain to Howells, January 28, 1882, *Letters*, vol. I, p. 416.

41. Henry Stanley to Mark Twain, January 24, 1887, Mark Twain Papers.

42. Thomas K. Beecher to Olivia Clemens, May 25, 1884, Mark Twain Papers. Beecher went on to praise Livy's maintenance of a devout conscience "amid the apparent rationalism and speculation of Hartford society."

43. Mrs. E. J. Hamersley to Mark Twain, November 30, 1885, Mark Twain Papers.

44. Helen Post Chapman, in *My Hartford of the Nineteenth Century* (Hartford, 1928), p. 48, from which many of the details of subsequent paragraphs come, remembered that Mark joined the young folk in coasting, wearing his short sealskin cap and coat, dragging a pig-sticker and carrying a white pillow under his arm.

45. Arthur W. Shipman, remembering his boyhood in the 1870's, was glad, in 1920, to report to the Connecticut Historical Society (unpublished paper on file in its library) that he heard no one of the ball players ever say a word his mother could have objected to. Mark and Twichell went often, like many other adults, to the games. On one occasion a small boy stole Mark's English umbrella after it fell through the stands. Mark offered a reward of $5 for the umbrella, and $200 for the boy's remains, in the *Courant* of May 19, 1875.

46. Mark and Twichell learned to ride the bicycle and got up at five in the morning for a few weeks to make expeditions in the cool of the day to Wethersfield and West Hartford.

47. Mark told a Boston reporter that his lameness was like walking on stilts — as if he had wooden legs with pains in them. Twichell, Journal, vol. I (entry for November 17, 1874).

48. ". . . all Americans expect to go to Europe. I have a friend who says she should be mortified if she reached heaven and there had to confess that she had never seen Europe. It is one of the things that is expected of a person." Margaret DeBree in Warner's *A Little Journey*, pp. 72–73.

49. Warner, *A Little Journey*, p. 210.

50. Twichell to Mark Twain [May 1877], Mark Twain Papers.

51. William Lyon Phelps, *Autobiography with Letters* (New York, 1939), p. 111.

52. Twichell continues in his Journal, vol. I, pp. 96–97 (entry for May 7, 1875): "He had the strongest predilection to the stage and yielded to what he felt was his 'call' . . . He seems a right true and manly Christian youth and I pray God he may prove that the pursuits of an actor may not be inconsistent with the Christian profession."

53. General William B. Franklin, warm friend of Mark Twain and a West Pointer in Grant's class, came under criticism for injudicious command judgment in the Fredericksburg disaster. In 1865 he became general manager of Colt's Firearms Manufacturing Company and a director of the National Fire Insurance Company. His favorite anecdote: In the panicky retreat from Bull Run, he tried to rally the scattering troops, ordering one man lying at full length in a gully to leave off being a rabbit, to come out of his hole and fight. The soldier said calmly, "Yes, you want the place yourself, you son of a bitch." Condensed from unpublished portion of Mark Twain's autobiography, Paine No. 108 (Dictation of October 30, 1906), Mark Twain Papers.

54. Mark Twain to Franklin, endorsement on letter, H. B. Langdon to Mark Twain, April 27, 1876, Mark Twain Papers.

55. Franklin to Mark Twain, May 4, 1876, Mark Twain Papers.

56. Twichell, Journal, vol. IV, p. 4. (entry for January 9, 1880). The play was "The Professor," on which Gillette lost all the money Mark Twain had lent him. William Hooker Gillette (1855–1937) as a boy in Nook Farm amused himself building scenery and miniature stages, giving marionette shows, and playing in homemade plays and charades. After his appearance in "The Gilded Age," he played in stock companies in Boston, New York, Cincinnati, and St. Louis. Eventually he wrote a dozen unreadable but widely popular comedies. He played in "The Admirable Crichton" and "Dear Brutus." His greatest stage roles were of one pattern — the cool resourceful man of action in "Held by the Enemy," "Sherlock Holmes," and "Se-

cret Service." With the riches he eventually accumulated he built a monumental castle (most unlike the house in which he grew up), complete with miniature railroad, on the Connecticut River.

57. Olivia Clemens to Mark Twain, January 25, 1885, Mark Twain Papers.

58. Mark Twain to Howells, June 27, 1878, from Heidelberg, *The Portable Mark Twain*, Bernard DeVoto, ed., p. 754.

59. The Hooker Cash Book (Connecticut State Library) shows his total income and expenses from 1857 to 1875. More prosperous in the seventies than earlier, he was having great difficulties because of notes he had endorsed for unsuccessful townspeople.

60. Goodwin was an Episcopal rector of considerable wealth, who went abroad annually after 1871 and gave up his pulpit early to look after his family holdings, to nurse a slight heart ailment, and to pursue a philanthropic interest in civic betterment. He lived on Twichell's Woodland Street. He forced the recalcitrant New Haven Railroad to elevate the grade crossing there by collecting 40,000 proxies from Cousin J. P. Morgan and appearing blandly at a stockholders' meeting. He lived in "simple" luxury, it was said. See Sherrod Soule, *Francis Goodwin of Hartford* (Hartford, 1939).

61. Hartford lawyer and judge who held stock with Mark in the Paige typesetting machine.

62. Except at Twichell's. Journal, vol. III, p. 24 (entry for December 3, 1877): ". . . ours is the only house where the Club is entertained that is 'dry' in this way. May be, though, Dr. Burton's is another exception."

63. Twichell (Journal, vol. I, entry for December 13, 1875) doesn't say whether it is or not.

64. *Mark Twain in Eruption*, p. 240. Twichell, who usually referred to the substance of the essays, simply said of this meeting, held at his house November 21, 1881: "M.T. was essayist" (Journal, vol. IV, p. 101).

65. Trumbull "in the course of his remarks said that he had lately met Josh Billings in Boston, who, in a conversation, declared his conviction that you were by all odds the brightest light of humor in the land, and incomparably superior to all rivals on the platform, which I thought very handsome of him and a thing you ought to hear." Twichell to Mark Twain, May 8, 1871, Mark Twain Papers. This is the first letter of their correspondence that has been preserved.

66. Published in eight numbers (November 1891 to May 1893), then discontinued because "it was too much work," though the club remained active. The Watkinson Library of Reference has a complete file.

67. M.B.C., "Mark Twain as a Reader," *Harper's Weekly*, LV, 6 (January 7, 1911).

68. *A Club Corner*, I, 16.

69. Warner, *A Little Journey*, pp. 1–2.

70. Paine does not include this detail in his account of the incident (*Biography*, vol. II, pp. 600–612). Mark and Twichell soon found out the girl's duplicity when they inquired after the child, and they report it in the autobiography (unpublished, Paine, No. 108, Dictation of April 10, 1907, Mark Twain Papers) and the Journal (vol. III, pp. 4–7, entry for July 17, 1877). Later Mark fictionalized this event grotesquely as the Wapping Alice story and carried the marriage to completion to reveal that Alice was a man. He did not publish the sketch but incorporated it, with the true version as he remembered it, in his autobiographical dictations.

CHAPTER 4: IDEAS OF AMERICA · 1871–1891

1. Mark Twain to Orion Clemens, March 27, 1875, Mark Twain Papers. Mark accepted eventually Twichell's assessment of Beecher.

2. Fields, *Memories of a Hostess*, M. A. DeWolfe Howe, ed., p. 252; and Mark Twain to Mollie Fairbanks, August 6, 1877, *Mark Twain to Mrs. Fairbanks*, Dixon Wecter, ed., p. 209.

3. Twichell, Journal, vol. II, p. 118 (entry for November 7, 1876).

4. Henry C. Robinson was defeated for the governorship.

5. Wilson, *Crusader in Crinoline*, p. 604.

6. Twichell, Journal, vol. III, p. 129 (entry for March, no day, 1877). The "trying incident" was another Democratic majority in Congress.

7. Twichell wrote of Hayes: "The Chief Magistrate received us with cordial simplicity and made an altogether pleasing impression on me — a plain, strong, sensible looking man, utterly unaffected in his deportment." Journal, vol. IV, pp. 17–18, n.d., [1880].

8. "I am sleepless now o' nights in anxiety lest the republican ticket should be defeated," Warner wrote T. R. Lounsbury on November 3, 1882 (Warner Papers), stating the condition that afflicted him before every election.

9. Cashier of the Phoenix National Bank and one of Mark's businessman cronies.

10. Paine, *Biography*, vol. II, p. 778.

11. Twichell, who sponsored a Chinese educator named Yung Wing and who was intimately involved in the latter's Chinese Educational Mission (based in Hartford), repeatedly intervened to attempt alteration of unfriendly Chinese policy. He brought Mark in as his assistant when it was necessary to take his intervention to the White House through General Grant.

12. Unpublished portion of letter to Howells, August 31, 1884, typescript copy in Mark Twain Papers, the remainder of which appears in *Letters*, vol. II, pp. 443–444, under date of August 21, 1884.

13. Twichell, Journal, vol. V, pp. 50ff (entry for September, no day, 1884).

14. *Ibid.*, p. 52.

15. Mark states that he and Francis Goodwin and Twichell consummated their "hellish design" to vote for Cleveland (*Mark Twain's Autobiography*, vol. II, p. 21) but his inclusion of Twichell was erroneous.

16. Twichell, Journal, vol. V, p. 52.

17. *Mark Twain's Autobiography*, vol. II, p. 15.

18. To the later regret of such commentators as Edgar Lee Masters. See Masters's *Mark Twain: A Portrait* (New York, 1938).

19. Mark Twain to a Mr. Burrough, November 11, 1876, *Letters*, vol. I, p. 289.

20. Horace Bushnell, *The Age of Homespun* (Hartford, [1851]), p. 123.

21. Fields, *Life and Letters of Harriet Beecher Stowe*, p. 294.

22. Batterson was a self-made man among Hartford's Yale graduates. Born in 1823, he began as tombstone cutter, became a contractor, incorporated the New England Granite Works in 1875, and built the Library of Congress in Washington, the State Capitol of Connecticut, and the Soldier's Monument at Gettysburg. When he conceived of accident insurance on the English model, he insured for two cents a Hartford banker journeying from the post office to his home. The characteristic alliance of culture and business is nowhere better illustrated than in Batterson's self-cultivation. He trained himself as a linguist, translated the *Iliad*, wrote poetry (principally *The Beginnings*, a book-length reconciliation of evolution and religion in blank verse) better than Mrs. Stowe's at least, studied geology avidly and law in order to avoid litigation, and collected paintings and sculpture. He was a trustee of Brown University, collected three honorary M.A.'s, and belonged to at least fifteen national societies for the advancement of such assorted studies as Biblical exegesis and statistics.

23. See Mark's speech on accident insurance, *Sketches New and Old*, pp. 274–276, in which he welcomed dinner guests "to a city whose fame as an insurance center had extended to all lands, and given us the name of being a quadruple band of brothers working sweetly hand in hand — the Colt's arms company making the destruction of our race easy and convenient, our life insurance citizens paying for the victims when they pass away, Mr. Batterson perpetuating their memory with his stately monuments, and our fire insurance companies taking care of their hereafter."

24. *Hartford, Conn. as a Manufacturing, Business, and Commercial Center*, pp. 45, 20.

25. Temperance was not a noticeably Puritan characteristic. In 1845 Hartford county produced 75,000 gallons of cider brandy and 300,000 gallons of gin in 114 distilleries. Much of it was consumed locally. In 1880 only four distilleries were operating. Charles Hopkins Clark, "The Growth of the County," *The Memorial History of Hartford County*,

Connecticut, J. Hammond Trumbull, ed. (2 vols., Boston, 1886), vol. I, p. 211.

26. George Ade, "Mark Twain and the Old Time Subscription Book," *Review of Reviews*, XLI, 703–704 (June 1910).

27. Unpublished portion of letter from Mark Twain to Elisha Bliss, January 28, 1870, *Letters*, vol. I, p. 169, Mark Twain Papers.

28. The American Publishing Company distributed his *Gabriel Conroy*. In an angry letter of March 1, 1877, Mark Twain Papers, Harte charged that the sales of his book were negligible because the company was run only in Mark's interest, that other books were printed only to cover up that fact.

29. Warner to Helen Hunt Jackson, July 20, 1874, Warner Papers.

30. Mark Twain to Joel Chandler Harris, August 10, 1881, *Letters*, vol. I, p. 402.

31. When the Patent Office investigated Mark's "Adjustable and Detachable Strap for Garments" because of interference from another applicant with the same important idea, Mark swore to John Hooker, notary public, that he had got the idea in bed on August 13, 1871, and included Orion's statement that Mark told Orion about it on August 18 — no, August 11 — 1871 and submitted the contradictory evidence with intense anxiety lest his patent be defeated. See George Hiram Brownell, "Mark Twain's Inventions," *Twainian*, III, 1–5 (January 1944).

32. Mark Twain to his mother, February 17, 1878, *Letters*, vol. I, p. 319.

33. Leland Stanford to Mark Twain, March 31, 1885, Mark Twain Papers, said that he had spoken to the Sultan about it and knew he was interested and that the whole project ought to be very profitable.

34. First published in *The Portable Mark Twain*, p. 776.

35. "When I knew Warner, he was a tall, good-looking fellow, gray but vigorous. My first recollections of him were in Florida and New Orleans about 1885. You can bet that he got copy enough out of the trip to make it pay. He made everything pay. For a literary man of imagination, he was the canniest I ever knew; he even beat Bayard Taylor." Henry Holt, *Garrulities of an Octogenarian Editor* (Boston, 1923), p. 101.

36. Twichell, Journal, vol. II, p. 144 (entry for February 11, 1877).

37. The cashier and president were sent to the penitentiary at Wethersfield for five and six-and-a-half years, respectively. Twichell was terribly troubled as he helped the stricken family, his neighbors. A few months after the trial, a son died; the father was brought under guard from the penitentiary to be with him; his remorse was excruciating to witness. In the following year he was released from prison by the pardon of President Hayes, petition for which Twichell had reluctantly signed, fearing that his parishioner was not reformed.

38. Stowe, *Poganuc People*, p. 317. Practically everyone in Poganuc (Litchfield) earned "a decent and comfortable living. Such were our New England villages in the days when its people were of our own blood and race, and the pauper population of Europe had not as yet been landed upon our shores."

39. Warner, *Fashions in Literature*, p. 162.

40. Burr was publisher of the Hartford *Times*, uncle of Ella Burr McManus, who in turn edited a five-day journal called the *Bazar Budget*. Bulkeley was a Hartford politician and occasional mayor.

41. *Bazar Budget*, June 4, 1880, p. 10.

42. *Ibid.*, June 3, 1880, p. 3.

43. "It is a part of the national kindliness which is inherent in American women, and which no one prides herself on as anything uncommon in the way of good breeding, to put her company at ease, to avoid family or private topics that shall isolate the visitors from the conversation, to study the tastes and inclinations of the guests, and to make them feel that their enjoyment is uppermost in mind." *Ibid.*, June 1, 1880, p. 2.

44. "Two Editions of Spring," *Ibid.*, June 3, 1880.

45. *Ibid.*, June 4, 1880, pp. 1–2. For text, see Appendix; for comment, see pp. 188–196 below.

46. *Ibid.*, p. 4. Not published elsewhere.

47. N. Maria Landfear, *Reminiscences of Father Hawley* (Hartford, 1877), pp. 36, 42.

48. Twichell, Journal, vol. I, p. 58 (*Courant* clipping, n.d.).

49. Quoted in Landfear, *Reminiscences of Father Hawley*, p. 76.

50. *Ibid.*, p. 72.

51. Twichell, Journal, vol. IV, pp. 54ff (entry for November 13–16, 1880).

52. Hooker, *Reminiscences*, p. 232.

53. Caroline Severance of Boston brought the women together. See Alma Lutz, *Created Equal: A Biography of Elizabeth Cady Stanton 1815–1902* (New York, 1940), p. 182; and Isabella Beecher Hooker, "The Last of the Beechers," *Connecticut Magazine*, II, 291–295 (Spring 1905).

54. Later published in pamphlet form (Hartford, 1870).

55. Miss Burr, sister of the *Times* publisher, was interested in suffrage even earlier than Isabella.

56. *History of Woman Suffrage*, Elizabeth Cady Stanton, Susan B. Anthony, and others, eds. (4 vols., New York, 1881–1902), vol. III, p. 323.

57. Lutz, *Created Equal*, pp. 182–183.

58. Isabella wrote Mrs. Stanton: "I fully expect to accomplish far more by a convention devoted to the purely political aspect of the woman question, than by a woman's rights convention, however well managed; and this because the time has come for practical work . . ." Lutz, *Created Equal*, p. 207.

59. *History of Woman Suffrage*, vol. III, p. 73.

60. *Ibid.*, vol. IV, p. 116.

61. *Ibid.*, vol. III, p. 99*n*.

62. Hartford *Courant*, March 17, 1871.

63. Beyond Thomas Hooker, John's "lineage takes root in one of England's most honored names, Richard Hooker, surnamed 'The Judicious'; and I have been accustomed to say that, however it may be as to learning and position, the characteristic of judiciousness has not departed from the American stock." *History of Woman Suffrage*, vol. III, p. 101.

64. Catharine E. Beecher and Harriet Beecher Stowe, *The American Woman's Home*, pp. 317–318.

65. Bushnell's words in this paragraph are from *Women's Suffrage: The Reform Against Nature*, foreword, pp. 166, 167, 177, respectively.

66. Hooker, *The Bible and Woman Suffrage* (Hartford, 1870), p. 17.

67. Hooker, *Reminiscences*, p. 114.

68. Written to the press in 1871; reprinted in Hooker's *Reminiscences*, p. 344.

69. Hooker, *Womanhood: Its Sanctities and Fidelities* (Boston, 1873), pp. 9–10.

70. Women must also govern the sex education of their sons in such a way as to avoid such crises as that which arose in the home of one of her neighbors, where a child watched sexual intercourse between two servants.

71. See "The Temperance Crusade and Woman's Rights" in *Europe and Elsewhere*, pp. 24–30.

72. "I will ask you to help me pay expenses of other speakers from New York & Boston & the hall — all which I have assumed in order to make the sessions free." Isabella to Mark Twain, May 3, [1883?], Mark Twain Papers.

73. Most explicitly in the introduction of *The Portable Mark Twain*, pp. 17–18.

74. "My Platonic Sweetheart," *The Mysterious Stranger* (New York, 1922), pp. 287–306.

75. Paraphrased from an unpublished portion of the autobiography, Paine No. 108, pp. 1878ff. (Dictation of March 1, 1907), Mark Twain Papers.

CHAPTER 5: LITERATURE IN HARTFORD · 1871–1891

1. Edwards grew up in Hartford, but after he left for Yale in 1716, he did not return there to live.

2. The earliest secular writer and first poet of Hartford was Roger Wolcott (1679–1767), who wrote *Poetical Meditations, Being the Improvement of Some Vacant Hours* (New London, 1825).

3. He watched the complete *M'Fingal*, which first appeared in 1782, run through thirty editions.

4. For a list of the known titles, see *Connecticut Historical Society Bulletin*, VII, 2–4 (October 1940).

5. Goodrich, *Recollections of a Lifetime* (New York, 1856), pp. 391–392.

6. For her career see Gordon S. Haight, *Mrs. Sigourney: The Sweet Singer of Hartford* (New Haven, 1930). Mrs. Sigourney's voluminous correspondence with the world's literary great, with editors, czars, queens, presidents, and lesser citizens is preserved in the Connecticut Historical Society Library.

7. Quoted in Francis Parsons, *The Friendly Club and Other Portraits* (Hartford, 1922), pp. 97–98.

8. Whittier to Mrs. Sigourney, January 1833, Sigourney Collection, Connecticut Historical Society Library.

9. Emily Foote, *Flora and Other Poems* (Hartford, 1879), p. 345.

10. Lucy Bull, *A Child's Poems* (Hartford, 1872). Twichell once called upon the prodigy. He was disappointed, as he always was face to face with a literary celebrity, that nothing in her appearance distinguished her from anybody else.

11. Mrs. Cooke's short stories, published in magazines from the fifties to the seventies, were collected in *Somebody's Neighbors* (1881), *Root Bound* (1885), *The Sphinx's Children* (1886), and *Huckleberries Gathered from New England Hills* (1891).

12. Brownell's *Lyrics of a Day* appeared in 1864; *War Lyrics* in 1866.

13. Warner's enemy, James Dixon, was one of these. His sometimes graceful poems were the whimsies of the cultivated gentleman.

14. Erastus Wolcott Ellsworth (*Poems*, Hartford, 1855), a worker with his hands, constructed a long poem around the story of Theseus and Ariadne.

15. Inasmuch as the works described in this chapter are not taken up in chronological order, it may be helpful to refer occasionally to the Bibliography.

16. Boston, 1871. See pages 173–174.

17. *Saunterings* (Boston, 1872), p. 239.

18. Boston, 1874. By 1891 fourteen editions had been printed. The book is dedicated to Twichell, "Summer and winter friend, whose companionship would make any journey a delightful memory . . ."

19. *My Winter on the Nile* was published by the American Publishing Company in Hartford (1876), which issued the book also under the title *Mummies and Moslems. In the Levant* was published by J. R. Osgood in Boston in 1877.

20. Quoted passages are from *A Roundabout Journey* (Boston, 1884), pp. 281, 306.

21. Warner wrote Mark Twain as he was finishing *Studies in the South and West* (July 25, 1886, Mark Twain Papers) of Mark's trip West in that year: "We are all anxious to hear of your trip, because you have made it and not because I care a button for the Great West. Yet, I saw by a Chicago newspaper that you spoke well of the Mississippi." Howells, with Warner, looked back on his Western experience with distaste. Of a trip to Europe he felt forced to make to "reinstate" Mrs. Howells after her annual Spring collapse, he wrote Warner on September 2, 1882 (Warner Papers) that he hated to go. He would almost as soon spend a year in the Western Reserve. Mrs. Stowe never longed for Cincinnati, and Mark himself never contemplated resettling in the West he had left.

22. Paxton Hibben, *Henry Ward Beecher*, p. 229. Beecher had also endorsed a truss for $1,000 without being publicly criticized for breach of taste.

23. Such data were supplied from the researches of a Dr. Bernadino. I do not know how much the Santa Fe paid him.

24. The $10,000 contract must have appeared at this point.

25. Nothing could be less characteristic of the gentle and reserved Warner than this speech or gesture.

26. J. H. Harper, *The House of Harper* (New York, 1912), p. 553.

27. Collected in his posthumous *Fashions in Literature* (New York, 1902), pp. 31–76.

28. *Captain John Smith (1579–1631), Sometime Governor of Virginia, and Admiral of New England: A Study of His Life and Writings* (New York, 1881).

29. Mark Twain to Orion Clemens, February 21, 1868, *Letters*, vol. I, p. 150.

30. One of his schemes is a *reductio ad absurdum* of spiritualism. Sellers works on a device for materializing the dead to serve as cheap labor and for resurrecting departed statesmen in order to furnish the Congress with legislators who knew enough to come in out of the rain.

31. Mark insisted on daily reports on his royalties from each performance of his play. Its success prompted him to bring Howells down from Cambridge as a collaborator in other plays that did not materialize despite

their apparent potentiality as gold mines. See Howells, *My Mark Twain* (New York, 1910), pp. 22–23.

32. Harriet Beecher Stowe to James T. Fields, in Annie Fields, *Life and Letters*, p. 332.

33. Mark Twain always commanded the highest page rates of his day, and Warner continuously pressed his editors to raise his own. Mark used the rule of thumb that he should be paid double Warner's fees. When he found that *Harper's* paid Warner $100 a page (850 words) for his California articles — he was presumably unaware of the Santa Fe's subsidy — he raised his price to $200 a page. "If I aint worth, (commercially, not literarily,) double what Warner is, I want to be finding it out right away," he wrote Fred J. Hall from Europe on August 4, 1892 (George C. Smith Collection).

34. To secure British copyright for *The Gilded Age*, Mark and Warner drew up in 1873 a document solemnly swearing that their permanent residence was in Canada. They did not sign it, for Mark discovered that he could satisfy English law by spending a few days across the border, a practice all three Nook Farm writers followed for a long time — beating a path for Quebec to be there on the publication date of the volume they wished to register. Mark and Warner were extremely active for years in urging improvement of the protection by copyright law of authors' property rights in their productions. Their arguments are full of analogies with industry.

35. "Modern Fiction," published in book form in *The Relation of Literature to Life* (New York, 1895), pp. 151–152.

36. Mark Twain to Andrew Lang, n.d., [1889], *Letters*, vol. II, pp. 527–528.

37. A typical defense: "O my brothers and sisters! is there then nothing in the world to think of but literary effects? . . . Are the cries of the oppressed, the gasps of the dying, the last prayers of mothers, — are *any* words wrung like drops of blood from the human heart to be judged as literary effects?" Harriet Beecher Stowe, *Lady Byron Vindicated*, p. 4.

38. As part of her informal manner, Harriet made no effort to conceal the mechanisms of the novel: "As I before remarked, Mrs. Katy Scudder had invited company to tea. Strictly speaking, it is necessary to begin with the creation of the world, in order to give a full account of anything. But, for popular use, something less may serve one's turn, and therefore I shall let the past chapter suffice to arrange my scenery and act my little play, on the supposition that you know enough to understand things and persons." *The Minister's Wooing*, p. 11.

She confidentially warns her reader when sorrow is in the offing: "We are writing thus on and on, linking image and thought and feeling, and lingering over every flower, and listening to every bird, because just before us there lies a dark valley, and we shrink and tremble to enter it. But it must come, and why do we delay." *Ibid.*, p. 229.

It was like her to pause after a melodramatic turn of story to observe: "Well! we shall see what will come!" *Dred*, p. 81.

39. Warner's carelessness is probably the product of his journalistic habit of constantly producing new matter without extensively revising the old. Examples: The picture of a roast turning on a spit before an open fire "makes a person as hungry as one of Scott's novels." *Backlog Studies*, p. 19. "A red man had been skulking along the brow of this very hill and peering down through the birches where the boy was now perched on a tree, shaking his fist at the hated civilization [the Indian is shaking his fist; the boy is not] and vengefully . . . looking down into the valley." *That Fortune*, p. 5.

40. *The Relation of Literature to Life*, pp. 43–56. This essay was written in 1889.

41. Mark Twain to Howells, November 23, 1875, *Letters*, vol. I, pp. 266–267.

42. *The Art of Authorship*, George Bainton, ed. (New York, 1890), pp. 85–88.

43. *Pink and White Tyranny*, pp. 51–52.

44. *Ibid.*, p. 319.

45. Her point had a local applicability in that Connecticut divorce laws in 1870 were the most liberal in the United States, and more liberal than they are now. Under the leadership of Marshall Jewell, they were made stricter before the end of that decade.

46. *Pink and White Tyranny*, p. 320.

47. Quoted passages in this paragraph are from *My Wife and I*, pp. iv, 3, 5, 236, respectively.

48. Mrs. Cerulean and Miss Dangereyes in character and relationship are exactly paralleled by the Isabella Beecher Hooker–Victoria Woodhull partnership. I am sure that Harriet was aware of the resemblance. Audacia is not a very good portrait of Victoria from an unbiased point of view, but Victoria affected the conservative in her own time in the same way. Audacia edits a paper called *The Emancipated Woman*, equivalent to *Woodhull and Claflin's Weekly* that was later to publish the Henry Ward Beecher–Elizabeth Tilton scandal. Harriet thought of both as ignorantly indecent, saying that Audacia's paper is "an exposition of all the wildest principles of modern French communism." *My Wife and I*, p. 257.

49. *Ibid.*, p. 258.

50. *Ibid.*, p. 35.

51. *We and Our Neighbors*, p. 86. Mrs. Stowe's comment is naïve and not quite intelligible, but it seems to me she comes close here to sensing the contrast between the relatively simple uniformity of pre-Civil War society and the complex disintegration of the earlier social codes that took place afterwards — an idea more usable than the mutation in human nature which she postulates here but elsewhere shows no sign of really believing.

52. Quoted passages in this paragraph are from *We and Our Neighbors*, pp. 106, 196, 419–420, respectively.

53. *Oldtown Folks*, pp. 109, 166.

54. Quoted passages in this paragraph are from *My Summer in a Garden* (Boston, 1871), pp. 8, 73, 76, 63, respectively.

55. *Ibid.*, p. xii.

56. These papers first appeared in the *Atlantic* and were later published in book form (Boston, 1872).

57. Quoted passages in this paragraph are from *Backlog Studies*, pp. 28, 143, 105, 215, respectively.

58. *Ibid.*, p. 161. This favorite idea of Mark's (involved also in the genesis of *Tom Sawyer*) refers specifically to the "Story of the Bad Little Boy" and "The Story of the Good Little Boy," written about 1865 and published ten years later in *Sketches New and Old*, pp. 44–45. Howells refused to print them in the *Atlantic* on the grounds that they would cost him the rest of his paying subscribers. I have already referred to the likeness of Mark Twain that appears in the form of an andiron in one of the illustrations in *Backlog Studies*.

59. Quoted passages are from *Backlog Studies*, pp. 17, 248, 224, respectively.

60. *Fashions in Literature*, p. 134.

61. *The Relation of Literature to Life*, p. 73.

62. *Washington Irving*, p. 5.

63. "Thoughts Suggested by Mr. Froude's Progress," *The Relation of Literature to Life*, p. 204.

64. See "Equality," *The Relation of Literature to Life*, pp. 57–98.

65. See "Some Causes of the Prevailing Discontent," *Fashions in Literature*, pp. 157–192.

66. *Their Pilgrimage*, pp. 216, 91.

67. J. H. Harper, *The House of Harper*, p. 207.

68. *As We Were Saying*, p. 76.

69. *As We Go*, pp. 23–24.

70. *A Little Journey in the World* (New York, 1889), was followed by *The Golden House* (1895) and *That Fortune* (1899). For mention of the second and third volumes of this trilogy, see pages 225–226.

71. Warner comments on the sale of pews to high bidders, saying that the Puritans "were very shrewd, but it had not occurred to them to give the best pews to the sitters able to pay the most money for them. They escaped the perplexity of reconciling the mercantile and the religious ideas." *A Little Journey*, p. 11.

72. It is interesting that the legislative chicanery of this novel is advanced over the outright bribery satirized in *The Gilded Age*. Henderson's partner thought his enterprises were for the public good and concealed even from himself the fact that he was corrupting Congressmen. The exploitation of the country by big business, Warner is saying, was more subtly managed in the 1880's than in the cruder period after the Civil War and thus harder to combat.

73. The cost of his special train "would have built and furnished an industrial school and workshop for a hundred Negroes; but this train was, I dare say, a much more inspiring example of what they might attain by the higher education." *A Little Journey*, p. 338.

74. Quoted by W. D. Howells in a letter to Charles Dudley Warner, January 17, 1890, Warner Papers.

75. *The Gilded Age*, vol. I, p. xxi.

76. In at least one place, contempt for the electorate becomes explicit, in connection with Mark's disgust with the jury system — a part of his early reservation about the common people. Of the jury drawn from the populace to try Laura Hawkins for the murder of her seducer, Mark, not Warner, writes: "Low foreheads and heavy faces they all had; some had a look of animal cunning, while the most were only stupid. The entire panel formed that boasted heritage commonly described as the 'bulwark of our liberties.'" *The Gilded Age*, vol. II, p. 231.

77. Colonel Sellers was Mark's contribution to the book, just as Ruth Bolton, the young lady who wanted to be a doctor, is Warner's. The collaboration of Warner and Mark was very close — much more so than Paine indicates in the division of chapters (*Biography*, vol. I, p. 477). Each of the authors wrote versions for most of the incidents sketched out beforehand and read them to Livy and Susie Warner, who chose between them. Warner wrote to Whitelaw Reid on April 7, 1873, "We have hatched the plot day by day, drawn out the characters, and written it so that we cannot exactly say which belongs to who; though the different styles will show in the chapters." (Royal Cortissoz, *Life of Whitelaw Reid*, 2 vols., New York, 1921, vol. I, p. 272.) See also Ernest E. Leisy, "Mark Twain's Part in *The Gilded Age*," *American Literature*, VIII, 445–447 (January 1937).

78. A sample of Warner's contribution: "And the world never knows how many women there are like Alice, whose sweet but lonely lives of self-sacrifice, gentle, faithful, loving souls, bless it continually." *The Gilded Age*, vol. II, p. 325. Warner fortunately outgrew the maudlin tendency of his first fiction.

79. *The Gilded Age*, vol. II, p. 308.

80. John Hoben, "Mark Twain's *A Connecticut Yankee*, A Genetic Study," *American Literature*, XVIII, 197–218 (November 1946).

81. Quoted in Paine, *Biography*, vol. II, p. 840.

82. *A Connecticut Yankee*, pp. 233–234, 237.

83. "Well there are times when one would like to hang the whole human race and finish the farce" (*ibid.*, p. 303) and "I reckon we are all fools. Born so, no doubt" (*ibid.*, p. 352) illustrate more than a sense of humor.

84. R. U. Johnson of the *Century Magazine* wrote Mark on August 15, 1889, Mark Twain Papers, in answer to a letter from Mark, "Mum's the word about the political bearing of the book."

85. One example will suffice. The original version of a passage on poi eating in Hawaii appears in the Sacramento *Union*, May 21, 1866, as follows (quoted by Ivan Benson in *Mark Twain's Western Years*, Palo Alto, 1938, p. 146): "Many a different finger goes into the same bowl and many a different kind of dirt and shade and quality of flavor is added to the virtue of the contents. One tall gentleman, with nothing in the world on but a soiled and greasy shirt, thrust in his finger and tested the poi, shook his head, scratched it with the useful finger, made another test, prospected among his hair, caught something and eat it; tested the poi again, wiped the greasy perspiration from his brow with the universal hand, tested again, blew his nose — 'Let's move on, Brown,' said I, and we moved." Five years later this passage appeared in *Roughing It*, vol. II, p. 199, shortened to the first sentence.

86. Mr. Brown's girl, for example, picked her nose with a fork. These unfortunate sketches have been resurrected by Franklin Walker and G. Ezra Dane in *Mark Twain's Travels with Mr. Brown* (New York, 1940).

87. Quoted by George R. Stewart, "Bret Harte upon Mark Twain in 1866," *American Literature*, XIII, 263–264 (May 1941).

88. Mrs. Fairbanks to Mark Twain, July 26, [1880], Mark Twain Papers.

89. Note here, as in Warner's criticism, that the genteel critics were not attempting to vitiate Mark's vigor of diction and unique use of the American language, that in fact they recognized and praised it.

90. E. P. Parker to Mark Twain, December 22, 1880, Mark Twain Papers.

91. Albert Bigelow Paine, "The Prince and the Pauper," *Mentor*, XVI, 8–10 (December 1918). The statement in this account and in his *Biography*, vol. II, pp. 597–598, that Mark

wrote 400 MS. pages at this time and then dropped the project for three years is erroneous. Mark did not begin writing until late in the winter.

92. The following sources are acknowledged in the documentation that accompanies the published book: Hume's *History of England*; Timbs's *Curiosities of London*; *The English Rogue*; J. Hammond Trumbull's *Blue Laws True and False;* J. Heneage Jesse's *London, Its Celebrated Characters and Places.* In addition he reminded himself in unpublished study notes (Mark Twain Papers) to look at Harriet Martineau's *Little Duke* for a coronation and to borrow a tournament from Sir Walter Scott.

93. *Mark Twain to Mrs. Fairbanks*, p. 218 (February 5, 1878).

94. Published only in the Hartford *Courant*, June 21, 1912.

95. Without saying what the blot was, Parker tells the story in the Hartford *Courant*, June 21, 1912. There is little doubt that the blemish referred to is the following passage of *The Prince and the Pauper*, p. 102 (Tom Canty, mistaken for Edward VI, asks a courtier about the funeral of Henry VIII):

"What day did he say the burial hath been appointed for?"

"The 16th of the coming month, my liege."

" 'Tis a strange folly. Will he keep?"

This passage is elaborated in at least two dramatic versions of the book; Mark's faith in its humor was unshakeable.

96. J. T. Goodman to Mark Twain, October 24, 1881, Mark Twain Papers. Goodman was fully as disappointed in the book as he had expected to be and wrote Mark on January 29, 1882, to stay in the vein of *The Gilded Age* and *Tom Sawyer*. "No one but a mere romancer should travel out of his age."

97. The original edition is a perfect example of the taste of 1881. Between its heavily embossed covers are 192 illustrations, in which the boys look like delicate girls in ballet costume. Mark was inordinately fond of the drawings. He wrote Ticknor that they far surpassed his expectations. "They are as dainty and as rich as etchings," and "the more I examine the etchings, the more I am enchanted with them." Mark Twain to Ticknor, August 1 and August 14, 1881, Yale University Library.

98. Mrs. Fairbanks was all in favor of such elements if they were subordinated properly and were not the whole discourse. Her comments here are from a letter to Mark without date, Mark Twain Papers.

99. *Mark Twain's Notebook*, p. 191.

100. Hartford *Courant*, April 22, 1910.

101. Henry C. Vedder, *American Writers of Today*, p. 94. Laurence Hutton, good friend of Mark's, also regretted that "*The Prince and the Pauper* was rejected by the great mass of non-thinking readers, when it appeared in 1881, because it was Mark Twain's, and was not 'funny.' " See his review of *Joan of Arc* in *Harper's*, XCIII, 684, Supplement 2 (September 1896).

102. "Then is thy grandam not overkind to thee, I take it." *The Prince and the Pauper*, p. 13. Of using a courtier as court taster: "Why they did not use a dog or a plumber seems strange." *Ibid.*, p. 45.

103. " 'If thou do but touch him, thou animated offal, I will spit thee like a goose!' said Hendon." *Ibid.*, p. 79.

104. "Snags and sand bars grew less and less frequent, as Tom grew more and more at his ease." *Ibid.*, p. 39.

105. In one of the most interesting exceptions, Mark's sentimental susceptibility to remorse appears. Tom Canty rebuffs his mother when she recognizes him on the way to the coronation. " 'I do not know you, woman!' The words smote upon the king's soul as the strokes of a funeral bell smite upon the soul of a surviving friend when they remind him of secret treacheries suffered at his hands by him that is gone." *Ibid.*, p. 243.

106. *Literary Leaders of America* (New York, 1904), p. 272.

107. Richard Burton, *Little Essays in Literature and Life* (New York, 1914), p. 202.

108. *Washington Irving*, p. 288. For the moment on the defensive, Warner added that he could not bring himself to exclude the moral element "from a literary estimate, even in the face of the current gospel of art for art's sake." *Ibid.*, p. 302.

109. "Uncle Lot" (later name of "A New England Tale"), *The May Flower and Mis-*

cellaneous Writings (16th ed., Boston, 1869), p. 9. This first story is about the familiar chestnut-burr character (spikes outside, softness within) who finally becomes reconciled to God's will after the death of his saintly son. The concluding moral: "There's a great deal that's worth having in this 'ere life, after all . . . that is, if we'd only take it when the Lord lays it our way." *Ibid.*, p. 42.

110. Doctor Hopkins is a New England abolitionist who fearlessly splits his congregation by insisting that its slaves be freed. Once Harriet makes the point that there was a militant abolitionist in New England, she drops the abolition theme entirely and never in later years refers to it in her printed books.

111. *The Minister's Wooing* (Boston, 1898), p. 62.

112. See page 31 above.

113. Mrs. Kittredge forced little Mara to touch the cold flesh of a corpse laid out in her dark parlor, announcing over the girl's screams: "I tell ye, children's got to learn to take the world as it is; and 'taint no use bringin' on 'em up too tender. Teach 'em to begin as they've got to go out, — that's my maxim." *Ibid.*, p. 57.

114. Annie Fields, *Life and Letters of Harriet Beecher Stowe*, pp. 199–200.

115. *Oldtown Folks*, p. iii.

116. *Ibid.*, p. 228.

117. *Ibid.*, p. 261.

118. *Ibid.*, p. 391.

119. *Oldtown Fireside Stories*, p. 27.

120. *Poganuc People*, p. 178. Harriet gives herself, of course, an "organization" (this time "vibrating" and musical) similar to that of all her young heroines, most of whom have part of herself in them.

121. *Ibid.*, p. 316. *Poganuc People* is not always literal autobiography. Lyman Beecher's deference to the revolution against Calvinism among his children did not take place until after he had left Litchfield to try to save Boston from the Unitarians.

122. *Ibid.*, pp. 374, 375.

123. Boston, 1887. Warner was to use his experience in Charlemont, Massachusetts, again in the opening pages of *That Fortune* (1899).

124. W. D. Howells asked Warner whether he knew that *Being a Boy* was one of the best novels ever heard of (October 21, 1877, Warner Papers).

125. *Being a Boy*, p. 164.

126. *Mark Twain's Letters to Will Bowen*, Theodore Hornberger, ed. (Austin, Texas, 1941), pp. 18–19.

127. Published by Bernard DeVoto as a supplement to his essay "The Phantasy of Boyhood: *Tom Sawyer*," in *Mark Twain at Work*, pp. 3–44.

128. Mark Twain in an unmailed letter to a prospective dramatist of *Tom Sawyer*, *Letters*, vol. II, p. 477.

129. To try to prove direct influence of Aldrich's earlier book (1869) on *Tom Sawyer* would be pointless, but both owe something to the flood of Sunday School books that Aldrich refers to in his title and that Mark Twain had in mind at one point or another in *Tom Sawyer*. For the connection between *Tom Sawyer* and the satire of Sunday School books, see Walter Blair, "On the Structure of Tom Sawyer," *Modern Philology*, XXXVII, 75–88 (August 1939).

130. *Letters*, vol. I, pp. 229–230.

131. *Life on the Mississippi*, p. 193.

132. Mark Twain to Livy Clemens, May 17, 1882, *Letters*, vol. I, p. 419.

133. Mark Twain to Howells, August 9, 1876, *Letters*, vol. I, p. 283. Mark continued: "I like it only tolerably well, as far as I have got, and may possibly pigeonhole or burn the MS when it is done."

134. Mark Twain to Howells, July 20, 1883, *Letters*, vol. I, p. 434; and Mark Twain to Orion Clemens, July 21, 1883, *ibid.*

135. Except to a few who knew how to write. Thus Joel Chandler Harris wrote Mark: "I think that its value as a picture of life and as a study in philology will yet come to be recognized by those whose recognition is worth anything. It is the most original contribution that has yet been made to American literature." June 1, 1885, Mark Twain Papers.

136. See Bernard DeVoto's important essay, "Noon and the Dark: *Huckleberry Finn*," *Mark Twain at Work*, pp. 45–104.

137. *Huckleberry Finn*, p. 160.

138. *Ibid.*, p. 120.

139. *Ibid.*, p. 303.

NOTES TO CHAPTER 6

CHAPTER 6: THE DISSOLUTION OF NOOK FARM · 1891–1918

1. Mrs. Stowe to Olivia Clemens, December 28, 1890, Mark Twain Papers.

2. Mrs. Stowe to Oliver Wendell Holmes, February 5, 1893, in Wilson, *Crusader in Crinoline*, p. 636.

3. After Sarah had reread the beginning of *The Pearl of Orr's Island* in 1889, she wrote Mrs. Fields that she had found it "just as clear and perfectly original and strong as it seemed to me in my thirteenth or fourteenth year, when I read it first. I never shall forget the exquisite flavor and reality of delight that it gave me . . . It is classical — historical . . . Alas, that she couldn't finish it in the same noble key of simplicity and harmony." Sarah Orne Jewett to Mrs. Fields, July 5, 1889, *Letters of Sarah Orne Jewett*, Annie Fields, ed. (Boston, 1911), p. 47.

4. Mark, Livy, and Clara were at the time concluding a world lecture tour undertaken to pay Mark's creditors after the bankruptcy of the C. L. Webster Publishing Company. Susie had remained behind and was visiting the Warners, with the old family servant, Katy Leary. Very soon after Mrs. Stowe's funeral, Susie was to die of spinal meningitis in the Clemens house.

5. J. B. Pond to Mark Twain, July 3, 1896, Mark Twain Papers.

6. John inserted a squirelike notice in the *Courant* which added to the general invitation the comment that "The old servants of the family will be there as guests, and the honest traders with whom we have long dealt, and their wives and children." Hooker, *Reminiscences*, p. 179.

7. In his eightieth year, John was knocked down by a bicycle, and his hip was broken. He recovered to resume the long tramps of which he was very fond, but he never looked upon cyclists with favor.

8. Hartford *Courant*, February 12 and 13, 1901.

9. Isabella Beecher Hooker, "The Last of the Beechers," *Connecticut Magazine*, IX, 295 (Spring 1905).

10. *History of Woman's Suffrage*, vol. IV, p. 296.

11. Isabella Beecher Hooker to Mark Twain, August 25, 1905, Mark Twain Papers.

12. Not all of Warner's friends knew of his friendship for Isabella. Mrs. Fields wrote to Warner (n.d., Warner Papers) in connection with a Harriet Beecher Stowe memorial that ought to be signed by the "right names": "*Must* we ask Mr. Hooker to sign or any of that bad, bad, mad, company?"

13. On December 7, 1904, Isabella addressed a Doctor Richardson about her administration of earthly affairs. He replied: "Nothing could be more gratifying to me, dear Madame, than to be called into your Cabinet council, and permit me to say that the proposition you have just outlined to Miss Foote in regard to the President seems to me to be full of promise." Isabella then wrote: "Thank you, dear doctor. Now for a personal matter. My beautiful hair which is half my stock in trade seems to be thinning on my forehead, just where baldness would be a helpless blemish. Can you suggest any remedy?" The doctor answered: "Not at present, dear Madame, but I will take it into consideration if you will give me time." Hartford *Courant*, March 20, 1908.

14. John Hooker, she claimed, had intended to leave her $10,000 but decided to leave his $70,000 estate to Isabella, who promised to leave Katherine the $10,000 in her own will. Instead Isabella left her granddaughter $1,000 to spend in "little charities" in memory of her grandfather. The Superior Court set aside the will on March 25, 1908. Hartford *Courant*, March 26, 1908.

15. *The People for Whom Shakespeare Wrote* (New York, 1897), p. 175.

16. *That Fortune* (New York, 1899), p. 372.

17. *Ibid.*, p. 8.

18. It is interesting, in view of Warner's traffic with the Sante Fe railroad, that Philip indignantly turns down the suggestion of a scheming journalist to include "line scenery" in his novel, get his characters to travel on the trunk lines, and then persuade the willing railroads to print the novel and scatter it all over the country. Later he is offered wealth

by a railroad magnate; he refuses it again. Phil continues to work on his novel about a lovely girl, "such as might walk out of the Bible," as Warner perhaps wished *he* had done instead of boosting California for the Sante Fe.

19. *That Fortune* is more strikingly than its predecessors an incidental plea for continuance of the genteel tradition. Both T. R. Lounsbury and Charles Eliot Norton asserted their pleasure, at the time when Dreiser and other naturalists were beginning to write, in a book that contained refined characters. Lounsbury wrote Warner on July 3, 1899 (Warner Papers): "I confess more & more to a fondness in my novel-reading for nice people, & I was glad for once in a modern novel to have the two leading characters persons you could spend your time with . . . both agreeably and profitably." However, he noted a glaring indiscretion: "No Englishman could possibly say '*bloody* cold' to a lady (p. 296) . . . Why in the English papers it is printed, when quoted, as 'b----y' and it would be a thousand times worse than speaking to an American girl of her leg." Norton wrote on July 31, 1899 (Warner Papers): "I wish your book might have as many readers as 'David Harum.' The success of that book is a curious comment on American civilization. It is a book to do more harm than good."

20. John Hooker wrote to Warner of *That Fortune* (July 6, 1899, Warner Papers): "It is admirable — immensely to your credit. Not only is the story very interesting (merely as a story) and exceedingly well told, but filled with a high moral lesson. It is most excellent in this respect. Wall Street cd not have its Nemesis better presented, with its certainty and terribleness. Get on him every time."

21. See "The Indeterminate Sentence" (1899), in *Fashions in Literature*, pp. 225–252. Warner was a member of the Connecticut Commission on Prisons and of the National Prison Association, and vice-president of the New York Association of Prison Reform.

22. Mrs. Annie Fields to Warner, April 2, 1885, Warner Papers.

23. Twichell, "Qualities of Warner's Humor," *Century*, XLV, 378–380 (January 1903).

24. Twichell, Journal, vol. VII, pp. 68–75.

25. Mark had wired to Charles H. Clark: "Bunce, Robinson and now Warner. I feel the stroke. He was one of the old, old friends. This is a bereavement, which falls heavily not only upon the family and friends but upon all the country. I wish to be at the funeral. Give me the date." *Courant* clipping, n.d., Parish Memorabilia, vol. V.

26. The Brooklyn *Eagle*, for example, said: "He and dear old General Hawley were like brothers and Mark Twain and Dr. Twichell . . . and the rest of the Hartford coterie made a circle of influence and of affection upon which it is more than a personal calamity that the shadows of mortality must fall." Reprinted in the Hartford *Courant*, October 24, 1900.

27. Reprinted in the Hartford *Courant*, April 10, 1901.

28. Joseph H. Twichell, "Qualities of Warner's Humor," *Century*, XLV, 380 (January 1903).

29. Twichell to Olivia Clemens, April 18, 1893, Mark Twain Papers.

30. Mark Twain to H. H. Rogers, December 27, 1894: "We shall try to find a tenant for our Hartford house; not an easy matter, for it costs heavily to live in. We can never live in it again; though it would break the family's hearts if they could believe it." Paine, *Biography*, vol. II, p. 994.

31. Lilly Warner to Olivia Clemens, June 9, 1899, Mark Twain Papers.

32. Twichell to Olivia Clemens, June 7, 1900, Mark Twain Papers. Only the previous month, however, Mark had written Twichell (March 4, 1900, *Letters*, vol. II, p. 697) implying that though so many old friends were gone (Henry C. Robinson had just died) they would come home. "The friends are passing, one by one; our house, where such warm blood and such dear blood flowed so freely, is become a cemetery. But not in any repellent sense. Pure dead are welcome there; their life made it beautiful." He did not believe he could ever play billiards on the top floor again, however; some other use would have to be made of that room.

33. An undated clipping, Hartford *Courant*, enclosed in a letter from Whitmore to Mark Twain (April 19, 1902, Mark Twain Papers) contains an editorial comment on the advertisement: "The sale indicates what has

been considered probable for some years, that the author does not intend to make Hartford his home again. He has recently bought a house at Tarrytown, N. Y., and will practically abandon Hartford to its fate." Since its sale the house has been roughly treated, despite the valiant efforts of a handful of Hartford citizens to preserve it. It was bought in 1903 and occupied until 1917 by Richard M. Bissell, president of the Hartford Fire Insurance Company. Then it housed for a time the Kingswood School for Boys. In 1920 Hartford real-estate men bought it for $51,000, intending to cut it into apartments. When approached by private citizens who wished to purchase it as a memorial, they raised the price to $300,000. The Connecticut Attorney General invoked "eminent domain." (See *Literary Digest*, LXV, 36–37, May 29, 1920.) Today the house is, on the ground floor, the quarters of a branch of the city library; the other floors are apartments after all, financing the maintenance of a rather shabby memorial to its first resident and suggesting very little of the magnificence that once characterized its appointments.

34. Mark Twain to Twichell, January 19, 1897, *Letters*, vol. II, p. 641.

35. Susie Clemens was apparently a brilliant girl, and her death occurred under pathetic circumstances. Disease struck her suddenly. Before she died, her mind cracked and she became blind. Her parents were in London, and before Livy could reach America the girl was dead. But without minimizing the pathos of this accident, I think it obvious that the response of her parents was more than ordinary grief; its prolongation was a symptom of a more fundamental unhappiness. For years the family perpetuated pain by refusing to celebrate the birthdays of the other children or to recognize festival holidays like Christmas and Thanksgiving.

36. Jean's personality deteriorated tragically during attacks which heartbreakingly late were finally diagnosed as epileptic. She died suddenly on the day before Christmas 1909. Her death was the final disaster of Mark Twain's life.

37. Twichell to Mark Twain, November 2, 1897, Mark Twain Papers.

38. Twichell to Mark Twain, July 3, 1905, Mark Twain Papers.

39. Twichell to Mark Twain, August 24, 1900, Mark Twain Papers. Twichell went on, "But Charley Warner will cry you Amen to every word you say. He is sure the world is going to the dogs — especially since Mr. Brockway [leading experimenter in rehabilitation] has been forced out of the Elmira Reformatory."

40. The last four passages quoted are from letters of March 13, 1905; December 9, 1901; September 28, 1902; and June 13, 1905, respectively, Mark Twain Papers.

41. "I've written another article; you better hurry down and help Livy squelch it." Mark Twain to Twichell, January 29, 1901, *Letters*, vol. II, p. 706.

42. Twichell to Mark Twain, July 25, 1904, shortly after Livy's funeral, Mark Twain Papers.

43. Mark Twain to Sir Walter Besant, February 22, 1898, Berg Collection, New York Public Library.

44. DeVoto No. 31, Mark Twain Papers.

45. Twichell, *John Winthrop* (New York, 1891), p. 234.

46. "Mark Twain," *Harper's*, XCVIII, 816–827 (May 1896). Twichell wrote of the request from *Harper's*: "Reluctantly I consented to undertake it. H. [Harmony] thought it due to M. T. whom we had known and loved so long, and from whom we had received so many kindnesses and bounties that I should, especially as he has fallen into financial troubles and had a special present claim on us for anything that might be construed as the office of friendship. I did the best I could, but wished much that I might have done better." Journal, vol. VI, p. 182 (n.d., 1896).

47. Hartford *Courant*, December 21, 1918.

Bibliography

BIBLIOGRAPHY

The Hartford Writers

Batterson, James G.
The Beginnings (Hartford: privately printed, 1901).
Bull, Lucy Catlin
A Child's Poems (Hartford: privately printed, 1872).
Burton, Nathaniel Judson
In Pulpit and Parish (New York: Macmillan, 1925).
Burton, Richard
Dogs and Dog Literature (Hartford: Connecticut Humane Society, 1895).
Memorial Day and Other Poems (Boston: Copeland and Day, 1897).
Literary Leaders of America (New York: Charles Scribner's Sons, 1904).
Rahab: A Drama in Three Acts (New York: Henry Holt, 1906).
Little Essays in Literature and Life (New York: Century Company, 1914).
"The Mystery of Personality," *Bookman*, LII, 333–337 [433–437] (January 1921).
"Mark Twain in the Hartford Days," *Mark Twain Quarterly*, I, 5 (Summer 1937).
Bushnell, Horace
God in Christ (Hartford: Brown and Parsons, 1849).
The Age of Homespun (Hartford: privately printed, [1851]).
Nature and the Supernatural (New York: Charles Scribner, 1858).
Christian Nurture (New York: Charles Scribner, 1861).
Christ and His Salvation: In Sermons Variously Related Thereto (New York: Charles Scribner, 1864).
The Vicarious Sacrifice, Grounded in Principles of Universal Obligation (New York: Charles Scribner, 1866).
Women's Suffrage: The Reform Against Nature (New York: Charles Scribner and Company, 1869).
Work and Play: Or Literary Varieties (New York: Charles Scribner and Company, 1871).
Moral Uses of Dark Things (New York: Charles Scribner's Sons, 1893).
Cabell, Isa Carrington
Seen from the Saddle (New York: Harper and Brothers, 1893).
Foote, Emily
Flora and Other Poems, Grave and Humorous for the Domestic Circle (Hartford: Brown and Gross, 1879).
Hooker, Isabella Beecher
The Relation of Woman Suffrage to the Home and to Morality (Hartford: Woman Suffrage Association, n.d.).
A Mother's Letter to a Daughter on Woman Suffrage (Hartford: Tracts of Connecticut Woman Suffrage Association No. 2, 1870).
Womanhood: Its Sanctities and Fidelities (Boston: Lee and Shepard, 1873).

"The Last of the Beechers: Memories on My Eighty-Third Birthday," *Connecticut Magazine*, IX, 286–298 (Spring 1905).
Diary (May 1876–January 1877), unpublished, Connecticut Historical Society Library, Hartford.

Hooker, John
The Bible and Woman Suffrage (Hartford: Tracts of Connecticut Woman Suffrage Association No. 1, 1870).
An Account of the Reunion of the Descendants of Rev. Thomas Hooker . . . Held at Hartford, May 16, 1890 (Salem: Salem Press, 1890).
Some Reminiscences of a Long Life: With a Few Articles on Moral and Social Subjects of Present Interest (Hartford: Belknap and Warfield, 1899).
Cash Book, 1857–1875, unpublished, Connecticut State Library, Hartford.

Parker, Edwin Pond
History of the Second Church of Christ in Hartford (Hartford: Belknap and Warfield, 1892).

Sigourney, Lydia Huntley
Lydia Huntley Sigourney Papers, unpublished, Connecticut Historical Society Library, Hartford.

Stowe, Calvin Ellis
Common Schools and Teachers' Seminaries (Boston: Marsh, Capan, Lyon, and Webb, 1839).
Origin and History of the Books of the Bible (Hartford: Hartford Publishing Company, 1868).

Stowe, Harriet Beecher *
The May Flower and Miscellaneous Writings (1843; Boston: Fields, Osgood and Company, 16th ed., 1869).
Uncle Tom's Cabin: Or, Life Among the Lowly (1852; Boston and New York, Houghton Mifflin, 1896).
A Key to Uncle Tom's Cabin: Presenting the Original Facts and Documents Upon Which the Story is Founded (1853; London: Thomas Bosworth, 1853).
Sunny Memories of Foreign Lands, 2 vols. (Boston: Phillips, Sampson, and Company, 1854).
First Geography for Children (Boston: Phillips, Sampson, and Company, 1855).
Dred: A Tale of the Great Dismal Swamp (1856; Boston and New York: Houghton Mifflin, 1893).
The Minister's Wooing (1859; Boston and New York: Houghton Mifflin, 1898).
Agnes of Sorrento (1862; Boston and New York: Houghton Mifflin, 27th ed., 1890).
The Pearl of Orr's Island: A Story of the Coast of Maine (1862; Boston and New York: Houghton Mifflin, 1896).
House and Home Papers (by Christopher Crowfield) (Boston: Ticknor and Fields, 1865).
Little Foxes (by Christopher Crowfield) (Boston: Ticknor and Fields, 1866).
Queer Little People (Boston: Ticknor and Fields, 1867).
Religious Poems (Boston: Ticknor and Fields, 1867).
The Chimney-Corner (by Christopher Crowfield) (Boston: Ticknor and Fields, 1868).

* If the edition I cite is not the first, the year of the original edition immediately follows the title.

Men of Our Times (Hartford: Hartford Publishing Company, 1868).

The American Woman's Home, Or, Principles of Domestic Science: Being a Guide to the Formation and Maintenance of Economical, Healthful, Beautiful, and Christian Homes (with Catharine E. Beecher) (New York: J. B. Ford and Company, 1869).

Oldtown Folks (1869; Boston: Houghton Mifflin, 1897).

Lady Byron Vindicated: A History of the Byron Controversy from its Beginnings in 1816 to the Present Time (Boston: Fields, Osgood and Company, 1870).

Little Pussy Willow (Boston: Fields, Osgood and Company, 1870).

My Wife and I: Or, Harry Henderson's History (New York: J. B. Ford and Company, 1871).

Oldtown Fireside Stories (1871; Boston: Fields, Osgood and Company, 1872).

Pink and White Tyranny: A Society Novel (Boston: Roberts Brothers, 1871).

Palmetto-Leaves (Boston: James R. Osgood and Company, 1873).

We and Our Neighbors: Or, the Records of an Unfashionable Street (1873; Boston and New York: Houghton Mifflin, 1898).

Women in Sacred History (New York: J. B. Ford and Company, 1874).

Betty's Bright Idea, Also Deacon Pitkin's Farm, and the First Christmas of New England (New York: J. B. Ford and Company, 1876).

Poganuc People: Their Loves and Lives (1878; Boston: Houghton Mifflin, 1884).

A Dog's Mission, Or The Story of the Old Avery House and Other Stories (New York: Fords, Howard, and Hulbert, [c. 1880]).

Trumbull, J. Hammond

The True-Blue Laws of Connecticut and New Haven and the False Blue-Laws Invented by the Rev. Samuel Peters (Hartford: American Publishing Company, 1876; edited by Trumbull).

The Memorial History of Hartford County Connecticut, 1663–1884, 2 vols. (Boston: Edward L. Osgood, 1886; edited by Trumbull).

List of Books Printed in Connecticut, 1709–1800 (Hartford: Case, Lockwood and Brainard, 1904).

Twain, Mark *

"Forty-Three Days in an Open Boat," *Harper's* Magazine, XXXIV, 104–113 (December 1866).

The Celebrated Jumping Frog of Calaveras County and Other Sketches, John Paul, ed. (New York: C. H. Webb, 1867).

The Innocents Abroad, Or, The New Pilgrims' Progress: Being Some Account of the Steamship Quaker City's Pleasure Excursion to Europe and the Holy Land: With Descriptions of Countries, Nations, Incidents and Adventures, as They Appeared to the Author (Hartford: American Publishing Company, 1869).

"Henry Ward Beecher's Private Habits," *Connecticut General Advertiser*, II, 2 (January 15, 1870).

Mark Twain's (Burlesque) Autobiography and First Romance (New York: Sheldon and Company, 1871).

Roughing It (Hartford: American Publishing Company, 1872).

The Gilded Age: A Tale of Today (with Charles Dudley Warner) (Hartford: American Publishing Company, 1874).

* First appearances in magazines are included here only for articles not subsequently published in book form.

BIBLIOGRAPHY

Number One: Mark Twain's Sketches (New York: American News Company, 1874).
Practical Jokes with Artemus Ward (London: John Camden Hotten, [1874]).
Mark Twain's Sketches, New and Old (Hartford: American Publishing Company, 1875).
The Adventures of Tom Sawyer (Hartford: American Publishing Company, 1876).
A True Story, and the Recent Carnival of Crime (Boston: James R. Osgood and Company, 1877).
Punch, Brothers, Punch! and Other Sketches (New York: Slote, Woodman and Company, 1878).
A Tramp Abroad (Hartford: American Publishing Company, 1880).
1601. Conversation, as it was by the Social Fireside, in the Time of the Tudors (no publisher, [c. 1880]).
The Stolen White Elephant, Etc. (Boston: James R. Osgood and Company, 1882).
The Prince and the Pauper: A Tale for Young People of All Ages (Boston: James R. Osgood and Company, 1882).
Life on the Mississippi (Boston: James R. Osgood and Company, 1883).
Adventures of Huckleberry Finn (Tom Sawyer's Comrade) (New York: Charles L. Webster and Company, 1885).
A Connecticut Yankee in King Arthur's Court (New York: Charles L. Webster and Company, 1889).
The American Claimant (New York: Charles L. Webster and Company, 1892).
Merry Tales (New York: Charles L. Webster and Company, 1892).
The £1,000,000 Bank Note and Other New Stories (New York: Charles L. Webster and Company, 1893).
Tom Sawyer Abroad (by Huck Finn) (New York: Charles L. Webster and Company, 1894).
The Tragedy of Pudd'nhead Wilson, and the Comedy, Those Extraordinary Twins (Hartford: American Publishing Company, 1894).
Personal Recollections of Joan of Arc (by the Sieur Louis de Conte, her page and secretary) (New York: Harper and Brothers, 1896).
Tom Sawyer Abroad, Tom Sawyer, Detective, and Other Stories Etc. Etc. (New York: Harper and Brothers, 1896).
Following the Equator: A Journey Around the World (Hartford: American Publishing Company, 1897).
How to Tell a Story and Other Essays (New York: Harper and Brothers, 1897).
"James Hammond Trumbull: Tribute of a Neighbor," *Century*, LV, 154–155 (November 1897).
"Letter Declining the Herald's Fund for His Benefit," *Critic*, XXXI, 8 (July 2, 1897).
The Man That Corrupted Hadleyburg and Other Stories and Essays (New York and London: Harper and Brothers, 1900).
English as She is Taught (Boston: Mutual Book Company, 1900).
"To the Person Sitting in Darkness," *North American Review*, CLXXII, 161–176 (February 1901).
Edmund Burke on Croker & Tammany (New York: Economist Press, 1901).
"A Defense of General Funston," *North American Review*, CLXIV, 613–624 (May 1902).
A Double Barrelled Detective Story (New York and London: Harper and Brothers, 1902).

"Mrs. Eddy in Error," *North American Review*, CLXXVI, 505–517 (April 1903).
My Debut as a Literary Person, with Other Essays and Stories (Hartford: American Publishing Company, 1903).
A Dog's Tale (New York and London: Harper and Brothers, 1904).
Extracts from Adam's Diary (New York and London: Harper and Brothers, 1904).
"Concerning Copyright," *North American Review*, CLXXX, 1–18 (January 1905).
"The Czar's Soliloquy," *North American Review*, CLXXX, 321–326 (March 1905).
"John Hay and the Ballads," *Harper's Weekly*, XLIX, 1530 (October 21, 1905).
King Leopold's Soliloquy: A Defense of His Congo Rule (Boston: P. R. Warner Company, 1905).
"Letter to Samuel Hopkins Adams on Quackery," *Collier's*, XXXVII, 16–17 (September 22, 1906).
Eve's Diary (New York and London: Harper and Brothers, 1906).
The $30,000 Bequest and Other Stories (New York and London: Harper and Brothers, 1906).
Christian Science, with Notes Containing Corrections to Date (New York and London: Harper and Brothers, 1907).
A Horse's Tale (New York and London: Harper and Brothers, 1907).
"Letter about the Japanese Schoolboy," *Collier's*, XLI, 22 (August 8, 1908).
"A Capable Humorist," *Harper's Weekly*, LIII, 13 (February 20, 1909).
Is Shakespeare Dead? (New York and London: Harper and Brothers, 1909).
Extract from Captain Stormfield's Visit to Heaven (New York and London: Harper and Brothers, 1909).
Mark Twain's Speeches (New York and London: Harper and Brothers, 1910).
"Letter to the Editor of the Spectator Concerning John C. Hotten," *Bookman*, XXXIII, 114–115 (April 1911).
The Mysterious Stranger, A Romance (New York and London: Harper and Brothers, 1916).
What Is Man? and Other Essays (New York and London: Harper and Brothers, 1917).
Mark Twain's Letters, Arranged with Comment by Albert Bigelow Paine, 2 vols. (New York and London: Harper and Brothers, 1917).
The Curious Republic of Gondour and Other Whimsical Sketches (New York: Boni and Liveright, 1919).
The Mysterious Stranger and Other Stories (New York and London: Harper and Brothers, 1922).
Europe and Elsewhere, Albert Bigelow Paine, ed. (New York and London: Harper and Brothers, 1923).
Mark Twain's Speeches, Albert Bigelow Paine, ed. (New York and London: Harper and Brothers, 1923).
Mark Twain's Autobiography, Albert Bigelow Paine, ed., 2 vols. (New York and London: Harper and Brothers, 1924).
"Sam Clemens in 'Sideburns' to 'Dear Friend Annie,'" *Literary Digest*, LXXXIX, 36–46 (May 8, 1926).
Sketches of the Sixties (with Bret Harte) (San Francisco: John Howell, 1926).
The Adventures of Thomas Jefferson Snodgrass, Charles Honce, ed. (Chicago: Pascal Covici, 1928).

Mark Twain's Works, Stormfield Edition, 37 vols. (New York and London: Harper and Brothers, 1929).
"A Mark Twain Retort," Nathaniel S. Olds, ed., *Saturday Review of Literature*, VIII, 722 (May 7, 1932).
Slovenly Peter, Der Struwwelpeter (New York and London: Harper and Brothers, 1935).
Mark Twain's Notebook, Albert Bigelow Paine, ed. (New York and London: Harper and Brothers, 1935).
"New Letters of Mark Twain," John R. Schultz, ed., *American Literature*, VIII, 47–51 (March 1936).
Letters from the Sandwich Islands Written for the Sacramento Union, G. Ezra Dane, ed. (Palo Alto: Stanford University Press, 1938).
The Washoe Giant in San Francisco, Franklin Walker, ed. (San Francisco: George Fields, 1938).
Letters from Honolulu, John W. Vandercook, ed. (Honolulu: Thomas Nickerson, 1939).
Mark Twain in Eruption, Bernard DeVoto, ed. (New York: Harper and Brothers, 1940).
Mark Twain's Travels with Mr. Brown, Franklin Walker and G. Ezra Dane, eds. (New York: Alfred A. Knopf, 1940).
Mark Twain's Letters to Will Bowen, Theodore Hornberger, ed. (Austin: University of Texas, 1941).
Republican Letters, Cyril Clemens, ed. (Webster Groves, Missouri: International Mark Twain Society, 1941).
Mark Twain's Letters in the Muscatine Journal, Edgar M. Branch, ed. (Chicago: Mark Twain Association of America, 1942).
"An Unpublished Mark Twain Letter," Lawrence Clark Powell, ed., *American Literature*, XIII, 405–407 (January 1942).
Washington in 1868, Cyril Clemens, ed. (Webster Groves, Missouri: International Mark Twain Society, 1943).
"Letter from the Recording Angel," Bernard DeVoto, ed., *Harper's* CXCII, 106–109 (February 1946).
Mark Twain: The Letters of Quintus Curtius Snodgrass, Ernest E. Leisy, ed. (Dallas: Southern Methodist University Press, 1946).
Mark Twain, Business Man, Samuel Charles Webster, ed. (Boston: Little, Brown and Company, 1946).
The Portable Mark Twain, Bernard DeVoto, ed. (New York: Viking Press, 1946).
The Mark Twain Papers, unpublished, General Library, University of California, Berkeley, California.
The Morse Collection (Frear Gift), unpublished, Yale University Library, New Haven.
Mark Twain Memorabilia, W. S. Morse, collector, unpublished, Connecticut State Library, Hartford.

Twichell, Joseph Hopkins

Memorial of Samuel Mills Capron (Hartford: Case, Lockwood and Brainard, 1874; edited by Twichell).
"Concerning Charles Lamb," *Scribner's Monthly*, XI, 720–726 (March 1876).

"The Grand Mission of America," *Our National Centennial Jubilee*, Frederick Saunders, ed. (New York: E. B. Treat, 1877), pp. 128–130.
"Harriet Beecher Stowe," *Authors at Home*, J. L. and J. B. Gilder, eds. (New York: Cassell and Company, Ltd., 1888), pp. 315–322.
"Charles Dudley Warner," *Authors at Home*, J. L. and J. B. Gilder, eds. (New York: Cassell and Company, Ltd., 1888), pp. 325–332.
"A Modern Saint," *New Englander and Yale Review*, II, 381–395 (June 1889).
"The Christian Layman," *Congregationalist*, LXXV, 104 (March 20, 1890).
John Winthrop, First Governor of the Massachusetts Colony (New York: Dodd, Mead and Company, 1891).
Some Old Puritan Love-Letters — John & Margaret Winthrop, 1618–38 (New York: Dodd, Mead and Company, 1893).
"The Minister as an Angler," *Outlook*, XLI, 1018–1020 (June 9, 1894).
"The Victorious Bible," *Outlook*, LI, 850–852 (May 25, 1895).
"Mark Twain," *Harper's Monthly*, XCII, 816–827 (May 1896).
"Dr. Bushnell in the Woods," *Outlook*, LXV, 261–265 (June 2, 1900).
"Personal Reminiscences," *Bushnell Centenary* (Hartford: Hartford Press, 1902), pp. 70–85.
"Qualities of Warner's Humor," *Century*, LXV, 378–380 (January 1903).
Coleridge Patteson of Melanesia, A Modern Knight (New Haven: privately printed, 1906).
Frank Woodbridge Cheney, Address, May 29, 1909 [Hartford, 1909].
Keith-Falconer of Arabia: A Christian Soldier (New Haven: privately printed, 1911).
Civil War Letters of Joseph Hopkins Twichell, April 22, 1861–March 8, 1863, unpublished, Yale University Library, New Haven.
Journal, 1863–1918, 12 vols., unpublished, Yale University Library, New Haven.
Parish Memorabilia of the Asylum Hill Congregational Church, 1865–1918, 14 vols., unpublished, Connecticut State Library, Hartford.
Letters to T. R. Lounsbury, 1873–1913, unpublished, Yale University Library, New Haven.

Warner, Charles Dudley

My Summer in a Garden (Boston: James R. Osgood and Company, 1871).
Backlog Studies (1872; Boston: James R. Osgood and Company, 1873).
Saunterings (Boston: James R. Osgood and Company, 1872).
The Gilded Age: A Tale of Today (with Mark Twain) (Hartford: American Publishing Company, 1874).
Baddeck, and that Sort of Thing (1874; Boston: 14th ed., Houghton Mifflin Company, 1891).
My Winter on the Nile, Among the Mummies and Moslems (Hartford: American Publishing Company, 1876).
In the Levant (Boston: James R. Osgood and Company, 1877).
Being a Boy (Boston: James R. Osgood and Company, 1878).
In the Wilderness (Boston: Houghton, Osgood and Company, 1878).
Captain John Smith (1579–1631), Sometime Governor of Virginia, and Admiral of New England (New York: Henry Holt and Company, 1881).
Washington Irving, American Men of Letters Series (Boston and New York: Houghton Mifflin Company, 1881).

BIBLIOGRAPHY

A Roundabout Journey (Boston: Houghton Mifflin Company, 1884).

Their Pilgrimage (New York: Harper and Brothers, 1887).

On Horseback: A Tour in Virginia, North Carolina, and Tennessee (Boston and New York: Houghton Mifflin Company, 1888).

A Little Journey in the World: A Novel (New York: Harper and Brothers, 1889).

Studies in the South and West; With Comments on Canada (New York: Harper and Brothers, 1889).

As We Were Saying (New York: Harper and Brothers, 1891).

Our Italy (New York: Harper and Brothers, 1891).

"American Literature," *The United States of America,* Nathaniel Southgate Shaler, ed., 2 vols. (New York: D. Appleton and Company, 1894), vol. II, pp. 395–414.

As We Go (New York: Harper and Brothers, 1894).

The Golden House: A Novel (New York: Harper and Brothers, 1895).

The Relation of Literature to Life (New York: Harper and Brothers. 1895).

"Lord Byron," *The Warner Classics* (New York: Harper's Weekly Club, 1897), pp. 11–31.

The People for Whom Shakespeare Wrote (New York: Harper and Brothers, 1897).

That Fortune: A Novel (New York and London: Harper and Brothers, 1899).

Fashions in Literature and Other Literary and Social Essays and Addresses (New York: Dodd, Mead and Company, 1902).

The Warner Papers, unpublished, Watkinson Library of Reference, Hartford.

Index

INDEX

INDEX

INDEX

INDEX

INDEX